Southern Writers
at Century's End

Southern Writers at Century's End

Jeffrey J. Folks & James A. Perkins

Editors

THE UNIVERSITY PRESS OF KENTUCKY

Publication of this volume was made possible in part
by a grant from the National Endowment for the Humanities.

Scholarly publisher for the Commonwealth,
serving Bellarmine College, Berea College, Centre
College of Kentucky, Eastern Kentucky University,
The Filson Club Historical Society, Georgetown College,
Kentucky Historical Society, Kentucky State University,
Morehead State University, Murray State University,
Northern Kentucky University, Transylvania University,
University of Kentucky, University of Louisville,
and Western Kentucky University.

Editorial and Sales Offices: The University Press of Kentucky
663 South Limestone Street, Lexington, Kentucky 40508-4008

01 00 99 98 97   5 4 3 2 1

Library of Congress Cataloging-in-Publication Data
Southern writers at century's end / Jeffrey J. Folks and James A.
   Perkins, editors.
       p.   cm.
   Includes bibliographical references and index.
   ISBN 0-8131-2032-2 (alk. paper)
       1. American literature—Southern States—History and criticism.
2. Southern States—Intellectual life—20th century. 3. Southern
States—In literature. I. Folks, Jeffrey J. (Jeffrey Jay), 1948- .
II. Perkins, James A., 1941-
PS261.S617   1997
810.9'975'09045—dc21   97-14744

Contents

Part II. Old Friends

Acknowledgments

The editors are grateful, above all, to the many contributors whose essays appear in this volume. We appreciate their patience and cooperation throughout the book's process of review and editing. They have been understanding and supportive at every point.

Many others have contributed their advice to this effort. James H. Justus read the manuscript at an early stage and was gracious enough to compose an eloquent foreword. Others, certainly too numerous to list, offered suggestions on authors who should, or should not, be included. We would also like to express our appreciation to the staff of the University Press of Kentucky for their continual encouragement and expert editorial advice.

For permission to reprint, we are grateful to *Southern Review* for David Madden's essay on Barry Hannah; to *Mississippi Quarterly* for James A. Perkins's essay on Robert Drake; and to *South Atlantic Review* for Lucy Ferriss's essay on Andre Dubus.

We would like to acknowledge the invaluable editorial assistance of Nancy Summers Folks, who contributed to every stage of manuscript preparation.

We like to believe that in this last quarter of the century, we know and are untouched by everything; yet it takes only a very small jolt, at the right time, to knock us off balance for the rest of our lives.

—Andre Dubus, *"Rose"*

Foreword

JAMES H. JUSTUS

One of the minor issues in Southern studies that lost relevance about a decade ago—for which we should all be grateful—is whether or not the Southern Renascence ended in 1955. The Southern Renascence itself—which truly existed despite its inaccurate nomenclature—was premised on the assumption that writing from the South was distinctively different from that generated in other parts of the country. And one of the defining traits always listed, usually with the highest priority, was Southerners' heightened sense of place. And the revered text that ratified the critical consensus, the one that explicitly enunciated what critics had been implicitly assembling from the work of Faulkner, Porter, Wolfe, and others, was Eudora Welty's fine essay of 1956, "Place in Fiction." Never mind that this impeccably place-centered writer had called place one of the "lesser angels," and never mind that her examples were Flaubert, Mansfield, Brontë, and Hemingway along with Faulkner. "Place in Fiction" became the second most-quoted-from essay by the historians of Southern literature. (The first, Allen Tate's "The New Provincialism" of 1940, was the Rosetta Stone for "explaining" the remarkable efflorescence that began just after World War I, the "backward glance" that allowed modern Southern writers a perspective on their home region unavailable to their predecessors.)

One of the wry observations about the Southern Renascence, by both participants and scholars, was that there was a writer lurking in every Southern village, threatening to be discovered. In terms of practical criticism, however, the same eight or ten names claimed the spotlight, and, of these, Faulkner was, after World War II, the undisputed headliner. What is striking about the fiction of the last few decades is its diversity of setting, which merely reflects of course a more important phenomenon of this writing: the widely dispersed origins of its authors. There is as yet no voice as strong as Faulkner's among his successors, nor any imaginative geography equal to the unique fertility of Yoknapatawpha. But the storytelling cadences are distinctive and betray fewer anxieties about their unavoidable model than did Flannery O'Connor, Truman Capote, and their generation. And what may be lost in the tenacity and intensity of one mythic Southern county is commendably replaced by a refusal to elevate Southern place into something higher than a lesser angel. There are still a few haunted landscapes left over from the Southern modernists, but even they seem haunted by up-to-date ghosts raised by a stock car-and-insurance-and-VFW culture. There is little deference to be seen—either among themselves or for their predecessors—in the constructed worlds of Georgia (Hood, Walker), Kentucky (Mason), Tennessee (Drake, McCarthy, Marius), North Carolina (Chappell, Edgerton, Gibbons, Kenan, McLaurin, Pearson, Smith), South Carolina (Humphreys), Mississippi (Ford, Grisham, Hannah), or Louisiana (Burke, Dubus, Wilcox).

If traditionalists, in defining the particular slant of modern Southern fiction, insist upon the dominance of the organic community, its collective idiosyncrasies, its mores and morals, its dirty secrets and common report, its accrued wisdom and handed-down superstitions, its tolerance for reiterated stories from family archives, then the great period known as the Southern Renascence has passed. The Civil War in its fiction is finally over. The backward glance from a twentieth-century war that now compels Southern storytellers to reevaluate their region is Vietnam.

Contemporary Southern fiction is frankly engaged with contemporary social problems, especially race relations and the struggle of the poor and marginal working class to wrest some meaning out of their lives beyond survival itself. Its familiar space for the italicizing of the problems tends to be a mobile home, not a ruined mansion. It is a fiction of social dislocation, dealing often with the fragmentation of family following divorce, with the psychologically wounded seeking healing rituals to overcome familial incoherence.

It is ironic that John Grisham—the very model of what one of my friends calls the new authopreneurs—should be the one writer who boldly overcame the anxiety that O'Connor expressed for her generation by setting up shop right on the tracks of the Dixie Special. But perhaps being unawed by Faulkner, even in the 1990s, requires an agenda in which Oxford is irrelevant as fortunate geography. "When you're writing suspense," Grisham confesses, "you can't spend a lot of time on persons, places, or settings." I suppose we should be grateful that most of his fellow Southerners don't write "suspense." For most of his writing generation, I find little diminution in interest from their predecessors in particularizing persons, places, and settings. Even that straddler of North and South, Anne Tyler, examines all the woeful effects of placelessness and dislocation without sacrificing any of the memorable incisiveness of her settings: they may be "impaired" or merely "remnant places" (in Leonard Lutwack's terms), but they are the consequences of time spent imagining and inscribing them. Bobbie Ann Mason's Vietnamized Kentucky may be more an imaginative construct than it is Rand-McNally cartography—but, if so, her chronicles of rapid social change and its human costs are as firmly conceptualized and finely detailed as the more literalized characters and their ordeals in Tim McLaurin, whose interest, according to a friend, is in "a bunch of rednecks who fight and cut each other" in North Carolina.

By World War II, the common reader's response to Southern fiction already being celebrated by critics and academics was one based on the most natural need of the ordinary reader: that literature be inspirational, or at least consoling, in its depiction of the social scene. Serious Southern fiction was never that, of course. What garden-variety readers did not look for in the 1950s (or now, even in the impressive corner bookstore on the Oxford square) was a novel that engaged moral reality, especially if the conclusions of the authors happened to be darker than the most vocal pessimists of the Junior League. If some of the truisms of the Southern Renascence seem hopelessly dated in the writing of contemporary Southerners, the dark vision—Walker Percy said it was an old tradition oriented "toward tragedy"—is still darkly with us.

Richard Marius's narratives are as locally based as his great predecessors', but the old piety of place so common to the agrarian generation is no longer operable—his three novels are studded with transregional philosophical and religious questionings. The shaping Catholicism of James Lee Burke and Andre Dubus threads its way throughout their fiction. In Dubus, ordinary male-female relations are usually depicted in the context of Christian doctrine about the human relationship to God; the sacrament of the Eucharist and human sexuality are somehow equated in astonishing feats of analysis. The detective fiction of Burke is layered over with the older stories of the vulnerable hero battling his own internal demons without notable success; and because of external demons—Reaganism, American arrogance in foreign policy, corruption at all levels of government—a dour Cajun protagonist entertains no possibility for moral improvement in individuals and no melioristic vision for history, even the Southern variety.

It would be wrong to dismiss contemporary Southern novelists as homogenized mainstreamers in the national talent pool. Fictional settings no longer resonate with the liturgical undertones of the South as sacred place, but they are never merely invoked as necessary ingredients in the craft of fiction—following the writing-workshop rule that action must occur *somewhere*. Even Grisham's Memphis and New Orleans show that place is important to what happens because it is a lived-through, lived-in piece of geography before it is articulated as fictive scene. Towns are seedier than they once were in earlier Southern fiction and the occasional cities have streets that are as mean as their Northern and Eastern counterparts. Kentucky coal mines and Vietnam veterans and Job Corps and labor strikes and ubiquitous trailer parks constitute a South more familiar to us from life situations than from books, but, thanks to the postmodern generation, they now are known as imagined venues as well.

Introduction

JEFFREY J. FOLKS AND JAMES A. PERKINS

We began this collection with the intention of bringing together those authors of Southern narrative who began to publish their most significant work only after the mid-1970s. In planning this book, we sought essays that would introduce and analyze a varied group of the foremost Southern writers, including well-known artists such as Alice Walker, Richard Ford, Cormac McCarthy, and Anne Tyler, and more recent or lesser-known figures such as James Wilcox and Tim McLaurin. Some of our authors have only just begun their careers, having published only a few books, while others, later in life, have continued their narrative writing. The ages of these authors vary, but while some have published important work before the seventies, we believe that all of the writers represented in this collection have published the bulk of their significant work since 1975. From the beginning, then, we have focused on those writers whose achievements have come largely in the fourth quarter of the twentieth century.

While we have included essays on many of the finest contemporary Southern authors, it is impossible to represent all the deserving writers who match this description in a single collection. By intention, we did not include those writers who, though still producing important work after 1975, had established their reputations earlier. (One thinks of Ernest Gaines, Walker Percy, Reynolds Price, Elizabeth Spencer, William Styron, Peter Taylor, and Eudora Welty, among others.) As for those we have included, the variety of styles and subjects in their work is representative of the breadth of contemporary Southern narrative. Nevertheless, we still have a fairly long list of very good Southern writers who are not discussed in this volume. We recommend that readers interested in contemporary Southern narrative consider the work of the following writers: Lisa Alther, Pat Conroy, Fannie Flagg, Ellen Gilchrist, Marianne Gingher, Winston Groom, Allan Gurganus, John Holman, David Huddle, Gayl Jones, Ed McClanahan, Jill McCorkle, James Alan McPherson, Lewis Nordan, Jayne Anne Phillips, Padgett Powell, Ferrol Sams, Robert G. Shacochis, Susan Richards Shreve, and John Kennedy Toole.

The twenty-one authors we have included write in a variety of styles and with a range of artistic intentions. Working within well-established narrative traditions, today's Southern writers continue to find absorbing ways to respond

1

to their regional culture and to relate their art to larger issues. Questions of sense of place, of community, and of voice continue to be important in their writing. As it has been for preceding generations of Southern writers, Southern society is a fertile social landscape from which new forms of narrative art may be cultivated.

We have organized these twenty-one essays into two categories. For the younger and, in most cases, lesser-known writers, we offer introductions to their work as a whole. Sue Laslie Kimball's "Tim McLaurin: *Keeper of the Moon*" and Mary Bozeman Hodges's "T.R. Pearson: Debatable Heroes" provide an introduction to, and overview of, these new writers' works and include a useful bio-bibliographical survey. Hodges, for example, presents Pearson as a humorist whose writing displays an abiding "disappointment in people." Touching on each of Pearson's novels through *Cry Me a River* (1993), she demonstrates that his satiric writing portrays human beings as dominated by lust, hypocrisy, selfishness, and greed.

In the case of another younger writer, Randall Garrett Kenan, Doris Betts's fine essay is an appreciation of the blossoming career of her former student at the University of North Carolina. Randolph Paul Runyon's essay on John Grisham, which focuses on the author's first four novels, is one of the first attempts to address Grisham's work as serious fiction. In "James Wilcox: The Normality of Madness," Hugh Ruppersburg locates Wilcox's novels within a Southern narrative tradition of alienation and "cultural dissolution" that includes such notable recent examples as John Kennedy Toole's *A Confederacy of Dunces* and Gurney Norman's *Kinfolks: The Wilgus Stories*. Struggling futilely against the meaninglessness and decay of their environment, Wilcox's characters are overwhelmed by the chaos and disorder of life. As Ruppersburg writes, "psychological turmoil and spiritual crisis are not only deeply related but more or less indistinguishable" in Wilcox's fictional world. Similarly, essays on Kaye Gibbons, Mary Hood, John Burke, and Clyde Edgerton, in ranging broadly across the works of each author, provide an introduction to the writers' emerging careers.

For those more established writers, our essays analyze a single work or a narrow theme or technique within several works. James Grove's essay on Anne Tyler's *Morgan's Passing* addresses the sense of place in one of Tyler's lesser-known novels. As Grove writes, alluding to Eudora Welty's classic essay "Place in Fiction," "a sense of place is essential for fiction since it helps make character sing by confining and defining it." Writing out of the marginally Southern setting of Baltimore, Maryland, Tyler connects place with many of the ambivalences of character and theme in her narrative. The disorder and uncertainty of Tyler's protagonist, Morgan Gower, are painfully embedded within his inescapable consciousness of Baltimore as a border city. To the end,

Morgan's character "remains persistently elusive," and his "malady" of place-lessness challenges any simple reading of the novel.

Randolph Paul Runyon's "Fred Chappell: Midquestions:" examines the complex narrative structure of *Midquest* in connection with the related novels *I Am One of You Forever* and *Brighten the Corner Where You Are*, in which characters from the narrative poem recur. Runyon explicates the poem's "trail of miscues" and considers the "strange misstatements" of its Preface leading to the "quandary" that "the reader may never be quite sure what he or she sees is what the poet sees." The stubborn resistance to explanation and conceptualization in Chappell's artistic temperament is reflected in the structure of his narrative.

In "Cormac McCarthy: Restless Seekers" John Cawelti offers a close assessment of four major works (*Suttree, Blood Meridian, All the Pretty Horses,* and *The Crossing*). In its breadth of coverage and its incisiveness, Cawelti's essay affords an evaluation of the entire body of McCarthy's work. He offers insights into how McCarthy's writing fits into both Southern and Western traditions, an issue of regional identity also addressed in "Richard Ford: Postmodern Cowboys" by Jeffrey Folks. By examining the evolution of McCarthy's career, Cawelti offers support for his assessment of McCarthy as a writer "many consider the most important living Southern writer."

In his retrospective essay on Barry Hannah's *Geronimo Rex*, David Madden considers Hannah's first novel ("the best first novel I've ever reviewed") in light of narrative issues arising from his later fiction. As Madden demonstrates, Hannah's use of style and language in his first novel is brilliant but "one misses the play of a conceptual imagination over the wobbly mass of raw material." This conceptual force, Madden believes, enters Hannah's narrative only in his subsequent writing, including *Nightwatchmen* (1973), *Airships* (1978), and *Ray* (1980).

Other essays focus narrowly on single works: Carroll Viera's treatment of millenialism in Richard Marius's *Bound for the Promised Land*, Elizabeth Pell Broadwell's analysis of Appalachian communities in Lee Smith's *Fair and Tender Ladies*, and Albert Wilhelm's study of the legacy of Vietnam in Bobbie Ann Mason's *In Country* are thematic interpretations of single novels. Lucy Ferriss's work on Catholicism and gender in Andre Dubus's fiction and James Perkins's study of the railroad and its place in Robert Drake's short stories treat narrowly defined issues within several narrative works by a single author.

As a relatively traditional society that has seen rapid social change since the end of World War II, the South has experienced an awareness of change, and of accompanying problems and tensions, greater than that in other regions of America. Until recently, most Southerners lived with the memory of an agrarian past, but while Faulkner, for example, wrote with some assurance that readers, at least in the South, could distinguish an adze from a scythe, or a harrow from a plow, contemporary writers cannot. The rapid Southern transformation to modernity has produced a greater sense of disorder and conflict than elsewhere. Southern culture, quite simply, has moved further in a shorter period of time than have other regional cultures in America, and this fact has not escaped the notice of Southern writers at the end of the century. As Fred Hobson remarks in *The Southern Writer in the Postmodern World*, recent Southern writers locate their fiction "in a world of popular or mass culture, and their characters' perceptions of place, family, community, and even myth are greatly conditioned by popular culture, television, movies, rock music, and so forth" (10).

Hobson's observation concerning the importance of popular culture may be supported by examining several of the authors represented in this book. In the title story from her important first collection, *Shiloh and Other Stories*, Bobbie Ann Mason narrates Norma Jean Moffitt's decision to separate from her husband, Leroy. A sense of the devaluation of myth and tradition is found in every aspect of the Moffitts's lives, from Leroy's popsicle cabin sitting atop the television set like "a rustic Nativity scene," to Norma Jean's name (after Marilyn Monroe's "real" name), to the crucial visit to the Shiloh battlefield, where an afternoon is spent driving "aimlessly through the park," with the Moffitts impressed only by its immensity but unable to "see it as a battlefield," or to connect it in any way with an historical past.

As David Aiken reminds us in his essay on Mary Hood, Southern writing after 1975 is connected with a public culture often characterized by confusion and violence: the war in Vietnam, Watergate, and the Cold War and its aftermath are crucial events in this period. Some of the central images emerge on the television screen: the first televised war in history, public protest and official corruption, political and social instability. The Vietnam War, that pivotal historical event for many writers in the late twentieth century, figures explicitly in such stories as Andre Dubus's "Molly," in which, as Lucy Ferriss points out, Molly's mother "discourses in long monologues about things like sex and the Vietnam War." A refrain for many is, in the words of Molly's mother, "if it weren't for the war . . ."

In the Preface to *The Fable of the Southern Writer*, Lewis P. Simpson concludes with an intriguing suggestion, elaborated in his chapter "A Fable of White and Black," that the "Southernness" of African-American literature is a topic of central concern not only for Southern studies but for American culture generally. Referring to Fred Hobson's *The Southern Writer in the Postmodern World*, Simpson addresses Hobson's point that African-American fiction retains "quintessential" Southern and even "agrarian" qualities. For the African-American Southerner, and indeed for those African-American authors such as Toni Morrison and Ishmael Reed, whose experience of the South is largely indirect, the writing of fiction reflects, at least imaginatively, an intimacy with the land, an identification with nature and the physical environment, an emphasis on the necessity of an extended family and a supportive community, and a legacy of struggle against social oppression and a consequent immersion in history.

Winifred Morgan's essay on Alice Walker's *The Color Purple* and Doris Betts's introduction to the writing of Randall Garrett Kenan are thoughtful studies of important African-American writers who might well be considered in the terms suggested by Simpson. Walker's novel is set among the black residents of a small South Georgia community. As Morgan demonstrates, Walker's narrative transforms the particular racial and gender tensions of this milieu into significant imaginative art. The fiction of Kenan, according to the author's own admission, owes much to the culture and locale of rural North Carolina. If Kenan's fiction is intended "to underscore the importance of old values," as Doris Betts asserts in her essay on her former student, it does so in narrative forms that are distinctly innovative. Incorporating Southern oral history and folklore, shifting between history and fictionalized autobiography, including nonfictional prose accounts of Southern rituals such as hog-killing or tobacco harvesting, Kenan's *A Visitation of Spirits* should be recognized as a version of magical realism, as Terry McMillan has suggested. Kenan's collection of stories, *Let the Dead Bury Their Dead*, is, as Betts writes, "often erotic, often crossing fact with fantasy."

In a 1983 article, Hugh Holman noted that Southern writing must escape the "devastating" influence of the past, especially the influence of William Faulkner and his major successors, whose accomplishments and literary reputations might intimidate the beginning author and blind the critic to original work written outside the conventions of the past. Holman argued that contemporary Southern writing would find an adequate reception only when critics responded openly to "the fresh, the vital, and the new" (xxi). We hope that the essays in this collection respond to new writing in the spirit of openness that Holman suggests, while at the same time recognizing the continuity and importance of Southern literary tradition. Contemporary Southern writers have indeed discovered fresh ways to continue writing original and distinctive narrative. In different respects, each of the writers we have included has contributed to a continuing tradition of narrative that draws on the South's cultural and human complexity. Our hope is that the essays in this collection will provide new insight into Southern narrative of the last few decades.

PART I
New Faces

Randall Garrett Kenan

TIM SMITH

Myth and Reality in Tims Creek

DORIS BETTS

The chinquapin, a Southern edible nut like a miniature chestnut, grows within a burr on a small bushy tree. As a child, I picked and ate many in pastureland in Piedmont, North Carolina, strung some as beads. Randall Garrett Kenan saw but did not eat them as a boy growing up thirty years later in the unincorporated community bearing that name, Chinquapin, Cypress Township, with its own post office and one "high" and one "low" Baptist Church, located in the southeastern part of southeastern Duplin County, North Carolina.

When Kenan was born in 1963, that county, 822 square miles of small towns imbedded among woods, swamp, and farms, settled by Scotch-Irish in the early 1700s, already had in its population of Kenans aplenty—white, established, often wealthy. The family had stamped its surname on Kenansville, the county seat, and was known for two hundred years of leadership and philanthropy to the state. The first white Kenan immigrant ancestor, a member of the British House of Commons, was listed in the 1790 census as owner of thirty-seven slaves; some of these became the novelist's forebears. The Duplin chapter of the United Daughters of the Confederacy is named for a Kenan. Duplin was one of only seven counties in North Carolina that voted never to repeal secession. That old Southern family added new money when one of the Kenan girls married Henry Flagler, founder of Standard Oil and father of

Miami, Florida. In 1971, when a volume of Duplin County history and government was compiled, white Kenans, Sprunts, Hills, and Herrings continued to be well-known surnames in Kenansville, Faison, and Rose Hill. Randall Kenan, then eight, was sharing with lesser-known Kenans a mostly agricultural and communal way of life, though there were nearby chicken plants and pickle factories. In the county history there was little indication that African-American descendants of slaves had been steadily living out their own complex histories alongside the descendants of slaveholders, their names and stories intertwined.

Into Duplin County, Randall Kenan, born in Brooklyn to a mother who could not afford to keep him, came first as a six-week-old baby to Wallace, then to Chinquapin to be reared by his father's kin. His father was eventually arrested for manslaughter; Kenan told Dorothy Allison in a conversation printed in the *Village Voice Literary Supplement* (188 [September 1993]: 26) that he had vivid memories of visiting him in prison. In the 1980s, Kenan would look back on that close-knit rural childhood as an adult living again in Brooklyn, where he would invent characters who resemble members of his extended Kenan family, to whom he dedicated both novel and story collection. In these fictions about race, love, gender, and religion in an invented York County and unincorporated community of Tims Creek, Kenan has presented the double histories of the proud white Cross family (of Crosstown, North Carolina), which takes its turn at being merely backdrop for the upstage story of the proud black Cross family. Though his work is fiction, its very existence acts as a response to that highly selective Duplin history in which so few black citizens appear.

Not surprisingly, Kenan once told a New York interviewer that North Carolina was "ambiguous. It's hard to distinguish between myth and reality." That remark serves as a useful introduction to the way he sorts, juxtaposes, and layers both myth and reality in his work.

As a youth, Kenan attended integrated East Duplin High School in Beaulaville, where he played trumpet and was a Smithsonian scholar. He has described these years in his interview with Allison as a "bifurcation" (26), his integrated school life running parallel to an insular home life where it was never discussed. The division was so strong that at school he was known by his first name, Randall, and among aunts and grandparents by his middle name, Garrett.

As a teenager, he also corresponded with a military physicist at NASA and almost patented a conversion device for changing light into electricity, but told book editor Betty Hodges of the *Durham* (N.C.) *Herald-Sun* that "it had no application." Still, he was avidly reading books by Arthur Clarke and Isaac Asimov, and at age seventeen entered the University of North Carolina at Chapel Hill, planning to earn a physics degree and write sci-fi thrillers on the side. Here he took African-American studies with the late Professor Sonia Stone, for whom the campus Black Cultural Center is named. He joined the campus gospel choir and wrote a short play about the difference between gospel songs and spirituals.

During his sophomore year, "just for fun," Kenan took his first fiction-writing workshop, with Max Steele, then director of UNC's creative writing program, and also started reading Toni Morrison—a combination that moved him rapidly from physics to metaphysics and from science fiction to literary fiction. In various interviews he has praised Steele and other English Department professors (Daphne Athas, Bland Simpson, Lee Greene, Louis Rubin) for their encouragement during his undergraduate years. The summer after his junior year, he went to Oxford to study English literature and drama criticism and sealed his intellectual fate. That year he also worked for Signal Books in Carrboro, North Carolina.

By the time he entered the senior honors writing seminar I taught, Randall Kenan had already developed the style and tone he needed to tell the Cross family stories. For any teacher, it was a dream-seminar in which one's chief duty was to stand out of the light of talented young students. With Kenan in that year-long class were two other gifted and very different writers who became friends. All three were producing work that they would publish soon thereafter: Tim McLaurin (*The Acorn Plan, Woodrow's Trumpet, Keeper of the Moon*) and Sharleen Baker, whose first novel, *Finding Signs*, Kenan would end up editing for Knopf. Some of the stories he wrote that senior year later became part of his own published work.

In December 1985, he finished at North Carolina and received his degree in May, with an English major, honors in creative writing, a minor in physics, and this teacher's highest expectations.

That summer when he went to seek his fortune in New York, he carried good wishes and letters of recommendation from many faculty members, very different from the letters Ralph Ellison's protagonist bore. They included my note to Toni Morrison—with whom I was only slightly acquainted, but who did take an interest in his obvious talent and ambition. These helped him make his own way, with her, with other writers, and also with his first employer. He took the first job he could get in publishing, as a receptionist at Random House, then moved up quickly to assistant to the vice president, Ashbel Crane, and to assistant editor.

In the meantime he kept on with his fiction writing: nights, weekends, while riding on the subway, revising his prose in stages as it moved from long-hand drafts in ink to typescript and onto computer. At age twenty-six he published his first novel with Grove Press, *A Visitation of Spirits* (1989). It was praised by Gloria Naylor, and reviewed favorably almost everywhere. George

Garrett called him "one of the best writers of his generation" (6). In his home state, reviewer Michael Gaspeny (*Greensboro* [N.C.] *Daily News*) wrote: "It's as if Edgar Allan Poe, Alex Haley, and John McPhee were competing for space in this autobiographical first novel." Its plot does make rapid-fire shifts from supernatural horror to African-American family roots to evocative short essays about killing hogs and barning tobacco. "Truth is," George Garrett said in the *Chicago Tribune* (6), "Kenan tries pretty much of everything and pretty much gets away with all of it, too."

But since protagonist Horace Thomas Cross, age sixteen, commits suicide in the end, "autobiographical" is too strong a description, though there are similarities between character and author, between the real Duplin County and the invented York County. Horace, like his creator, is black, brilliant, rebellious, and gay. He feels very much an outcast, first by race in Southern white society but more seriously by his sexual preference within his religious and orthodox family in Tims Creek, where traditions are already collapsing as the young leave home for urban, often northern, opportunity.

None of the Crosses is quite ready to have the male-female tradition collapse, however. Kenan has said that he wants his fictions to underscore the importance of the old values, "work and compassion and love," but Horace loves his own gender and feels condemned thereby. At Thanksgiving dinner, 1983, the Crosses (who have been mostly ministers and teachers since Emancipation) are shocked not only because Horace has been hanging out with white boys, but because he comes to the holiday table wearing an earring in his left ear. "Life the way Horace wants it ain't condoned" (*Visitation* 253).

To summarize *A Visitation of Spirits* as sequential plot will undo its kaleidoscopic structure and yet, because setting, themes, and even some characters recur in his second work, some outline of its content is required. Each of the novel's five sections ("White Sorcery," "Black Necromancy," "Holy Science," "Old Demonology," and "Old Gods, New Demons") contains fragments that skip in time and space, and many are introduced by assorted epigraphs that break the reader's focus into even smaller parts. But the main story line switches back and forth between (1) a present level, December 8, 1985, and (2) Horace's crucial demon-ridden night of April 29-30, 1984, during which he suffered either a mental collapse or an occult possession that ended when he shot himself with his grandfather's gun. Within this main bifurcation, the style and narrating points-of-view also shift. Some segments are objective, even presented as playscript; other episodes are told in an omniscient nineteenth-century voice which addresses the reader as "you."

However, the main alternating narrators are James Malachai Greene, a preacher and school principal living out the respectable Cross family tradition, and young Horace—bookish and homosexual, who, finding his nature condemned by Jimmy's church, turns to its opposite, black magic, and calls up the Ultimate Accuser. Jimmy and Horace, the two youngest members of the Cross family, tell their generation's story. They are contrasted to but still loved by the family's two oldest members, Aunt Ruth, age ninety-two, and her brother-in-law, Zeke, Horace's grandfather, whose oral history reaches back before the Civil War.

Barely has the reader met these characters when, as early as page six, the first digression occurs—a short essay on old-time hog-killing addressed to "you" and entitled "Advent." This apparent shift in content and tone actually starts the myth/reality mixture. A factual account of slaughter and smokehouse is used to call up in the reader the ghosts of butchered hogs, the memory of older times when community food was obtained by communal work. But just as the reader begins to adapt to Kenan's method, this essay ends and the next segment leaps out of general time and back to the morning of April 29, the day Horace Cross first decides to use sorcery to metamorphose himself from an unhappy human to a red-tailed hawk. His spell chants up, or he fantasizes, a member of Satan's High Court who says to him, "Come!" And, wearing only a borrowed coat and carrying his grandfather's gun, Horace follows this spirit to revisit his own short life the way Scrooge followed the Ghost of Christmas Past.

In "Black Necromancy," Jimmy Greene's first-person "confessions" change the subject; they recount his biography, eulogize his dead wife, examine his role now as the first black principal of an integrated school in York County. In a realistic episode on December 8, 1985, Jimmy is driving Ruth and Zeke to the V.A. Hospital in Fayetteville, where Cousin Asa Cross is dying. Zeke then narrates much of this trip, allowing Kenan an opportunity to reproduce eastern North Carolina dialect, which is often interracial: "gone" for "going to," "won't" for "was not," and such well-worn examples as: "if I'm lying, I'm flying," "don't vex me, boy," and the promise to do something very soon, that is, "directly."

In this section, too, Kenan uses an old man's memory to trace the Cross family history from slavery to the day Zeke's wife, Retha, took on the care of their young grandson, Horace. This section of realistic background contrasts with the melodramatic events and poetic style of Horace's last night seventeen months earlier. In a sharp changeover, Horace recalls details of his baptism; then his real memory expands into a dream-fantasy of the congregation calling him "Oreo! Faggot!" The demon also makes him remember his school life and sexual awakening. At 2 a.m. on what has tipped past midnight into April 30, 1984, Horace steals a car that belongs to one of his teachers.

In "Holy Science," the flashbacks come first through Jimmy Greene, who can never now forget that time in 1983 when Horace attempted to confide in him and seek help. In a replay of their scripted dialogue, Jimmy hears himself assure Horace he will outgrow his same-sex desire and be "perfectly normal." The matriarch Ruth picks up the narrative thread of their December 8 visit to Asa's hospital bedside, before the novel shifts backward again to the fateful night, 2:40 a.m. at the high school, where Horace's demon makes him relive his ninth-grade affair with Gideon Stone, when "for the first time he realized the difference between knowledge and experience, and that there is more than one way to know" (*Visitation* 155). But he must also relive with pain his rejection not only of Gideon but of his own sexuality.

In Part Four, "Old Demonology," Jimmy Greene's "Confessions" continue to detail his love for his wife, Anne Gazells Dubois, who died at age thirty-seven, but this time with pain of his own, he reveals how he found her in bed with another man. After the Thanksgiving dinner playscript previously described, the novel resumes the December 8 return trip from the hospital for Ruth, Zeke, and Jimmy, including a humorous restaurant scene, with a car breakdown and a quarrel and reconciliation between the two elders. For the first time, the plot outcome is more than foreshadowed; it is specified with the words, "If Horace had not died" (*Visitation* 208).

By now on Horace's final April 30 night, the clock has ticked down to 4:45 a.m. Horace is led by his demonic spirit to visit another crucial spot in his personal history, the Crosstown amphitheater, where he worked as an eleventh-grader for the local historical production, "Ride the Freedom Star," a two-and-one-half hour musical saga of an American family—the other Cross family, of course, the white Cross family. The theater had been built by the town, aided by a grant from the Cross Endowment, and the play was written (badly) by a family member, Philip Cross. The drama had sixty characters, three intermissions, and only used black characters as happy slaves, buffoons, primitive preachers, or singer-shouters in church choirs. Kenan intends all the irony of its titular "freedom" applied narrowly to those white Americans who immigrated to York County from the British Isles, but not applied to slaves who had been kidnapped from Africa and who sometimes escaped northward, navigating by the constellations.

Interestingly enough, in the real Duplin County, where Randall Kenan grew up (though almost two decades before he was born), a real outdoor pageant called "The Duplin Story" was performed in 1949 and 1950 and underwritten by a Kenan family foundation. That play, seventeen scenes of three minutes each, was written by Sam Byrd of nearby Mt. Olive, North Carolina, the actor who had portrayed Dude Lester in the long Broadway run of *Tobacco Road*. Its two acts, also, covered primarily the history of white settlers who became leading white families. In it, black residents performed largely as minor characters or rendered choral sound effects. North Carolina's governor attended one of the performances.

In the fictional life of Horace Cross, the summer theater job introduced him to gay male actors. He had an affair with Antonio Santangelo—part Italian, part Puerto Rican—and then with two other cast members. Confused, tormented by guilt, unable to invest his full self and capacity in love, Horace was becoming both promiscuous and unfulfilled. Revisiting the theater on this mad night of April 30, Horace encounters his own shadow self, who sits applying white greasepaint at a mirror. Then he is led to relive a night of debauchery at a final cast party held in the cemetery where the Scotch-Irish Crosses are buried.

Now both the night and the novel are rising to climax. When the demon makes Horace revisit that same graveyard, he is also offered a vision of African-American racial history. He shoots his own white-faced, actor-doppleganger, but lacks the strength to throw off the demon's influence, to respond to this larger vision and mature into one of those heroes who knows the grim past but can contribute to a better personal and communal future.

There follow some quick recollections of how, after that wild party, Horace's school grades slide downhill as do his hope for his future. "So this is it," his personal demon says (*Visitation* 235) as the night's "visitations" come full circle. "It is time."

In the last section ("Old Gods, New Demons"), Horace's "Confessions" again seem at first to digress. He describes the old way of killing a chicken, either by neck-wringing or with an ax: ("it would run and run fast, in a kind of womanish strut, as if somebody had told it some bad news and it was trying to run away and not hear it, all the while running with no head and blood just a-streaming red over its dusty white feathers" [*Visitation* 245]). It's a prophetic picture. But these six-and-a-half pages of rhythmic "I-remember" sentences seem to cascade like those in Ambrose Bierce's "Occurrence at Owl Creek Bridge," to pile up like the instant whir of a life passing before one's eyes, a life with its own bad news, whose original promise has in some ways been butchered like a hog or decapitated like a chicken. This section ends: "I remember me" (251).

Surely, all that remains for the final segment, 7:05 a.m. on April 30, 1984, is that Jimmy Greene will find Horace behind Tims Creek Elementary School, naked inside his borrowed coat, will vainly and too late try talking him into life rather than death, only to witness the gunshot blast into Horace's head and to scream.

But then, surprise! Instead of "The End," there appears on page 254 another three-page segment, "Requiem for Tobacco," an essay in omniscient prose addressed to "you," a counterpart to the hog-killing episode that was called "Advent, or The Beginning of the End." Here, too, the process of harvesting and curing tobacco as a community enterprise is reproduced in quiet, factual narrative—the movements required in hard, hot work, the sensory detail, a harvesting long since taken over by machines, and also a recognition of the death of that way of life, a death that is as much worth remembering as Horace's. "It is good to remember," says the novel's final sentence, "for too many forget" (257).

The novel's summary has been lengthy because there is no good way to explain exactly what Kenan does except by seeing him do it, bringing his individual vision to bear on Southern folklore and local history.

After publication of this first novel, which he has called a "cautionary tale," Kenan became all writer rather than part-time editor, teaching creative writing at Vassar, Sarah Lawrence, and Columbia, receiving a fellowship from the New York Foundation for the Arts and one from *Reader's Digest* to the MacDowell colony. He completed the twelve stories, also containing angels, ghosts, and demons, for his collection, *Let the Dead Bury Their Dead* (1992), working with editor Alane Mason, another product of UNC's senior honors writing seminar. Some of these stories were originally potential sections of *A Visitation of Spirits*; others develop the people and situations already set in motion there.

It is not only useful to read the volumes back-to-back, but some may wish that the title story of *Let the Dead Bury Their Dead* had been a preamble to rather than the final story in the novel, since these last fifty-one pages with footnotes, both real and invented, purport to be an oral history of Tims Creek (1854-1985) recorded in 1985 by the late Reverend Jimmy Greene (dead in a car wreck, 1998) in taped conversation with those same two Cross elders Ezekiel Thomas and Ruth Davis Cross, but made two months before Jimmy escorted them on the novel's long hospital trip December 8, 1985. Did Jimmy—who became the town's historian—respond in a small way to part of Horace's vision? The "R.K.," who with the aid of grants has organized and published Jimmy Greene's "papers," is identified as Reginald Gregory Kain and not author Kenan, although the story is dedicated to Kenan's real contemporaries, Nell Painter and Randy Page.

If the history of Tims Creek, with its mythologized black slave hero-leader (called Menes or Pharaoh), is an antidote to the lopsided mythology of Crosstown's pageant, it also recalls both Toni Morrison's *Song of Solomon* and the historical Nat Turner. Part of the writer-reader game will be this very pursuit of texts within texts, facts within fictions, mixed myth and reality. I tallied a few points when recognizing (among footnote sources from John Hope Franklin, Arna Bontemps, and William Styron) the apparently dead-serious citation of scholar Joseph A. Cincotti. (Joe Cincotti, also a gifted honors writing student at Chapel Hill, is currently on the staff of the *New York Times*.)

This title story then (or oral history/legend/artifact) makes its own contribution to a standard theme in American literature: What is reality? But Kenan puts his own English on that ball—Southern English, Black English, gay English—and makes old questions new with his personal version of magical realism, causing Terry McMillan to call him "our black Marquez."

For example, the botanical footnotes supplied to the narrative by R.K. about the persimmon tree (not the chinquapin!) are accurate and "real"; Canaan Plantation, home to the white Crosses in York, may or may not resemble Turkey Branch Plantation or Liberty Hall, which were homes to white Kenans in Duplin; the Southern Historical Collection at UNC-Chapel Hill is certainly real, and some volumes cited are, and are not, stored in it. Verbatim diaries of Rebecca Cross sound authentic but are invented, although they do mention the real chinquapin. The fictional white—and gay—Phineas Cross is said last century to have stumbled on what must have been the real Northeast Cape Fear River in Duplin and compared it with the Thames (Tims Creek—get it?) and so on. This "history" also introduces the Elihu McElwaine family, which figures in some of the other eleven stories set in Kenan's Yoknapatawpha, and who are destined to become central characters in his next novel.

As if serving as a corrective to Horace's suicide, the epigraph to *Let the Dead Bury Their Dead* is from Katherine Anne Porter's *Pale Horse, Pale Rider*, in which Miranda—near death during the 1918 flu epidemic—nonetheless fights through to life. These dozen stories, often erotic, often crossing fact with fantasy, also move beyond defeat. For instance, "The Foundations of the Earth," a title taken from God's challenging question to Job, has a post-Horace Cross theme with a happier resolution. Here Maggie Williams, six months after her grandson's funeral, can accept the fact that he had a white male lover whose smile "would make cold butter drip" (67), and thaws out her bias. This story and "Cornsilk" are among Kenan's favorites because they are the oldest in the collection and he "worked on them the hardest." He calls "Cornsilk," a story about the incest taboo, an even more "cautionary tale" than the novel. Here a first-person, heterosexual narrator recalls his passionate but doomed love affair with his half-sister.

In March 1991, when Kenan read for one of the first times with his family in the audience, he chose to read "Angel Unawares," perhaps indebted to Max Steele's story about a woman who lays a large blue egg that hatches into an angel. Here an Asian angel named Chi, which in Chinese and Korean means both angel and personal spirit, falls out of the sky into John Edgar Stokes's front yard. When Stokes's old dog Shep is wantonly killed by the wicked white

Terrells, Stokes, age eighty-six, shoots all their prized coon dogs and then is carried off to Heaven before he can be prosecuted.

Characters from the novel do reappear in the Tims Creek stories. The Reverend Hezekiah Barden, who is one of Maggie's visitors in "Foundations of the Earth," and who in the novel was the Baptist predecessor to the Reverend James Malachai Greene, is also the hypocritical narrator of "Ragnarok," an old Norse word equivalent to Armageddon. He is preaching a eulogy while his secret thoughts review his long, adulterous affair with the deceased.

In "The Strange and Tragic Ballad of Mabel Pearsall," the title character, a tormented schoolteacher who believes her run-around husband has fathered a child by another woman, actually baby-sits that child and ends up heaving the infant to its death. This story is reprinted in *The Christ-Haunted Landscape* (1994) along with a Kenan interview.

In "This Far," the historical Booker T. Washington comes in 1915 to Tims Creek to visit the McElwaine twins whom he knew at Hampton. Excerpts from Washington's *Up from Slavery* depict him as an accommodationist to whites in contrast to the unrelenting activism of the McElwaines, who have apparently seen and adopted that responsible racial vision offered Horace near the end of *A Visitation of Spirits* and have responded by organizing local schools, also by supporting Frederick Douglass, W.E.B. DuBois, and the new NAACP.

In other stories, a fifty-one-year-old woman in Newark, New Jersey (originally a McElwaine from Tims Creek), spends a vivid sexual weekend with a young boy; Essie cares for, and disciplines, a boy in her care. One white narrator, Ida Perry (in the story "Tell me, Tell me") is as haunted as Horace Cross ever was, but this time by the ghost of a small black boy who, by accident, witnessed her having sex with her boyfriend, Butch, back in 1937 at Emerald Isle Beach. Butch drowned him in the sea for punishment.

Not only does Kenan reverse the major white and minor black characters in his revised histories, but he also reverses stereotypes. In his York County, the blacks are usually educated, polite, civilized; whites on the fringes of their lives are the primitive savages. The Terrells kill an old man's dog. Percy Terrell in "Run, Mourner, Run" (whose title echoes a Harriet Tubman song) lies, steals, and blackmails to acquire more land and uses Dean Williams as if he owned him. Butch callously drowns a child.

One of Kenan's stories, "The Virtue Called Vanity," from *The Boston Review* (fall 1992), though not included in this collection, was chosen by Robert Gingher for his anthology of stories by North Carolinians, *The Rough Road Home* (1992). Here, another Tims Creek native, Geneva Hudson, age seventy-five, after witnessing a street-gang stabbing, decides to leave the safe Hillcrest Rest Home and take her chances on living a more vivid life outside.

As Dean Williams once responded to rhymes, she is activated by the blues lyrics of Koko Taylor's "Earthshaker."

In the spring of 1994, Kenan published his first nonfiction book, *James Baldwin*, which opens a series of twenty-nine young adult biographies (edited by Martin Duberman for Chelsea House) subtitled "Lives of Notable Gay Men and Lesbians." The frequent question in Baldwin's work is certainly echoed in Kenan's own themes: "Isn't love more important than color or gender?" Baldwin, whose mother would never tell him his father's name, giving his title *Nobody Knows My Name* an ironic double meaning, was—like Horace Cross— black and gay, pulled between judgmental religion and the youthful sexual desires it condemned and, said Baldwin, also "afraid of the evil within me." But unlike Horace Cross and much more like Kenan himself, Baldwin decided that "despair is a luxury only white men can afford."

Also during 1994, besides teaching and giving readings, Kenan was completing a second nonfiction book under option to Knopf, *Walking on Water*, an attempt to do with facts on a national scale what his fiction has already done in Duplin/York counties: redress the balance by presenting the untold story of black citizens as more than minor characters in a white society. For a year he traveled to Canada, New England, Alaska, and the desert Southwest, applying the techniques of V.S. Naipaul and Bruce Chatwin in delineating the diverse worlds of contemporary African-Americans. He has contributed numerous articles and reviews to magazines and has a second play in progress, the first having been performed in 1983 by a UNC student workshop.

Also under option to Harcourt is a novel tentatively titled *The Fire and the Baptism*, set in Tims Creek, Chapel Hill, and New York City. It will pick up the footnote from page 332 in the story collection stating that Elihu McElwaine, the last McElwaine of Tims Creek, killed a man in Chapel Hill while studying at UNC in 1963 and then disappeared. The projected plot involves McElwaine's kidnapping of two children—one black, one white—and his disappearance with the ransom money. In the novel, the lives of these kidnap victims will intersect twenty years later.

All these various fiction and nonfiction projects illustrate what Valerie Minor wrote of Kenan's work in *The Nation*, that "reclaiming life history—whether through apparition or scholarship—is a healing process of personal and cultural recovery" (28).

Kenan, in the fall of 1994 at age thirty-one, became the first William Blackburn Professor in the English Department at Duke University and, in 1995, received a Guggenheim Fellowship to continue that reclaiming and healing of myth and life history in his prose. Few American writers a decade out of college have produced so much, so fast, and so well. So meteoric has been

Kenan's rise to authority that when Toni Morrison won the Nobel Prize, the *Los Angeles Times* called him for a comment.

Unquestionably influenced by Morrison, he shares her sense of a writer's tribal responsibilities and has absorbed into his own vision and modified the way her characters, too, accept the supernatural while remaining firmly rooted in the real world. He has, also, a similar interest in how individuals do or do not fit into their communities. Both writers use elderly people as timeless markers of continuity and hard-won wisdom.

When Morrison, in *Playing in the Dark*, suggested that the story of "a black person, the experience of being bound and/or rejected" could become "a means of meditation—both safe and risky—on one's own humanity" (53), she might have been setting Kenan's agenda. And when she said that earlier literature had created the American as "new, white, and male," she might have been summarizing Kenan's York County historical drama about the white Cross family or, indeed, its real counterpart, the "Duplin Story" about the white Kenan family. White history, too, is mythological, lopsided, overblown. And *Uncle Tom's Cabin*, as Morrison has made clear, "was not written for Uncle Tom to read or be persuaded by."

Kenan brings to Morrison's "othering" his own high intelligence, a gift for lyrical prose as well as an ear for down-home speech, and an eye for earthbound reality. But he is also fortunate to be publishing his own first book a generation after Knopf had rejected James Baldwin's *Giovanni's Room* as "repugnant." In fact, Kenan's sexual scenes offer a broader, less restricted eroticism than Baldwin's, a joy of sex for straight as well as gay participants, in bodies not only black but white, within either young flesh or flesh that is older but ain't dead yet, an often celebratory sexuality lived out by very physical individuals whose specific genitals and skin become universalized. In Kenan, the sex, the family values, rural life, religious conflicts become—as Morrison advised—a means of "meditation . . . on one's own humanity" (53).

After his first novel was published, Randall Kenan answered one journalist's question in his home state by saying that his goal in life was "to be a good man," and added with a smile, "but I also need to find out what that means."

Whether in a Tims Creek church or in the mind of a troubled boy, in the biography of a writer who would never live in America after King's assassination, in the stories that pursue durable loves, close-knit families, a truer past history, and a more just present society, Kenan continues in his postmodern fictions to meditate—and to make his readers meditate—on their diverse humanity, on what being a good person really means.

Mary Hood

The Dark Side of the Moon

David Aiken

"The artist must possess the courageous soul. . . . The soul that dares and defies."

—Kate Chopin, *The Awakening*

Mary Hood's hair was as red as the clay from which her north Georgia characters are drawn when she started writing poems and short stories more than twenty-five years ago. She spent the first ten years of her career collecting rejection slips for works she had carefully placed on yellow legal pads with an old ink pen. These stories she revised at her typewriter and mailed out, hopeful an editor somewhere would accept her early efforts and give them a final resting place on the printed page. Mary Hood's hair has lost most of its redness, and her work—far from being that of a beginner—is now eagerly awaited by editors, reviewers, and readers.

Hood's first collection of short stories, *How Far She Went* (1984), won both the Flannery O'Connor Award for Short Fiction and the *Southern Review*/Louisiana State University Short Fiction Award. In 1986, "Something Good for Ginnie" won the National Magazine Award in fiction. In 1987, *And*

Venus Is Blue won the Townsend Prize for Fiction, the Lillian Smith Award, and the Dixie Council of Authors and Journalists Author-of-the-Year Award. In 1994, Hood was a Whiting Writers Award winner. Her stories have been anthologized in *Best American Short Stories, Editor's Choice, New Stories from the South, The Pushcart Prize Anthology, The Literary Dog,* and *Georgia Voices: Fiction.* They have been translated into Swedish, French, Japanese, and Dutch. Her prose has appeared in *Harper's Magazine, North America Review, Art & Antiques,* and *Southern Magazine.* Her stories have been published in *Yankee, The Georgia Review, Kenyon Review,* and *Ohio Review.* Her first novel, *Familiar Heat,* was published by Knopf in 1995.

When asked about early influences on her writing, Hood speaks candidly of her response to reading a true account of the Oregon settlers, the Quaker Whitmans, and their deaths at the hands of Indians. She read the Whitman biography while in elementary school at a time when she much preferred sports biographies. She says the book changed her eight-year-old life because it destroyed her illusions about reading as a means of escape from mundane reality. It prompted her to consider issues she is still confronting in both life and work. Hood speaks of her awakening: "I asked all sorts of questions about truth, about books, about what has to be, what has to be told, about justice, about God's care." She claims the experience also changed her choice of reading material for years: "I read silly stuff, nurse books, books with plucky heroines . . . formula books . . . so I would never fall off the high wire again." Then she adds, "But you can tell from my short fiction that I was branded from that early point. I really believe that. Truth is truth. How things ought to be is not always what we get" (Hood, "Real Life" 8).

Since Hood is dyslexic, reading has never been a simple pastime. "For me," she says, "the story of my reading is as important as the development of my writing." Displaying the candor typical of her short stories, she says, "There was no time to read in college. I finished in three years, going summers as well. After college, I read. My education began. Balzac, Turgenev, Chekhov, Dickens (whom I'd read all along, as my best friend, comforter, and delight), I.B. Singer, Katherine Anne Porter, Katherine Mansfield, Willa Cather, Virginia Woolf, Flannery O'Connor, Eudora Welty, Ernest Hemingway. Stories, always the short thing, if possible." Her library includes "shelves and shelves" of poetry which she read for "years and years." Poetry, she says, taught her compression, brevity, and clarity. She admires Virgil, prefers the *Georgics,* enjoys Chaucer and Shakespeare. She has also learned much from naturalists, saying of them, "They are poets, really." Thoreau is a "desk-top indispensable" as is the King James Version of the Bible. These books and authors represent only a few she has studied: "I do not seek out the easy ones, the ones that please my temper. I raise the bar and try for a higher jump," adding, "I hope that every book teaches me something; reading ought to have that much in its favor" (Letter to David Aiken and Della Jean Aiken).

After saying "my reading life and writing growth are linked," Mary Hood is quick to point out, "a lot of what and how I write comes from life itself." She confirms her own decision to write true-to-life stories when she exclaims, "People who write because of what they have lived—and not understood— not accepted—not forgiven—now there's a text!" (Letter). Her daily experience of people in the hills of Georgia and her unblinking fidelity to life as she knows it are the origins of the gutsy, down-to-earth writing of a uniquely gifted Southern author, whose forte is dialogue so real it rings true in the reader's ear.

Except for brief travel out of state, Mary Hood has spent her life in Georgia. She knows as much about the flora and fauna of Cherokee County, where she has lived in an area called Victoria since 1976, as she knows about the neighbors she first met as a polling officer in her local precinct, which at the time had less than five hundred people. Her early stories were set in her own community, which once had a ferry, a mill, a small village, family cemeteries, and an agrarian way of life—all buried now under Lake Allatoona. When she was writing the stories collected in *How Far She Went*, old Victoria was already gone, and Hood's little Victoria area was enduring the pressures of being subdivided. As trees were being cut and bulldozers were moving closer, Hood recorded the turmoil and dislocation in a few stories that well-wishers thought would never find an audience. On more than one occasion, people suggested that she might fare better by writing about uptown things and high-dollar stuff because little Victoria was not big enough to appeal to the modern reader interested in cities, glamorous lifestyles, and progressive ideas. Hood continued to express in her work a personal sense of sadness over the loss of a rural setting teeming with wildlife and independent people to the shopping centers and subdivisions. With a touch of Southern humor and perhaps a little defiance, she inscribed her first collection of short stories: "For little Victoria, big enough."

When not working as a polling officer, Hood tried an assortment of jobs: substitute teacher, library assistant, clerk in a department store; and for a long time she supported herself by painting portraits, rural scenes, and dogs. Hood's painting, which she began as a means to learn the inner workings of a crafts fair, was a forerunner to her short stories. Done by request and often painted on rustic implements such as old hand saws, her visual art was experimental in nature and a reflection of her region. Neighbors repeatedly asked her to paint pictures of deceased pets—"sometimes like saints with the radiance around their faces" (Hood, "Real Life" 6). Some of these pet owners became the subjects of Hood's expanded artistic endeavors, although not as much in paint as in carefully selected words.

The length to which Mary Hood goes in order to report the truth should not go unnoticed. Only a very careful reader will guess the extensive research she pours into her stories. In speaking, for instance, of her creation of character, Hood says, "It's like a collage. I don't even take living body parts. I take bottle caps and features and it's just a mess. I think that other writers take real, whole people. I always take emotions" (Letter). Herein lies the secret to Hood's memorable characters. A reader may have to imagine what a character looks like, but he or she is rarely left to wonder what a character is feeling. Whether cool disdain, concealed rage, calm assurance, quiet pleasure, or smug satisfaction, the reader easily identifies with the feelings Hood's characters experience.

Mary Hood excels not only in dialogue but also in wit and detail. Yet it is her ability to pass the head and hook the heart that leaves her readers deeply moved, even though much of what they have read comes closer to nightmare than to daydream. Set frequently in the foothills of Georgia, her stories illuminate the lives of quintessential Southerners who rarely flourish but somehow manage to survive. Her characters are the descendants of small-town people: shopkeepers, mill workers, truck drivers, and junk dealers. Often displaced and almost always financially hard-pressed, familiar with hard work, failure and firearms, her characters, young and old, have "pretty well gone to seed" (*Venus* 21) by the time we meet them.

Rhonda in "After Moore"—the lead story in *And Venus Is Blue*—is still in her teens when she greets her father-in-law for the first time: "I'm gonna call you Daddy," she announces, "because I never had a real one." Then Rhonda "hugged him fiercely, and didn't shy away from his rough beard, cud of tobacco, or the stump of his left arm. He never would tell her how he lost it. 'I'm no hero' is all he'd say" (*Venus* 21). But, as Hood makes clear, Rhonda and her father-in-law are heroic in holding on to the pieces of their fractured lives. Their combined efforts salvage a family, and their very "seediness" is what is needed to foster new life in a sadly dysfunctional group of kinfolk tottering on the brink of dissolution. They are also typical of the kind of characters Hood portrays. They slide, shadow side showing, right into our hearts, where we are surprised to find we can forgive them their mistakes and love them past their flaws.

Most of Hood's characters strike the reader as the moon strikes Delia in "And Venus Is Blue" the first time she sees it through a telescope: "It was so much more of a moon than she had suspected, huge, luminous, cold and unexpectedly true, not some little coin of light to carry in a mental pocket and know odd facts about but a world to itself, unknowable, with a dark side" (*Venus* 264). This is as good a description of Hood's work as it is of her characters. Her stories are short; observed from a distance, they might seem small collections of odd facts. On closer inspection, they assume large proportions. Under telescopic lenses, they prompt us to examine some big mysteries and to ask some important social questions: What is love? What is truth? Is evil born or made? Can cruelty be converted to kindness? Will money bring happiness? Is our society making it difficult to sustain family harmony? What price have we paid for progress? These and similar questions are at the heart of Mary Hood's artistry. Indeed, it is the blend of the existential and the social that makes her fiction compelling.

To examine these issues, Hood takes us out of the city, away from the ivory towers, far from the public experts in religion and society. She puts us in places where the only night lights are gifts of nature, not gadgets someone could make, sell, or buy. She does not allow us to steady our minds "on symbolic infinity rather than the universal sort" (*Venus* 265). Universal is where she aims, and universal is what we see in her work. She is at home in the dark, at peace with paradox, and perfectly capable of examining our shadows without fear.

Elizabeth Inglish in "A Country Girl" asks a journalist, "Are you writing a story story or a true story?" (*How Far* 54). One would never have to ask this question of Hood. Truth is her passion, her specialty. She knows the difference between what passes for truth just because it is written in a book or spoken by an expert and what is true because it fits and has been personally experienced. She also knows that there is a kernel of truth hidden in many a lie, and that sometimes lies are shadowy ways of expressing the deepest truths.

"After Moore" is one of Hood's finest works. It is buckshot with lines so funny the reader is forced to laugh while reading the gruesome details of a marriage gone bad in a big way. As social criticism, "After Moore" excels. The story, which begins with Moore, Rhonda, and their three sons talking to a family counselor, abounds with lies of every kind. Rhonda carries a fake I.D. Moore tells waitresses his sons are his brothers. Rhonda discovers her husband's "little book with names and dates" in his wallet, which she claims she looked through "not spying, just exercising a wifely prerogative." Moore declares "I've only been fired three times for my temper." Then he adds, "The real reason is I drink a little sometimes" (*Venus* 10). A few well-worn social lies are included. When Rhonda says of Moore, "He never did without anything nice he could owe for," Moore says, "You've got to go into debt to get ahead." No doubt Moore spends a lot trying to turn his life around: "I've been dried out, shrunk, reformed, recovered, rolfed, revived, acupunctured, hypnotized, and chiropractically adjusted" (*Venus* 29).

Mary Hood is fond of saying, "The world speaks. I listen and write what I hear" (Letter). Her collected work to 1997 is a testimony to experience. Like Delia in "And Venus Is Blue," who must confront the suicide of a father she loves deeply, we are forced by Hood to face unsettling facts in our own society. When Delia prays, "Not my daddy, not *my* daddy—not my *daddy*" we are left with our own echoes: not my world, not *my* world, not my *world*. Yet, having once caught sight of the truth, we cannot shut her books. We become kin to the hounds that fill her stories; our animal natures with their instincts for survival leap to life. And like Delia, we don't want to admit the possibility of suicide. We want to know who did the wounding and where, when, how, and why it happened. We look for someone or something to blame. We point one finger at shadows and find three pointed back at ourselves.

Mary Hood leaves the reader no rights, wrongs, or rules to follow. She neither praises nor blames her characters. She makes no excuses for their behavior. She gives them no A's for effort and offers no blue ribbons for good behavior. Nor does she cross losers off as lost souls or hand out F's penned in black to those who seem to have failed for lack of trying. In every story, Hood's persona remains the compassionate but scrupulously unbiased reporter who steadfastly shuns the role of judge. Aimed at the gut, her stories hit hard and leave gaping holes in the rosy tissue of our romantic notions. Like bullets of ice lodged in the belly, they may melt as we warm to the sting of their meaning, but we won't soon forget the force of their impact. Filled with more questions than answers and more truth than fiction, Hood's stories take on a haunting quality impossible to shake off.

In "The Goodwife Hawkins," Vinnie's last words one evening are "Hawk! Please don't." She says nothing more "till noon the next day, because Hawk taped her mouth shut with two-inch-wide adhesive and stood her against the refrigerator door, at attention, while he sat at the dinette table, pouring whiskey into his coffee and aiming the pistol at her good heart" (*Venus* 127). Many of Hood's characters have lost their homes and their locales. They often live on impoverished lots of land littered with trash and ringed by encroaching, though uninhabitable, progress. What was touted as benefit and blessing has become a curse, not unlike the living death Vinnie is left to endure as her once powerful and wealthy husband declines from the man he once was. From the title of the story to its last pitiful line, Hood reveals a world that flounders: Vinnie, Hawk, their children, their friends, their church, their community, and finally the collective society in which we also dwell.

Vinnie doesn't look like much of a good wife at first: "As soon as she touched Hawk's cold shoulder she knew he was good and dead, not sulking." We are shocked to find her not calling for an ambulance but rather going outside, "buttoning her sweater as she surveyed the damage. The yard looked bad, the hard-won lawn rain-trampled, its bright rye gone under the autumn's castings" (*Venus* 121). We find it hard to believe that Vinnie is going to clean up storm damage in her yard before she tends to the details of having her husband's body prepared for burial.

Gradually, though, our sympathies switch as we learn what Vinnie has endured. We witness her feeble attempts to get help: doctors and church members overlook her honest, if understated, appeals for assistance. We see her sink to the bottom of the same bottle Hawk was drinking from when his car hits a cattle truck head on, leaving him changed, "something gone wrong in his brain" (*Venus* 125). We see Vinnie, drunk at the wheel, having wrecks of her own. Even knowing that Hawk has had a head injury, followed by a stroke, we are reluctant to forgive what he does to his wife, as he trips her, hurls food at her, and shoves her head into pieces of furniture until she lies unconscious.

Then Hood puts us in their bedroom where Hawk has locked himself away from visitors. We see him, unable to dress himself, his body covered in blood where he has rolled in glass from a mirror shattered by his walker. We see him as Vinnie finds him, after she forces the lock with an ice pick: "He shook so hard she thought he was having a chill. 'I don't want them to see me like this,' he said. She realized he was crying" (*Venus* 136).

Like many of her stories, "The Goodwife Hawkins" puts God on trial with painful portrayals of human suffering. On the surface, God seems to have failed many of Hood's characters, because they often have good reason to be pathetic, sorry, and mean. But in Hood's fiction, the narrative persona paradoxically becomes the counsel for the defense. Hood depicts individuals like Vinnie living in, through, and beyond pain and suffering; doing the best they can; doing what they feel is right even if it is hard; forgiving rather than blaming; and letting their pain soften their hearts to a point where they are rendered redeemable.

Until shortly before its publication, the second volume of Mary Hood's stories was going to be called "Finding the Chain." Then, from her home Hood mailed her editor "And Venus Is Blue." He had had no idea what she was working on to conclude her collection. He read it, came back to his office, plopped it on the desk, sat down, and said "Jesus Christ!" (Lecture Notes). This novella would not only change the title of the collection, but it would also be the crowning achievement of the first part of Mary Hood's career. It is her most experimental story and surely one of the most powerful written recently by a Southern author. No one reads it even halfheartedly without being moved, and those who study it attest to its artistry and power.

The plot is simple enough. James Racing has committed suicide. Delia, his only child and the daughter of his first wife, must be told. What follows is Delia's day-to-night automobile journey from her residence in Maryland to her father's home in Pinedale, Georgia. The novella consists of nine sections, framed by "Daybreak" and "Midnight," which are related through the central intelligence of Webb Brannon. He is the brother of James's second wife, Carol, the foreman of James's construction crew, and Delia's first love. The seven internal sections, "Dawn: Delia, Age Two" through "Night: Delia, Age Seventeen" are gleaned from Delia's subconscious reservoir, which is busy pushing memories to the surface as she speeds down the highway.

In Delia's murky inner world of fantasies, memories, and dreams mixed with perceptions of the present, the reader enters a spaceless realm where time spirals. During the journey to Georgia, the reader is engrossed in Delia's inner world, where time and space have little relevance and where thoughts are experienced on a level of feeling rarely encountered in the mundane world. The epigraph is our guide: "Imagine a photograph album, with a bullet fired pointblank through it, every page with its scar. Murder attacks the future; suicide aims at the past" (*Venus* 203). Each of Delia's selected memories ends with the death of her father and is splattered with his blood. The impact of James's death reaches back to imprint itself on every memory of her past. So will his suicide reach forward to splatter her future. Its reality overshadowing all reason, James's death now has within Delia no beginning and no end.

The summer that Delia arrives at the airport—looking so much like her mother, Toni, that James is reminded of the pain of losing his first wife and only child in an unwanted divorce—James lives up to his last name by racing to Pinedale "like it was life or death to get Delia safely home." Along for the ride, his mother, Ma Jo, warns him, "You can't outrun it. You have to outlive it" (*Venus* 268). This wisdom is sewn in each of Hood's short stories. It is essential knowledge some of her characters learn and some do not. Those who learn go forward with their lives. Those who don't learn spiral downward.

Delia's mother leaves James partly because he does not provide enough to suit her. After she leaves, James redoubles his efforts, working harder, longer hours than anyone around him. He gives Delia expensive gifts while depriving himself of medical care and vacation time. In speaking of the telescope James bought Delia, Ma Jo says, he "paid on it for months, the best he could find to owe for, and he was always so proud." Then she adds, "that was how it had to be with James, nothing too good for his Delia" (*Venus* 264).

Delia's given ages and the insertion of factual detail provide a precise time frame for Hood's novella. During the Christmas vacation of her fifteenth year, Delia goes with her Georgia family up a ridge to view the comet Kohoutek. This comet, named after the astronomer who discovered it, was first seen on March 7, 1973, and was visible from earth through early 1974. Since we know Delia is two years old during "Dawn" and eighteen during "Midnight," the time of the story stretches from spring 1960 until spring 1977. In the story we are repeatedly told that "Delia listened." Emphasis is also placed on Delia's problem with her eyes. What Delia sees and hears is broader in scope than the wrenching crises of her family circle, for elements in the story remind the reader that Delia's youth is the time when televisions and radios were replacing fireflies and crickets as evening entertainment in even the smallest towns.

In 1960, television was entering American homes. There were 99 million televisions in the world; 85 million of these were in the United States. By 1970, there were 231 million televisions. What was seen and heard from 1960 to 1977? The Cuban Missile Crisis; the assassinations of JFK, Martin Luther King, and Robert

Kennedy; Watergate; Vietnam War scenes; race riots in major American cities. The race to space and the moon race became part of the Cold War between the United States and the Soviet Union. Pollution had become a problem everywhere. In 1969, Neil Armstrong walked on the moon, and rains in California caused mudslides which destroyed ten thousand homes and killed one hundred people. The energy crisis of 1973 added an additional one hundred thousand to the ranks of unemployed in the United States, and the dollar was devalued for the second time in two years. Worldwide inflation caused dramatic increases in the cost of fuel, food, and materials. In 1974, the United States Mariner 10 satellite transmitted detailed pictures of Venus and Mercury while a Russian space probe landed on Mars.

Set in this time period, Hood's stories imply a troublesome question. Was all the racing worth it? By portraying some of the assaulted people of the sixties and seventies, Mary Hood reveals a society that is failing to fulfill its promises.

In "A Country Girl," a young woman finds her bliss in a small rural town where red clay is solid under her bare feet, where wildlife is abundant, and where she is surrounded by extended family. She sits quietly on the porch, composing music in her head. "And some had the impression she was a fool" (*How Far* 66). But was she? After reading all of Mary Hood's stories, we are left to wonder if what individuals lost under the urgency of personal and collective racing was not the environment, the stability, and the humanity we were defending. Mary Hood's stories imply existential and social questions: in the flurry to compete, have we wasted our resources and compromised our ideals?

Although "Finding the Chain" precedes "And Venus Is Blue," this charmingly humorous work offers a hopeful resolution to some of these problems and could well have been placed at the end of the book. Cliffie's second husband, Ben, takes their family back to Cliffie's homeplace, a log cabin in the Georgia mountains, which she is going to have to sell. The trip becomes humorous because of the seemingly endless, though innocent blunders of Ben, his dog, Cliffie's two children by a previous husband, and the baby she has had by Ben. Though Ben "couldn't imagine what there was about red mud for Cliffie to love and miss" (*Venus* 186), he secretly digs up a crate-full as a surprise Christmas gift for his wife. He is helped by a stepson who is eager to please his mother but as reluctant to accept a stepfather as Cliffie is to accept Ben's dog as a family member.

Returning to the cabin in order to collect all the things "she could not bear to part with," Cliffie wants her family "to love the place as she did" and "to know everything, all the little stories" about it. There isn't much her helpers haven't managed to break, damage, or lose before they join together to search for a chain missing from the porch swing Cliffie wants to take home as a reminder of her father. About to abandon the search, "they closed ranks against the coming dark, against the soft, random [snow] flurries, against the idea of giving up" (*Venus* 200).

This story ends under a night sky in Georgia and puts a light face on the moon. It suggests there is time to save something of a more humane life by reclaiming the principles we lost on the dark side of our race to the moon.

In *Familiar Heat*, her third book, Hood leaps triumphantly from short story writer to novelist. Set in Sanavere, a small fishing town on the Florida coast, the novel is complex and riveting. Weaving together the life stories of more than a dozen fully developed characters, Hood works from the basic premise that love never fails. Shrimpers, fishermen, priests, shopkeepers, a net mender, a charter boat captain, a baseball star, a stone cutter, and a housekeeper all swirl around the figure of Faye Parry, who "wasn't ashamed of Parry's A-1 Dry Cleaning and Laundry, or of growing up over the shop."

As the book opens, Faye is the nineteen-year-old wife of Vic Rios, a Cuban charter boat captain who has earned a "devil-in-a-white-shirt reputation." Faye's mother, "a naturalized war bride, convent-educated, with a French father and a Vietnamese mother," does not approve of her daughter's marriage to a man she considers a "foreigner," even though Vic—like Faye—was born in Sanavere. When Faye is kidnapped and raped, her four-month-old marriage begins to unravel. She is deserted by her husband and pursued by a young baseball star until a car accident alters her life forever. "Her left leg and pelvis as smashed as her skull," Faye must move from coma to the consciousness of a drooling infant. All memory of her past is gone. Brain damaged and physically handicapped, she has little more than a childlike innocence to sustain her as she struggles to relearn everything from walking and talking to reading, writing, and relating to others.

Although several marriages in various states of distress are explored in *Familiar Heat*, Hood does not confine herself to romantic or married love. God's love, love of vocation, love of place and community, love of art, music, nature, and animals, love of parents, children, and friends are all put under the microscope. In 451 pages of earthy prose laced with the sad, the funny, and the lyrical, love triumphs as the generous people of a small town help to restore Faye Parry's life.

Mary Hood is not alone in suggesting that cures for social problems rarely rest in the hands of officials and experts. But she is typically Southern in suggesting that individuals can do what agencies cannot. She creates characters specific and real, who, like the moon, have both light and dark sides. She removes labels and invites the reader to do the same.

Hood does not write about alcoholics; she writes about Moore, Vinnie, Hawk, and Candy—men and women with problems, one of which just happens to be drinking to excess. She does not write about the elderly; she writes about Floyd who does not want to be a burden to anyone and yet is not able to function on his own. Nor does she write about victims of divorce and suicide; instead she writes about Toni who leaves her husband because she wants more money, glamour, and fun than he can provide and who is so concerned about her appearance that she dies an early death rather than have a mastectomy. She writes about James, a master craftsman, a loving man, who copes poorly with the loss of his first wife, who overworks to give his daughter whatever he thinks will please her, who goes into debt and does not take vacations or keep doctor's appointments, and who finally commits suicide. And she writes about Delia, who loves both of her parents, who must shuttle between them while trying to grow up, and who must eventually deal with her mother's cancer and death as well as her father's suicide.

Readers of Mary Hood's fiction will notice that her stories are varied and sometimes experimental. "After Moore" begins with privileged information revealed to a family counselor and expands beyond his office where the action unfolds as if still being related to a professional who has for all practical purposes vanished. "Finding the Chain" is narrated by a family of five. "And Venus Is Blue" challenges the notion of linear time. While such techniques are appropriate and praiseworthy, they pale beside Hood's skill in presenting dark subjects without inflaming her readers. Focused as they are on our common humanity, her stories bypass the issue of blame and carry the reader to a point where forgiveness is not only desirable but possible. Mary Hood's fiction suggests that we can salvage ourselves and our world, day by day, one person at a time.

James Wilcox

The Normality of Madness

HUGH RUPPERSBURG

Mental disorder has traditionally served in Southern literature as a signifier of social and cultural decay. In William Faulkner's *The Sound and the Fury*, Benjy Compson, described in the Appendix to that novel as a mongoloid idiot, is incapable of speech, reason, or the ability to differentiate between past and present. He is the emblem of a once noble Southern family's decline, of the Old South's decay, of modernist horror. Other congenitally handicapped characters in Faulkner's work, such as Tommy in *Sanctuary* and Ike Snopes in *The Hamlet*, hold similar meanings. Mentally aberrant characters allow a literary work to redefine mental normalcy: Benjy, in part, serves that purpose, as do Lucynell Crater in Flannery O'Connor's "The Life You Save May Be Your Own," Lily Daw in Eudora Welty's "Lily Daw and the Three Ladies," or Peyton Loftis in William Styron's *Lie Down in Darkness*. More significant, however, than these obviously mentally deficient or ill characters are those who appear normal on the surface, but who often suffer from some form of madness that renders them as incapable of reason as Benjy or Lucynell. Benjy's brother, Quentin, is a prime example. For these characters, madness is an expression of alienation from the community, from conventional values, from tradition and history, from the serene state of well-being that society is supposed to bestow on its inhabitants.

As the characteristic stance of modernity, alienation is the characteristic stance of modern Southern literature. But as a symptom of the individual Southerner's relation to mainstream American culture, it has been evident from a very early point in the development of Southern writing. Even in the twentieth century, writers including Faulkner, O'Connor, and Welty lived in a South which could still boast, with some assurance, of its regional distinctiveness and its mainly rural, agricultural lifestyle and economy, despite the factory smoke and Bronx accents beginning to filter in from the North. The South portrayed by these writers, whatever its defects (which for the most part these writers recognized), provided an alternative to the prevailing culture of the North. In the late nineteenth century, this alternative was defined by the myth of the Old South, while through much of the twentieth century, it took the form of a myth of an agricultural Eden. It is worth noting that throughout the course of Southern writing, those characters who suffer alienation also tend to be dispossessed and excluded from the mainstreams of Southern and American life. As Southerners they tend to be economically disadvantaged members of the lower class. They are clearly not part of the Southern elite, and in one way or another they are aware of their dispossession.

In the last thirty years, the distinctive cultural alternative once offered by the South has significantly diminished as the region has grown increasingly homogenized. The massive sprawling suburbs of Houston, New Orleans, Atlanta, and Charlotte, with their high percentages of inhabitants born outside the South, with no real sense of an identity rooted in region or place of birth, dramatically reflect this homogeneity. These changes have left a clear mark on Southern writing, and they have largely deprived it of the myths that formerly gave it a regional identity separate from mainstream American literature. Other changes, most especially the inclusion of African-American and other minority writers in Southern literature, have also contributed to this change and have brought the fundamental paradigm of Southern cultural exclusivity into question. In effect, it is this context in which many, if not most, contemporary Southern writers work.

Southern writing since 1960 has been much more concerned than previously with life in the city or town, even with suburban life, and one might well argue that superficial geographical differences are the only elements distinguishing the fiction of Walker Percy or Josephine Humphreys or Bobbie Ann Mason from their Northern contemporaries. Yet contemporary Southern writing is still marked by the same subterranean, disjunctive tensions that have marked it throughout its history, though both the source and the tenor of these tensions have changed. What often seems missing in contemporary Southern writing is that sense of a cultural alternative, that Southern community with its own set of values. Much Southern literature, even by politically liberal writers, has tended to view the world from a conservative, agrarian perspective. From this perspective the commercialized, industrialized world, especially as embodied in the North, is not a hospitable place for the individual or a meaningful lifestyle. This is not to say that all Southern literature defends a Southern status quo. Many modern Southern writers have taken strong stands against racism, for instance, and they have taken exception to their region in other ways. But they also have found in the South an alternative to what many regard as depersonalizing and hostile in much of the rest of the world.

In much recent Southern writing this alternative is conspicuously absent: the South offers no more solace than any other region, and the characters in many of these books live a limbo existence without a past to look back to or a future to anticipate. They suffer depression, nervous collapse, and fundamental disorientation. We find hints of such a South, though not yet fully realized, in the Compson family of *The Sound and the Fury*, though in that novel the Compsons have the consolation of a supposedly noble ancestral past to look back to. Increasingly, the characters of modern Southern writing have no such past, or they have lost it entirely, and the vacuum that was the past lies at the core of their discontent. Post-Reconstruction writing may have taken its strength from Old Southern myths, and early- to middle-twentieth-century Southern writing may draw sustenance from the perceived values of agrarianism, but much contemporary writing finds its subject in the cultural hollowness of Southern life.

In a deeply satiric and ironic way, John Kennedy Toole's *A Confederacy of Dunces* (1980, written in the mid-1960s) examines the discrepancies between modern Southern life and the traditional Southern past. New Orleans, where the novel is set, epitomizes these discrepancies. It is an old Southern town whose history runs back to the eighteenth century, but in post-World War II America, it has taken on a character considerably removed from the traditional Southern mainstream. Its central character, Ignatius J. Reilly, fancies himself a medievalist in revolt against the modern world. He considers New Orleans the center of western civilization, though he rails at the same time against its corruption. The traditional, rural South he regards as a "heart of darkness" seething with barbaric rednecks. Reilly is a genuine eccentric, isolated from reality, always plotting revolutions and personal vendettas that cannot succeed, convinced that vague and unseen forces conspire against him. He is not wholly mad, perhaps, but he is close to it. He self-consciously proclaims his alienation from contemporary life, and his madness is a manifestation of that alienation. But he is also a victim of the modern world in ways he has never considered. The source of this novel's comedy is a disordered world on the verge of madness, of complete and utter collapse. Ignatius J. Reilly rails against the cultural collapse of his world, and though he rejects the traditional rural South, he assumes the posture in this novel of a Southern agrarian both in his valuation of the traditional past and in his attitude towards the modern.

Gurney Norman's collection of stories, *Kinfolks: The Wilgus Stories* (1977), offers a more muted and somber examination of this theme. They are set in the coal-mining country of modern Kentucky. Even in their best days, the families of this region led a hard existence. Norman describes a time (apparently mid-twentieth century) when the coal has run out, the mines have closed, and the ravaged land left behind offers nothing to sustain the families. Norman's stories are organized around a boy's growth towards maturity in the midst of the gradual disintegration of his family. Chronic depression, alcoholism, unemployment, and violent arguments are the bane of his family's existence. The family's collective psyche is fragmented. Because most of the characters have never known anything better than what they have, they accept their bitter lot and do not consider leaving or seeking some way to improve the conditions of their lives.

In *A Confederacy of Dunces* and especially in *Kinfolks*, madness is both a product and a symbol of cultural dissolution, and of the absence of any counterbalancing alternative. This is certainly the case in the novel *Modern Baptists*, by Louisiana writer James Wilcox. Published in 1983, *Modern Baptists* was Wilcox's first novel, and he has since written five others: *North Gladiola* (1985), *Miss Undine's Living Room* (1987), *Sort of Rich* (1989), *Polite Sex* (1991), and *Guest of a Sinner* (1993). The first four occur in a small, remote town called Tula Springs, in the midlands of Louisiana. Tula Springs is a typical rural Southern town which, with the diminishing importance of the agricultural South, has lost whatever vitality and character it once had. It is like the town in Eudora Welty's *The Ponder Heart*, isolated by the departure of the railroad from the stream of modern life. In *Modern Baptists* Wilcox specifically links the decline of Tula Springs to the logging industry: "The last time a train had come down these tracks was in 1908, when Tula Springs was an important logging town. But after most of the pine and cypress were chopped down, the lumber company pulled out, and the railroad became nothing but a dividing line between the side of town where Mr. Pickens lived and the side of town where Mrs. Wedge went every Tuesday to pick up her maid" (8).

Most important, Tula Springs has lost the sense of community that once might have given its citizens a feeling of place and identity. The characters of *Modern Baptists* and Wilcox's other novels have no central point to turn to. This is his major theme: the search of the citizens of Tula Springs for purpose and meaning in a world where neither exists. Much of *Modern Baptists* concerns his characters' efforts to establish connections and make sense of themselves. This theme is implicitly stated in the epigraph to the novel, from Psalms 89:47: "Remember how short my time is," although the entire verse, and the one immediately following, is specifically pertinent to the novel: "Remember how short my time is: wherefore hast thou made all men in vain? What man is he that liveth, and shall not see death? Shall he deliver his soul from the hand of the grave?" This is a question that each of the major characters implicitly confronts, but which Carl Bobby Pickens, the main character, most fully faces.

Much of the humor in this droll, imaginative, and comic novel results from the subtly ironic satire that Wilcox directs at Tula Springs and its people. Characters and landscape are presented without much authorial commentary, as commonplace fact, with no ironic context to inform us that something about them is askew. A characteristic example is this description of the downtown area of Tula Springs:

> Next to Sonny Boy was a tin-roofed Laundromat, then three empty buildings, one of which—the old wooden hotel built by the lumber company—had a sign promising that it would soon be the home of JoJo's Health Food Emporium (the sign had been promising that for the past two years). Ajax Feed and Seed, across the alley from the hotel, had all sorts of signs painted right on the cinder blocks in letters that dripped—Purina Chow, Cash and Carry, Mash Spaciel—and if you looked hard, you could see underneath a coat of whitewash, Suck Eggs. After Ajax was a Western Auto and a shoe store that never had the size you wanted. Then came Iota's Poboys, a shack no bigger than a tollbooth on the Lake Pontchartrain Causeway. [8]

Wilcox concludes his description of Tula Springs by turning to the City Hall, a nineteenth-century building in serious disrepair: "The state had condemned City Hall, and for good reason: Although it was admittedly a handsome old building, after several fires it ended up being Greek Revival with twelve stately columns, it was downright dangerous" (9). Such humor is reminiscent of Eudora Welty and Harry Crews, especially of Crews, though both Welty and Wilcox tend towards understatement while Crews is a decided overstater. Humor in these descriptions derives from the disjunctive tension between the present in Tula Springs and its past. Even though the town's lagging modern economy is apparent in the businesses that dot the downtown area, it is not at all clear that the past was a significantly better time for the town. The only architectural character in the City Hall is the result of haphazard efforts at restoration after fires.

The hotel built in a time of prosperity is to be replaced by a health spa. Clearly, Tula Springs is in decline. At the same time, it is never really clear that it has ever been much more than banal, dull, and fairly normal. In an odd way, Wilcox emphasizes its dreary normality, as if to suggest that it is a world that should be familiar to us because it is the world we inhabit.

The novel's title refers both to the characters who populate the novel as well as to the spiritual dryness of their world. Although they pay lip service to religious belief, it no longer provides them with spiritual sustenance. All of them are looking for sustenance of one sort or another. They are recognizable types who, for the most part, belong to the middle or lower-middle class. There is little distinctive about them. They lack special talents and are not especially attractive or generous or selfish. At moments, the protagonist, Carl Bobby Pickens, verges on the repugnant. He is an overweight, short, balding bachelor in his early forties who lives alone in his mother's house. On the one hand, he fears any upheaval in his careful, sheltered life, yet on the other he feels oppressed and suffocated. He is a contemporary Prufrock who rarely asserts himself, although he thinks about doing so constantly, until his breakdown, when he does assert himself, with comically disastrous results. He seeks only to have his life continue on unchanged and unruffled. A number of events upset him: his doctor tells him that he has a malignant mole on his back. He is fired by the Sonny Boy Bargain Store where he works as assistant manager. He is accused of stealing a watch. And his half-brother, F.X., paroled from the state penitentiary, comes to live with him. Although the mole turns out to be benign, Bobby's brief contemplation of an early death, coupled with the loss of his job and the appearance of F.X., precipitates a major crisis. Bobby himself is the prime modern Baptist of the novel. He has, the novel often reminds us, a remarkable sense of right and wrong, yet despite his constant efforts to avoid doing wrong, he somehow always manages to get into trouble. Moreover, his efforts to do the right thing never bring him the rewards that he thinks should come to him. When he considers becoming a preacher, he plans to start a church that will rectify these wrongs:

> Mr. Pickens knew that once he got his preaching diploma, he would open a church for modern Baptists, Baptists who were sick to death of hell and sin being stuffed down their gullets every Sunday. There wasn't going to be any of that old-fashioned ranting and raving in Mr. Pickens's church. *His* Baptist church would be guided by reason and logic. Everyone could drink in moderation. Everyone could dance and pet as long as they were fifteen—well, maybe sixteen or seventeen. At thirty, if you still weren't married, you could sleep with someone, and it wouldn't be a sin—that is, as long as you loved that person. If you hit forty and were still single, you'd be eligible for adultery not being a sin, as long as no children's feelings got hurt and it was kept very discreet. [145]

Bobby's half-brother, F.X., could be the hero of his own novel, and he is as richly and satirically portrayed as Bobby. (In fact, F.X. appears as the some-time lover of the protagonist of Wilcox's fifth novel, *Polite Sex* [1991], set in New York City.) If Bobby has been hoping for fulfillment within the narrow confines of Tula Springs, F.X. has sought fame in Hollywood. His "real aim in life," Wilcox tells us, "was to be a celebrity, preferably a film star. . . . The last job he had . . . was in a revival of *Come Blow Your Horn* at a dinner theater near Ozone. Although he had a starring role, they made him sing a song in between the acts pushing the house drink, Cajun Catnip" (81). Never successful as an actor, his career has spiraled steadily downwards since his divorce from his second wife and his arrest for trying to sell cocaine to an actor. An athlete in high school, F.X. banks on his good looks to make him a star. Unfortunately, he soon becomes involved in selling cocaine again in Tula Springs and is severely beaten by a drug salesman from New Orleans, whom he undersells. This event F.X. conveniently uses to mark the end of his career, though his physical appearance is not permanently damaged.

Despite their differences, Bobby and F.X. share the desire to achieve their own individual versions of the American dream. Both engage in a meaning-less series of hollow gestures that they hope will move them closer to the ideals they long to achieve. Bobby prides himself on his grammar, on the fashionable tie he buys at a local clothing store, on his attendance at an opera at a nearby college. F.X. reads Shakespeare ("I got Shakespeare out of the library today, like *King Lear* . . . you know, heavy" [84]) and lifts weights, both activities that he vaguely associates with the success as an actor he hopes to achieve.

Virtually every character in the novel is searching for fulfillment and sat-isfaction (a search common to Wilcox's characters throughout his fiction). Aware of the American ideal of personal and professional success purveyed by the media, they fail to grasp its illusory, mythic nature, and they are held miserably in its sway. Wilcox offers in this novel a cast of characters who might populate some medieval tableau, a Chaucerian assembly of failures, ne'er-do-wells, and pathetic dreamers. Toinette Quaid, an eighteen-year-old beauty who works behind the candy counter at the Sonny Boy Bargain Store, longs desperately to escape Tula Springs. She falls in love with F.X., partially be-cause of his physique, partially because she shares his dream of Hollywood suc-cess. Her best friend is Burma LaSteele, also a Sonny Boy clerk. She is engaged to a thirty-five-year-old music major named Emmett Orney, who has a taste for pornography and undergraduate co-eds. And there is Donna Lee Keely, a young, self-styled liberal lawyer intent on demonstrating to Tula Springs her superior talents and social commitment, but unable to live too far from her parents, and never happy unless she is helping some unfortunate victim.

Focusing mainly on Bobby, F.X., Burma, and Donna Lee, Wilcox develops an increasingly complex tangle of relationships and neuroses. Bobby's passion for Toinette, his increasing irritation with F.X., who, it turns out, owns the deed to his house, his vague resentment of the man Burma intends to marry—all of these and more drive him to the breaking point. For a time he acts openly mad. He tries selling shoes, turns briefly to evangelism, then begins working as a legal secretary. The fundamental problem in his life is his sense of meaninglessness, of void, though he would never use such words to describe how he feels.

In one way or another the unarticulated apprehension of the void is a problem for everyone in the novel, though Bobby is most deeply afflicted. When he discovers that Toinette and F.X. are plotting to convince the police that she raped F.X. as a publicity stunt designed to bring him the attention he needs to get his break in Hollywood, when he further learns that they mean to blackmail him into testifying against Toinette, when his short career as a door-to-door shoe salesman and an evangelist come to naught, when he is suspected of beating F.X. nearly to death, and when finally he is discovered by Toinette's mother praying in the dark with a nude Emmett Orney, Bobby simply cracks and runs out the door into the night screaming "Hellfire and tarnation." This is not so much the breaking point for him as it is the climactic expression of what has been happening to him throughout the novel.

Other characters experience similar crises. F.X. claims that his acting career has been ruined by the beating, and he and Donna Lee fall in love. Donna Lee holds a biracial Christmas party for the poor children of Tula Springs at the town's former recreation center, only to discover that the center is the site of a toxic waste dump (toxic waste storage is the main industry in Tula Springs). Burma breaks off her engagement with Emmett, suspects that she is in love with Bobby, loses her job, and is taken up as a social cause by Donna Lee. What hope of resolution is there for these characters, Wilcox seems to ask. Can their lives ever improve? We can find the answer by comparing *Modern Baptists* to the novels of Walker Percy. Insanity or emotional instability as an expression of the modern individual's disaffection from the world was one of Percy's main themes. For Percy's protagonists, recovery from mental and spiritual malaise and subsequent reintegration into the world come about at least partially as the result of romantic love. This is certainly the case in *The Moviegoer* (1961). Human love, and the spiritual love to which it is linked, is a transforming agent that enables Percy's protagonists to develop a new and sustaining perspective. Wilcox's novels, especially the Tula Springs novels, do not offer much hope of transcendence. His characters must make do with what they have. Their only source of meaning resides in the small circle of relatives and acquaintances with whom they live their lives, and these are the same people, of course, who make them miserable.

At the end of *Modern Baptists*, Bobby achieves an understanding of sorts with the gruff and indifferent F.X., and the prospect of attending a Christmas Eve gathering at the house of Donna Lee's parents, where the refugees from the toxic waste of the recreation center have retreated, convinces him to go on. For him there is no alternative to living, short of suicide (which he briefly considers), but to continue living. The book's conclusion makes clear that this resolution is no victory, that it lacks any redemptive character, and that it does little to diminish the despair that has gripped his life. His only consolation lies in his discovery of a particular kind of kinship with his brother:

> The two brothers stood there a moment in the dim, cramped living room that was their home. Looking down at that damn plastic-covered love seat, Mr. Pickens felt that no one could ever understand his bitterness and defeat. But then, glancing over at his brother's face, he saw written there, in eyes black with pain, a story that was somehow like his own. . . . As they were walking down the sidewalk that cut the front yard in half Mr. Pickens was suddenly overcome with doubt again. He stopped, gazing up at the stars. It hurt a lot to look at them, those shameless stars, but he couldn't help looking. Then he felt an arm, around his shoulder—"Come on, son, they're waiting for us"—and with this yoke, which was easy, he was able to continue on his way. [239]

This is a surprisingly dark conclusion to such a comic novel, yet it is not quite so dark as it might be. The slight promise of reconciliation suggests that there may indeed be some rescue from the despair Bobby feels, but the book does not linger on that hope. Wilcox's later novels are much clearer in their suggestion that human relationships, however muddled and misdirected, may offer the only real protection from the emptiness of modern life.

In his second novel, *North Gladiola*, Wilcox examines a different strata of Tula Springs society: the Catholic middle class. The main character is a woman in her early fifties named Ethyl Mae Coco, the mother of six children, founder of the Pro Arts string quartet, and a struggling Catholic. Reminiscent of a number of the middle-aged women who populate Flannery O'Connor's short fiction, Mrs. Coco struggles to pursue her artistic ambitions, to keep her family intact, and to survive. The comic entanglements of *Modern Baptists* grow far more complicated in *North Gladiola*: they include a dead Chihuahua, a fiftyish Korean graduate student and member of the Pro Arts quartet named Duk-Soo who is secretly in love with Mrs. Coco, an incompetent psychiatrist, a schizophrenic teenager named Ray Jr., and a Samoan Catholic priest. Out of these and other disparate threads, Wilcox weaves an absurd and comic modern tapestry.

In a way similar to *Modern Baptists*, the plot of *North Gladiola* follows Mrs. Coco's struggle to maintain order in the face of increasing chaos. Her marriage is faltering, the neighbors suspect her of an affair with Duk-Soo, a beauty-shop proprietor suspects her of murdering a beloved pet, and she worries over her children, spread across the country, all but one of whom have moved far away, probably, Wilcox implies, to escape her interference. Yet Mrs. Coco, considerably less the caricature than Bobby Pickens, is no pasteboard character. She is a rich and vivid creation. She constantly violates, usually unwittingly, the same moral precepts she attempts to impose on her husband and children and neighbors, yet she is genuinely concerned with living a moral existence and doing good for others. Her befuddlement is more the consequence of the kind of life she attempts to live in the sort of world she happens to inhabit. She is a moral, religious, and artistic soul in a world that resists all three impulses. Because she herself is of that world, because she lacks the requisite moral fiber and artistic talent, she is torn by conflicting forces, driven to sin on the one hand, compelled to resist sin on the other, never quite able to see herself as she really is.

The result is that she misjudges and mistreats most of the people around her. She suspects Duk-Soo of molesting Ray Jr. and is horrified to discover that he might be in love with her. She has driven all but one of her children away, and the one who remains, George Henry, is clearly the damaged consequence of her well-intentioned mismanagement. His first marriage is a failure, and when he is on the verge of marrying a second time, Mrs. Coco tells him that she will not attend the ceremony because of the Catholic prohibition against divorce. When that marriage fails to happen, and George Henry decides to remarry his first wife, Mrs. Coco refuses to attend that wedding as well, even though she had longed for it.

North Gladiola demonstrates what *Modern Baptists* only hints at, and what Wilcox's later novels, especially the most recent ones, insist on: that psychological turmoil and spiritual crisis are not only deeply related but more or less indistinguishable. Once again, reconciled relationships provide some protection against the world's coldness.

Curiously, Wilcox carefully links the world of *North Gladiola* to that of *Modern Baptists*: Bobby Pickens appears again as the legal secretary of Donna Lee Keely's father (he is responsible for many of the rumors about Mrs. Coco), the owner of the dead Chihuahua is Burma LaSteele's mother, and Toinette Quaid appears in a beauty contest. They appear briefly, as if to draw a deliberate link between the concerns of both novels. Similar links and relationships exist among Wilcox's other novels. For example, the main character in his fifth novel, *Polite Sex*, set entirely in New York City, is a native of Tula Springs, and her occasional lover is F.X. Wilcox's most recent novels take place entirely in New York City, and the transition between Tula Springs and Manhattan is surprisingly smooth: life for New Yorkers is no more or less complicated than it is for the residents of small towns in rural Louisiana. (Only in his most recent novel, *Guest of a Sinner*, is there no link at all to Tula Springs.) One of the central themes that emerges from Wilcox's fiction is the clear sense that he is writing about the same spiritual and psychological landscape, regardless of where his characters might live geographically. Still, his earlier novels seem more comic than his later ones, perhaps because we are not accustomed to encountering the angst of modern life in the inhabitants of small towns such as Tula Springs, while modern angst is common in the fiction of large cities.

An interesting comparison to the fiction of James Wilcox lies in the books of Don DeLillo, a somewhat older novelist who came to prominence in the same decade as Wilcox. DeLillo's three recent novels, *White Noise* (1985), *Libra* (1988), and *Mao II* (1991), portray individuals against the backdrop of an American cultural and historical scene that not only informs their consciousness but controls it. DeLillo's characters have no existence apart from their culture and its defining institutions. The main figures in *Libra* and *Mao II*, for example, are the products of images of success and meaning projected by the national media. But the comparison seems most interesting in the case of *White Noise*. The family of Jack Gladney, a professor of Hitler Studies at a midwestern university noted for its department of popular culture, takes its identity from television images of family life, emotional well-being, and current events. Television has in fact replaced religion in DeLillo's novels as the central source of meaning and the defining images of existence in modern life. When Gladney's family is exposed to a toxic cloud of gas, they gauge their reactions by reports on television. Instead of looking out their window to view the cloud drifting towards them, they rely on radio and television news reports for information. In this sense, at least, their existence is wholly artificial, lived entirely within the social and technological context of their culture.

The characters in Wilcox's novels are similarly informed by, created by, their culture. All the major figures in *Modern Baptists* respond in one way or another to the images of success projected by national media. F.X., a would-be actor, in particular models himself on Hollywood images of beauty and success, as does Toinette Quaid. F.X. constantly watches television. Burma LaSteele and Bobby Pickens are self-consciously *not* the embodiments of popular images of beauty and success, and in one way or another their dissatisfaction stems from their awareness of the distance between the realities of their own lives and the American images of the Ideal.

Modern Baptists and *North Gladiola* set a pattern in plot and theme that Wilcox has followed throughout his later fiction. Although his most recent novels, *Polite Sex* and *Guest of a Sinner*, occur in New York, they continue to explore the lives of characters struggling to maintain order in a chaotic world. Wilcox does not exploit New York in the same comic way he exploited the world of Tula Springs, but his ability to portray complex characters in a way that is realistic, subtle, and still comic has matured considerably. *Modern Baptists* and *North Gladiola* remain his most comic and entertaining works.

In James Wilcox's fiction, madness is the defining metaphor of modern life, of the individual's relation to the modern world. It is a response by individual characters to their apprehension of the absence of meaning in modern life, to their growing sense of atrophy and entropy. The primary traits of Tula Springs are the essential traits of modern America and the modern world. Tula Springs is the world in microcosm, and Bobby Pickens is Everyman. Along with its comedy, its droll style, and its vivid characters, the universality of Tula Springs and its citizens helps to explain this book's success. *Modern Baptists* explores the insanity of modern life, the angst and neurotic uncertainty that grips us all. In this sense, James Wilcox is not a regionalist. As a chronicler of the modern age, he works as much in the tradition of Updike, Bellow, Cheever, and Malamud as he does in that of Faulkner, Percy, Welty, and Crews.

John Grisham

Obsessive Imagery

RANDOLPH PAUL RUNYON

Born in Arkansas in 1955, and raised in numerous towns throughout the South until his parents finally settled in Southaven, Mississippi, John Grisham has achieved remarkable success as a writer of compelling mysteries, all of which involve lawyers and take place almost entirely below the Mason-Dixon line. *A Time To Kill* (1989) is set in Ford County, a fictive northwest Mississippi locale to which he would return in *The Chamber* (1994), though the latter transpires primarily at the Mississippi State Prison at Parchman. Memphis is the setting for *The Firm* (1991), *The Client* (1993), and *The Rainmaker* (1995). *The Pelican Brief* (1992) has Louisiana roots, and *The Client* has some crucial scenes in New Orleans. Grisham's most recent novel, *The Runaway Jury* (1996), is set in Biloxi, Mississippi.

Though his Southern settings are probably not what attract most readers to his fiction, they are a fairly constant feature of his work. That his novels reveal a network of consistently intriguing literary imagery is perhaps less apparent at first reading.

In interviews Grisham has in fact tended to deprecate the literary value of his bestsellers. "This isn't serious literature," he told *People Weekly*, alluding to *The Firm*. He has often said he wished he could be allowed to write more of the kind of fiction his first novel exemplifies. "My motives were pure when I wrote *A Time to Kill*. It's better because you can almost smell the biscuits and the eggs and the grits and hear the chatter in the Coffee Shop; the people are better, the setting is better; you can feel the sweat sticking to their shirts in the July heat around the courthouse" (*Newsweek* 15 March 1993). This appreciation for atmosphere has no place in the formula for suspense Grisham divulged to *Writer's Digest* (July 1993): "You have to start with an opening so gripping that the reader becomes involved. . . . The end should be so compelling that people will stay up all night to finish the book. . . . You take a sympathetic hero or heroine, an ordinary person, and tie them into a horrible situation or conspiracy where their lives are at stake. . . . No flashbacks. . . . When you're writing suspense, you can't spend a lot of time on persons, places, or settings." Persons, places, and settings, if not flashbacks, are what his first novel is full of; the book is at the same time, as Grisham writes in an "Author's Note" to the Dell reprint, highly autobiographical. "I no longer practice law, but for ten years I did so in a manner very similar to Jake Brigance. . . . Jake and I are the same age. . . . Much of what he says and does is what I think I would say and do under the circumstances. . . . We've both lost sleep over clients and vomited in courthouse rest rooms" (xi-xii).

What Brigance, and thus Grisham, believes is that a father's premeditated murder of his daughter's rapists is morally defensible, even after they have been apprehended for the crime and have every likelihood of being convicted and sentenced to the state penitentiary (where, we are told, they will be raped until dead by outraged inmates). This, however, is not the moral issue the novel seems to want to raise; rather, because the father is black and the rapists are white and the state is Mississippi, the more immediate question is: Can Carl Lee Hailey get a fair trial from an all-white jury (which the district attorney is skillful enough to procure)? Has Southern society evolved enough by now that such a thing is possible? Can Jake Brigance succeed in making a father's rage more compelling than his race? To the extent that the book is read as a "Southern" novel, the racial issue will appear paramount.

Perhaps an even deeper, and thus more hidden, moral issue is raised by Brigance's foreknowledge of the crime. Carl Lee Hailey told him he was going to kill, and even said he thought he could get away with it if Brigance would agree to be his lawyer, for Brigance had once successfully defended Carl Lee's brother by convincing the jury that the man he killed had deserved to die. Hailey even asked him details about how prisoners are transported between the courtroom and the jail; with that knowledge he was able to leap out of a broom closet and fire upon the prisoners with an automatic rifle as they were being led down a flight of stairs. Before the murder, Brigance's wife Carla cannot understand how he can sit on this knowledge; Jake eventually does the right thing by alerting the sheriff, but Ozzie Walls—who happens to be the only black sheriff in the state—does not think Carl Lee would really do it. Jake's foreknowledge may not seem terribly important in the novel, but in the context of what we so far have of Grisham's oeuvre it begins to look like the seed for what will blossom into the innocent stumbling onto the truth that would prove so life-threatening for Mitchell McDeere, Darby Shaw, and Mark Sway in the three books to come.

In *The Pelican Brief* that foreknowledge takes the form of something that bears a remarkable resemblance to writing itself as Socrates defined it in the *Phaedrus*: the orphan text, set loose by its father—or mother, in Darby's case—into a world where it can only get into trouble: "Once a thing is put in writing, the composition, whatever it may be, drifts all over the place, rolling here and there, getting into the hands not only of those who understand it, but equally of those who have no business with it; it doesn't know how to address the right people, and not address the wrong" (Plato 521; translation modified). It is, as Jacques Derrida points out in his analysis of Plato's terminology in the dialogue, a *pharmakon*, a dangerous drug that can easily turn into a poison; a "*supplement*" too (in Derrida's terminology): an addition, be it ever so slight, that can upset the whole system. Certainly the White House is in turmoil, likewise Victor Mattiece's industrial-criminal organization.

Two Supreme Court justices have been assassinated on the same night. Chief Justice Runyan has set all the Court's law clerks to searching the files of upcoming cases to determine who could profit from such a crime. Runyan does not know that he has a rival in Tulane University law student Darby Shaw, who searches the record of the two dead justices' decisions to determine what they could have had in common, which turns out to be a penchant for ruling in favor of environmental causes. She connects this to some local Southern history: Louisiana oil tycoon Victor Mattiece has been blocked by a judge's injunction from drilling in the Louisiana wetlands, notwithstanding the suspicious death of a lawyer for the other side. When the case makes its way to the Supreme Court, a couple of new justices would be useful to his cause, and, Darby surmises, he must have thought it best to deal with that now, while a Republican President unlikely to be reelected is still in office.

But Darby is not at all convinced she is right. "I had [a suspect], but now I'm not so sure," she tells her law professor and lover Thomas Callahan. "I spent three days tracking it down . . . and printed out a thin rough draft of a brief which I have now discarded." He can't believe she has left his bed for three days for something she's now thrown away. "It can't be done," she concludes, "at least not with legal research. There's no pattern, no common thread" (90). Realizing, perhaps, that an author is not always the best judge of her own work, Callahan saves the brief from destruction, finds it "fascinating," and soon has occasion to show it to an old law school chum, motivated as much by the desire to show off his young mistress as by a sense of civic duty. Gavin Verheek just happens to be special legal counsel to F. Denton Voyles, director of the FBI.

Somehow Mattiece finds out about the contents of the brief, and a bomb that was meant for both of them kills Callahan in his car. "It fell into the wrong hands, wouldn't you say?" she would later say to Verheek (136), alluding to the brief, but echoing what Socrates once said about any written text. Later, to *Washington Post* reporter Gray Grantham, she would characterize it as "lethal" (266). "Where is the brief now?" Darby had asked Gavin. "Here and there," he had replied (135), in an unwittingly platonic way. Verheek had given it to someone else at FBI headquarters. "The brief had been passed upward all day until Voyles read it and liked it" (114-15). Not because it would be any help to the investigation; indeed, "he viewed it as a long shot, unworthy of serious attention" (115), "one notch above a practical joke" (141). But Voyles was at war with the president, who was mentioned in the brief, and saw it as a way to discomfit the White House, where he would pretend to take it very seriously indeed.

Just after she is made aware of the first fatal effect of the text to which she had given birth—the death of her lover in the explosion that was meant for her—Darby Shaw appears strikingly maternal: Wandering about dazed in the hospital where the police had taken her, "she looked like some child's mother" (134). For Socrates too, authorship confers parenthood. The wandering text, he goes on to say in the passage from the *Phaedrus* cited above, "always needs its parent to come to its help, being unable to defend or help itself." But of course the problem is that once consigned to writing, there is nothing the parent can do to keep it from mischief. Grisham lays stress as well on Darby's status as an author, the brief transforming her from law student to writer: "She told the facts succinctly, and made them interesting," thought Gavin Verheek. "Fascinating, really." "It dragged a bit" in the middle "but he kept reading. He was hooked." Though "implausible" it was "highly readable" (111). The head of the CIA gives it a review that suggests a parallel between Shaw and Grisham, whose success in writing enabled him to give up the practice of law: "very imaginative and a fine work of fiction. I think its author should forget about law school and pursue a career as a novelist" (224).

The Pelican Brief features another writer, the co-protagonist Gray Grantham, who writes for the *Washington Post*. Darby gets in touch with him, and arranges a meeting in a New York hotel in which she conveys to him the essence of the Pelican Brief. Its name, which it acquired during its passage through the FBI, derives from the endangered species that stood in the way of Mattiece's exploitation of the Louisiana wetlands, all outlined in the brief. Darby had given her only copy to Callahan; the version on her computer had been erased, and the floppies stolen, by Mattiece's operatives. But to undo the mischief her brief had caused (that is, its having called her to the attention of Mattiece, who is doing his best to put her away) she has to recreate the text from memory. Fortunately, she has sufficient power of recall: "I've rewritten most of it in longhand," she tells Grantham, to whom she is orally reciting its contents. She re-creates the brief, and this, combined with confirming evidence obtained through a lawyer at a Washington firm (who had provided Mattiece the analysis whose conclusion led to the demise of the two Supreme Court judges), will lead to the *Post* article that will bring all to light. Consequently, there will be no need for Mattiece to pursue her further, though she will still need Voyles's help to go into hiding to ensure her safety.

An author can stumble onto the truth without realizing it, can be right without knowing why, as Darby's brief abundantly shows. As Socrates said to Meno, leading him on, "if a man judges correctly which is the road [to Larissa], although he has never been there and doesn't know it, will he not also guide others aright?" (381). Similarly, the author of *The Pelican Brief* may not realize it, but his novel re-creates the outline of what Socrates says about writing in the *Phaedrus*. Plato's protagonist calls writing a *pharmakon* when he tells the story of its origins in Egypt (the country where, as it happens, Mattiece will disappear at the end of the novel [423]). The god Theuth, proud of his discovery, presents the new invention to King Thamus. "O king . . . my discovery provides a prescription [*pharmakon*] for memory and wisdom." The king, in his wisdom, rejects the gift. "If men learn this, it will implant forgetfulness in their souls; they will cease to exercise memory because they rely on that which is written, calling things to remembrance no longer from within themselves, but by means of external marks" (520). Though Socrates appears to adopt Thamus's condemnation of writing, he nevertheless leaves open the possibility of something like a good kind of writing, its better twin: Isn't there another sort of discourse, he asks, "that is brother to the written speech, but of unquestioned legitimacy? . . . The sort that goes together with knowledge, and is written in the soul of the learner, that can defend itself, and knows to whom it should speak and to whom it should say nothing" (521). Though he goes on to say that what he means is "living speech," it nevertheless has a "written" component, for it is "*written* in the soul."

Now the Pelican Brief, lost but not forgotten, written as it were in Darby's memory, comes remarkably close to incarnating what Socrates is describing. At least its second version does, the one Darby recites to Grantham and writes out from memory. Furthermore, as a *pharmakon*—in the full context of Derrida's elucidation of the text (based on a close reading of the network of related words in all of Plato's works)—once writing is set loose upon the world the only workable antidote is more writing. It's too late for anything else. And this purpose the *Post* article, whose writing and publication are the novel's denouement, admirably serves.

In *The Client*, the orphan text is, literally, an orphan. Or at least would like to be. Mark Sway came close to killing his father the night he "damned near took his head off with the baseball bat. A perfect shot to the nose" (155). The eleven-year-old, who lives with his mother and younger brother in a trailer park, becomes the repository of a dangerous piece of information when a mob lawyer tells him where his boss buried the body of Senator Boyd Boyette, then commits suicide. No one knows that he knows this, and he tries to conceal his presence at the scene, but the mobster boss suspects that he knows, and so Mark's life is in danger. The parallel with *The Pelican Brief* is obvious; similarly in *The Firm*, when Mitchell McDeere discovers that his new employer launders money for the Mafia, it becomes a question of "do they know that I know (that they know [that I know])." In a highly negative review of the film of *The Pelican Brief*, Anthony Lane in *The New Yorker* asks, "Why do people read John Grisham? They say that he forces you to keep on flipping the pages, but then so does a Rolodex. . . . I remember the awed shock that overcame me as I realized what the pivotal event of *The Firm* [he means the book] was going to be: *photocopying.*" Lane goes on to complain about "the lure of office machinery," missing the point that *of course* Grisham's book is about photocopying (McDeere copies some ten thousand pages of the firm's files to give the FBI enough evidence to indict)—because, like *The Pelican Brief*, it's about the dissemination of text.

Mark Sway's oedipal effort shows that *The Client* is about a whole other issue as well. Curiously, the only scrap of biography on the dust jacket is "He coaches Little League baseball in Oxford, Mississippi"; Grisham, who told the *Newsweek* interviewer that as an adolescent his consuming passion was the same sport Mark put to such a special use (Grisham's "eighth-grade teacher noticed 'special qualities' in him; prime among them were fierce self-confidence and a drive to be No. 1. But he devoted those resources to baseball"), indeed makes his past and present baseball prowess part of the public text of his life. One might well wonder if he is not inviting his readers to speculate about whether there is more than a baseball connection between the author and his child protagonist. One would be, however, on safer ground reading texts than lives, and there is quite enough material for analysis in the novels to show that fathers, good and bad, are an integral part of the typical Grisham plot.

The senior Sway was an abusive father, especially when drunk; the junior Sway swung in self-defense, and in a vain attempt to protect his mother. Half the oedipal ordeal is discovering oneself in bed with one's mother; the father inflicts something like this on the son when he strips Mark's mother naked and throws her into the street, and then, despite the bat's blow to his nose (and the boy's "trying to land a good one in the crotch"), strips him naked too: "Not a bit of clothing. I guess he wanted me in the street with my mother, but about

that time she made it to the door and fell on me" (155). After this scene recollected from four years before (Grisham beginning with *The Client* to violate
his rule against flashbacks), this thoroughly bad father disappears from the scene,
his place more than filled by the evil—and, as his nickname implies, castrat-
ing—Barry The Blade. As the name of his victim implies—Boyd Boyette—
the Blade kills little *boys*. It is his eyes that cut, and pierce: "To the average
person, the sight of Barry The Blade's eyes cutting and darting and searching
for violence would loosen the bowels" (21).

The firm in *The Firm* is "a big family, of sorts" (18). Mitchell McDeere
would discover just how close-knit a family when he learns that it is owned by
the Mafia. No one in the firm can divulge the secret; no one can leave. After a
few years the new associates undergo a rite of passage: they are told the truth,
their childlike innocence forever gone. Led like a lamb to the slaughter,
McDeere is charmed at his interview by the aptly named Oliver Lambert, of
the two senior partners the kindly "grandfather of the firm" (3). Only later,
when he is locked in for life, does he meet Nathan Locke, the evil father (or
grandfather) with the sinister eyes. "Mitch . . . knew for certain he had never
been within a hundred yards of Nathan Locke. He would have remembered.
It was the eyes, the cold black eyes with layers of black wrinkles around them.
Great eyes. Unforgettable eyes. . . . Knowing eyes" (72).

Our only glimpse of Victor Mattiece shares some features with Mitch's
first view of Nathan Locke. It takes place through the eyes of Matthew Barr,
sent by Fletcher Coal, the power behind the president, to ask if the Pelican
Brief is true. His blindfold removed, Barr sees a Howard Hughes-ish figure,
gaunt and bearded. But then Mattiece turns his back to conduct the interview.
At its conclusion Mattiece turns back to face his interlocutor, no longer piti-
able but frightening. The first things we see are his eyes: "Mattiece turned
slowly and looked at Barr. The eyes were dark and red" (350). When Nathan
Locke spoke, McDeere noticed his "eyes narrowed and the black pupils glowed
fiercely" (72). In both scenes, the eyes, at once dark and glowing, black and
red, convey the essence of the man, and in both we are not allowed to behold
them until the right theatrical moment.

A *Time to Kill* stands apart from the subsequent three novels for a number
of reasons, but one of particular relevance here is that it is the only Grisham
story in which the protagonist has achieved paternity. Jake and Carla Brigance
are the doting parents of four-year-old Hanna (though she is "the only child,
and there would be no others" [19], given her difficult birth). Jake has to be a
father, and of a daughter; otherwise, he could not so readily put himself in the
shoes of Carl Lee Hailey. While the Klan, as a criminal organization with a
long memory whose crimes tend to go unpunished, does resemble the Mafia
(or the long arm of Victor Mattiece) of the other novels, Brigance is not at its

mercy to the extent that the other protagonists are; nor is he caught in the grip of an evil father whom he must slay or escape. Mitchell McDeere, however, is; and in contrast to Jake Brigance, he is unable to become a father himself until he can deal with his own. "Babies are encouraged" by Bendini, Lambert & Locke, Kay Quin tells Abby McDeere (26), but that's because they become hostages to the firm's terrible secret. Having discovered the secret, Mitchell and Abby will have no children until they can make their escape. In this they are following the advice of F. Denton Voyles: "Don't have any kids in the near future. They're easy targets" (240). Besides, the couple's ardor for making love has been chilled by the realization that every sound they make is picked up on the bugs planted throughout the house; the eyes (in this instance, the ears) of the father are indeed oppressive.

Given that Mitchell cannot yet attain fatherhood, and thus remains trapped in a childhood prolonged by the father he must destroy, Grisham's *The Client* is less a departure from than an intensification of his earlier work. For the hero is quite literally a child. Having already proved his ability to strike at his dad, Mark immediately progresses to what appears to be the next necessary step in Grisham's scenario for maturation: coming to terms with the mother. But before he can encounter her in the form of lawyer Reggie Love, like the hero of a fairy tale faced with three doors and obliged to make, by luck or by wit, the proper choice, he must choose a lawyer. He had heard ambulance chaser Gill Teal make his pitch to someone else, and seen his ads on TV, so Teal was his first choice. He knew he wouldn't be happy with someone named "J. Winston Buckner. F. MacDonald Durston. I. Hempstead Crawford. The more names Mark read [on the office building doors], the more he longed for plain old Gill Teal" (77).

Luckily, he is ill-treated by Teal's secretary, and thus continues his search (otherwise, given Grisham's penchant for funny but accurate naming, he would have chosen a lawyer whose name sounded too much like "guilty") until he finds Reggie Love's nameplate on her door. Fifty-two years old, though less than five years out of law school, Reggie has "very short, very gray hair" (80) and is, despite her name, a woman. Given what we know about Mark, Grisham, and the national pastime, it is intriguing that the boy should say to himself "It was strange calling this lady by *a baseball name*" (82), thinking of Reggie Jackson. Indeed, an almost obsessive attention is paid to Ms. Love's first name. "Where in the world did she get a name like Reggie?" New Orleans District Attorney Foltrigg asked, "thoroughly baffled by it." A colleague informs him that her original name had been Regina, adding, "I guess she got Reggie from Regina, but I've never asked" (108), as if it were not perfectly obvious that she had. Mark, still puzzled, would later ask Reggie's mother the reason for the change (187).

"The first thing he noticed about her was her hair," Grisham tells us about Mark's first glimpse of Reggie. "It was gray and shorter than his. . . . He'd never seen a woman with gray hair worn so short" (81). Women in Grisham's novels are in constant danger of drastic haircuts. In *The Firm*, Mitchell McDeere tells his wife Abby that she must cut her hair "extremely short" and change its color in order to elude the police and the mob. Under her direction, his brother Ray gives her "a boyish cut, well above the ears, with bangs" (449), anticipating the Reggie Love look, which is likewise "very short above the ears . . . with bangs" (81). For the same motive, Darby Shaw has recourse to the same technique: "It took two painful hours with dull scissors to cut it off yet leave some semblance of style. She would keep it under a cap or hat until who knows when" (156). She will call it, jokingly, "sort of the punk look," but also, with accuracy, a self-mutilation. "If she lived another two days, she would cut some more. . . . If she lived another week, she might be bald" (203).

That this sort of mutilation is almost an obsession in Grisham is evident from the fact that it even takes place in *A Time to Kill*, where it is not, as elsewhere, performed by the woman herself for the sake of a change of identity (Reggie Love apparently did it to make a break with her past), but done *to* her in a sadistic way. The gorgeous and brainy Ellen Roark, who magically appears on Jake Brigance's doorstep to assist him in the defense of Carl Lee Hailey, just as suddenly disappears from the novel when she is kidnapped by the Ku Klux Klan and forced to suffer a number of indignities, of which the final one is the violent infliction of a bad haircut. "With his knife, he cut her hair. He grabbed handfuls and hacked away until her scalp was gapped and ugly. It piled gently around her feet" (433). When their eyes first met, Jake had not failed to notice the glory of her hair: "The noon sun burned brightly and blinded her as she looked up in his direction. It also illuminated her light, goldish red hair" (294). (Darby's had been, incidentally, of a similar, though more somber, hue: "Her thick, dark red hair was now in a paper sack in the closet" [156].)

If all these close-cropped coiffures begin to resemble each other, so too does Reggie Love, who becomes a mother to Mark Sway to the extent that a practicing attorney can, calling to mind the one real mother a Grisham protagonist is granted, Mitchell McDeere's in *The Firm*. They are but a year apart in age, and both have (prematurely, one could say, at that age) gray hair that is conspicuous for its absence. McDeere does not talk to his mother in the novel, just gazes at her from a taxi in the parking lot of the restaurant where she works. "Her gray hair was pulled tightly and hidden under the Waffle Hut bonnet. She was fifty-one, and from the distance she looked her age. Nothing worse" (206). Similarly, to Mark Sway, Reggie Love, who is "fifty-two," "wasn't old and she wasn't young" (81).

Why is it Grisham keeps making the hair of these women disappear? Freud has an answer that seems compelling. In Medusa of the long serpentine locks he found the mother, particularly from the son's point of view. "The terror of Medusa is . . . a terror of castration that is linked to the sight of something. Numerous analyses have made us familiar with the occasion for this: it occurs when a boy, who has hitherto been unwilling to believe the threat of castration, catches sight of the female genitals, probably those of an adult, surrounded by hair, and essentially those of his mother" (Freud, "Medusa's Head," 212). Perseus, the story goes, cut off her head because the sight of her turned men to stone (which Freud interprets, logically enough, as a certain sexual firmness); he could only regard her indirectly through the mirror of his shield. Grisham's women get their hair hacked off instead of their heads. But the hair is precisely what Freud found most menacing anyway: multiple penises (actually, writhing serpents) that made men feel threatened.

Grisham's heroes, then, must not only do away with or get away from their fathers, but must remove the threat their mothers pose as well by cutting their hair, hiding their sex, making them look like boys. Mark Sway accomplishes this by replacing his young mother (the one his father made him be naked with) with one whose hair is shorter than his and of an age more appropriate to the mother of a typical Grisham protagonist (Reggie Love is prevented from grandmother status by having a mother of her own, Momma Love, who fully plays the grandmother to Mark). Mitchell McDeere takes care to see his mother only when her hair is hidden by the Waffle Hut hat, and makes his wife cut hers off to ensure their escape from the Firm (whose name, like so many in Grisham, acquires its own second sense). Jake Brigance's tortuous route to courtroom success does not neglect to pass through a parallel episode in the form of Ellen Roark's ordeal.

The Pelican Brief might not seem to fit this pattern, given its female protagonist: How could she be a son? Yet, given, too, that (as Grisham told Mathews in *Newsweek*) he wrote that novel "partly to convince [his wife] that he could invent a strong woman," he nevertheless found a way to bring in a stand-in for the more typically male character on the lam from a menacing father. Gray Grantham, like practically everyone else, has an intriguing name, all the more so for its doing what the names of Grisham's other male protagonists do not do, which is to evoke his own: GRANTHAM/GRISHAM (what they have in common evokes writing itself, the Greek *gramma*). As someone remarks in *The Client*, "Where do they get these names?" (49). Or with more pertinence, as Gavin Verheek once remarked to Thomas Callahan, apropos of Darby Shaw, "You could always pick names, Thomas. I remember women you turned down because you didn't like the names. Gorgeous, hot women, but with flat names. Darby. Has a nice erotic touch to it. What a name" (75). Darby Shaw does have an evocative name, not only for its androgyny but also for its possessing half the letters of Mark Sway's first name and three-quarters of his last: DARBY/ MARK SHAW/SWAY. If *The Pelican Brief* were a dream, Freud would have remarked that all this commentary on Darby's name that Grisham puts into what Gavin says to Thomas is a displacement serving to conceal the real issue, which would be the extra-textually evocative quality of the name of her colleague and fellow-writer Gray Grantham. Grantham's first name (in addition to the alliteration it forms with his last) duplicates that of another protagonist's double, the strangely twinlike brother of *The Firm*'s hero, the convicted felon *Ray* McDeere. "Were it not for a scar on Ray's forehead and a few wrinkles around the eyes [which recall the "layers of black wrinkles" surrounding the eyes of the dread father Nathan Locke (72), suggesting the potentiality for seeing the father within one's own reflection], they could pass for twins" (133). In fact, the novel's denouement is triggered by Lamar Quin's spotting Ray and thinking it could be Mitchell.

Grisham's delight in names is Dickensian, giving us Judge Noose (a hanging judge?) in *A Time to Kill,* along with rural characters like Cobb, Maples, and Grist. "Brigance" suggests both "brig" (as in "jail") and brigandage; appropriately so, as Brigance is enough of an outlaw to break the law to win his case. Curiously, his wife and his client have the same name: Carla and Carl. In *The Firm,* besides Locke and Lambert, there are the two FBI agents Tarrance and Tarry, who both exemplify why McDeere does not trust the FBI: Wayne Tarrance (always called by his last name) for his incompetence, Tarry Ross (customarily known by his first) for his treason. About as blatant as Judge Noose is Middle Eastern terrorist Khamel, who kills the justices and tries to assassinate Darby Shaw. Though the accent may fall on the second syllable (and does so in the film), it's hard not to read it the other way. In the same book, the FBI and CIA communicate through the occasional secret tryst of a Trope and a Booker, each of whom may well wonder if the other's name is for real. "His real name was Trope, and he wondered if Booker was a real name. Probably not" (239). The joke may be that, while both may exist only in the realm of language, it's Trope that sounds the more purely rhetorical.

While Runyan is more than willing to take the credit for ordering the Supreme Court's law clerks to set about finding the killer of his two colleagues by searching the docket of upcoming cases, he had not been the first to propose it. Justice Thurow had in the beginning instructed his own law clerks to do so, and proposed that the rest join in, but the Chief Justice thought it "a bit premature." He finally relented, yet insisted on waiting until the following week to start. Grisham's heroine, of course, discovers the truth (though without fully realizing it) long before either Thurow or Runyan do. Yet, that a *Thurow* should be a rival to Grisham's protagonist, and that there is some question of who had the idea first, is surely not due to chance, as Grisham has taken pains to point out to his public that if he and fellow legal thriller novelist *Turow* were both working on the same kind of thing at the same time, it was purely due to chance: "I must disclaim any inspiration from Scott Turow. A month before *Presumed Innocent* was published, my agent in New York received the first draft of *A Time to Kill,* my first novel. I swear. My agent can verify this, under oath if necessary" (Grisham, "The Rise of the Legal Thriller" 33).

Then there's courtroom stenographer Gregg in *The Client,* who no doubt also knows shorthand. Mark, as orphan text, repository of fatal information (practically Bellerophontic in its danger to the bearer), is equally well named, for a *mark* is a piece of writing, even if only the least amount of text that can still deserve the name. "Mark Sway" would thus become "Mark's Way," the way of a mark, the errant path traced by a wandering orphan text.

But it's the name of the one recurring character in Grisham's post-*Time* novels that deserves the closest scrutiny: F. Denton Voyles, director of the FBI for forty-two years (though clearly not J. Edgar Hoover, as mention is made of the Hoover building). His constant presence in these three novels is increasingly reassuring, for he is the good father, the counterpart and worthy opponent to all the bad ones. The narrator of *The Pelican Brief* suggests the extent to which Voyles could be the double of the mobsters who so persistently pursue Grisham's protagonists: "All dressed in dark coats," Voyles and his entourage entering the offices of the *Washington Post* "resembled a Mafia don with bodyguards. . . . Though not striking, F. Denton Voyles was a presence" (403).

An interesting progression can be detected from *The Firm* to *The Pelican Brief* to *The Client*: more and more, Grisham's protagonists come to trust the FBI, in particular Voyles. Mitchell McDeere trusts him not at all, the novel ending with his flight from both the Bureau and the Firm. Darby Shaw, however, observes of Voyles, "I didn't like him at first, but he sort of grows on you" (420). Her words mean more than she realizes, for he evidently grows on Grisham too, in the context of the progression of which I speak. Darby accepts the offer of Voyles's private jet to get out of town; trusting his promise not to have her followed, she will then take a commercial flight to parts unknown. Mark Sway goes the whole way, not just—like Darby—in the manner of his flight, departing in the FBI plane, but also in its destination, placing himself and his family fully in Voyles's hands, trusting to the ability of the Bureau's witness protection program to hide them forever from the mob.

Darby in fact realizes that she was wrong not to have put her faith in the FBI from the beginning. "If she had trusted Gavin after the first phone call, he would be alive and she would never have held hands with Khamel," the assassin who tracked her down and almost killed her. "There comes a time when you give up and start trusting people" (416). Yet in *The Pelican Brief* Voyles is not entirely without blame. Had he not decided to use the Pelican Brief against the president in a relatively meaningless political skirmish, despite his initial impression that it was of no value to the investigation, then nothing would have happened to Callahan, Verheek, or Darby Shaw. (Though in that case the murders might never have been solved.)

In *The Client*, however, he is entirely faultless, even if some of his agents (Trumann and McThune, putty in Reggie's hands) display incompetence. Something happens, then, between *The Firm* and *The Client*, both in terms of the protagonists' increasing level of trust in Voyles and in his increasing worthiness of that trust—something like a narrative between the lines, or in this case between the books. As in many good tales, its end is in its beginning, in *The Firm*. An extraordinarily bizarre parallel within that novel signals its presence: in the sole scene of personal contact between McDeere and Voyles, "Voyles sat close to Mitch" on a park bench near the Vietnam Veterans Memorial, "their legs touching." Later, in a bar in the Cayman Islands, Tammy Hemphill, Mitchell's confederate, will seduce firm associate Avery Tolar by allowing him to move "his chair closer to her. Now their legs were touching." Such an enjambment, banal if understandable in a scene of seduction, slightly unsettling yet not especially remarkable in a meeting between the director of the FBI and a potential informant, is suddenly charged with potential significance when one realizes it has happened twice in the same novel. Tammy wanted Avery to succumb so that she could photocopy the documents in his Cayman Island condo; Avery wanted to get Tammy to bed; each had designs on the other. In the plot of the novel, Voyles wants Mitchell to sing; Mitchell wants a way out. As a Grisham protagonist, however, Mitchell wants reconciliation with the father; and it could be, at least one can sense the hero's (and perhaps the author's) desire that it be so, that the father feels the same way.

Can Grisham's penchant for meaningful names provide one more piece of evidence? Mitchell McDeere traces his origins to a fictional *Danesboro*, Kentucky. Voyles's middle name, which he has elevated to prominence by reducing his first to an initial, could be its distant double: Denton, as in Den + town, recalling Dane's + boro, Dane's (or Danes') town: a patronymic placename. And then there is *Voyles*: On the last page of the novel, Mitchell tells his wife, "I have a confession to make. . . . The truth is, I never wanted to be a lawyer anyway. . . . Secretly, I've always wanted to be a sailor" (501). Indeed, his decision not to trust the FBI to provide him a safe haven from the Firm has resulted in his having been forced to become a sailor, a kind of Wandering Dutchman, spending the rest of his existence (and Abby's) in more or less constant transit from one to another of the thousand English-speaking islands of the Caribbean. "Just tour the islands for the rest of your life," he's told. "There are worse things" (497). It is not an entirely happy ending (and the film provides a vastly different one). Abby doesn't like it, and, at least in the beginning, "She slept alone" (499). This protagonist is still the wandering son; only his later incarnations will find rest in the father's arms. But even here, in *The Firm*, Mitchell's "confession" of his secret desire is at least the gesture of a return to the father's domain, for—as his strangely twinlike brother Ray would know, since he spent his time in prison learning foreign languages, including French—*voyles* (*voiles*) are *sails*.

After the publication of *The Client*, Grisham told the *Newsweek* interviewer that while "what I'd really like to do is just go back to Ford County and never leave," his contract with Doubleday required him to write three more legal thrillers. *The Chamber* and *The Rainmaker* are evidently the first two installments. Both show signs of having been written by an author who feels constrained by his straitjacket of a contract.

The Chamber adopts two conventions inherited from its sure-fire predecessors—a young lawyer-hero destined to succeed against impossible odds and a dread omnipotent enemy lurking in the shadows, like the Mafia in *The Firm* and *The Client*, Victor Mattiece's criminal syndicate in *The Pelican Brief*, and the Ku Klux Klan in *A Time To Kill*. But this time the hero fails, and the threat from Rollie Wedge, a Khamel-like terrorist who once worked for the Klan, fails to materialize. Adam Hall, though he spends the entire novel trying to save his grandfather from execution for a bombing in 1967 that killed five-year-old twins Josh and John Kramer, is not able to do so. While the novel is a tract against the death penalty, few readers perhaps are likely to have wanted him to succeed in saving Sam Cayhall from death. But the ending nevertheless does not give what one has come to expect. More disappointing, and perhaps inexplicable except in the larger story of a novelist's frustration at being forced to perform an act he'd rather decline, is the dangling thread of Rollie Wedge. Wedge sneaks into Adam's favorite aunt's house and into the Memphis branch of Adam's law firm; he even manages to pay a visit to Sam Cayhall on death row, posing as his brother. There, he threatens harm (to Adam, presumably, and to his Aunt Lee) if Sam reveals his role in the bombing. Though Sam keeps his pledge of secrecy, Adam is made aware of the menace Wedge represents. The reader, whom the previous novels have led to expect that Adam Hall will save his grandfather, is also likely to expect a confrontation between Hall and Wedge. But, strangely, nothing happens—though the novel ends on a curious note of dread, in a cemetery as a grave-digging backhoe approaches. "It was coming their way," the last sentence intones, as if Lee and Adam were about to be crushed. But the reader is perfectly aware that Rollie Wedge is not at the wheel.

The Rainmaker's young lawyer-hero fails too, but only by succeeding all too well. The insurance company he sues on behalf of a client whose son dies for lack of a leukemia treatment the policy should have covered is bankrupted by the jury's award. Rudy Baylor had done too good a job at the trial. He only asked for ten million; they gave his client fifty, with the result that he never saw a dime. At first, the Great Benefit Insurance Company seems to assume the role of the omnipotent shady organization against which the hero must do desperate battle. But little by little it may dawn on the reader, as it does on Baylor, that his victory is assured, and has been for some time. A hostile judge drops dead, replaced, as Baylor himself observes, by "an incredibly sympathetic trial judge," and this is followed by "one lucky break after another at trial" (389). Some time before the end, it becomes no contest, and the fun goes out of the battle. This time, Grisham has fought back by gradually deflating expectations.

But then, just twenty pages from the end, a totally new story seems to begin, though it is in fact the culmination of something that had been building up for a long time. Rudy Baylor had become infatuated with Kelly Riker, a battered wife he met in a hospital cafeteria. He has finally persuaded her to divorce her brutal husband, and they go to her former apartment to pick up her effects. Cliff Riker suddenly appears swinging a baseball bat. Rudy wrests it away and brings it crashing on his head, twice. The second blow was probably unnecessary from the standpoint of self-defense, and it kills Riker. Rudy lets Kelly take the fall, and persuades the state not to prosecute. In an ending reminiscent of *The Firm*, *The Pelican Brief*, and *The Client*, he and Kelly drive off into the West, Rudy having decided to abandon the practice of law for some more honorable profession.

That murderous swing of the baseball bat may be the culmination of something more than the subplot. What Mark Sway did with a bat to his father in *The Client* gave us a glimpse at the oedipal subtext that emerges with explosive force here. Mark was with his mother in their trailer; his father was coming in the door. "I damned near took his head off with the baseball bat. A perfect shot to his nose. I was crying and scared to death, but I'll always remember the sound of the bat crunching his face. He fell on the sofa, and I hit him once in the stomach. I was trying to land a good one, in the crotch, because I figured that would hurt the most. . . . I was swinging like crazy. I hit him once more on the ear, and that was all she wrote" (155). The parallel passage in *The Rainmaker* is remarkably similar, though with a different sequence of events: "I can hear and feel his testicles pop as he explodes in an agonized cry. . . . I swing hard and catch him directly across his left ear, and the noise is sickening. Bones crunch and break. . . . My second swing starts at the ceiling and falls with all the force I can muster. I drive the bat down with all the hatred and fear imaginable" (414). Though Cliff Riker is actually younger than Rudy, he nevertheless seems to represent the same figure against whom

Mark Sway struck his blows, the father whom Grisham's hero finally slays, whose wife he successfully steals. *The Chamber*, which in the end becomes barely more than the protracted killing of the father's father, may perhaps be read in this oedipal light.

In *The Runaway Jury*, Grisham's most recent novel as of this writing (and evidently the third and final legal thriller his Doubleday contract required him to write), he solves the problem posed by Rudy Baylor's too-great success in persuading a jury to make an immense award to a plaintiff. This time the object of the lawsuit, a tobacco company, will not be made bankrupt by the outcome, and the defendant's behind-the-scenes champion, Rankin Fitch, is bribed into not pressing too hard for an overturn on appeal. Jeff Durr, the apparent hero at the beginning of the novel, gives way to the real heroine, Gabrielle Brant, out for revenge after both her parents died from cigarette-induced lung cancer—and, appropriately for a Grisham heroine, coiffed with ever-shorter hair (399). The villain Fitch, along the lines of Nathan Locke and Victor Mattiece, has "nasty eyes" (307-8). If he plays the evil father in this latest installment of Grisham's ongoing oedipal triangle, Jeff is his son, while Jeff's girlfriend Gabrielle becomes the woman who seduces not the son but the father, inverting the normal order of events—seduces him, that is, into believing she's an "angel" (318, 399) who is working to assure the verdict he desires.

Plenty more material remains to be explored by readers who realize that Grisham's works are imbued with some interestingly obsessive imagery. One direction for further study is surely the twins who crop up with persisting frequency: Ray and Mitch McDeere in *The Firm*, whose twinship is more apparent than real; Josh and John Kramer in *The Chamber*, the five-year-old twins murdered, unintentionally, by the (grand)father who must die; Ronny Ray and Donny Ray Black in *The Rainmaker*, the latter "murdered" by the insurance company that refused to pay for the bone marrow transplant that could have been made from the perfect match his brother made. Intriguingly, the repeated "Ray" of their names matches that of Mitchell McDeere's twinlike brother in *The Firm*.

It will be rewarding to follow these threads of obsessive imagery as Grisham continues to develop as a writer. If indeed *The Runaway Jury* is the last legal thriller he will have to write, at least for a while, then we will be able to see what he can do when released from the constraints of the genre. Or will it turn out that such constraints—like rhyme and meter in poetry—make for better art?

James Lee Burke

"...always the first inning"

WILLIAM BEDFORD CLARK AND CHARLENE KERNE CLARK

Pursuing a craft driven by contradictions, American writers both dream of and dread success, the "bitch goddess" William James rightly identified as a national obsession. In our culture, where the misleading dichotomy between "high" and "low" art yet persists against the even more pernicious assaults of the "new theory," it is still customary to distinguish between artistic and popular—which is to say *commercial*—success. Writers, save for rare exceptions, yearn for a receptive audience, but a widespread readership and the financial gain that accompanies it are too often taken as signs of meretriciousness. The onus is compounded if an author elects to work in an identifiably "popular" genre like the gothic tale, science fiction, or—more to the point—the crime novel.

The *grande dame* of fiction-for-art's-sake, Katherine Anne Porter, once remarked to her nephew, Paul, that detective novels were "the perfect way to kill time, for those who liked their time dead" (Machann and Clark 28). As a Southerner, Miss Porter clearly misspoke herself. Detective fiction was, by most accounts, the invention of a chauvinistic Virginian, Edgar Allan Poe, and the evolving conventions of the form offered perennial grist for the respective mills of Mark Twain and William Faulkner. The obvious debt Miss Porter's friend,

Robert Penn Warren, owed to the hard-boiled school of crime fiction in his masterful *All the King's Men* has long been recognized, and Walker Percy's last book, *The Thanatos Syndrome,* is, among other things, a sleuthing thriller in the great tradition. Indeed, it can be, and has been, argued that there is something in the Southern sensibility, with its brooding awareness of a broken world and its preoccupation with violence, that makes detective fiction particularly congenial.

As an author of detective novels, James Lee Burke has come to know unusual success, but his achievement has been decidedly literary as well as remunerative. To be sure, prior to his introduction of Dave Robicheaux, the Cajun hero of nine novels (as of 1996), Burke's career resembled that of dozens of similarly uncelebrated fictionists, authors who emerge from creative writing programs and assume, in turn, a chain of teaching appointments while regularly publishing "serious" novels that attract a measure of critical praise before being quietly remaindered and consigned to the proverbial limbo of the out-of-print. But it would be a mistake to assume that Burke lifted himself out of relative obscurity by striking a cynical accommodation with the readerly marketplace, for the Dave Robicheaux chronicles are less an accommodation than a culmination of intensely personal creative forces that have fueled Burke's imagination from the start.

However undervalued, Burke's earlier work showed him to be an unusually serious and gifted writer, whose concern with the problem of evil—social, psychological, and metaphysical—was all-consuming, and his seriousness and native gifts have not been compromised. Indeed, Detective Robicheaux himself, one of the most complex and engaging characters in contemporary American fiction, was not the product of some sudden happy inspiration; he gradually evolved from a series of prototypical Burkean characters who were likewise haunted by demons within and without and straining to be whole. From the mid-sixties on, James Lee Burke was gradually shaping a distinctive vision to counter the sinister vacuity of postmodernity, and in hitting upon the fabulistic possibilities of the crime novel, he realized the perfect vehicle for articulating that vision. He stands as one of the most perceptive "diagnostic" novelists writing at present, locating and probing the psychic and societal pathologies that abound in the latter decades of the apocalyptic twentieth century. Burke's prognosis is guarded, at times quite grim, but his fiction counsels a stubborn resistance in the face of galloping dissolution. In keeping with the stoic wisdom of the twelve-step program both author and protagonist pursue with dogged fidelity, the Robicheaux novels concede that battles are frequently lost, though the long war may yet be won. As Burke puts it in his short story "Lower Me Down with a Golden Chain," the closest thing he has written to an explicit manifesto, "it's always the first inning" and, in the best existential sense, "courage and faith are their own justification" (*Convict* 130).

Burke's first novel, *Half of Paradise* (1965), is, by contrast, a naturalistic fiction that all but out-Dreisers Dreiser. It traces the grinding down and defeat of three separate protagonists, and its final vision is a despairing one. Burke's signature interest in popular music is manifest in the story of J.P. Winfield—a former cropper who makes good as a country singer only to have drugs bring him to a brutal and shameful end reminiscent of Hank Williams. Like music, race is a recurrent Burkean motif, and in Toussaint Boudreaux, a maimed black prizefighter/stevedore who is unjustly sent to prison, Burke succeeded in creating a particularly striking character. Ruthless destiny also sends Avery Broussard, the troubled scion of an aristocratic but ruined family, to the work farm.

Prisons and jails are an obsessive element throughout Burke's canon, as are the nightmarish effects of war on the combatant's psyche. (Among the inmates at the prison camp is one LeBlanc; maddened by warfare in the Pacific, he anticipates the Korean and Vietnam syndromes that affect protagonists in the later novels.) For Burke, institutions of correction are emblematic of institutions in general. They dehumanize inmates and guards alike and foster the very bestial impulses they are meant, theoretically, to check.

Already in this first novel, Burke's evocative talent for depicting place, whether it be the landscapes of his native Gulf Coast or the seedy streets of the modern urban South, is fully in evidence, and his Hemingwayesque attention to the details of how *things*—common human activities—are done is likewise present to a marked degree. What is missing is any note of hope or affirmation. The committed love between man and woman will be a positive source of strength in the later fiction, but here Avery's rediscovery of his potentially saving relationship with his former lover, Suzanne, is cut short by a senseless wrong turn (quite literally) that lands him back in the mechanistic, if absurd, grip of a malign fate.

Much is made in *Half of Paradise* of Avery's apostasy from the Catholic faith of his childhood, and, given the inescapable religious dimension of the Dave Robicheaux saga, it is tempting to speculate that the dark nihilism at work in the novel reflects a similar crisis of faith on the part of the novelist himself. Like his cousin, Andre Dubus, for whom Catholicism serves as a ubiquitous (though not always explicit) informing principle, James Lee Burke was a product of parochial schools in French Louisiana, and he is, at his best, a religious writer by instinct as well as orientation. Indeed, in his ultimate embrace of the detective novel, Burke would seem to confirm the extent to which his career may be regarded as a quest for a restoration of belief, for the theological implications of that form are embedded in genre itself, as two admirable studies, Erik Routley's *The Puritan Pleasures of the Detective Story* (1972) and Robert S. Paul's *Whatever Happened to Sherlock Holmes?: Detective Fiction, Popular Theology, and Society* (1991), persuasively attest. The events chronicled in Burke's second novel, significantly titled *To the Bright and Shining Sun* (1970), are, if anything, more horrendous than those portrayed in his first, but the narrative ends with the possibility of deliverance rather than imprisonment, and the presence of a suggested numinous realm beyond the sufferings of hard quotidian reality represents an important advance over the naturalistic *malaise* of its predecessor.

Set in the violence-ridden coal fields of Kentucky—a region Burke recreates as convincingly as he does South Louisiana, *To the Bright and Shining Sun* tells the story of Perry James, a miner's son prematurely conscripted into a world where injustice breeds injustice and deadly force feeds upon itself. As is the case throughout his fiction, Burke is insistent upon the dignity and innate worth of individuals even as he is suspicious of institutions. (After a crucial vote, the union betrays the miners with as much ruthlessness as the companies.) Still, Perry does find a brief period of respite as a member of the Job Corps, a fact that no doubt reflects the author's background in social work and a certain residual New Frontier idealism. Perry's final triumph, however, depends solely upon his own capacity for heroic action. Sickened by brutality and sadism, albeit the objects of such violence may themselves be guilty of no less heinous acts, he intervenes to save the lives of his father's assassins. Fleeing for his own safety as a consequence, he is paradoxically liberated from the confining hills and hollows of his Appalachian past and faces the tenuous promise of a better future at the novel's close.

Burke's next novel is, structurally speaking, more coherent than the previous two, but, in certain respects, its coherence is bought at the expense of the moral complexity that makes *To the Bright and Shining Sun* so compelling. *Lay Down My Sword and Shield* (1971) draws upon what might be termed the Matter of Texas in the Burkean canon. Like several of his more successful short stories (and like *Two for Texas* [1982], Burke's pulp Western which, in the density of its historical detail, transcends most examples of that genre), *Lay Down My Sword and Shield* deals with the Holland family, whose line includes a veteran of San Jacinto, a Texas Ranger who once bested John Wesley Hardin, the outlaw, and a sequence of prominent ranchers. Born into the Texas establishment, the novel's protagonist, Hack Holland, is contemptuous of the powers-that-be. Nonetheless, he finds himself running for Congress at the insistence of his social-climbing wife and stolidly respectable brother.

Hack is another of Burke's loners. His sensitive nature is masked behind a facade of cynicism that hides the psychic wounds he sustained as a prisoner of war in Korea and as a result of his father's suicide. He is, like every major

Burkean hero, an alcoholic seemingly bent on self-destruction, until circumstances conspire to enlist him in social action. Drawn into the cause of exploited pickers in South Texas by his involvement with an enticing hippie chick and by the example of an activist priest, Hack finally manages to cut himself free from a venal system (subject as it is to the sinister manipulations of a nuclear arms merchant) when he resolves to face down the truth about himself without shame.

Yet the conflicts in *Lay Down My Sword and Shield* are a bit too ideologically reductive. The sixties sensibility which to a varying extent undergirds the whole of Burke's writing is too uncritically present in this novel, though the author's descriptive writing and dialogue are handled with growing skill. In the years that have intervened since the book's publication, Hack's eventual role as an ACLU attorney seems less than a fully satisfying solution to what is, in the last analysis, an existential dilemma, though his new marriage and celebrative fatherhood are ultimately more promising signs.

In terms of Burke's evolution as a writer, however, his choice of a first-person narrative voice in *Lay Down My Sword and Shield* represents an important technical shift which prepares the way for the Robicheaux novels that will follow. Hack Holland, bearing witness in his own words, can be a master of tough-guy sarcasm at one moment and a rhapsodic nature-poet at the next, but the final weakness in the novel is the protagonist's myopic self-righteousness. Detective Robicheaux, on the other hand, will be righteous without ever succumbing to moral smugness. He sees the beam in his own eye only too vividly.

Though the narrator of Burke's third book anticipates Dave Robicheaux, the detective hero's immediate harbinger is the deeply flawed Iry Paret in *The Lost Get-Back Boogie* (1986), a paroled killer transplanted from Louisiana to Montana. The lines between good and evil in this fourth novel defy ideological compartmentalization. Old Mr. Riordan's environmentalism, for instance, is infected by a virulent streak of radical individualism which blinds him to the legitimate claims of other hard-working men as he fights the polluting menace of the paper mill, and he imprudently toys with the idea of raising nutria, a misguided scheme that Iry warns him has already wreaked ecological disaster in South Louisiana. Once again, institutions, symbolized by the county sheriff's office and the lumbering concerns, are portrayed as corrupt or dangerously irresponsible or both, but it is a festering *inner* corruption and suicidal irresponsibility that finally destroy Iry's gifted friend, Buddy Riordan.

Consciously or not, in *The Lost Get-Back Boogie*, Burke moves beyond the simplistic politics of his third novel. It is worth noting the gap of a decade and a half that separates the publication of the two books (including the nine years it took to place *Boogie*). In a recent telephone interview, Burke spoke of these intervening years as a period of frustration and discouragement. He even had trouble publishing his short fiction, and it was during this time that he brought out his only real potboiler, the paperback *Two for Texas* mentioned earlier. Not until Louisiana State University Press issued his collection of stories, *The Convict*, in 1985 did his career move forward again. But the clear evidence of the later fiction itself suggests that this long interval of dryness and relative silence was hardly wasted. Burke's struggle with alcohol and what one might suppose to be an accompanying crisis in confidence with respect to his literary vocation brought him to a new and deeper maturity. By the mid-eighties, he had come to understand the world and the men and women who are condemned to suffer through it in what might best be described as spiritual terms, and, henceforth, no ready set of ideological tenets would suffice. (This development is succinctly illustrated by the title story in *The Convict*.) Burke had learned that evil might claim membership in more than one party simultaneously and that the good must be pursued with vigorous discernment.

This is not to say that Burke's fundamental "politics" were altered. His contempt for Reaganism, the military/industrial complex, and Yankee imperialism in the Third World (particularly Latin America) would remain a constant. The basis for Burke's dissent, however, becomes more than mere secular partisanship. The strong moral strain that pervades the Robicheaux chronicles stems from a reassertion of Burke's religious sensibility, informed by the Catholic Church's "fundamental option for the poor" and the spirit of the major social encyclicals. Burke's explicit loyalties are with the progressivist wing of the Church, which devotes itself to social justice. On various occasions he has voiced his admiration for Father Dan Berrigan, the Catholic Worker movement, and the work of the Maryknollers, but his concern for the metaphysics of good and evil and his attention to the drama of individual redemption mark him as a traditionalist by instinct. The immutability of natural law serves as the unspoken foundation for his vision. In a world that has lost its moorings and given itself over to systemic and random terror, Burke and his character, Dave Robicheaux, meet force with force to reestablish, as best they can, the antique virtues.

The locale of the Robicheaux novels—New Orleans and the bayou country to its west—has long exerted a strong pull on the collective American imagination. Its lush, semitropical landscapes and climate suggest, on the surface, a kind of fecund paradise, and it is peopled by individuals who (at least as stereotype would have it) embrace a life free of the Puritan repressions and grasping ambitions of the dominant Anglo culture. But the pastoral dream of South Louisiana generates its own dark antithesis, a nightmare realm of primeval reptiles and freakish perversions where evil lurks beneath the luminous beauty of the swamp lilies.

A passage near the beginning of *The Neon Rain* (1987) encapsulates this dialectic quite nicely. Fishing on Bayou Lafourche in a reflective mood approaching Edenic peace, Dave makes a grotesque discovery:

> The shore was thickly lined with cypress trees, and it was cool and quiet in the green-gold morning light that fell through the canopy of leaves overhead. The lily pads were abloom with purple flowers, and I could smell the trees, the moss, the wet green lichen on the bark, the spray of crimson and yellow four-o'clocks that were still open in the shade. An alligator that must have been five feet long lay up close to some cypress roots, his barnacled head and eyes just showing above the waterline like a brown rock. I saw another black swelling in the water near another cypress, and I thought it was the first alligator's mate. Then an outboard boat passed, and the wake rolled the swelling up into the cypress roots, and I saw a bare leg, a hand, a checkered shirt puffed with air. [10]

The body, that of a rural black girl undone by a web of urban corruption she could scarcely fathom, defiles the natural order and precipitates Robicheaux's descent into a putrid underworld where even a man's trusted partner may prove to be an unabashed killer.

Burke has an avowed, if largely nostalgic, kinship for the principles of Jeffersonian agrarianism, with its strong bias against the city as an enemy of human virtue and fulfillment. So when Robicheaux abandons New Orleans in favor of New Iberia, his relatively bucolic hometown, at the conclusion of *The Neon Rain*, the reader is led to suppose that the Cajun detective has left behind the moral squalor for which his case-file is a sordid "microcosm." The subsequent novels soon disabuse protagonist and reader alike of that comforting notion. There is no place to hide from the tentacles of dehumanizing modernity. Their reach is global, as the second Robicheaux book makes manifestly clear.

The novel *Heaven's Prisoners* (1988) begins with one of Burke's typically vivid and evocative descriptions of a beatific, if unpredictable, nature, but the scene is soon disrupted when disaster literally comes crashing out of the sky and sets in motion a series of mounting complications, culminating in the graphically depicted murder of Robicheaux's wife, Annie, a Mennonite girl from Kansas whose love for the liquor-plagued detective had been a powerful redemptive force in his recovery. Despite some apparent canonical irregularities in their marriage, Dave's union with Annie seems to admirably meet the test of a sacramental relationship within the terms of traditional Catholic "personalism," and the domestic arguments between husband and wife over the appropriateness of combating violence with violence constitute an important dimension of the novel's moral center.

In one of his typical moments of reflection, Dave concedes the degree to which violence offends the moral imperative written in the human psyche: Violence is "always ugly, it always dehumanizes, it always shocks and repels and leaves the witnesses to it sick and shaken. It's meant to do all these things" (*Heaven's Prisoners* 108). Yet the way of Dave Robicheaux is the militant *via activa* in deadly spades, and he must live with the knowledge that Annie is dead "because I couldn't leave things alone" (*Heaven's Prisoners* 139), an admission that drives him into a frenzied binge after a year of determined sobriety. Dave deplores violence even as he recognizes the irresistible allure it holds over him. His problem is one Saint Augustine wrestled with: how to kill in a just cause without killing his own conscience, "the unblemished place [within] where God once grasped our souls" (*Heaven's Prisoners* 240). It is a challenge indeed.

In D.H. Lawrence's classic formulation, "the essential American soul is hard, isolate, stoic, and a killer" (Lawrence 68). Dave Robicheaux may perform acts of brutal vengeance, and he *is* a killer—though always in self-defense (often, however, after forcing, gunslingerlike, a fatal confrontation). Still, he is never a *hard* man. His stoicism is a defining trait, but, unlike Hemingway's, it is informed by a tenacious refusal to surrender the last vestiges of a tattered religious faith. Dave's melancholy alcoholic's temperament does indeed condemn him to a painful sense of alienation and estrangement, but he (in contrast to Leslie Fiedler's archetypal American male protagonist) is a most reluctant *isolato*. Dave's loneliness is all the more torturous because he craves the peace of domesticity and the reciprocal entanglements of women and children. The shade of his alcoholic, but loving, father, killed in a drilling accident in the Gulf, frequently comes to him in memory and dream, and perhaps the most important wisdom that ghost has to impart is this: "'The bad thing is when you make yourself alone. Don't never do that, Dave, 'cause it's like that coon chewing off its own foot when he stick it in the trap'" (*Heaven's Prisoners* 137).

What is, at its foundation, a *spiritual* yearning in Dave Robicheaux often expresses itself in terms of a pronounced sexual hunger, but it is a sanctified love that Dave is after. His occasional illicit copulations provide only a momentary release. Fulfillment, on the other hand, demands a matrimonial commitment. Sex and the natural consequences of the sexual act are positive goods in Burke's world view, which is why the perverse abuse of the Other through any act of predatory self-gratification frequently serves as a readily identifiable badge of unmitigated evil.

At its most extreme, this negative eroticism finds its twisted consummation in the adrenal rush the sociopath feels gazing into the eyes of his victim, an orgasmic thrill Dave Robicheaux recognizes but has learned to deny himself at any cost. In a world where the will to power has come to define most relationships, women and children inevitably become the most vulnerable prey. Conversely, the unqualified love of a man for a defenseless child confers a special grace, as is poignantly demonstrated by Dave's protective tenderness for his surreptitiously adopted Salvadoran daughter, Alafair, in *Black Cherry Blues* (1989), and even the brutal Tony Cardo in *A Morning for Flamingos* (1990) proves redeemable, largely due to his capacity for selfless concern when it comes to the needs of his crippled son, Paul.

Some readers regard *Black Cherry Blues* and *A Morning for Flamingos* as a falling off from the two preceding books, and it is certainly true that the third and fourth novels in the Robicheaux series depend less on philosophical asides on the part of the protagonist and more on the hard action and unlikely coincidences one associates with the genre. In a more positive way, it is possible to see this pair of novels as a movement away from reportorial verisimilitude toward a freer embrace of fabulation and *romance*.

Be that as it may, *A Stained White Radiance* (1992) and *In the Electric Mist with Confederate Dead* (1993), with their elements of magical realism and echoes of the Grail legends, are major fictive statements that function as sober admonitions and bracing calls to action. This is no less true of *Dixie City Jam* (1994), in which a Nazi submarine sunk off the Louisiana coast in World War II serves as a disturbing emblem of hatreds (ancient and modern) which forever threaten to rise to the surface in new permutations. In these books, and in *Burning Angel* (1995) and *Cadillac Jukebox* (1996), Burke can reveal, in Boschian terms, the systemic network of public and private evils that, old as humankind itself, come together with unprecedented virulence in the late twentieth century, and he can bolster his reader with the encouraging assurance that the pieces of a shattered world can be reclaimed and restored. Like his Scholastic coreligionists of an earlier age, whose wisdom is once again being widely reasserted as an antidote to the chaotic relativism born of Nietzsche, Marx, and Freud, Burke shows that evil is, by its nature, a negation, denial, and diminishing of a creation God Himself had pronounced *good*. Thus sociopaths, drug dealers, arms merchants, and politicians blinded by *hubris* are alike aligned against life. In the high value Burke places on family and community and on the passionate empathy for those who suffer, he is unmistakably a Christian writer, but these same qualities also mark him as a recognizably *Southern* novelist who (despite his ostensible liberalism) shares with the Nashville Agrarians a sense that history is by no means melioristic.

Like every major Southern writer since the Civil War, James Lee Burke handles his regional *donnée* with a great deal of ambivalence and ambiguity. He loves his native land, and he refuses to dissociate himself from the tragedy and undeniable heroism of its past. At the same time, he refuses to rationalize away the horrors of slavery or the mutually demeaning system of racial injustice that eventually replaced it. This uncomfortable tension has been at work in Burke's fiction since the start of his career, but it comes perhaps as close as possible to an empowering resolution in the sixth Robicheaux novel, *In the Electric Mist with Confederate Dead*, in which the mysterious body of a forgotten black murder victim becomes the compelling symbol of a shameful past that will continue to haunt the present until justice is finally done. Moreover, the presence of the ghost of John Bell Hood in the novel establishes a solidarity between what was best in the Old South and what is most required in the New. The maimed Confederate general regrets that the courage and honor of decent men were formerly employed in an unjust cause, but he implies that these same virtues ought to be turned against present evils that are no less an assault on the inviolable dignity of the human person. Slavery was evil because it systematized the ruthless use and abuse of innocent men, women, and children. There are dominant forces at work in the modern world that are no less reprehensible, and the traditionalist *ethos* of the South is a way of confronting the enemy from an entrenched higher ground.

"The philosophical novelist," wrote Robert Penn Warren many years ago, "is one for whom the documentation of the world is constantly striving to rise to the level of generalization about values, for whom the image strives to rise to symbol" (*Essays* 58). James Lee Burke has a legitimate claim to just such a designation. His detective fiction is anything but an escapist art. Rather, its mode is confrontational. The reader, no less than the protagonist, is forced to face, explore, and challenge the peculiar horrors, little and great, that define our shaky moment in time. Distrust and terror would seem to dominate the collective American experience in the final decade of the second millennium, and Burke's success — popular *and* artistic — derives from his prophetic capacity to articulate authentically the fears and tentative hopes of a people in crisis.

T. R. Pearson

Debatable Heroes

Mary Bozeman Hodges

T.R. Pearson has forged his way into the late-twentieth-century literary world with the novels *A Short History of a Small Place* (1985), *Off for the Sweet Hereafter* (1986), *The Last of How It Was* (1987), *Call and Response* (1989), *Gospel Hour* (1991), and *Cry Me a River* (1993). In the manner of Mark Twain, Pearson's criticism of human nature goes down with a dose of humor, and like Twain's humor, Pearson's lies both in the situations he creates and in the narrator's voice. Unlike the innocent Huck, however, Pearson's narrators and major characters are all too aware of the depraved nature of humankind, reflecting that depravity themselves. They are searching for answers to the human condition, something that says life is worth living, but they can laugh at themselves and at others in their search.

Unlike Twain's works, however, which seem to reflect a greater and greater disillusionment with humanity, Pearson's first novel reveals as much disappointment in people as do his later works. In fact, he probably reflects less disillusionment in *Gospel Hour* than in any of his other novels, from his first, *A Short History of a Small Place*, to his most recent, *Cry Me a River*. At the beginning of *Gospel Hour*, the reader is introduced to the main character, Donnie Huff, who works as a logger but occasionally stays home after a drinking binge; to Donnie's mother-in-law, Opal Criner, who holds herself superior to the rest of the degenerate family; to Donnie's son, Delmon, who takes pleasure sucking on everything from Lorna Doones to rocks; to Donnie's wife, Marie, who spends her time in the kitchen smoking cigarettes and ignoring the rest of the family as though to escape her overbearing mother; and to Donnie's dog, Sheba, who lives in a crawl space under the house and only comes out occasionally to voice her displeasure. After this introduction to everyone in Donnie's family, the reader is convinced that these people have few redeeming qualities.

This opinion is reinforced when the scene jumps to a logging incident in which Donnie goes off a cliff into a river, riding a dilapidated John Deere skidder (a piece of logging equipment) behind which he is pulling a heavy (too heavy for the skidder) walnut log. The description of the skidder's crash into the river goes on for pages and pages of Pearson's long, winding sentences, with Donnie as mesmerized by the fall as are his four logging buddies, including Little Gaither, who owns the logging operation and who has illegally cut down the valuable walnut tree which pulls Donnie and the skidder into Big Reed Creek. Though the event could have been told in a page or so, throughout the many pages the elaborate yarn reveals the depraved nature of all the men, beginning with the episode in which Little Gaither cuts down the tree which "wasn't his to cut" (20).

In his greed for profit at the expense of his men's safety, Little Gaither orders Donnie to haul one half of the heavy log behind the ancient skidder. As Donnie and the skidder are being pulled by the walnut log over the cliff into the creek, the men climb down the bank, but in the spirit of true brotherly love they are reluctant to get wet in order to retrieve the dead (or possibly alive) body of their friend. Little Gaither finally wades in, not because of Donnie, but because of his sunken skidder. He only looks for his employee, who is somewhere in the water with the skidder, when one of the other men from the bank asks Gaither if he sees any sign of Donnie, at which time Little Gaither reaches deep into the creek and pulls Donnie up by the hair (but only up to his eyebrows) to show that Donnie is there. Donnie's breathing apparatus is still under water until one of the loggers observes that "elevating a man's topnotch and forehead out from the water was [not] truly much of an improvement over total submersion as far as any life-sustaining variety of respiration went" (29). Little Gaither is annoyed and gripes that he has to do everything, but he lifts Donnie up to the bridge of his nose, revealing Donnie's eyes, one of which is open and one closed, frightening the men into telling Gaither to put Donnie back where he found him.

If there is any glimmer of hope that he can be moved by any feeling other than pure greed, it is totally destroyed when Little Gaither is so disgusted at the loss of his skidder, not to speak of his stolen log, that he attacks the blue-green body of Donnie Huff, even though one of the men tries "to persuade Little Gaither that a man couldn't be dead and a troublesome blameworthy son-of-a-bitch both at the same time together" (32). Donnie finally revives on the creek bank, no thanks to any of his logging buddies, who do nothing to help him. The folksy language, ironic understatement, and satirical tone of Pearson's narrator make the reader laugh at this ridiculous story.

After more of the humorous yet shameful account of the event by a narrator who makes the reader laugh at and at the same time feel revulsion for Donnie's "friends," Donnie's mother-in-law, Opal Criner, reveals that people are indeed ruled by some human emotions other than greed and selfishness. She introduces the traits of hypocrisy and self-righteousness. Opal, who has up to this point in her daughter's marriage considered Donnie basically a bum, decides he must have had some sort of out-of-body experience and that maybe he'd even seen Jesus.

Opal, as her name suggests, seems to have only a vague view of the hereafter, but decides from all she has heard it must be a wonderful place, not to speak of the fact that she would look extremely pious to her peers if her son-in-law had entered the pearly portals, and she determines to convince Donnie that he has had such an experience. She takes him to the Reverend Mr. Worrell who, she believes, can determine "a genuine sign . . . from your regular insignificant and unportentous variety" (49).

However, when the narrator introduces the reader to the married Reverend Mr. Worrell, he mentions that the good reverend has been worried with lewd thoughts concerning a check-out lady at the Food Lion, and then right away makes another detour from Donnie's story on the road to the hereafter. The narrator directs the reader's attention to the Reverend Mr. Worrell's visit to the home of one of the members of the community who has recently begun to make wooden sculptures, having retired and begun to drive his wife crazy until she demanded he find a hobby.

The man begins to make sculptures one day when he "attacks" a cherry log which will not succumb to his attempts to split it. In an outburst altogether as demented as the actions of the loggers, "he knocked that length of wild cherry over onto the ground where he beat and pounded at it and kicked it and stomped on it and paused only shortly to inform it how disagreeable in fact he found it to be" (51). Once it is split, he decides a part of it looks like a nose, so he decides to carve some more and comes up with the idea of using his up-to-that-time-still-boxed "cute, tiny chain saw" (51). He proceeds to sculpt a face, and when he finishes he says in words that ring of biblical tones, "It is done" (53).

With this creation, which the "sculptor" thinks looks like Tennessee Ernie Ford, he fanatically begins to create likenesses of Teddy Roosevelt, Hank Williams Jr., Maybelle Carter, and Douglas MacArthur, to mention only a few. By the time the Reverend Mr. Worrell comes to "witness" to this gentleman, he has a front yard full of images. The reverend is convinced that the sculpture of Willie Nelson is Christ, which shows about how much of the hereafter and of Jesus the Reverend Mr. Worrell actually knows and about how much the so-called sculptor has really arrived at his calling.

All these digressions take many more pages and seem to wander from the main story line, and indeed the Reverend Mr. Worrell's personal experience is not necessary to move along the story of Donnie Huff's trip to the hereafter. But since it is at the Reverend Mr. Worrell's church service that Donnie "sees the light" of his experience, it is important to know that the good reverend is himself far from perfect and has been more recently inspired by sexual thoughts than by spiritual ones and that his vision of Christ is actually a vision of Willie Nelson in wood created by an ex-trucker-turned-artist with a "cute, tiny chain saw."

A visit to the Reverend Mr. Worrell's Laurel Fork Full Primitive Missionary Holiness Church also reveals the hypocritical nature of the people who attend his church and who, in Job-like fashion, all elaborate on their various sufferings and on the fact that their burdens are completely undeserved. When the reverend finally lights on words from which the reader feels an answer might be found, "It's easy enough to love a man for his righteousness . . . the challenge is to love him in spite of his sin," a Mrs. Gloria Hawks shoots down that hope by saying that "there were some things even a Christian couldn't love a man in spite of" (78). But still there is the hint, larger than Mrs. Gloria Hawks, that if a person *could* love another in spite of his failings, there might be some sort of salvation for the human condition.

It is to this Bible hour at the Laurel Fork Full Primitive Missionary Holiness Church that Opal takes Donnie in the hopes that he will be inspired to remember his "experience." The reader's assessment of people, which has already been appreciably lowered, is lowered further when Donnie, who is not convinced at all that he has had any kind of heavenly experience, becomes inspired at the church meeting by Miss Cindy Womble and "her sizable hooters as she expressed to him her anxiety as well which inspired in Donnie Huff a sense of evangelical duty coupled with a notion of just where he'd be pleased to press and lay his face" (117-18).

For a hundred pages or so, Donnie learns the art of witnessing and healing from his mother-in-law and from the Reverend Mr. Worrell. Finally Donnie admits to his wife Marie that he is tired and asks her if a man couldn't just die and be revived and be like he was before, even though everybody wants something more from him. She tells him that just the fact he was saved from death was testimony enough that he was worth saving, and since she is not prone to testifying, she pulls "his face flush against her GOBBLERS" and gives him the only salvation she knows to give, and the only one Donnie knows how to receive (341).

After Donnie's last tent service, during which he tells the congregation that it should just be enough that he died and came back, their response to his true testimony continues to lower the reader's already deteriorating estimation of people. Donnie is told that the golden trumpet will sound to call only the faithful (which does not include Donnie). When Donnie and his son, Delmon, are driving away from the tent meeting, they cannot hear the words of the preacher, only "his voice rising and falling by turns and mingling so with the lowly organ strains as to sound almost like Gospel" (355), but not quite.

So Donnie Huff has found no answer, unless perhaps that there is no answer, only an ethereal glimpse of one, and the closest real answer on earth is perhaps given at the end when Donnie goes in to his wife at the kitchen sink, which is their way of telling each other to go to bed in a household which includes their son and her mother. Donnie and Marie leave Delmon sucking on his cookie, watching the news on TV and hearing about "somebody somewhere lying in the road under a sheet, a fellow sprawled face down beside a streak of pavement . . . as he [Delmon] heard, above the sirens on the TV, above the vigorous lamentations of the kin . . . a lone girlish shriek of delight" (360). And perhaps that sound of pleasure from Delmon's mother (which he associates with the sucking of his cookie) is what gives him security in a world of insecurities and perversities, as it does to Donnie, his father. Marie, who cooks supper with a cigarette dangling from her mouth and who is cynical about her mother's hypocritical religiosity, is the "eternal femme," as much as there can be such a person in Pearson's world.

No one in the novel is perfect, not even near perfect; actually all are degenerate, lewd, hypocritical, self-absorbed, or all of the above. Nevertheless, the reader laughs at the characters' base natures and their futile attempts to find meaning in life, suggesting that while Pearson is judging everyone, he's not judging them too harshly nor without mercy. By presenting people in their failings and still being able to maintain a sense of humor, Pearson suggests a sort of salvation.

Cry Me a River is another story of depravity told in the voice of another good-old-boy narrator who lets the reader laugh with him and at him, but the subject matter is more depressing and the glimmer of hope at the end is even less bright than in *Gospel Hour.* The narrator and main character is a local-yokel cop called only "officer" who is degenerate enough himself that he understands the many misfits that he comes across every day in his line of work. Like Donnie Huff, he also has a dog, a disgusting animal who goes to the dump every day, eats from her findings there, and comes home at night to regurgitate her meal in his apartment. The symbolism is obvious, as the narrator himself figuratively "eats" of the trash of the town and regurgitates his stories of corruption to his listeners.

The narrator begins his tale, explaining how everyone loves to hear of the town's "own tragic episode which had gotten to be an object of civic pride suggesting like it did that we were, after all, under the surface of things, a community of passionate people who sometimes slaughtered each other for love" (2). Such a description of people's love of blood and guts and gore sounds all too familiar in a world in which people support violence in movies as a form of entertainment. Everyone in *Cry Me a River* is perverse, suggesting, of course, as Pearson does, that all people (not just criminals) participate in perversities.

The narrator begins to tell of a bloody, senseless murder that he and his sidekick Ellis discover, but he gets sidetracked as he introduces Ellis, an alcoholic and thief who becomes useful to the police, which says something frightening about people and their official efforts to control themselves. Ellis becomes helpful when he vomits on a young Latin American suspect who is fleeing the police. The felon "came to be paralyzed straightaway with disgust and collapsed to the pavement where he found likely occasion to contemplate the unforeseen vagaries of American law enforcement since he hailed after all from a primitive land where justice was surely not so swift and malodorous" (6). As in *Gospel Hour*, the sidetracking isn't really sidetracking at all, but a means by which Pearson, through his narrator, reveals even more disgusting behavior of human beings.

The narrative then moves to a call that the narrator and Ellis answer from a Mrs. Heflin, who "possessed a gift for spying prowlers and could concoct from a murky shadow and a couple of leafy limbs a most devious manner of ne'er-do-wells afflicted evermore with a spectacular array of unsavory intentions, set plainly on raping and pillaging and maiming and killing and raising just a general and extraordinary fuss" (7). The reader, unclear as to where the story is going, continues to hear more of this demented woman who constantly calls the police, convinced she has seen a villain behind her house who is like the "ruffian of the Sahara" (7) that she has read about in a book she purchased at the pharmacy. While they are searching for Mrs. Heflin's phantom prowlers, the narrator returns to the original murder, when he and Ellis find near the river the body of a fellow police officer with a hole blown in his face.

The narrator cannot keep from investigating the murder, though it is not his assignment. It is apparent to the reader that the narrator stays with the case, expecting to discover some motive, some aspect of human nature with which he can relate. Up to this point in his life as a policeman, he has been able to understand the criminal as well as the victim. No matter how disgusting the crime, the narrator has been able to see the criminal as a fellow human being with shortcomings that he shares and that he can, therefore, understand. This crime is something different; he cannot see a human motive for it.

As in Pearson's other novels, everyone in *Cry Me a River* is perverse, even those who represent the law. A newly introduced police officer, Dewey, makes the reader wonder how bad the criminals can be compared to a police officer who dangles suspects by their heels over a gorge until they confess and who once dangled a suspect too long and lost him. The narrator says, "Dewey determined to treat as the merest manner of technicality [the dropping of the suspect] and wouldn't allow himself to indulge in doubts and recriminations, guessed that boy should have spoken up sooner, been prompt for once and timely like all those hoodlums otherwise" (15). For his action, Dewey receives a reprimand and at the same time the greatest respect of the law enforcement community. The reader is unsure which unsavory characters are going to be significant in the story, since it seems that everyone is degenerate.

The narrator/police officer himself steals evidence, a nude picture of a woman, from the murder scene. As well as using it as a clue, he is sexually aroused by it. The victim of the crime, a fellow police officer, a fellow *married* police officer, had obviously also been sexually aroused by it, as well as by the woman whose likeness it portrays. But the narrator can accept that; lust is a human trait he can understand. The ability to blow off someone's face for no apparent reason is not. He, like Pearson's other characters—and like the reader—wants understanding of human depravity.

In this novel, too, there is little hope, less even than in *Gospel Hour*. The narrator himself finally sees the murderer kill someone else by blowing away the victim's face, and he still sees no answer, no reason, as he thinks he should. Nevertheless, through part of the book, the reader has been able to laugh at the narrator's voice and at his humorous explication of his adventures. But the humor stops at the last murder, and even telling it in a funny way cannot take away the hopelessness it suggests; there has been no love, even sexual love, that has offered any relief satisfying enough to be an answer, as was a possibility in *Gospel Hour*. If Pearson offers any salvation for perversity in this novel, it is that, for the most part, the narrator understands and cares for people in spite of their failings and in the fact that he can laugh at himself and others and can make the reader laugh.

A Short History of a Small Place is an even more depressing story of the weak and depraved nature of human beings. Instead of being a history of a town's crime, it is a story of its madness. Like Pearson's other narrators, the child Louis speaks in the language of small-town Southern people, and he also seems to have trouble telling one story without getting sidetracked to other stories. In fact, Pearson is sometimes criticized for rambling. William Schafer attacks Pearson's style in *A Short History* as "the literary equivalent of 'pickin' and grinin'" and adds that it might best be described as "'sittin' and jawin'" (320). But Pearson says he tries to approximate the way people in the South tell stories and get sidetracked in episodes that seem "not much to the point" (*Moveable Feast*), but which, of course, are very much to the point. This is the case again in *A Short History*. The "short history," which is not so short—but which is hardly, as Schafer says, "glacially slow"—is the history of madness in a small Southern town, a history which focuses on those characters whom everyone considers "peculiar." And, to the reader, those who are not officially considered peculiar are still peculiar.

Louis begins the story by telling of his father's view of Miss Pettigrew, a woman who obviously has lost her mind and who stands on an oak stump in the front yard ranting "something about Creon . . . and the stink of corpses" (3). By having the child-narrator basically repeating a story that his father tells him, Pearson can still use the good-old-boy language and humor, and he can have the narrator expose perversities that Louis alone cannot understand. Yet Louis's words flow naturally when he says, "Daddy said . . ."

When his father leans against a door facing and says simply "Madness" in response to the bizarre incident of the woman on the stump, it is a comment appropriate to the events of the rest of the novel, which all hinge on Miss Pettigrew's strange actions and later suicide (4). The child-narrator is naturally interested in the fact that Miss Pettigrew owns a chimpanzee which wears clothes, and the story seems to sidetrack while Louis tells about the monkey.

Miss Pettigrew has decided her monkey must be more civilized if she is to keep it, so she has had clothes made for it. The town is intrigued by the clothed chimpanzee, and when the monkey gets out of the house and heads for the flagpole, the townspeople gather round to watch, and what they see is the monkey darkening its trousers at the top of the flagpole in front of God and country. This becomes a regular occurrence, and finally the idea of the monkey's wearing pants is abandoned, and it still runs to the top of the flagpole to defecate with its bottom half bare, showering those too close. One of the unfortunate souls yells "'Shitshitshitshitshit' like a steam engine" (110). Like Jonathan Swift's scatological passage in Part IV of *Gulliver's Travels*, in which Gulliver, who is hiding under a tree, is showered with excrement by the Yahoos above, Pearson suggests that people are "full of it" by having the townspeople watch a half-clothed chimpanzee climb upon a flagpole to defecate and urinate and by having them showered with the results.

This sidetracking does not seem so much like sidetracking following Louis's father's voiced opinion of "madness" after all, but the narrator does return to the even weirder story of the wild woman who, wearing a bedsheet, reenacts the siege of Thebes, playing all roles at once and occasionally interrupting herself to agonize on the role of kings, and again the reader is reminded of Creon, who destroys his son and his son's bride-to-be, Antigone. Half of the

town is watching with "curious expressions . . . except for the hint of merri-
ment, and . . . good money was on Miss Pettigrew who was pulling away from
the sheriff with her bedsheet sailing and popping behind her" (6).

Then the sheriff, representing the law, enters the story, "probably a little
too much encumbered with the implements of law enforcement . . . with all
his free-swinging attachments threatening to beat him senseless" (7). The sheriff
"used his arms to clear out a berth for his pistol butt and the shaft of his night-
stick. He had a badge on his hat and a badge on his shirt pocket and a badge in
a wallet on his left hip, and . . . he was dripping with bullets, festooned with
them" (6). The reader is not sure who is more mad, the townspeople who are
enjoying such a scene, the wild chattering chimpanzee who does his business
atop a flagpole, the people who watch the monkey at the risk of being showered, the sheriff who is so weighted down with his law-enforcement implements that he is rendered ineffectual, or the ranting woman (Miss Pettigrew)
acting out a Greek tragedy in her nightclothes on a stump in the front lawn.

From the account of Miss Pettigrew's performance, the narrator roams to
other "peculiar" folks of the town, including the three "sisters," triplets who
aren't triplets, one of whom isn't even a sister to the other two. Finally the
"sisters" are carted off to a mental institution, and everybody is "a little too
happy, a little too quick to laugh, everybody but Sheriff Browner" (17) who
later kills himself, suggesting to the reader that if one can't laugh at the ridicu-
lousness and perversity of the human condition, one can't stand living. The
sheriff is found slumped over the bathtub "with his head entirely under water
and nothing in the world to hold him there, Daddy said, except his own desperation" (22). The narrator's father's description of the sheriff's mental state
is that "the sheriff went to the well [and] he drank too deep" (18-19).

As always in Pearson's novels, representatives of the church appear every
bit as corrupt, inept, and incapable of helping anyone as any other representative of the community. At Miss Pettigrew's funeral, the Reverend Mr. Richard
Crockett Shelton can't find his notes when he is called upon to make his comments, "and Daddy recollected that in the course of his hunt the reverend
managed to come out with five completely separate, purely unrelated, and
entirely insignificant statements none of which, taken singly, was particularly
offensive, but all of which, taken as a group, were magnificently inconsequential. . . . Daddy said it was the most appropriate burial prayer he'd ever heard
since we all died a little in listening to it" (352).

The narrator notes that so many of the people of Neely have become "mad"
that a reporter tries to do a story on the phenomena, and he comes up with the
theory that maybe the insanity is because of fluoridated water (51). The reporter warns "against long stopovers in Neely since life there tended to bore
folks to distraction" (52). When the narrator says, "Daddy said it [the town]

was better than the madhouse" (52), the reader is already convinced it is a madhouse of a town, that maybe all towns are, because the characters seem all too familiar in their insanity.

Louis, as well as his father, seems to be trying to find answers for the desperation of the "peculiar" people, since the history is a story of those bizarre members, especially Miss Pettigrew. The way the town feels about the Pettigrews is about as strange as the Pettigrews themselves, whom the townspeople see as aristocratic and somewhat above the rest of them. The people don't want their idols to be touched by tragedy, and when Louis's father tells of Miss Pettigrew's raging on a stump in a bedsheet, "Momma assured us it [the bedsheet] was probably good linen" (42). If there are no answers for the aristocratic Pettigrews or for the sheriff who represents the law, there is the obvious question of how there can be any answer for anyone else. But "Daddy said it was still madness" (42).

The narrator says when Miss Pettigrew jumped off the town's water tower after her escapade on the front lawn, his mother wouldn't even talk about it because she didn't want to hear of "fate and courage and the trials of existence" (52), so his father talks about those concepts with him. And, Louis says, "Daddy was considerable proud of Miss Pettigrew" (53). Louis says his father's idea of suicide is that suicide isn't cowardice, as people believe, but "Daddy said you have to be brave. He didn't see any other way for a man to bugger fate except by his own hand, and I always got the feeling Daddy would have tried it himself if he didn't have to die from it" (52).

Everyone in the town speculates about Miss Pettigrew's demise, but even the time of her death is becoming vague by the end of the novel when the narrator says it has been "near about two years" (396). So the reader doubts if any accounts are accurate, let alone anyone's interpretation of the events leading up to her leap from the water tower. It is also not clear whether her fall from the tower is her baptism, thus her salvation, or simply her fall, in the traditional sense.

Therefore, not much of a reason is found for Miss Pettigrew's "madness" or for the madness in the world, but in the last part of the book, simply entitled "ME," Louis recalls a conversation he once had with Miss Pettigrew when he was trying to sell her toothbrushes. She asks him, "Do you ever go out in the summertime and lie on your back in the grass and look up at the sky?" (374). His father also tells him at the end of the book "You have to bend some . . . you have to sway a little every now and again, don't you know" (399). He also says that the world is "a disagreeable and unfortunate fact, but . . . it is a fact" (399). Again, if there is any hope for Pearson's characters, it is simply in acceptance of the world and its madness and of people in their human (or animalistic) shortcomings, and in being able to laugh at it all.

Pearson is often criticized for his portrayal of the severity and perversity of human deprivation. He himself says of his novel *Call and Response*, which begins with an amazingly vivid account of a carnival peep show in which a woman projects a pecan from the gyrations of her vagina, that his mother began reading the book and had to stop. He isn't sure whether or not she ever finished it, but he says he sees no way to show such baseness and at the same time "sanitize it" (*Moveable Feast*). After all, it seems to be that part of human nature which Pearson seeks to understand and accept. Otherwise, there's the obvious question with which his characters struggle—what's it all about? Even in the carnival strip show full of debauched people, there is a hungering thirst for something that makes life worth living. Misguided as the search may be, it is a search for meaning, nevertheless. In this respect, *Call and Response*, which seems to many the bleakest because of the details of the sexual scenes, is probably less discouraging in terms of hope for people than some of Pearson's other novels. Again, if there is any salvation, it is in the ability to laugh and love, even if love is only a temporary, sexual love.

Paul Gray's review of *Off for the Sweet Hereafter*, another story of lust and crime, focuses on Pearson's humorous style and his tendency to digress from the main plot line. He suggests that while Pearson's style "can be genuinely funny . . . the discovery and enjoyment of such moments call for considerable patience" (64), but he doesn't go as far as Schafer, who calls Pearson's rambling style "a tsunami of nearly aimless storytelling" (320). William Vollmann in his *New York Times Book Review* piece, "The Search for Miss Polaroid," also discusses Pearson's digressions. In fact, he says that *Cry Me a River* is "about two-thirds digression by weight," but unlike Gray, Vollmann doesn't suggest one needs patience to plow through them. Rather, he says "the digressions are delicious" (11). In fact, he adds that they are like chocolates, "and 200 or 300 pages more of them would gladly have been consumed with no loss of appetite" (12). As Somerville writes, "few reviewers have failed to note that Pearson has a knack for writing that produces laughter" (346).

But there are reasons for the elaborations of Pearson's stories and for the down-home quality of his narrators, who are entertaining enough in themselves. The mini-episodes and his colloquial style all add to Pearson's message about human nature, which is questionable at best and totally despicable at worst. Like Cormac McCarthy's digressions in *Child of God*, Pearson's digressions do come together when the reader realizes that all these smaller stories are present for reasons other than providing humor and authenticity. McCarthy's episodic style, like Pearson's, is a way of showing that the "normal" people are every bit as deranged as the depraved characters they help create by being fascinated with their oddities.

In his fiction, Pearson reveals the essential corruption of human nature and the eternal search for some kind of meaning. With his stylistic skill, Pearson makes his point clear: if there is any meaning in life—or perhaps just a way to survive—it can only be gained by caring for and accepting others and by being able to laugh at everyone's weaknesses. His humor and satire and authenticity of time and place enable his message to be understood and accepted by a public that recognizes every form of degenerate creature Pearson presents.

Tim McLaurin

Keeper of the Moon

SUE LASLIE KIMBALL

Tim McLaurin and Huck Finn enjoyed similar childhoods; they would have had a great time together. Beard Station, just east of Fayetteville, North Carolina, has much in common with Hannibal, Missouri. Both are near a river; the families are working class; the children do not own expensive toys; and their games are richly imaginative. While McLaurin loved his father and still mourns his loss, his family dreaded the days and nights when their "Pap" had imbibed too freely. Huck's Jim becomes McLaurin's boyhood friend, LJ (always written without punctuation) Williams, whom he hired more than once—in the mode of Tom Sawyer—to mow the scrubby McLaurin lawn in return for a sandwich of Merita white bread, baloney, and a dab of mayonnaise. Young Tim never let LJ know how much he longed for one of the Williams's sandwiches of fat homemade biscuits and salt pork.

Counterparts of Hannibal's Injun Joe were two East Fayetteville Lumbee boys. As soon as the boys announced proudly that they were Indians, Tim and LJ pretended to be impressed. "That must mean you can run fast!" they teased. Tim and LJ planned a four-boy race, which they allowed their visitors to win because the hosts had prepared a pit covered with brushes at the finish line. The game culminated in the ultimate humiliation: Tim and LJ peed on the victors in the pit.

While Tom Sawyer planned a raid on "Spanish merchants and rich A-rabs" for the members of his gang, Tim and LJ pretended that they were jungle natives hunting lions and rhinos in their pine woods, their weapons spears cut from reeds. From a well-worn copy of *National Geographic*, they copied war paint, theirs concocted of Carolina red clay, purple pokeberries, and a tube of old lipstick. When game was scarce, says McLaurin, they might ambush the infrequent pickup trucks or tractors that used the road through the pine thicket. They would follow the vehicles, make jungle noises, flash their spears, and retreat.

As Huck and Jim always felt safe when the two of them were on the raft and in mid-river, Tim McLaurin says that camping and canoeing on the river are what he has done all his life and where he finds peace. In a heavy rain, he is elated: "I was dry and warm under my poncho. I had to bail the canoe once in a while with an empty Spam can. Like a worm still in his cocoon, I have likened myself to these few days, protected against the elements by my wraps, my tent, the time drawing closer to emerge" (*Keeper of the Moon* 14).

Admirers of Twain have long marveled at Huck's poetic descriptions of the sky, of the foliage along the river, and of the island. Two of McLaurin's three books begin with comparable descriptions:

> An evening fog is settling on the river, and in her fingers of vapor I see the spirits of one thousand memories. The rain has stopped after three days of gray skies and pewter water; the clouds are beginning to break and I have seen a sliver of the moon in the west. Beavers are sounding their warnings up and down the river. They slap the water with their tails, and you'd think someone had thrown a large rock in the water. [*Keeper of the Moon* 13]
>
> A chilly spring rain had been falling for two days when the clouds finally broke in the west. [*Woodrow's Trumpet* 11]

And in the *last* paragraph of *The Acorn Plan*, McLaurin's first novel, we read, "The eastern sky was flaming from the remnants of the past storm. . . . A waning moon balanced the sunrise from the west, the oval huge and silver" (189-90).

As is true in Hannibal, religion is important to the inhabitants of Beard Station. Huck receives his religious education from Miss Watson, who tells him all about the "bad place." Huck can't see any advantage to going to the good place with his mentor and decides to go for hell. Tim's mother and his Granny were Primitive Baptists, whose congregation met once a month and whose hymns were sung without accompaniment. On a typical Sunday, two or three preachers might show up and talk for hours if they felt God's call. Once a year, the association met for a picnic of fried chicken and ham, vegetables, lemon and cherry pies, and banana pudding. Then the adults, on their knees, washed each other's feet.

Noting that a Southern atheist is rare because Southerners believe that "somehow this chaos is controlled by one who knows a good bit more," McLaurin admits, "I have spent a good part of my life searching through the back alleys of my mind for a definition of how I might describe God" (*Keeper* 38). Certain that he was "high on the list of sinners," young Tim learned to concentrate on a BB-shot hole in the church window so he would not be tempted to answer the call of "Just as I Am" and what he considered "angel duty" (*Keeper* 40).

Pap, Huck's alcoholic father, no angel himself, beat his son as long as he himself could stay on his feet. Tim's alcoholic father once whipped his youngest son Bruce with a belt despite "Mama's" attempts to stop him. Mama McLaurin herself was the chief disciplinarian, and she was quick with words and quick to forgive. One of her favorite threats was, "Boy, I'll cut the pure blood out of your legs with a switch," but the children all knew that she wasn't serious. McLaurin admits, "If I never received many whippings during my childhood, it was not from good behavior" (*Keeper* 23).

While McLaurin claimed in a recent interview that he doesn't read, he does. He added, "They say you have to be a reader to be a writer, but that isn't true" (Interview). He might not read fiction regularly, but he certainly reads hungrily about subjects that interest him. When he received, as a grade-school boy, a gift of a high-powered German telescope from an uncle, he read every book in the school library on astronomy and became the neighborhood authority. When his class wanted a money-making project, Tim took his telescope to school and charged ten cents per child for a good look at the stars. When he caught his first snake, he read everything he could find about reptiles, and later, he actually became a traveling snake handler—a "carney."

He became a writer because he recognized that East Fayetteville is a rich source of stories, characters, and dialect; because one of his grandmothers was a storyteller; and because he was "trying to sort out what was important and what wasn't" ("What I Learned" 29). His failure to be an avid reader is evident only in his punctuation and spelling; he has to have a good editor. One of his professors at the University of North Carolina, when he was a twenty-seven-year-old junior, was Doris Betts, who recognized early that Tim had a "knack" for writing, and who red-penciled all his papers with comments such as:

> Tim, use your dictionary. Learn to punctuate. And for heaven's sake, learn the comma rules!
> Tim, I don't ever want to explain *one more time* the difference between "its" & "it's." You're bright; just learn it & prevent my apoplexy. ["What I Learned" 30]

In spite of the shrill tone and the abundant red marks on his papers, McLaurin says that he learned more about how to craft a sentence from Betts than from anyone.

Actually, before McLaurin entered the Peace Corps because the "wander bug bit again," Max Steele, a professor of English at UNC, gave him advice about his writing, one part of which was, "Read all those books you neglected when you were smoking dope and chasing girls in high school." Back from his Peace Corps assignment in Tunisia and once again a student, McLaurin found himself intolerant "of sitting at a desk with nineteen-year-olds." They wrote about "broken dates and coming of age," while he wrote about "returned veterans, whore houses, divorces, and old scars" ("What I Learned" 29).

McLaurin had shown some of his early writing to a friend in Raleigh, who commented, "I like the writing, but who wants to read about a bunch of rednecks who fight and cut each other? Most people who buy books couldn't relate to them" ("Dreamers"). Her criticism "haunted" him because he realized that every story he wrote had "a drunk or a truck driver or a barroom fight in it." While he was in Tunisia, however, a friend had handed him a book he had bought at the American Embassy and said, "I think you'll like it" ("Dreamers" 5G).

McLaurin *did* like *Ironweed* by William Kennedy because it was about "drunks and street people and the hard life of Albany, New York." *Ironweed* won for Kennedy the Pulitzer Prize and the National Book Award, and it offered hope to McLaurin, as did another book he read while he was in Tunisia, *The Autobiography of Malcolm X*. These stories "of misfits and deadbeats and heroes showed me," says McLaurin, "that my own 'redneck,' hard-living Southerners have stories to tell and that their lives are important as long as I write from the heart." And thus he received the encouragement to continue work on what would become *The Acorn Plan*, which is about country people "mired in ignorance and shackled by drugs, booze, bad jobs, poverty and rage. But they survive on dreams, grit and hope" ("Dreamers" 5G).

Billy Riley, protagonist of *The Acorn Plan*, works in a pet shop while he is on parole for having almost killed a Fort Bragg soldier in a drunken brawl. He falls in love with Cassie, a Fayetteville stripper, and they double-date on a fishing-trip picnic with Billy's Uncle Bubble and his once-homeless friend, Wilma. Worried about Billy's excessive drinking, Uncle Bubble quits his job in the cotton mill to try to drink all the wine in the world as a lesson to Billy. The title of the novel comes from Billy's philosophy. When Cassie says, "I think it's grand how nature can take something as small as an acorn and make it grow into a tree that size," Billy argues that nature isn't fair. "Look how many acorns there are on the ground. They can't all grow into big trees. Maybe just one in a million." He worries about the ones that don't make it. "Wouldn't you think that all acorns are created equal?" (112). Almost everyone in East Fayetteville, and certainly those who cared for him, expected Billy to be a "big tree"—his Aunt Ruby, the fat, lovable truck-stop waitress who had raised him when his mother died, his Uncle Bubble, who had given him a German telescope, and Cassie, whose ambition to be a ballet dancer causes her to leave for the city.

A strange reversal: Mark Twain grew ever more bitter and depressed and angry, declaring eventually that he hated "the damned human race." This despair and fury were brought on by a series of bad investments, the deaths of his beloved wife and two daughters, and the failure of his publishing firm. McLaurin lost his father, whom he writes of lovingly; suffered a rare form of cancer called multiple myeloma, endured chemotherapy, had two bone marrow transplants from his brother, Bruce, and incurred staggering expenses; feared that he would not live to see his children, Christopher and Meaghan, grow up, yet his work is ever more optimistic. Uncle Bubble and Billy fail to survive in *The Acorn Plan* and both Woodrow and Nadean die in *Woodrow's Trumpet*, but they have realized their dreams. They have raised acres of watermelons, held barbecues for all of their neighbors and friends, and built a swimming pool, adding sand, pink plastic flamingoes, and a real palm tree in inland North Carolina. Their young friend, Ellis, who is like an adopted son to them, blows Woodrow's trumpet—his hunting horn—at story's end in an affirmation of hope.

Keeper of the Moon delights, not only because of the abundant humor, but also because we see the unprecedented determination of McLaurin to defeat cancer and survive to canoe and to visit his cabin retreat built on the family farm. Even when he was in Seattle and undergoing treatment, McLaurin retained his sense of humor, noting that he had to find grits in the ethnic section of the Safeway. "They had 'em next to the tabouli and couscous," he said (quoted in Skube, "One Writer's Long Wait"). Of the autobiographical *Keeper of the Moon*, McLaurin, who has certainly been near death, says, "It's not about death or almost dying. It's about life" (quoted in Miller, "An Adventure," 2E).

The doctor who first diagnosed the bone marrow cancer was not optimistic. He told McLaurin, then thirty-five, that he might die within two or three years and that to expect ten years more of life would probably be "pushing it." A four-mile-a-day jogger until that moment, McLaurin declares, "I decided in that first minute I would not face this disease in a passive mood, but would confront it as the thing it was—an intruder. I felt more pissed-off than afraid, more hassled than victimized." Convinced that "hope and positive thinking are very strong medicine," McLaurin fully believes that he will beat the disease and recover ("Fighting Back" 5). The courage that allowed him to imagine the "chemotherapy melting the myeloma cells away like acid" is evident in his last books. McLaurin believes that the fact that he has "pushed himself into areas that required strong physical and mental stamina" ("Fighting Back" 8) will stand him in good stead: he has been a Marine, a snake handler, a Peace Corps volunteer, a writer, and an outdoorsman. Each experience demanded the dedication that he now devotes to staying alive.

Of *Woodrow's Trumpet*, his second novel, McLaurin has said that there are two major themes. One is the theme of home—home as a place, "like in our case, where it's tied to the land and a tradition." North Carolina, and particularly Fayetteville, are still "home central" to him, he added. The other idea of home, he pointed out, "is where you rest your hat," and that place can change in a mobile society. "That's the concept of home," he said, but he wonders if it is possible to "carry home from place to place" (quoted in Joyce, "Tough, Gentle," 50). Nadean, in *Woodrow's Trumpet*, expresses her creator's idea when she says, "Home stays in just two places—on the land where you were raised, and always, always, in the back of your mind" (157). The subject recurs in Nadean's thoughts and conversation: "My mama told me once there weren't no such thing as home, but now I know better" (153) and "Home always be home, even if you gone for seventy years" (153).

The other theme of *Woodrow's Trumpet* is a satire of middle-class America. Liberals Jeffery and Mary Stewart have moved to the Whispering Pines subdivision, a community "perfect for up-and-coming young professionals" and built to surround Woodrow's inherited ten acres. The Stewarts see themselves as progressive when they invite Woodrow and the black ex-prostitute and recovering addict, Nadean, to dinner, but they rebel at Woodrow's reconstruction of a Florida beach in his backyard because they fear it will affect their property values. They are, thinks McLaurin, typical of the much-educated people in Chapel Hill who espouse causes as long as they're "a hundred miles or a few thousand miles away" (quoted in Joyce, "Tough, Gentle," 50). A reviewer in the *Raleigh News & Observer* has called *Woodrow's Trumpet* "a morality tale of the changing South" and "a brilliant mirror by which we see ourselves, darkly" (Richards, "Through McLaurin's Mirror" 4D).

Potpourri: When McLaurin reads from his works, he sometimes milks snakes and drinks the venom. He has been known to bite a rattle off a snake and spit it into the audience. His children are comfortable with the pythons, rattlers, and other snakes that have lived in their carport, and he has taught a class called "The Last Great Snake Show." He has his wife's nickname, "Katie-O," tattooed among hearts and flowers on his upper right arm. He has been a carpenter, a painter, and a Coca Cola salesman. He was a forward air-controller and a rifle expert in the Marines. Seven of the eleven patients who were in the Seattle Veterans Hospital when he was receiving treatment have since died. He carries a plastic bag of dirt from the pasture behind his boyhood home. He drinks less since his cancer treatment, but he admits to "the peace that begins after guzzling two or three beers": "Chug that first beer, down another nearly as fast, settle back in the seat, and enjoy the soft, warm cloud as it settles over me" (*Keeper* 226). He once told an interviewing reporter to stop the car so that he could lift a box turtle out of the road and harm's way. He was the first subject of a PBS series about Southern writers.

Keeper of the Moon ends with a one-sentence paragraph: "I have told you of home" (316). McLaurin has told us of home in three books, but his most recent novel, *Cured by Fire*, is about two men who start in North Carolina but wander westward, ending in California. Unlike the protagonists of the earlier books, the wealthy man and the migrant worker of *Cured by Fire* leave home as they go on a quest that is actually a search for answers to their respective religious doubts. As the two fictional characters ponder the nature of God, the author, a one-time Primitive Baptist who terms himself an unorthodox believer, will surely find some satisfactory answers to his own questions.

Richard Marius

"The Brooding Mystery"

CARROLL VIERA

Richard Marius—novelist, historian, educator—became a writer during his high school and college years when he worked as a reporter for his hometown newspaper, *The Lenoir City* (Tenn.) *News*. In his essay "How I Write," he credits his newspaper experience with teaching him that a writer must be concerned with truth: "Report the wrong second prize winner in the Garden Club's contest for the best dry arrangement, and see what happens. . . . You get an outraged gardener sometimes weeping on the telephone or, worse, standing over your desk shaking a mean-looking trowel in your face" (149).

Marius's commitment to truth has dominated his academic writing. As a young scholar he served as an editor of the Yale edition of the complete works of Sir Thomas More, laboring to produce accurate texts and introductions to More's writing. His biographies of More and of Martin Luther, as well as his scholarship on topics as varied as Woodrow Wilson and Civil War poetry, challenge many assumptions of earlier historians.

Truth, however, is often elusive. "The good biographer's judgments must be ambiguous," Marius contends, "because ambiguity is the stuff of real human life" ("Reflections" 199); and the historian's task is always complicated by the fact that "evidence for past events is always incomplete and fragmentary, like a jigsaw puzzle washed out of a shipwreck and cast upon a rocky beach by the waves" (*Short Guide* 5).

This elusive, fragmentary quality of truth is a recurring theme in Marius's fiction. In *The Coming of Rain*, many of the characters struggle to achieve a coherent view of reality. The protagonist attempts to arrange his fragmentary knowledge "in some pattern which made room for the mystery he could not understand" (377). The heroine's account of her past is "a chaos of things fetched out of her memory" (113). An attorney has once considered the law a force that gives order to life's "chaotic fragments" (170), but he comes to regard events and objects in his life "as unconnected in his mind as particles of dust suspended in the atmosphere" (162).

After the War, which reintroduces many of the characters of *The Coming of Rain*, also explores the problem of inferring a pattern from fragmentary knowledge. At the outset of his narrative, the protagonist, who compares his story to "a mosaic," concedes that he "cannot account for everything. Parts of my story vanish in the dark. I once yearned to know how they ended. No more. I am resigned to some things—resigned to my destiny, the fragmented story I tell here" (4).

Marius's concern with perceiving unity and reality through fragmented clues, a concern that persists throughout his nonfiction as well as his fiction, is nowhere more evident than in his second novel, *Bound for the Promised Land*. Early in the novel, the protagonist, Adam Cloud, gazes into the fragment of a mirror too small to reflect his entire face at once. "He saw broken fragments as he moved the mirror around—his eyes, his chin, his mouth, his cheekbones. He remained a mystery to himself. He wondered how all the pieces fit together" (25).

Adam's efforts to define his own identity and to understand life send him west in search of his father. In his physical journey toward California and his psychological journey toward a mature perception of reality, he confronts questions of good and evil, of predestination and free will, and of orderly patterns and random occurrences.[1] These questions are posed by four guides—two false, two true—who disclose alternative ways of shaping reality into patterns which successively collapse as new alternatives arise.

Marius underscores the spiritual nature of Adam's quest by borrowing the title of the novel from a hymn popular among Protestant fundamentalists and by using one stanza and the chorus as an epigraph. In equating the Promised Land with the New Jerusalem and the crossing of the Jordan River with a passage through death to eternal life, the hymn defines reality in traditional Christian terms.

As a member of a fundamentalist community and the child of a fanatically devout mother, Marius knows Southern religion from the inside.[2] In his freshman year at the University of Tennessee, however, his childhood faith was shattered when he read W.T. Stace's "Man against Darkness," an essay which argues the purposelessness of the universe (Marius, Interview by Randy Brison). He attempted to recover his faith and to fulfill his mother's dreams for him by attending two Baptist seminaries, but these attempts failed. In fact, his seminary experiences verified for him the darker side of fundamentalist

mentality and its traits of hypocrisy, self-righteousness, hysteria, predestinari-
anism, and belief in instantaneous conversion.[3]

Like the young Marius, Adam is an atypical member of his community.
Nudged from his familiar world by his mother's death, he defies local custom
by burying his mother on their farm rather than in the churchyard, by disre-
garding the community's expectation that he marry Sylvia Roberts, and by avoid-
ing his church. His fantasies of remaining in Tennessee with Sylvia dissolve
when he dreams "of taking a journey, of riding on a rocky path beneath the
battlements of castles that flung high turrets into the clouds like the pictures
in a book of fairy tales he had seen once for a precious hour" (25). His search
for his father, "a stranger, remote and spellbound in some enchanted realm
the boy could never enter" (3), further beckons him toward this fairy-tale world,
a world epitomized by an aspiring but inadequate mentor, Harry Creekmore,
who creates reality—including his own identity—rather than searching for it.
Harry's romanticism presents the first significant challenge to Adam's fundamentalism, but Adam clings to his community's construct of reality, insisting,
when Harry calls him "a real Christian," that he "ain't never had no experience. You got to have a experience to be a real Christian. I ain't never shouted"
(36). Nevertheless, Adam's capacity for transcending this rigid perception of
reality is metaphorically suggested: after he sells his Bourbon County farm, it
"looked like the Garden of Eden. It was sin and death to leave" (27).

The allure of Harry's world, though manifested in Adam's dream, remains
largely dormant. Harry is given to "theatrical sighs" (57), wonders if Nashville
has a theater, and contends that a play is "true when you see it" (41); but Adam
maintains, "We ain't got time for such like in Bourbon County" (34) and mar-
vels that "anybody wants to go spend a night looking at something that ain't
true" (41). And yet Harry functions as an external projection of Adam's inner
impulses: Adam wavers between disgust with Harry's lies and admiration for
the way "Harry made lying truly an art" (51).

The inadequacy of Harry's vision, however, is reflected by his myopia.
Though glasses have improved his physical vision, they have deprived him of
a blurred but beautiful and colorful world, which he replaces with increasingly extravagant illusions of becoming mayor of Nashville, mayor of San Francisco, governor of California, president of the United States. When challenged,
he retreats into a "soft and private universe where only his imagination could
penetrate and nothing could attack him" (96). He cannot recognize in Ishtar
the malice immediately apparent to Adam; and, when she endangers him in
Nashville, he withdraws into intoxication, leaving Adam to rescue him.

Adam and Harry's flight from Nashville and from Ishtar and their crossing
of the Cumberland River again invoke the Edenic myth and the implications
of the title of the novel. The ferryman, a fusion of Charon from Greek mythol-

ogy and the Porter from *Macbeth*, demands a coin for his services and then curses them until Adam knocks him unconscious. Adam, who has never fought before, feels a surge of joy, a response which recalls the first Adam's immediate response to sin; but his joy dissolves into a sense of darkness: the moon is "a crescent against the eastern dark," the frogs and the insects create "a crescendo of trembling discord," "within the tall forest the darkness was so thick that Adam could not see his hands" (69), and the hour is "unholy." Adam's entry into this mysterious darkness elicits severe self-scrutiny: "*Maybe I'm bad*" (70).

The Cumberland River is one of many boundaries between Adam's childhood and his maturity, each boundary marking an irreversible transition. Adam's longing "for the kindling of dawn in the east" signifies his continued search for meaning; and the road he follows, "winding, climbing, and descending through fields and through corridors of spectral trees," suggests a moral and psychological maze. Significantly, he realizes, "I can't never go back." Adam is right. He can never return to his simple life in East Tennessee, where innocent girlfriends have names meaning "woodlands" and where homes are shaded by apple trees.[4]

Adam's night blindness parallels his lack of self-perception and his tenuous grasp on reality. As he rides through the night, he remembers his father and "a trivial vision, a light gleaming abruptly and steadily in the far deep of the woods, lingering for a while, then going away and leaving a mystery" and a question: "And what was there in the dark?" (70). Much of the novel explores the question "What was there in the dark?"—in the western wilderness, beyond civilization, in the psyches of the characters. The answer, Adam will learn, evades easy formulaic reduction.

Traveling through Kentucky, Adam continues to search for coherence, bringing up "the pieces of his old life one by one to dismiss them" (73-74) and not knowing "exactly what he was doing" (74). The crossing of the Mississippi, which marks the end of his life in the East, is invested with a significance that Adam does not yet perceive. Though this crossing is "a very simple experience . . . a conglomeration of simple experiences . . . that moment would always be so keen in his mind that it became nearly a talisman of memory. He would always entertain the fantasy of going back to that magic river at that place and so reversing all the processes of age and time" (75).

The "conglomeration of simple experiences" at Cape Girardeau gives way to the alien world of the Jennings family, whose shattered wagon wheel, another emblem of fragmentation, joins their destinies to Adam's and Harry's. Jason Jennings's Emersonian Idealism, which he had adopted at Yale in rebellion against his mother's Calvinism, diametrically opposes Adam's dualistic fundamentalism. Jason also advocates a Jeffersonian agrarianism, already invalid in the market economy of mid-nineteenth-century America. Both of his creeds prove as illusory as Harry's fairy-tale romanticism. In fact, Marius begins to discredit Jason by depicting a symbiosis in which Harry fuels Jason's dream of an Arcadian farming community and Jason encourages further extravagance in Harry's lying and illusions.[5]

Jason reaffirms his ignorance through his Emersonian belief that "being close to nature makes you strong and good" and through his superficial Primitivism which includes stereotypes of noble savages. Like his other concepts, these perceptions come from books, not from experience, and they are so rigid that when he first encounters Indians who do not conform to his perceptions, he concludes that they are not "real Indians."

Adam immediately rejects Jason's illusions, pointing out that "if you're going out to California to farm, and if you can't farm, then it matters one hell of a lot if you know what you're talking about" (103), and even Harry concedes the truth of Adam's assertion and labels Jefferson "a liar" (101). Yet Jason eludes Adam's full comprehension: "The fire half-concealed his expression, and the shadows dancing upward over his eyes did not allow Adam to see him clearly" (97). This distorted vision creates an ambivalence toward Jason that echoes Adam's ambivalence toward Harry. Listening to Jason read of the Exodus, Adam indulges in a glorious fantasy of California, though the fantasy dissipates in his awareness that "he was in a meadow with ordinary people"(95); and he finds Jason's reading of the Bible "a splendid show" even if it is "vain and self-conscious" (139). Adam is shedding his identity as a Bourbon Countian who does not have time for "such like."

Though eventually recognizing Jason's insanity, at the eastern border of the Plains, Adam briefly adopts his monistic Transcendentalism: "he had never jumped and shouted with conversion in any camp meeting revival, and now he did not care anymore. Maybe God lived on the Plains, and perhaps here people did not have to strain for Him, and being here might be all the experience with God that anybody required" (140).

Jason's equating California and Arcadia, however, validates Adam's initial uncertainties about such an impractical vision. Though Arcadia evokes images of the Golden Age, its associations, as Erwin Panofsky demonstrates, are more sinister, for the original place of the phrase *Et in Arcadia Ego* "is a tomb," and *Ego* refers to the tomb and thus to death.[6]

These ominous associations of Arcadia pervade *Bound for the Promised Land*, intensifying as Ishtar and her husband overtake the Jennings party on a morning described in images of mystery that obscure Adam's vision: "the darkness still piled like veils hung down from infinity" (104). Appearing on "the little road that coiled away in the forest toward Cape Girardeau" and emerging from "long, thin shadows," their cart resembles "a tawny apparition of evil fantasy" (107). Significantly, Ishtar's first name denotes the Mesopotamian goddess of lust and war and her surname derives from the Old English *bana* ("murderer"). Marius reinforces this amalgam of associations by consistently using her full name. Again Adam underestimates her capacity for destruction, but he does see "her malice and her cunning" and, like the narrator, frequently describes her in reptilian terms. Harry, however, whose innocence and impotence before such evil is suggested by his white suit, cannot "seem to see her malice" and argues that "people are basically good" (111).

At Westport Landing, another boundary for Adam, Shawnee Joe McMoultrie abrades Adam's already fractured sense of order. When the trapper castrates an assailant, Adam exclaims, "We never done nothing like that back in Tennessee," adding a moment later, "I never seen nothing like it" (146). Adam's vision remains limited, his world still shrouded in mystery: over everything hangs "a prodigious and mysterious silence" (153), and the road West is "uncertain" (158).

Shawnee Joe's view of reality is founded in experience, not in dreams, books, or abstract speculations;[7] thus he becomes a suitable mentor and surrogate father for Adam, a guide into the Indian Territory, an "alien" land, a morally ambiguous world "beyond the reach of the law" (142) and "free of the conventional restraints" (209). Though perplexed by "the unfathomable foolishness of human beings he could not explain" (147), he discerns, even if he cannot account for, the Jennings brothers' incompetence, Ishtar's scheming possessiveness, Harry's masquerade as a doctor, and Rebecca's charades. Dismissing Adam's stern concept of religious experience as "a bunch of shit," he models an alternative flexibility. He disparages Adam's condemnation of Harry's lies, asserting that at his age "you don't know what's true and what ain't for nobody but yourself" (160); and he admonishes Jason that "they's some bends in the road" (154). Most important, he recognizes that "they's lots of things that don't make no sense, but they're true" (171), while Adam still grasps at mythic religious constructs.

Shawnee Joe's knowledge includes a recognition of negative forces which Adam only faintly intuits until their crossing of the Kaw River challenges his conception of nature. Though Adam is an accomplished hunter who can navigate by the stars, the Kaw alters his perspective: "the isolation, the danger, and the enmity of nature itself were things he had never before felt, never dreamed of in his worst nightmares" (168). The Kaw, as Samuel notes, "has turned everything upside down" (171).

The crossing promises a rebirth: the river is a "flood," Jason's wagon an "ark"; Adam thinks of "rising from the dank grave" and "standing at the resurrection" (168); and even Shawnee Joe feels young again. But the water has a "deadly murmur" (165), it terrorizes five-year-old Rachael "as though it had been an enormous brown snake" (170), and it further begrimes rather than cleanses the travelers. Nevertheless, having mastered the Kaw, Adam suddenly believes that he is "a man now" (169) and that a bond has been created between him and Jessica.

Adam sets out to affirm this bond through his first buffalo hunt. According to Shawnee Joe, it is this traditional rite of passage that transforms him into a man, but unknown to his companions, the transformation has derived from his killing of two Pawnee braves. Adam's encounter with the braves during his hunt not only verifies Shawnee Joe's warning that beyond civilization it is sometimes necessary to kill, but also forever divests Jason's Transcendentalism of validity. With the appearance of the Pawnee, Adam's perceptions of a benevolent landscape—"the sweet smell of the grass . . . the clean fragrance of the open air"—crumble. His illusions of noble savages also collapse, for the braves are scrawny and cowardly and carry ineffective weapons—a dull knife and a flintlock musket that won't fire. Gazing in "spellbound wonder" at one of the slain Indians, Adam does not recognize "the Indian he had imagined when he pondered those fleet huntsmen of the plains" or "the imaginary Indian people talked about in Independence or Westport Landing. It was like no picture of an Indian he would ever see. . . . He could not understand" (205). In this encounter with death, Adam's expulsion from Eden and childhood innocence is absolute. He returns to camp "with a growing and hopeless shame as if his very footsteps across the grassy night were an abomination to God," and he is overcome with guilt, believing that "in a just world where sin had its recompense, the Indians must kill him before dawn" but hoping "that morning would come with a liquid shining to wash away his sins" (207).

Later, at Alcove Springs, in an echo of his last night in Tennessee, "Adam looked into the dark beyond the magical forms of the trees and wondered what was out there." Events of the next day confirm what he has learned at the Kaw and during his hunt. Ironically, before Adam crosses the river with Rachael, Harry again calls him "a Christian and a gentleman," to which Adam once more responds, "I ain't never had no experience." But struggling against a current that "coiled around him like a thousand snakes," Adam discovers an innate evil beneath Rachael's illusory angelic appearance, a discovery which nullifies Jason's Lockean assumptions about formative environments. A diminutive version of Ishtar and Rebecca, Rachael displays her affinity for these incarnations of evil in her absorption of their obscenities, her gleeful malice, and her viperous behavior, which leads to her death in a river whose "snarling" enmity mirrors her own. Three days later, in a travesty of the Resurrection, her father finds her body "misshapen and decomposing. It stank of the muddy river and of its own putrefaction. . . . And Adam cursed God in his heart and willed to die" (225), his heart "made heavy by all he had *experienced*" (228;

my italics). In the days that follow, Adam's world is marked by "the snakes, the dust, the unending trail, the parching thirst" and his enduring awareness of Rachael's depravity, omens "of something more terrible lurking just beyond their sight" (236).

It is Jessica who supersedes Shawnee Joe as Adam's mentor and restores meaning into his life. Traits she shares with the trapper combine with traits of her own to qualify her for this role. Though Adam finds both of them enigmatic, he recognizes that they are "cut out of the same stuff" and are "hard and durable and tough" (254). Like Shawnee Joe, who has wanted "a good ride" out of life, Jessica has "always sought new things" (281). And like Shawnee Joe, she has no use for Adam's simplistic fundamentalism, which she regards as "vulgar beyond words" (284).

Because Jessica's capacity for mystery exceeds Shawnee Joe's, she gradually displaces him as Adam's mentor, becoming both signifier of, and guide into, a new level of reality. Despite their bond established at the Kaw River, she remains "mysterious," her face "still and inscrutable" (201), her expression "illusive and dark," her hair "a golden veil" (279). Just before their first intimate conversation, she appears beside the campfire "a dim and shrouded figure," with "shadows thrown over her features" (237). Adam "could not see her expression clearly in the shadows"; but though he "could scarcely see her," "he felt that there was something sympathetic in her expression, and yet he did not know" (236). She asks if he has "ever thought that nothing is the way it seems" (239), but she herself incarnates this mutability: he realizes her desire for him, but when he tries to kiss her, she struggles free, verbally lacerates him, and leaves him in the dark "more shattered and humiliated and more guilty than he had ever been in his life" (241). Again his hold on reality and his sense of identity are fractured.

Pondering "what might have been, how close things came to being different . . . a mystery close and unfathomable, shadows looming in the dark" (251), Adam retreats into nihilism: "life had become a speck in a soundless universe," and Rachael's "death was robbed of any mystery." But his memories of "the world where things hung together in a pattern" intrude upon the present and indicate his capacity for recovery. These memories include images of his father, with whom he "had sat in silent communion out on the porch of their cabin every summer evening, listening to the infinite choir of loud insects singing their immemorial song in the woods" (253), impressions which, significantly, Adam recalls in the language of religion.

The Platte River initially promises renewal to the entire Jennings party, but the river dissolves into one more emblem of fragmentation, "disorderly and dirty," composed of "a dozen rivers, all running crazily through brown, sandy gullies that made up its wide bed" (256). Jessica exclaims, "I wish I could see just one thing in my life that turned out to be what it seemed to be when I first saw it!" (256).

By the time the wagon train reaches the western border of the Plains, Jessica's coldness has faded. Though Adam thinks the hills "ain't much," Jessica finds them beautiful, "something to conjure with." Despite the trauma of a teenage pregnancy and of bringing up an illegitimate child, she is resilient. The concert that had precipitated her youthful tryst has remained a memorable moment, a spot of time. The music, she has told a baffled Ishtar, "was like something in my heart rushing out to meet what was coming in from the outside. Music within and music without. And there was a harmony when they met in my heart" (271). Though Jessica perceives a fusion of the inner and the outer for which Adam has been searching and though she locates the source of this fusion in her impressions, she does not attempt to define it. Her experience exemplifies the modern epiphany, in which, according to Ashton Nichols, "the moment of revelation is absolute and determinate but the meaning provided by the inspiration is relative and indeterminate" (xii). Jessica's epiphany also illustrates additional requirements, noted by Robert Langbaum: an origin in an actual sensuous experience and a transitory nature but "enduring effect" (40).

Adam too recalls epiphanic moments when Jessica asks, "What is the most beautiful thing you have ever seen in all your life?" (282). He thinks of her and also of simple activities shared with his father on Sunday mornings, activities infused with magic and meaning. In answering Jessica, however, he reduces the mystery to a prosaic "Sunday mornings, back home, in the spring" (282). Because he cannot adequately articulate the significance of these memories, Jessica misunderstands his response just as Ishtar has misunderstood Jessica's attitude toward music. When he tries to impose meaning upon his impressions, the mystery is "cut away" and his pattern collapses.

Jessica, like Adam, ponders questions of determinism, asserting that people are merely "chips on the flood" (284) and yet wondering if a God "can take all the accidents that happen to us and put them together in some pattern that has a purpose" (285). Her recognition of the indeterminacy of answers to these questions leads Adam toward a Humean vision, with its emphasis upon the primacy of unconnected fragments of sensory experience and of memory.

As Jessica knows and as Adam has increasingly perceived, the fragments that make up life include the negative, a perception further clarified for him at Ash Hollow. Though Jessica's daughter, Promise, compares Ash Hollow to Paradise, references to graves and to "relics of the great emigration" (302) subvert the allusions to Eden, to a chalice, and to water that is "like wine" (307); and here Adam gains insight into Ishtar. Earlier he had assumed a design, however inexplicable, beneath her malice; now he perceives that "she sowed destruction because destruction corresponded to the broken fragments that in their very disorder made up the only soul she possessed. And she had no motives beyond the chaos itself" (304). Adam also recognizes that she poses a real danger to Harry, who has evoked her enmity from the outset. Adam's awareness of evil now approximates Shawnee Joe's, and, reflexively mimicking a characteristic gesture of the trapper, he places his hand upon the weapon at his belt.

Beyond Ash Hollow another shattered wagon wheel adumbrates the further splintering of the Jennings party. When Jason's trip to Courthouse Rock temporarily removes him from the group, Jessica resumes her role as mentor. Her talk about "inconsequential things" elicits from Adam an understanding of "how important those inconsequential things had been in his own life" (323). Their conversation reveals to him not only "a mystery—how life is an intangible web woven invisibly between simple objects that mean little in themselves" but also a vision of the Plains as "the substance of an invisible magic that would make all of them into new creatures" (323).

Adam's attainment of Jessica's vision is dramatized in a lyrical passage in which they make love in the grass against "mute and magical" heat lightning. Significantly, he "did not fully understand her," in the dark "he could form no clear impression of her body," and "he could see her naked legs dimly." "Sometimes it seemed that the experience was all memory and no happening at all. A mystery." Once again the reader recognizes an epiphany, the full significance of which Adam does not yet apprehend: "Later he thought it was foolish to have glanced behind him at those suspended legs, to remember that sight above all others, but it happened that way, and he never forgot it" (326).

As Shawnee Joe becomes incapacitated and as Adam matures through his relationship with Jessica, Adam displaces the trapper as a force holding the group together. The precariousness of this hold is underscored by the tragedy at Mitchell Pass. In a final, incontestable assault on an Emersonian view of nature, Marius abruptly destroys Promise's impression of the pass as romantic even more forcefully than he has demolished her impression of Ash Hollow. The pass is cast in "black shadows," its features are "spectral and forbidding," its formations are "broken temples, fallen spires, streets . . . choked with debris" (329), and it is suddenly overhung with the darkest clouds Adam has ever seen. Almost instantly in a world "dimly seen," an unexpected storm dissolves "the sturdy shapes of things," transforming them "into vague, gray shadows, only swimming suggestions of themselves" (330). As the storm subsides, the "splintered" tongue of one of the wagons, "the tangled wreckage," and Ruth's "shattered arm" (332) presage the final disintegration of the group.

With his mythmaking, Harry has won Promise's love, sustained Jason's vision of Arcadia, and routed the Sioux. Now, in amputating Ruth's arm, he restores the illusion of a pattern, the pattern of a good story, in which "the conflicts were resolved, and good came out on top." But, soon afterwards, at Independence Rock, the shattering of Harry's glasses signifies the final crumbling of his world of romance as a tenable pathway to truth, leaving Adam to face "another mystery with terror at the heart of it." Adam's acceptance of terror as part of reality denotes his growth, though he still "did not understand himself, this alternation between terror and peace. He had endured haunting things, but they seldom haunted him once he had left them behind" (374).

By the time the group reaches South Pass, Shawnee Joe has lost his faith in the fragments of memory that have held his life together—sharing a pipe or whiskey in the wilderness, watching running rivers and roaring waterfalls, celebrating the pleasures of the rendezvous. Unlike Jessica who "can't stop hoping" but like the archetypal isolated frontiersman, he cannot adapt to a rapidly changing world. Finally he yields to a vision of evil that crushes his will to live.

Thus, Adam's reconciliation of terror and peace takes him beyond the level of experience exemplified by Shawnee Joe, a necessary stage in the attainment of maturity, according to Sigmund Freud, who notes that a boy finally transfers to his teachers the ambivalence earlier displayed toward his family (Freud, "Some Reflections," 244). Adam demonstrates this pattern by retaining only selectively what Shawnee Joe has taught him: in refusing to shoot Ishtar and Asa, he rejects Shawnee Joe's harsh survival tactics and ultimately rejoins a larger community.

Though Shawnee Joe allows his darkening vision to efface his sustaining Wordsworthian "spot of time," his recognition of the real presence of evil is validated in Marius's scrutiny of Rebecca. Repulsive and deluded, self-righteous and full of harmful lies, Rebecca has conspired with Ishtar to secure the allegiance of Rachael and to destroy Jessica. At Mitchell Pass, when Adam has admitted that he "ain't never had no experience," she has proclaimed that he will "burn forever in *hell!*" Adam's response has reflected a deterministic stoicism: "I reckon it does all right"; and when she has wondered, "Well, ain't you *worried* about it?" he has replied, "No, ma'am. I don't reckon so. What is to be will be" (343). Now, at South Pass, her absolute corruption is signified by the gruesome details of her cholera attack, the excrement that spews uncontrolled from her bowels being a physical manifestation of her moral corruption.

Stricken with cholera in South Pass, Adam recalls moments in Tennessee, memories which comprise another epiphany: "Now out here and dying, Adam thought that he possessed his father's love just as if the two of them had found each other in California! He did not have to seek Joel Cloud anymore"

(402). Though Adam and his father will be reunited in California, Adam's psychological search for him ends at South Pass when he can look within himself rather than to others for guidance.

As Adam recovers from near death in a symbolic resurrection, he must distinguish between dreams and reality. At Ishtar's instigation, the Jennings men really have hanged Harry, exposed Shawnee Joe in the sun to die, taken the oxen, tied Jessica up in Jason's wagon, and abandoned Adam, Promise, and Henry. But amidst Adam's horror of recognition, a cow wanders into camp; and, in another epiphany effected through sensory impressions, Adam smells her milk and recalls "the sweet, orderly regularity of the good life." Shawnee Joe and Jessica are gone, but Adam has absorbed their strength and resilience. Now he is ready to assume the care of Promise and Henry and to bring them safely to California.

In crossing the country, Adam has searched for a pattern of meaning, a pattern he initially believed attainable through religious conversion. When Harry has explained that after death, he would like to "look down at the world and see how it all came out," Adam has given his customary response: "I don't talk about religion . . . I ain't never had no experience." And yet he too has continually yearned to know how things come out: the fate of the ferryman in Nashville, of the Indian in St. Louis, of the Indian's assailant, of the castrated man in Westport Landing, and, especially, of Jessica. Shawnee Joe has cautioned him against such thoughts: "Ah, you can't ask questions like that. You ain't never going to know" (148).

In California, Adam comes to uneasy terms with his uncertainties, again finding serenity in "that limited, clear, good world where men told the truth naturally, spontaneously." His rigid adolescent attitude toward truth, however, has dissolved; and, out of concern for Promise, he lies to her about his relationship with Jessica. Moreover, his perceptions of the past begin to blur. When he recalls South Pass, "it was a puzzle to him that nothing ever came back and that intense experiences, glory, horror, and the petty details of ordinary life, dwindled alike to become fragments of color, smell, and disconnected sound, all fading, fading" (422-23).

Nevertheless, he does not entirely relinquish his attempts to impose meaning upon these fragments. For forty years he continues to hold himself responsible for Harry's death, until Henry stuns him by announcing that cholera is infectious rather than contagious and that their epidemic had likely been triggered by sharing the dipper that Jason had called their chalice, not by Adam's and Harry's venture to Independence Rock. Now "his entire conception of the past was breaking up," and he reiterates Jessica's yearning: "*I wish one time in my life things would be what they seem to be.*"

Adam's serenity is further jolted by Ishtar's reappearance and her disclosure that Jason had traded Jessica to Indians for five horses. But when Ishtar reveals that the Jennings brothers had been scalped, Adam muses that "it was not justice for what they had done to Harry, to Jessica. Not even revenge. Just something that had happened." The final image of the novel suggests that, like Jessica, Adam has accepted the indeterminacy of meaning: "the wind was blowing lines of water across the waves, so that the pattern was crisscrossed and in such constant motion that he could not fix his tired eyes upon it" (436).

Adam's quest has returned him to a dualistic universe where good and evil coexist; but his universe, devoid of providential order, is a secular and demythologized version of Bourbon County Protestantism, his dualism empirically derived from experience. And though he cannot force the fragments of his life into a coherent pattern, he has learned to find transcendent if elusive meaning in "specks of time" that give life beauty and wonder, as well as terror.

This acceptance is closely intertwined with clear vision, self-awareness, and attenuated expectations of life, inherent traits in Adam which have been honed through experience and through the tutelage of Shawnee Joe and Jessica. Life is filled with pain and disappointment, but emerging from "the brooding mystery" of this darkness are fleeting but memorable moments of epiphany: watching a deer "streak through the forest shadows like an illusion of dim light" (12), listening to stories beside a campfire, making love in the grass beneath "fitful illuminations of the blue lightning" (326), recovering a father and seeing the signs of love in his face.

In his essay "The Middle of the Journey," Marius alludes to his scrutiny in *Bound for the Promised Land* of predestination and of cause and effect, confessing that he himself sometimes wonders "if the world could be what David Hume supposed—merely a succession of things happening after other things so that all existence is reduced to such mystery that no mind can fathom it" (465).

But while *Bound for the Promised Land* ends with a Humean image, this image cannot offset a repeated emphasis upon many turning points, a change in any one of which would have altered Adam's life. This emphasis upon contingency, in subverting the image of the waves, places the reader in a position analogous to Adam's and illustrates Marius's assumptions that "it is a common intellectual experience to discover that the more closely we look at any text, the more it dissolves in front of our eyes" and that "all of us remember texts, if we remember them at all, as glittering fragments disconnected from the linear form in which we read them" ("On Laughing" 235).

Similarly, while Adam is left with a sense of discontinuous reality, the reader is left, in addition, with Marius's frequent evocation of mystery and use of epiphany. It is the reader who must interpret epiphanies, Ashton Nichols explains, and yet the interpretative process "is endless . . . because [epiphanies] do not completely contain or restrict meaning within themselves" (*Poetics of Epiphany* 29-33). Thus, transcending Adam's final vision, the reader perceives a mystery, which derives empirically from a web of experience preserved through fragments of memory and which contains sustaining power.

In Tennessee, Adam "was left groping in confusions of color and sounds and smells, all spinning in and out of each other, all revolving around a great pole star—the West" (28). Late in his life he stands at the end of his journey, gazing out beyond the edge of the continent, groping in similar confusion. As Harry Creekmore had said years earlier, "It's as far West as we can go" (101).

NOTES

1. Protagonists Samuel Beckwith in *The Coming of Rain* and Paul Alexander in *After the War* also search for connections with their fathers as they struggle to apprehend reality. References to veils, shadows, fragments, mists, and mosaics recur in all three novels along with contrasting references to patterns, designs, and destiny.

2. Marius discusses the religious influences of his youth in his essays "The Home That Lies Always in Memory," "The Middle of the Journey," and "Musings on the Mysteries of the American South." Marius suggests that the character of Eugenia Curry in *After the War* is based upon his mother ("Interview with Richard Marius" 117).

3. Marius's essays "Ruleville: Reminiscence, Reflection," "The War between the Baptists," and "Musings on the Mysteries of the American South" provide a detailed analysis of Southern fundamentalism. The defects of fundamentalism are further portrayed in the fanatics of the novels, the worst of whom are Protestant clergymen. In *The Coming of Rain* the Reverend R. Vernon Sizemore preaches "in tones dripping with unction," and the Reverend Thomas Bazely commits arson, rape, and murder. In *After the War*, one minister who officiates at Pinkerton's funeral is "a pompous, gluttonous-looking man," and the other, a long-winded fanatic. In the same novel a third minister is distinguished by his "greased hair," Mr. Pendleton is guilty of child molestation, and Mr. McEnroe is "a florid, oily fat man."

4. In an earlier draft, Adam does eventually return to the East. Marius deleted this material in the revision.

5. Jason's Transcendentalism clearly comprises one version of what W.T. Stace identifies as "philosophical expressions of romanticism, which was itself no more than an unsuccessful counterattack of the religious against the scientific view of things" (55). In an interview with Missy Daniel, Marius comments that he himself never embraced a romantic view of nature, and he recalls the harshness of nature and farm life in "The Home That Lies Always in Memory."

6. Marius originally intended to use "Once in Arcadia" as the title of *Bound for the Promised Land*. He also considered the phrase for the title of his third novel and

envisioned a dust jacket using a Poussin painting which illustrates its deadly connotations.

7. An anti-intellectual current runs throughout Marius's novels. His strongest characters—Brian Ledbetter, for example, who figures prominently as the moral center of *The Coming of Rain* and *After the War*—are intuitive rather than analytical; and his well-educated characters are often, though not always, destructive or ineffectual.

Robert Drake

MICHAEL O'BRIEN

The Railroad as Metaphor

JAMES A. PERKINS

Robert Drake was born in 1930 in Ripley, Tennessee, the county seat of Lauderdale County and about fifty miles north of Memphis. In his first teaching position at the University of Michigan, he showed Austin Warren a short story he had been working on. Warren encouraged the young Drake by saying, "I want you to bring me a new story to read every Monday" (Drake, "Appendix," 183). Drake continued to write and in 1965 produced *Amazing Grace*, his first collection of short stories. In a letter, Robert Penn Warren said that although Drake did not write at the "height of fashion," he had produced in *Amazing Grace* "[a] very veracious account of a world" (Warren quoted in *My Sweetheart's House* 184).

Over the years, Drake continued to write short stories (although not quite one every week) and produce collections of stories not quite at the height of fashion. The first major critical acclaim for his work came in a special session of the South Atlantic Modern Language Association on November 15, 1991, followed by a special issue of *Mississippi Quarterly* in the spring of 1992. In response to this late acclaim to his work, Drake has continued to do what he has always done, write stories about Woodville.

A railroad track runs through the center of Woodville, the fictional town

Robert Drake has chronicled in five collections of short stories. The railroad which Drake identified as the L&N in *Amazing Grace* is based on the Illinois Central, which cut through Drake's hometown of Ripley, Tennessee. As Drake recalled in "The New Bridge: *Cui Bono?*":

> Everything around us there, you know, revolved around a north-south axis. Situated on the main line of the Illinois Central Railroad—back in the days of passenger travel—and U.S. Highway 51—the principal Great Lakes to Gulf artery, we could go to Chicago or New Orleans without batting an eye. But God help you if you wanted to go to Arkansas and Missouri to say nothing of points farther west. Indeed, it has always been well nigh impossible to get to Nashville or Knoxville by public means at least. But then, as I have been saying for some time, West Tennessee is, in many ways, an extension of northern Mississippi. [2]

In his subsequent books, Drake identified the railroad by its proper name, the Illinois Central. But the name of the railroad is not important. The City of New Orleans still runs between Chicago and New Orleans but you have to call Amtrak to get a ticket. What is important is the idea of the railroad, the metaphor of the railroad, the possibilities that the "railroad" offers Woodville.

The railroad which runs through Woodville is unusual in Drake's work because it is one of the few physical objects he ever describes. Were physical description necessary for a sense of place, Woodville would be the Tennessee equivalent of Oakland, California, in Gertrude Stein's famous statement, "There is no there there." Who we are and where we are from are inexorably intertwined. Place gives rise to character. The obverse is also true. Character gives rise to place. To a great extent, *where* is the result of *who*, and the uniqueness of any place is the collective result of the uniqueness of its populace. In Drake's work, that uniqueness is captured, for the most part, through the recollection of stories and events, through tales told and told again, through an oral tradition that lived on front porches before air conditioning and television. As Patsy G. Hammontree pointed out in the title of her 1988 article, "Comic Monologue: Robert Drake's Community of Voices," in Robert Drake's stories, the ear dominates the eye.

In an interview published in the *Mississippi Quarterly*, Drake told Jeffrey Folks: "I don't *see* my stories, I *hear* my stories, more than anything. Somebody told me he couldn't imagine how my characters look, and I said, 'If you'll just listen to them, you'll know'" (226). Folks followed up with the question, "Do you see Woodville visually at all?" and Drake responded, "Well, yes. But not enough to make you see it. I think of it in my mind's eye, but I don't ever describe it" (226).

Even when there is a reasonable expectation that Drake would unleash a visual description, as in 1990, when he provided the text for a book of photographs, *Tennessee: A Photographic Celebration*, Drake uses his ear: "I myself am a West Tennessean, and I come from that part of the state which might seem least typical to some people. . . . And its speech is more like that of the Deep South—soft, liquid, often with a fine disregard for consonants. And when I open my mouth, strangers often mistake me for a Mississippian, a Georgian or an Alabamian" (4).

There are two major exceptions to this pattern of aural dominance in Robert Drake's fiction, two things that are visually described. The first is the Drake Brothers' store, found in "The Store," which was a late addition to *Amazing Grace* and which Drake says is "of course not fiction but absolutely fact: a memoir of Drake Brothers, the hardware and grocery store owned and operated by my father and my uncle, a very real institution in Ripley, Tennessee, and, along with this town and the Methodist Church, the beginning of everything there is to know about me and my world" (*Amazing Grace: Twenty-fifth Anniversary Edition* xiii). "The Store," an avowed piece of nonfiction, actually serves best as an introduction to *The Home Place: A Memory and a Celebration,* in the prologue of which Drake says, "This is the book I was perhaps born to write though I probably could not have written it until now" (vii). The second exception is the railroad, which is visually a strong enough element in Drake's work to have been used in the cover design for *Survivors and Others.*

The description of the railroad is not as compact or composed as the description of the store. The store is part and parcel of home. It is presented at the beginning of *Amazing Grace* as the place out of which the rest of Woodville grows. The railroad stretches out through story after story. It rumbles and shakes in our consciousness; it goes "tick tick" as the summer's heat expands the rails. It is seen through the passage of time. In the story "Under the Bluff" the narrator recalls: "But some of the older folks remembered when there was a regular passenger service, and you could get a boat at Boyd's landing and go down to Memphis or up to St. Louis or most anywhere in the world, especially when the roads were so mixed up in the winter that you couldn't get out of town to catch a train" (36). In "On the Side Porch" the narrator gives us a glimpse of the heyday of train travel while telling us about Evelyn Henning of Barfield.

> I had heard of her all my life, nearly, but usually as a rather exotic bird of passage: people down at Barfield (I lived six miles away in Woodville, the county seat) often didn't know what to make of her. Because without batting an eye, she came back there from what they could only assume was a glamorous life in Chicago and seemed perfectly content to exist in a town so small that people were still going down to the drugstore to have a Coca-Cola every morning at ten o'clock—and meet all their friends there—and, later on, watch the two I.C.

streamliners meet (on the double track) in mid-afternoon because Barfield was just about halfway between Chicago and New Orleans. [99]

America's railroads, of course, declined and in "Queen Anne Front, Mary Anne Behind," Tom and Louise King, heading off to college, have to flag down the nine o'clock express train (*My Sweetheart's House* 139). By the time we hear from Miss Sara in "The Fifth Wheel," the railroad has fallen on hard times: "I reckon the Greyhound bus still knows we're on the map, but I don't think there's a single good train that stops here any more" (120).

Some of the place names around Woodville, Fisher's Crossing and Haley's Switch, are names connected with the railroad, and the railroad provides the locale for all sorts of drama in Woodville, from the romance of the newlyweds, Sally Currie and Marcus Winslow in "A Cool Day in August" taking "the night train for Chicago" (*Survivors* 35), to the horror of suicides who jumped from the overhead bridge (*Amazing Grace* 142), to the scandal of the woman "who said she was a nurse" and who filed a breach of promise suit against a local doctor because in returning from a medical convention in Chicago she "left the day coach where she had been riding and moved into the Pullman with him *because she thought she deserved it*" (*Survivors* 159), to the humor of Mr. Howard, the drunkard, as reported in "Mrs. Picture Show Green":

> Why one time, Mrs. Green said she herself got up to take the early morning train for Memphis. When it came in, who should get off but Mr. Howard, who told her he had been coming out from Memphis on the late train the night before but had slept through Woodville, and the next thing he knew, he was up in Fulton, Kentucky, and had to wait there for the early morning local to come back down! [*Survivors* 52]

The railroad then, like the overhead bridge it made necessary, "was a sort of central fact about Woodville" (*Amazing Grace* 142).

The railroad did not mark a sociological division in Woodville. There were well-to-do folks as well as riffraff on both sides of the cut (telephone interview).

> Cousin Rosa and Cousin Emma Moss were Mamma's two old-maid cousins who lived up on the corner by the railroad bridge. When we sat on their porch in the summertime, you could hardly talk, the trains made so much noise chugging through the cut. Mamma didn't like having to talk between trains; but they were used to it and would always laugh and say, "There are always more trains when Lucille comes." [*Amazing Grace* 48]

Although Cousin Rosa loved the railroad and wanted "a ticket as long as your arm," Cousin Emma "hated living up on the corner by the railroad bridge" (*Survivors* 57).

In addition to his mother's cousins, "Uncle Urshel and Aunt Suzanne lived right on the railroad cut" (*Amazing Grace* 26). In the summer when Booker T. came back to Woodville to visit his parents, the narrator would play with Booker T.'s daughter, Alice Ann: "Alice Ann and I would sit out on the back porch eating ripe tomatoes that Aunt Suzanne kept in the icebox until they were real cold and watch the trains go by" (*Amazing Grace* 26).

Robert Drake watched trains as a child. He even secretly hoped to become an engineer (telephone interview). "Ever since I was a small boy growing up in West Tennessee on the 'Main Line of Mid-America,' as the Illinois Central Railroad likes to call itself, trains and all that pertains to them have been one of the great facts of my life" ("Trains in My Life" 23). He watched trains, and he put them in the daydreams of his narrator: "I was forever the young boy watching the Illinois Central mainline trains pounding grandly through our town (few of them actually stopped there) and resolving that someday it would be me on board, a spectator no longer but a real-live actor and, of course, the star of the show" (*Survivors* 60).

The narrator's parents were divided on the value of travel. His mother said, "I've got more to worry about right here in Woodville than I can attend to . . . and I haven't got time to go running around the world to see what other folks are up to" (*Survivors* 60). His father, on the other hand, had traveled on business to St. Louis, New York, and "once even to New Haven Connecticut—for a Winchester Repeating Arms convention of some sort" (*Survivors* 60) and was glad that he had done it and would not ever need to do it again.

The character Robert in "By Thy Good Pleasure" finds himself thinking about trains at the burial of his father in the Oakwood Cemetery in Woodville:

> Oakwood was down by the canning factory, and the railroad ran right along one side of it. And as we got out of the car, a long freight train zoomed by behind a triple diesel unit. And then all of a sudden right there while Brother Parks was pronouncing the benediction, I began to think about how I had always liked trains, ever since I was little, and how Daddy used to take me down to the station every Sunday between Sunday School and church so I could see the eleven o'clock passenger train from Memphis come by. Now there weren't any big old black steam engines chugging through anymore; there were just diesels, throbbing powerfully in a cool, restrained sort of way. It was strange that that was what I should be thinking about right there when we were burying Daddy. [*Amazing Grace* 152-53]

In "The Trains in My Life" Robert Drake asked rhetorically, "But why this fascination with trains, with noise, even dirt?" and then answered as follows:

I think now it all ultimately had something to do with the track, the rails—those gleaming streaks, so disproportionately small compared to the weight they bore, yet so ultimately and fundamentally important in directing, guiding, and controlling all that sound, all that energy. The rails too were the great connectors, which joined my small hometown to Memphis and Chicago and New Orleans and finally all the big wide world, Great Lakes to Gulf, sea to shining sea. [23]

Later in the same essay, Drake says:

We've got to "connect," as E.M. Forster commanded; and surely that is one of the things travel is all about—discovering the likeness in the dissimilar, the resemblances among the disparate. But sometimes I think it's only when we appreciate these differences, whether between peoples or countries, whatever, that we can really comprehend their essential and very real similarities. And that's why travel is broadening. [24]

A closer look at three of Drake's characters and at their responses to travel may bring this discussion of the railroad as metaphor into sharper focus. The three characters are Marcus Bascomb from "Mr. Marcus and the Overhead Bridge," Cousin Rosa Moss from "A Ticket as Long as Your Arm," and the narrator in "The Tower and the Pear Tree."

Certainly Mr. Marcus Bascomb is an accomplished traveler. After graduation from Harvard and additional study at Oxford, Mr. Marcus fought with the British in France in World War I. After the war, he remained in Paris "where he knew a lot of writers and artists" (*Amazing Grace* 144). Mr. Marcus liked to travel: "And now you heard he was in Spain or Italy or somewhere else over there" (*Amazing Grace* 144).

To the young narrator, "Mr. Marcus was the most 'romantic' figure that ever was—certainly around Woodville: a sort of cross between Rupert Brooke and Robinson's Richard Cory, who 'glittered when he walked'" (*Amazing Grace* 144). Since there is no suspense or foreshadowing in this story (it opens with a statement about the suicide of Marcus Bascomb) the choice of allusions here must serve other purposes. Rupert Brooke has become the standard coin for the loss of the young and talented. He and his fellow World War I poets have replaced Keats in the modern imagination as symbols of unrealized potential. Richard Cory on the other hand suggests always the public's bafflement at the suicide of a man who has everything.

Of course, not everyone believes that Marcus Bascomb had everything. Cousin Rosa Moss, who taught him "in the first grade and in the Baptist Sunday School" and who thought "the Bascombs were always a curious lot," believes that he had never been really happy: "I think that, for some reason, Marcus has always been afraid to let himself get mixed up in anything enough to love some particular person or some particular place, and you certainly do have to let yourself get mixed up in things when you do that. And that's why I think he keeps wandering around from one place to another so much" (*Amazing Grace* 145). Although he came back to Woodville once in a while, Mr. Marcus never stayed long. Cousin Rosa Moss, however, knew that he would be back: "But finally, he's bound to run out of places to go, and then I think he'll come back here to Woodville for good. Anybody that was born and raised in Woodville is mixed up in it forever whether he likes it or not. One thing's certain: Woodville will be right here waiting for him when he does get ready to come back" (*Amazing Grace* 145-46). Cousin Rosa Moss was right. Mr. Marcus came back, but he didn't have a home place, a sense of belonging. It is difficult to read Cousin Rosa Moss's prediction without hearing Robert Frost's lines from "The Death of the Hired Man": "Home is the place where, when you have to go there, they have to take you in" (Frost, *Complete Poems*, 53). When Mr. Marcus ran out of places to go, Woodville and the overhead bridge were right there waiting for him.

Mr. Marcus isn't the only person from Woodville to use the railroad to commit suicide. Mr. Campbell, in "All Dressed Up and Nothing on His Mind," is another: "But then one day in late fall, the year after he lost both his wife and his store, he drove out to Chipman's Crossing (on the way to see a client, they said) and got stalled on the track just before the fast train from Memphis was due; and it plowed right over him and the car and everything else. And some people said it was suicide, and some people said it wasn't, and nobody ever knew for sure" (*My Sweetheart's House* 157).

In "A Ticket as Long as Your Arm" Cousin Rosa Moss, who "taught the first grade for nearly fifty years—three generations in some families—and few people there could imagine learning to read or write from anybody else" (*Survivors* 61), loved to travel: "Cousin Rosa was big and bold, liked to venture out, go places, the farther away the better, and then come home and tell it all" (*Survivors* 64). She felt that travel cuts you down to size and makes you see that there are other people and places on this earth.

Cousin Emma, who, according to Cousin Rosa, "just wanted to be right in the middle of everything in town" (*Survivors* 57) thought "travel was fine, in small doses; but she didn't believe in building your whole life around it, and the best part of a trip was always getting back home" (*Survivors* 64-65).

While the Moss girls disagree about travel—with Rosa, who "thought riding a Pullman was the next thing to heaven," wishing for "a ticket as long as your arm" and Emma, who preferred to travel by bus, stating that "anybody that had been born and raised in Woodville, Tennessee, knew enough about human devilment to last him the rest of his life" (*Survivors* 65)—they never really leave Woodville: they might venture off somewhere to see something, but their roots remain in Woodville. Woodville is home. They are mixed up enough in it to love it as a particular place.

The narrator in "The Tower and the Pear Tree," the last story in *The Single Heart*, has settled in Chicago "in the Middle West—perhaps the most alien of all regions to the Southerner." Each spring he boards the Illinois Central in Chicago to go home to Tennessee. And that train takes him home immediately. "This is the railroad, above all others which has a distinctively Southern air with its brown and yellow and orange streamliners streaking back and forth between the Great Lakes and the Gulf over what it calls the 'Main Line of Mid-America'" (*The Single Heart* 167).

Although the narrator has found Chicago bustling, stimulating, energetic, driven, and healthy, he has also found it cold and uncaring, and he looks forward with increasing delight to his annual encounter with "an ancient pear tree which stands in the backyard of a modest house near the station" in Fulton, Kentucky, the last stop before home.

> Every year, I watched for the pear tree, sorry when spring was late and there were no blooms, rejoicing when I caught it in flower and comparing its performance then with that of previous years. Usually, some more limbs had died; but miraculously, there were always some new shoots sprouting from the old trunk, whose essential vitality never seemed to fail. And I would give thanks—I knew not why then—that it was still there, alternately blackening and silvering as the spring winds tossed it in the sun. [*The Single Heart* 170]

By the time the narrator tells the tale of "The Tower and the Pear Tree" he knows why he gave thanks that the pear tree was still there. "There was nothing of the tower about this tree" (*The Single Heart* 169). This lone tree taking strength from its roots stood against the ravages of age and weather to bring forth each spring what beauty it could manage to welcome the narrator to that particular place he had let himself get mixed up with, The Home Place, Woodville.

In her essay "Place in Fiction," which Robert Drake has assigned to his classes for a quarter of a century, Eudora Welty says: "Every story would be another story and unrecognizable as art if it took up its characters and plot and happened somewhere else" (122). When A.B. Crowder asked Robert Drake, "How do you think you'd be different as a writer if you were from Vermont or Michigan?" Drake responded with the question: "How could I answer a question like that?" ("Robert Drake" 121). Fortunately he doesn't have to. Robert Drake was born in Ripley, Tennessee, on October 20, 1930, and for more than thirty-five years he has been celebrating the particularness of that place through short stories about his fictional Woodville, a small town with a railroad track running right through it.

Kaye Gibbons

© JILL KREMENTZ

Her Full-Time Women

NANCY LEWIS

"I think the Southerner is a talker by nature," said Eudora Welty in an interview twenty years ago, "but not only a talker—we are used to an audience. We are used to a listener and that does something to our narrative style" (*Conversations* 94).

Storytelling is a Southern tradition. In local stores, on porch steps, the storyteller has had an audience of family and neighbors, and through generations of storytelling, much of local custom, character, and mores has been retained. Southern writers are proud of their past and of their literary heritage. In a changed and changing South, writing from an increasingly confused and complex background of shifting social scene, they've held on hard to their roots and maintained their distinctiveness. Despite the merging of the cultures of the North and the South, Walker Percy said in 1972, "perhaps it is still possible to characterize the South as having a tradition which is more oriented toward history, toward the family, toward storytelling and toward tragedy" (Welty, *Conversations* 95).

Contemporary Southern writers of fiction have been criticized for ignoring changes in the evolving South, the urbanization, the homogenization, and

112

the dissolution of family—that element on which so much Southern writing has leaned. They have been admonished for continuing to exploit the rural scene and presenting a disingenuous family image. In 1989, in a piece in *The Nashville Scene* titled "When Is Southern Literature Going to Get Real?" the author finds current writers Jill McCorkle, Bobbie Ann Mason, and others dated and unrealistic. He teases them for holding fast to an outdated perspective. But indeed there's been good reason for the Southern writer to keep a particular nostalgia and pride in the few regional differences that were strong enough to survive the outcome of the Civil War and the nationalism that followed. Though there's no longer the rural isolation of the past, there is a legacy of speech and custom, and the family bloodline still flows. But as Eudora Welty says, "now there are so many layers of life, so many blurrings, so many homogenous things together that you have to send a taproot down perhaps deeper" (*Conversations* 105).

There is a present flowering of Southern writers, perhaps a third generation Southern Literary Renascence that would include Allan Gurganus, Jill McCorkle, Randall Garrett Kenan, Lee Smith, and Gail Godwin. Among this third generation is Kaye Gibbons, a writer who has written five remarkable novels in ten years: *Ellen Foster* was published in 1987, followed by *A Virtuous Woman*, *A Cure for Dreams*, and in 1993, *Charms for the Easy Life*. A fifth novel, *Sights Unseen*, was published in the fall of 1995: the story of a girl growing up with a mother who lives on the edge of madness. As in her other novels, Gibbons develops her characters with affection and humor, and, allowing us to share their intimate emotions, makes us feel an almost proprietary sympathy with them. With a vernacular authenticity that leads us to believe she didn't need to do her homework, she has presented us with stories and characters most definitely real, uncontrived, and of their time. She has given us, in particular, some memorable women.

From the frontier days, Southern women have shouldered rugged responsibilities. Since men are "generally a bad and incompetent unobservant pack," women have tended to turn to each other for help, for good company, and for general local information. In *A Cure for Dreams*, even while favorable signs in prospective suitors are being looked for, "all this information was traded freely between women with daughters, like meringue secrets or geranium cuttings."

Kaye Gibbons creates women with backbone. We see them as an unspoken community, for they recognize the needs and strengths they have in common and perforce. They are experienced in "the areas of loneliness, abandonment, betrayal, and other furious pursuits" (214), as the narrator of *Charms for the Easy Life* observes in her mother and grandmother. We come to know them as individuals, learning self-reliance the hard way, facing misfortune with ingenuity and grit. As Gibbons shows us in *A Cure for Dreams*, they never "glorify in tribulation" (6), but rather seek a way out or a way to cope.

Ellen Foster, in the novel with that title, is the first of Kaye Gibbons's heroines, and she is eleven years old. The straightforward first-person narrative, dramatic for what she's telling us, never garish in the telling, is a story of pain and abuse, a recounting of her meeting with one harrowing situation after another, but it's told by a survivor. From the first pages, opening with the line "When I was little I would think of ways to kill my daddy" (1), we realize that Ellen is a remarkable, spunky little girl. Because her voice rings so true and because she's so clearheaded and honest and so funny to boot, we have absolute faith that she will find a way out of her troubles.

Ellen's brutal, drunken father is accountable for the suicide of her invalid mother. Orphaned soon after by his death from drink, Ellen must find a way of life for herself. Always practical, she realizes that in order to survive she must find herself a family. So she resolutely searches until at last she finds the right one, a kindly foster family from which she takes her last name. From the blessed comfort of her new home, where she tells us "I had me a egg sandwich for breakfast, mayonnaise on both sides. And I may fix me another one for lunch" (2), we are taken through her trials and are increasingly drawn to this plucky heroine.

After her father's death and a brief, happy stay with a sympathetic art teacher, she's placed by the court with her "mama's mama," a demented old woman who blames Ellen for her daughter's death. Having been through the heart-wrenching trauma of seeing her mother die, Ellen is then witness to her grandmother's death. She describes these two events to us in her own vivid but unembellished words. As she lies beside her mother, who has taken a fatal number of pills, she says "My heart can be the one that beats. And hers has stopped" (10). Staying with her declining grandmother, she's determined to keep the vindictive old woman alive. "I tried to make her keep breathing and when she stopped I blew air in her like I should have. She did not live but at least I did not slip into a dream beside her. I just stood by the bed and looked at her dead with her face pleasant now to trick Jesus" (79-80).

For a while she lives with her aunt and cousin, a spoiled and trivial pair who exclude her from their closely woven lives. She sees them clearly for what they are and knowing she's unwanted tells herself she'll treat their home as if it were a hotel. "If a girl was staying at my house that I did not want there, I certainly would be pleased as punch if she announced one night at supper that you will only be seeing me at meal times unless we happen to pass each other on the way to the toilet" (96).

Ellen is sensible and smart. She's smart enough to recognize the absurdity of the school psychologist's questions during their weekly sessions. Exasperated, she says "I do not plan to discuss chickenshit with you" (89). She's smart enough to search out the new mama she needs. "I looked her over plenty good too before I decided she was a keeper" (95).

And, in one of the most poignant parts of the story, her intelligence leads her to become aware of the racial prejudice she'd harbored in her relationship with her black friend, Starletta. In the early days, even though she likes Starletta and is grateful for her family's kindness, she cannot bring herself to eat with them. "No matter how good it looks to you it is still a colored biscuit" (32). By the end of the story, she realizes from her own experiences that racism led her to feel superior. Starletta has come to spend the weekend with Ellen and her new family. Resting together before supper, Ellen muses, "I always thought I was special because I was white. . . . When I thought about you I always felt glad for myself. And now I don't know why. I really don't" (125).

Kaye Gibbons's accomplishment in creating this totally believable and endearing character was an earnest of things to come. She showed us in her first novel that she has the writer's gift Eudora Welty talks of: "A writer's got to be able to live inside all characters: male, female, old, young. To live inside any other person is the jump."

Writing about Katherine Anne Porter's Miranda stories, Gibbons says that Porter's language "pulls the reader vertically towards submerged meanings and horizontally backward through time and memories." In all her novels, Gibbons shows a deft hand in juggling past and present, and in her second novel, *A Virtuous Woman*, we see how artful she is. Here there are two narrators: Ruby, who is dying of lung cancer, and her husband, Jack Stokes. In their plain language, the alternating narrative tells their story, before and after Ruby's death. Through Ruby's voice, as she prepares to die, and Jack's as he mourns her, we get to know them, their views of themselves and of each other. Through each voice recalling the same scenes, their sweet love story unfolds. We're caught up in the most important moments of their lives and the people central to them—a memorable cast of characters including a handful of really nasty ones. The proverb given us in the epigraph proclaims that the price of a virtuous woman is far above rubies. Ruby is indeed priceless. "Strength and dignity are her clothing" (Proverbs 31:10-25).

She is four months dead when the novel opens, and Jack tells us he's already finished the food she prepared and froze for him in her last months, the gesture of a strong as well as a virtuous woman: "I can't do much" (7), she tells us in her fragile state, "but I can do something. There's not a whole lot a woman can do from the grave" (7). Like other women in Kaye Gibbons's novels, she survived hard times by her own strength. "I know now," she tells us, "that this world is built up on strong women, built up and kept up by them, too, them kneeling, stooping, pulling, bending and rising up when they need to go and do what needs to be done" (13).

Jack, a childlike man with a sweet nature who introduces himself always as "Blinking Jack Ernest Stokes—stokes the fire, stokes the stove, stokes the fiery furnace of hell!" (3) is forty, twice Ruby's age, when they marry. Their love, based on a need for one another, deepens during a happy though childless marriage. Ruby knows she's "every bit of his experience" but she herself has already suffered from a disastrous match. We learn that at eighteen, babied by her fairly prosperous family, "lonesome and bored to tears" (25), she elopes with one of her father's migrant workers, a shiftless and surly man who degrades her and finally dies after a knife fight. During that brief marriage, Ruby works as a housemaid for the family who has hired her husband as a farm laborer. Here, where she is both prized and despised as coming from a higher social class than theirs, we meet the other characters central to the story. Tiny Fran, one of Gibbons's few unpleasant women, is the daughter of the household. Fat, pregnant, and unmarried when we meet her, spoiled and "mad at the whole world" (43), she is married off to one of her father's tenant farmers who takes her in exchange for the promise of forty-eight acres of good land. Her illegitimate son is a monstrous creation, a malicious rapist and woman beater who hangs Ruby's mule. The other child, neglected by Tiny Fran, turns to Ruby and Jack for nurturing, and becomes a treasure in their childless marriage.

The narrators are sympathetic people. We are attracted to them and touched by their hardships. They are plain country people; their speech rings of rural North Carolina, their metaphor is of the familiar. They are "versed in country things," as Frost puts it. Jack's mama, he says, "was a tough, hard woman, skin like a cat's tongue" (15). Tiny Fran, "getting into her feedsack of a bathing suit must've been like cramming mud into a glove" (100). Softened by love, Jack says, "I knew the sound of Ruby crying for babies the way I know a robin's call, the same way I know the sparrow's" (103).

Gibbons's characters have their own verbal idiosyncrasies, but much of their talk is regional folk speech familiar to anyone who has lived in the South, especially the rural South. Gibbons accustoms us early on to the cadences, peculiar rhythms, phrases, and provincialisms of her characters. The phrase "used to" replaces "once" or "at one time"; Jack says "used to he used to go sit at the store" (81) and "used to I wouldn't turn my hand over for green peas" (3). "Might could" or "might would" is often used instead of "might be able"; "I might could try for this girl" (20); "she might would could've joined the 4H" (62). We hear Jack say, "I was so tired I thought I might liable not to be able to . . ." (79) and "It wasn't anybody else there I gave a happy hurrah about" (80).

Her characters' speech is in no way contrived. It is natural and right. "When it comes to hearing and replicating the way people speak, Kaye Gibbons has perfect pitch," writes Anne Tyler on the cover of *A Cure for Dreams*, and other reviewers have noted her infallible ear. It is the voices of her characters that make them come alive.

A Cure for Dreams weaves a complex pattern of relationships, but the firm structure and the intimacy of scene and characters keep it within our grasp. We're quickly pulled into the lives of four generations of women, closely bonded by blood and by the very fact of their being women. Here, stronger than ever, is a feeling of party spirit and freemasonry.

Women's voices reverberate in all of Kaye Gibbons's novels and on the opening page of *A Cure for Dreams*, Marjorie, the first narrator, introduces us to her mother, Betty Davies Randolph, who has recently "died in a chair talking, chattering like a string-pull doll" (1). Marjorie says, "I had spent my life listening to her, sometimes all day, which often was my pleasure during snow and long rains—Talking was my mother's life" (1).

We hear Betty's voice comfortably narrating the family history to Marjorie, beginning with her grandmother, Bridget O'Cadhain, who, with her family, had come from Galway to Kentucky, to start farm life. Bridget's daughter, Lottie, tired of her meager surroundings, "perched on ready, hoping for a marriage proposal" (10), at sixteen marries a Welsh Quaker, Charles Davies, and they move to North Carolina. Charles is an ambitious man whose life becomes more and more obsessively centered on work in his farm and gristmill. He had expected his bride to share in the labor, but Lottie was not given to that traditional female involvement; she had married him for "love and rest" (13) and longed for babies. By the time Betty is born, Lottie has grown indifferent to Charles, and with no more babies coming, mother and daughter become increasingly close companions, sharing a life that hardly includes the driven husband.

Life at home being less than satisfactory, Lottie's energies, which are real and formidable, go into finding her own community, with little Betty always at her side, "her goal being to organize a gang of women for a habitual social hour" (30). These are lively meetings, full of gossip, politics, and gambling (this she tries to hide from Charles, who "hated gambling or anything at all involving the luck of the draw" [32]), and here we meet the women of Milk Farm Road. Betty tells us that her mother "remade herself into the Queen Bee, more or less organizing life through knowing everything" (100). She knows every household inside out and she dispenses help and advice to the point of officiousness, the justification for meddling being "anytime somebody's not looking after themselves it becomes your business" (97). But she is sagacious, sound, and of good heart, and her intimate and thorough familiarity with these neighbor women enables her to help them in extraordinary circumstances. She "knew the varying pitches of wives' wails" (43), and in one instance by hearing the cry of a woman whose husband has been murdered and by closely observing the domestic scene, she finds clues—a pie with one piece cut, a row of uncharacteristically messy stitches in a quilt the woman is making, the absence of burrs or dandelion seedwings from her cotton stockings—which lead her to deduce that the deed was done by the woman herself. Since the deputy sheriff investigating the crime has missed all these details and since the husband "was such a sonofabitch" (46), it's clear to Lottie that his wife had ample and justifiable reason to rid herself of a thoroughly bad lot.

Lottie is capable of keeping her own business to herself, of protecting herself from the nosiness of others. Her husband, Charles, undone in the Depression years by his failing farm and unsatisfied obsession with success, walks into the river and drowns himself. When a curious neighbor asks her how he was found, she replies, "Charles was discovered upside down, straight upside down on his head with the river rocks on either side, like bookends" (83). To satisfy the inquisitive questions of her Kentucky relatives, she creates a moving story of her husband losing his life while pulling a tramp from the path of a speeding train.

Strong as is her attachment to her mother, young Betty hankers to leave the confining boundaries of Milk Farm Road and see more of the world. She's encouraged by Trudy Woodlief, an exotic newcomer from Baton Rouge, introduced to us "with one leg high up on a bureau, smoking a cigarette and shaving her legs with lotion and a straight razor" (56). Trudy counsels Betty to leave her mother and Milk Farm Road, if that's what she wants, or to stop whining. Betty does have a try at the outside world. She gets as far as Richmond, Virginia, where an unhappy love affair sends her back home. Here on Milk Farm Road she marries and stays and talks. The last line of the novel is her daughter Marjorie's infant dream-memory of the moments after her birth. "But I wasn't sleeping, not for the sound of the women talking" (171).

Gibbons is increasingly adroit at handling time and place. In the stretch of years covered in *A Cure for Dreams*, there is no leap or disconnection; the conversational narrative transports us effortlessly from present to past and back again; the anecdotal style elucidates the past and introduces secondary characters.

Backgrounds become progressively more distinct in the novels, but though stage and scene are given in more detail, they are given only as needed for the development of the protagonists. Physical descriptions are spare—an occasional glance of green eyes, fresh lavender plaited into a braid of hair, a new dress with a row of lace at the throat—but each character is as vivid as if marked by a cicatrix.

In *Ellen Foster*, where the narrative is intensely inward, the time and place of the story are relatively unimportant. Landmarks have been sketched in to help us follow Ellen's journey from her unhappy parents' house to the clean brick house which is her home with her new mama and family and the setting for her new life. On the way to church, we pass houses and barns; then after going through "colored town," we see white houses and yards, but our concentration is on what happens to the small central figure.

In the works that follow we're made more aware of background (fields, farms, rural landscape, the houses on Milk Farm Road), and of the times when events take place. In *A Cure for Dreams*, "homes were in the grip of Mr. Hoover and his Depression" (30). *Charms for the Easy Life* brings us into the Second World War, when our heroines volunteer in a veterans' hospital, and we're given background details such as jitterbugging being outlawed on the Duke campus ("not so much for moral reasons as because of the numbers of students landing in the infirmary with dislocated shoulders" [199]).

These particulars are not gratuitous or unimportant. We need them for the development of the stories and characters. Perhaps it is the Southern storyteller's inherited practice of honing and editing to please the listener's ear that has given Kaye Gibbons her skill in economy and structure. Even in *Ellen Foster*, she avoids the mistake made so often by writers of putting into their first novels everything they've ever seen, heard, or observed. Gibbons is never wasteful or extravagant. Her characters are always in prime focus: above all, the women and the voices of those women.

Admittedly there are some sympathetic men in these novels, and when a good man does show up he's recognized as such and appreciated with good grace. Jack Stokes in *A Virtuous Woman* has great appeal; Charlie Nutter, a figure in *Charms for the Easy Life*, is a winner; and we have every reason to believe that Margaret, the narrator of the latter story, has chosen well in Tom Hawkings. (He is approved by Margaret's grandmother, Charlie Kate, one of Kaye Gibbons's most astute protagonists.) But on the whole, men are an inferior breed. Ellen Foster's daddy was "a mistake for a person" (49). Men are represented as an unpromising lot, just by their nature, as we see in the deputy sheriff in *A Cure for Dreams*, whose ineptitude "had more to do with the fact that he was a full-time male than it did with the fact that he was merely part-time deputy and neither bright nor curious" (46).

Intelligence and curiosity are, on the other hand, qualities we find in all Gibbons's central women figures, who are certainly reflections of herself, for as Eudora Welty remarks in *One Writer's Beginnings*: "of course any writer is in part all of his characters. How otherwise would they be known to him, occur to him, become what they are?" (101).

These women, like their creator, are smart, alert, and literate, and their literary interests and intellectual curiosity are made to seem as credible as their speech. Ellen Foster tells us: "I told the library teacher I wanted to read everything of some count so she made me a list. That was two years ago and I'm up to the Brontë sisters now" (9). She is excited by the bookmobile, and she spends secret hours with the little plastic microscope she bought and presented to herself for Christmas. Enthralled with what she sees on the slides, she feels she "could stay excited looking at live specimens day in and day out" (104). In *A Cure for Dreams,* the narrator, Betty, "had hit the first grade running and moved right on through like I was born to go to school" (51). Margaret, in *Charms for the Easy Life,* spends much of her time in the two years after high school reading Sophocles, Euripides, Homer, and Aeschylus. It is her grand-mother Charlie Kate's wonderful intelligence, as well as her healing powers and charismatic nature, that draws Margaret to her. "I became fascinated with her mind, enamored of her muscular soul" (46).

Charms for the Easy Life presents us with three generations of smart, strong-willed women: Margaret, the narrator; her mother, Sophia; and Sophia's mother, Charlie Kate, a character I'd match against any of the heroines I've admired in recent years. They are a vivid threesome, linked by blood and by their passionate natures. In the case of Charlie Kate and Sophia, the bond is made stronger when the men they have unwisely chosen, one way or another, leave them.

Charlie Kate, at twenty an accomplished and popular midwife, marries a man nowhere near her in spirit or intelligence and in 1910, moves with him and their daughter, Sophia, to Raleigh, North Carolina, where she becomes a curer of ills and a campaigner for good health and hygiene. When her hus-band leaves her, she has already established a successful practice "with sick people coming forth like the loaves and the fishes" (22). Sophia is her con-stant companion until she too marries a man far beneath her, handsome but a cad. Their child, Margaret, realizes, when her father dies, that it is not much of a loss. "I didn't think I'd have less of a life with him gone. I know my mother and I would have more" (49). Charlie Kate, who had so disapproved her daughter's bad choice in marrying that she refused to set foot in their house until begged to, on his death moves in with daughter and granddaughter, and their life together is the heart of the story. They are possessed of indomitable spirit and very much aware of their strength as women. As Margaret tells us, "If my grandmother could've populated the world, all the people would've been women" (93).

Charlie Kate's reputation as a self-made doctor continues to grow. Her genius is recognized by licensed medical doctors as well as by her patients, and she's proud of the fact that her fame has reached as far as the Outer Banks, where a leper hears of her healing accomplishments and walks a hundred miles to seek her help.

On her visits to the sick, Sophia and Margaret are her assistants, helping with every kind of grizzly operation; while at home, their daily life is occupied with voracious reading. "When a good book was in the house, the place fairly vibrated" (116). They approach reading with the vigor and passion with which they tackle everything. Margaret tells us that Charlie Kate "would sit for hours and contemplate the disappearance of the opening narrator in *Madame Bovary* with the same intensity with which she would line up a patient's symptoms and then labor over a diagnosis" (117). We don't wonder that Margaret can't bear the thought of leaving home to attend one of the fine colleges her school principal has proposed for her.

Charlie Kate is part of a tradition in the South of women healers whose cures and prescriptions are passed down from one generation to the next. In reading about North Carolina folkways and folk medicine, I've discovered that in some cases a certain amount of wizardry would seem to make the prescription questionable. A great deal of common sense, however, is usually behind these cures, plus intelligence and practicality. In a widely used volume called *Domestic Medicine, or Poor Man's Friend*, published in 1830 in Knoxville, Tennessee, the author, John C. Gunn, thanked God for having "stored our mountains, fields, and meadows with simples [medicinal plants] for healing our diseases" (15). Practical sense and economic necessity suggested the use of things at hand in the kitchen or garden, so remedies included local wild and cultivated plants, herbs, barks, and animals. One learns that sassafras bark or root thins the blood and prevents chills and fevers. Sage or horehound tea is good for general sickness, including colds, and bloodroot soaked in whiskey is used for liver trouble.

In her early days of healing, Charlie Kate refers to Gunn's medical manual and continues to increase her knowledge by keeping up to date with legitimate medical practitioners. "She refused to cross over the line from natural medicine into black magic, although, in many cases, if she had not combined useless folk remedies with treatments she judged to be therapeutic, her uneducated and overly superstitious patients would not have trusted her" (47). But although she's disdainful of voodoo and quackery and shows rationality and wisdom in her dealings with her patients, her prize possession is the charm given to her years ago by a lynching victim whom she had cut down and revived from near death. It is "the hind foot of a white graveyard rabbit caught at midnight, under the full moon, by a cross-eyed Negro woman who had been married seven times" (19). This is the talisman Charlie Kate has saved so many years and presents to her granddaughter, Margaret, to give to the man she loves (hence the book's title, *Charms for the Easy Life*).

The force behind all good writers remains the urgency to communicate. Doris Betts has said, "I write because I have stories I don't want to die with." Certainly one feels, reading Kaye Gibbons, that her stories had to be told, her characters born. One recognizes her unfailing ear, her dazzling control of the passage of time. However, in the increasing rewards of rereading, a conscious probing fails to reveal the sleight of hand that produced these works: the translation of her talents from the inside of her head to the printed page remains a mystery. Even gazing hard at a painting by Vermeer, it's difficult to believe that these seemingly life-size portraits are contained within a canvas scarcely twelve inches square. With similar wizardry, Gibbons, in a condensed number of pages, sweeps us into the lives of her ordinary people, and they become living and three dimensional as she creates for us not only their present world but the past that has made them what they are.

Eudora Welty, in *One Writer's Beginnings*, says,

> It is our inward journey that leads us through time—forward or back, seldom in a straight line, most often spiraling. Each of us is moving, changing, with respect to others. As we discover, we remember: remembering, we discover: and most intensely do we experience this when our separate journeys converge. Our living experience at those meeting points is one of the charged dramatic fields of fiction. [102]

It is the expression of Kaye Gibbons's inward journey that helps to explain the distinctive accomplishments of her fiction.

PART II
Old Friends

Barry
Hannah

Geronimo Rex in Retrospect

David Madden

"The best first novel I've ever reviewed." Several years ago, I ended a newspaper review of Barry Hannah's *Geronimo Rex* with that statement, and with the prediction that the next novel would be "a lasting contribution to literature." It remains the best first novel I have reviewed. First novels interest me as a literary phenomenon. I can look back on Susan Sontag's *The Benefactor*, Yves Berger's *The Garden*, Joyce Carol Oates's *With Shuddering Fall*, Steven Millhauser's *Edwin Mullhouse, The Life and Death of an American Writer, 1943-1954 by Jeffery Cartwright*, and the fictional memoir *Stop-time* by Frank Conroy. Here is a second, longer look at the first novel by the author of *Nightwatchmen* (1973), which comes close to fulfilling the prediction, *Airships* (1978), short stories, and *Ray* (1980), a short novel.

An early version of a chapter from *Geronimo Rex* appeared in the first issue of *Intro*, an annual publication that continues to present the best work from the nation's university writing programs. Comparison shows how much Hannah taught himself in the four years between the two versions. The early sophomoric cuteness of "The Crowd Punk-Season Drew" has been transmuted into a mature wittiness. Hannah made an intelligent decision when he shifted from the third to the first person, in which his inventive style works much more brilliantly. And he was wise to drop his hero's conscious image of him-

125

self as a cowardly punk; in the early version, a girl who is sexually excited by Harry's ugliness sees him as a Geronimo; in the novel, it is Harry who discovers and is activated by that image of himself.

So, even though Barry, like Harry, plays the trumpet and went to school in Mississippi and Arkansas, the novel, which begins in 1950 when author and character were eight years old, is not slavishly autobiographical. Hannah puts Harry through a complex network of moods; he is sullen, deceitful, envious, hypocritical, grudging, self-pitying, shy with girls, spiteful, pompous, self-righteous. One may wonder whether Hannah wants the reader to see his hero in *all* these ways.

When Harry kills a peacock, shoots birds maliciously, throws a huge firecracker into a black saloon, beats up a small trumpet player, ridicules girls who ignore him, shoots at a noisy organist, and bullies a graduate student in the library, Hannah seems to assume the reader will regard his hero's conduct as charming. Harry is so self-centered, we do not learn he has brothers and sisters until more than halfway through the novel. His self-disgust causes him to despise others, his self-contempt to express contempt for others.

Harry judges anything that moves. Having accepted a job injecting granulated nerve gas into dogs, he pitches a live cigarette into the lap of a man who enjoys such work. "I hated every minute of every effort of every bit of what I was doing" (289). It is difficult to sympathize with a man who would take such a job in the first place, or one where thousands of turkeys are killed each day, creating a canal of gut-muck, thigh-high. Harry judges his friend Silas for throwing an apple into a group of racists, an act typical of himself; then, when Silas asks Harry to write a poem for him, he tricks Silas by giving him a classic poem. A man who works off his own sense of worthlessness by doing a Geronimo war dance on top of parked Cadillacs seems miscast in the role of judge. (There is a very different version of that episode in *Intro*.)

Harry's juvenile boasting and preening become tiresome after one realizes that he is really conforming all the while; there is nothing drabber than the sight of a fundamental conformist indulging in feeble, often sneaky, acts which he celebrates as acts of rebellion or free-spiritedness. The author's own attitude is unclear. Harry comes through as a spoiled brat who has an eight-hundred-dollar checking account while he is in high school, who uses emotional blackmail to get a pistol, a fine trumpet, and a Thunderbird from his affluent parents, who, before he becomes Geronimo, thinks of himself as "Malibu" Harry. But before the car came the acne: "it was as if somebody had caught me in the hall and blasted off a shotgun loaded with BB's at my face, two or three BB's making it into my brain and festering there for years to make me crazy" (34). Perhaps so. Obsessed with guns and their cowardly power, he nurses criminal urgings and yearns to do physical violence. Unfair small-town rumors depict him as a sexual pervert. He imagines that his college teachers regard him as a fool, and his genius roommate calls him a rube and a "hero of the criminally stupid" (167). A repulsively fascinating character.

In college, Harry becomes what passes for a beatnik, an intellectual, a poet. Then he discovers Geronimo, who makes him "*drunk* with freedom to do *anything*" (161). In situations that offer possibilities of violence, he hears an eruption of Geronimo's "barking, yelping laughter" (331). He dreams about "old Geronimo, peering out miserably from a cage in the zoo of American History" (221). He wears a Geronimo kerchief around his neck, boots, and a Bogart raincoat in which he packs a gun, a "little pod of iron lying against my thigh" (168). Later, he grows a beard, wears cosmetic spectacles, and buys a reptile leather coat. "The pistol is just *there*," he tells his worried roommate. "I don't have to use it. It makes me feel like something may be coming any minute. I walk around, you understand, watching out turn after turn, like I was in a wild country. It sets a light on the things or people I see. I see what I see in the light of what it might be if I pulled out the gun, and what things would do, how things would change" (180).

All these means and expressions of power—the ready pistol, the intimidating costume, the dirty fighting, the identification with Geronimo, the trumpet blasting—are adolescent techniques for mental survival. All along, Harry is trying to find a more creative mode; we see him struggle from the "wretchedness" of his language to power as a poet, and his narrating voice predicts the happy ending. "I had the music, but not the words yet" (144). Our compassion for him is fitful, coming in such moments as when he fails his friends as a trumpet player in a black nightclub in Mississippi. "I always trusted my dreams before anything else" (117). We keep hoping his dreams will be less grotesque, less often at the expense of other people for, enthralled by the narrating voice, we become accomplices. The reader is moved when Harry tries to resurrect in his imagination three dead soldiers of World War I whose monument is smothered under vines that harbor snakes, and in those fleeting moments when he expresses affection for his mother and father.

Geronimo Rex rambles through a long autobiographical repertoire of characters and episodes. For Hannah's ability to depict Harry's relationships with an array of girlfriends, "marvelous" becomes a literary term. Ann Mick is a tough girl who works in Harry's father's mattress factory. "I was a fool over some rare idea like taking her out to my house and giving her a shower and letting her sit on the edge of my bed in a towel and holding her face in my hands" (50). But when he discovers his father is also enthralled, Harry says: "she put you in heat. You thought of a pig-run alley full of hoofmarks running between you and her" (60). Tonnie Ray and her group "were the giggling poultry of the recess yard, huddling here and there with their little egg-secrets" (48), frantic for "popularity." To Harry and his friends, she was Tonnie "the roach. The spittoon made out of the shell of a creepy insect" (100). Harry takes her to the senior prom, but puts her down in memory in every line. Lala Sink is the lovely, shy daughter of the town's richest man. "I imagined that her hard little brassiere was stuffed with hundred-dollar bills" (103). At a summer brass instrument clinic at NYU, Harry meets Sylvia, a technical virgin. Patsy Boone plays the flute in the Jackson symphony orchestra.

"Romeo of the Roaches" (200), Harry is "the type that can pick out obscure graces in a crippled hag." In college, he dates Bonnie, "who had had polio in one leg . . . but the other one was lovely, tan and firm" (130). A "virgin crippled witch" (133), she enjoyed breaking up couples who were about to get married. Sometimes Harry worries about his own behavior. "Who was I to give them my backside when they didn't suit my needs?" (127). He falls in love with a woman named Catherine who figures in some erotic love letters his roommate steals from Colonel Peter Lepoyster, a demented, aristocratic racist. The most important girl in his life is Peter's white-trash niece from Mobile whom he renames Catherine. Harry ridicules her for her terrible voice, her slump, her lack of intelligence, but he tries forcibly to sustain a "love for her delicate vulnerability" (308). In the two years they go together, they experience only one moment of genuine sentiment. She dies violently. Harry marries Prissy Lombardo, a miniature version of a woman in a Revlon photograph who had ravished him for a while. Prissy resembles a "pubescent Arab" (345) child "who did not call the police but followed me with wild concern everywhere I went" (348). At a party, among his teachers, he is afraid she will begin to talk. One's sympathy for Harry is fitful.

In one of the most fascinating chapters, we meet and listen to Bobby Dove Fleece, Harry's college roommate, a frail young man whose body seems to be "worked from above by some cynical puppeteer" (137), and who calls himself a genius and imagines his mother will ship him to Whitfield, asylum for the insane, if he makes one false move. He had made a big one the day he won a prize at the Science Fair, "and in a little excess of pride, I appeared in the garage in nothing but my jock shorts" (147), and some women reported him. A sickly fellow, "mucus would harden like antlers in his head and chest and he couldn't get out of bed. . . . Then he'd cough like somebody raking out an iron tomb" (148). He talks compulsively, in baroque syntax, of sex, inspired partly by a bunch of old love letters he stole from Colonel Lepoyster's mansion. The spirit of the letters takes hold of Harry, too. Meanwhile, Fleece meets Bet Henderson, a big girl who sings hymns spontaneously and to whom he makes love for a period of six years. When Lepoyster shoots at Harry, who is trying to sneak a look at Catherine, Fleece abandons Harry; to make up for this cowardly act, he later shoots Lepoyster in the knee when they sneak up to his house to harass him.

From the middle of the novel to the end, Peter Lepoyster is in and out of the narrative. One of his mottoes is "Treat every nigger as if he were a Jew and every Jew as if he were a nigger" (152). He appears wherever there is a demonstration for civil rights or a simple parade in which a black band is marching. When his Catherine ceased responding to his passion, he went sexually berserk and was sent to Whitfield, and was later released. Shot by Fleece, he regards himself as a "casualty of my convictions" (270). Peter is Hannah's most magnificent creation, more a product of his imagination, one hopes, than any of his other characters. Harry is afraid of Peter (perhaps sensing he is a more genuine exemplar of the Geronimo spirit than himself), but constructs a romantic image of him.

Another character who moves in and out of Harry's life—but from the beginning of the novel and over a longer period—is Harley Butte, a mulatto who works in the mattress factory for Harry's father. A student of Mr. Jones, who created the fantastic Dream of Pines Colored High School Band, Harley marches in the footsteps of his mentor, worshipping also the great Sousa. He denigrates the blues and jazz of the blacks that Harry takes up and is most happy wearing a pith helmet of canvas like the one Sousa wore in Haiti, leading his own band of black kids. "They were such snobs . . . riding too casually along, too confidently with that corps of drummers bombing down on what sounded like a hide stretched over the Grand Canyon" (187). The sight twice throws Lepoyster into a physical rage. Ten years older than Harry, Harley always seems to be reproaching Harry for wasting his life. The novel opens with a distinctively fine description of Jones's band and ends with an image of Harley's band playing his own music.

Even Hannah's minor characters are memorable after a decade. Harry's descriptions of his father, Ode Elann Monroe, who looks like Jack Paar, exude contempt and ridicule. "The old man faked three paragraphs of thought" (22). "The old man gets friendlier than a faggot Japanese when he approaches me on bad trouble" (57). The old man churns "himself into a dull butter of meditation about my life. Not one understanding sentence having passed between us" (59). Harry, of course, is the one who understands. "Very little has passed between us except money" (171) (from the old man to Harry, one notes). Ode is a pathetic snob, cowed by New York lifestyles, awed by Dream of Pines, Louisiana, money. Occasionally, Harry observes that his mother "still looked something like Elizabeth Taylor" (169).

Fleece's stepfather is General Creech of the National Guard, who every night pursues his own "original art form, that of violently ripping to shreds the newspaper of the day after reading every particle of it" (146). His mother, a religious woman, was "molded by panic ever since she was nineteen" (145).

Silas, who plays jazz cello, is another of Harry's friends at college. His father is "a millionaire in chemical fertilizers and also a big Baptist" (222). An enormous man, "what he liked best, I gathered, was for little girls to break into tears when he undressed" (238). One morning he wakes Fleece up to tell him he is in love with Bet, Fleece's girl. Fleece shoots him in the rear, but Silas and Bet elope. Mother Rooney is their ancient landlady who is finally killed in the crossfire of the boys' violent compulsions. Silas's idea of a joke is to vomit on Mother Rooney's bathroom floor and draw a face in it; his idea of restitution is to give her a pair of high-lace leather sneakers, taken off a dead lady wrestler.

Readers who crave relentless put-downs relish *Geronimo Rex* twice as much as I do. Not since Donleavy's *The Ginger Man*, Pinchon's *V*, Fariña's *Been Down So Long It Looks Like Up to Me*, not since Kurt Vonnegut stopped writing for *The Saturday Evening Post* and started dispensing black comedy judgments have so many put-downs been strung together in a single book. Often mean-spirited and small-minded, Harry is, finally, a more likable young man than any of the heroes of those pioneer efforts in the lowly art of the put-down. There is not enough compassion in this novel to nourish a bedbug overnight. When Tonnie Ray asks, "Harry, do you think God is really keeping up with me? Most of the time I feel like I'm just not . . . watched" (112), Harry peels off "a shattering belch," as though he were not a pathetic exhibitionist himself. The reader who does not need to nourish his own ego with such put-downs, may, by the end of the book, realize that Peter Lepoyster is a pathetic, not bathetic, creature upon whom Harry squanders not one pulse of compassion. Still, a celebration of life breaks through — in Harry's language. Reading this novel was a first in my experience: I simultaneously loved the effect of and despised the sensibility behind each line.

In Hannah's collection of bizarre episodes, there are stretches of fitful continuity, then new starts. The first third is set in Dream of Pines, Louisiana, whose blacks made Harry think of "dark fish breathing something different from what I did, some thick gas in brown water with the gases of the paper mills boiling on top of it" (88). Then he attends Herdermansever College near Jackson, Mississippi: "everything you need for a cemetery" (127). Hannah justifies taking us through the old this-is-what-it's-like-to-live-in-a-dorm routine again. But life in a tower in Mother Rooney's rambling old house on a kudzu-vine-matted cliff above the fairgrounds is even more interesting. Toward the end, we move on to Fayetteville, Arkansas, "a sort of flatland bum's dream of San Francisco" (334), and the university.

Among the episodes, readers are not likely to forget the slow death of an old dog and a mule who show up one morning on the edge of the subdivision; the pukey aftermath of the senior prom; Harry's sojourn in New York City before going to college; Harry's and Fleece's wild excursions to Vicksburg where Harry's ancestors lived, and where Fleece finds a cavalry pistol on the battlefield; attempts to steal Catherine's love letters to Peter; the jam session in a black nightclub at Vicksburg like "an old butane gas tank" (225); the explosion of violence at Peter's mansion and again later at his bungalow in town; the three encounters between Harley and Peter, twice during public parades and once at the fairgrounds where Harley is temporarily playing trumpet for the Harlem in Havana show.

Harry (and the author, one suspects) seems to revel in violence, right on through the contrived, but brilliantly rendered, implicitly melodramatic end. Hannah suggests a mandate to violence in his description of what boredom and inner void do to adolescents the summer after high school graduation in towns like Dream of Pines: "I have red welts all over me from standing nude with my air rifle and firing it against the wall almost pointblank, willfully suffering the ricochets when they come back" (118).

Interesting as he is, Harry Monroe does not develop enough as a character to hold all these episodes together. The reader's concentration is upon each episode or each line in isolation. After the three superb pages of the opening chapter, "Blue Spades," as prelude, the novel might more effectively have started with Book Two, in which Harry enters college.

Hannah's talent for narrative and structure cannot compete with the brilliance of his style, and thus the intensity of the reader's response is weakened. The novel lacks the force that focus would lend it. As lines already quoted suggest, the style *is* brilliant. Almost everything that language can do in prose without going berserk in an hysterically experimental way is done well in this novel. Language, more than bizarre characters and episodes, sustains interest. But Hannah's use of language is better *within* each line than *from* line to line. He fails to sustain continuity, except in attitude and tone.

More important, one misses the play of a conceptual imagination over the wobbly mass of raw material. Hannah's intelligence and style radiantly transform fragments of raw material, but not the whole narrative. The absence of a conceptualizing imagination is also felt in that short early version, which consists mainly of an episode not used in *Geronimo Rex*. The novel is comic, but it lacks a coherent comic vision. The statement "In my crowd, whatever gagged a maggot passed for humor" (60) sets the novel's own limits. No intellectual framework galvanizes the moments of wit that flicker and fade. In the works that have appeared over the past ten years, one can see Hannah develop an ability to control through conception, giving his energy a far more lasting effect.

EDITOR'S NOTE: A BARRY HANNAH UPDATE

At the time Madden's review, "Barry Hannah's *Geronimo Rex* in Retrospect," first appeared in the *Southern Review* (April 1983), Hannah had already published (in addition to *Geronimo Rex* [1972], which won the PEN/Faulkner Award for Fiction), *Nightwatchmen* (1973), *Airships* (1978), a collection of short stories, and *Ray* (1980), a novel. Since the early 1980s Hannah has continued to publish fictions that are dazzling and thought provoking. Whether he has yet produced the work of fiction that Madden predicted would be "a lasting contribution to literature" is still open to question. Madden was convinced that *Nightwatchmen* "comes close to fulfilling the prediction."

To date, Hannah has produced four additional novels: *The Tennis Handsome* (1983), *Hey Jack!* (1987), *Boomerang* (1989), and *Never Die* (1991) and three more collections of short stories: *Captain Maximus: Short Stories & Screen Treatment* (1985), *Bats Out of Hell* (1993), and *High Lonesome: Stories* (1996).

In most of his works, Hannah deals with violence, often the violence of war, in a darkly humorous manner that will remind readers of the later Twain. *Ray*, for example, recounts the tale of an alcoholic Alabama doctor who was a pilot in the war in Vietnam and who hallucinates about having been in the American Civil War. Or perhaps he is an immortal alcoholic Alabama doctor who served both in the Civil War and Vietnam. One of the beauties of Hannah's plots is that you are never quite sure what is happening, and even when you are quite sure, you don't think you are. As absurd and grotesque as Hannah's novels and stories are, the evening news seems to be catching up and keeping pace. Plots are not what's happening in the work of Barry Hannah, neither are characters. His characters, a string of gruff, mildly misogynist cases of arrested development, are memorable in the same way the people who show up on daytime talk shows are memorable; they are grotesques. And they are memorable, even when they are flat, twisted, incomplete, wounded, and whining. They are the way people we grew up with are, people we knew back in high school, people who stare back at us from the mirror. They are not at all unreal.

In our lives we get to know few people (or in many cases none) as well as we know well-developed fictional characters. Perhaps one reason we read fiction is to learn more about ourselves and others through their fully developed characters. However, these characters are the least realistic part of any novel. In our lives, we don't have (or take) the time to know people in depth. We deal with surfaces, with stereotypes, with masks, and with reflections of our own expectations.

For most of us, our only reason for believing in the complexity of characters is the complexity of our own tangled web of feelings and experiences, which we generally share with almost no one. If, in the future, we develop the skills or take the time to get to know people, if we open up and let them know who we really are, if we overthrow the shallow "have-a-nice-day" speakers in our lives, we may earn the right to question the shallowness of Hannah's fictional characters. Until then we should enjoy the accuracy of his depiction of our absurd situation.

If he promises us only a painful glimpse of ourselves in a shattered mirror, why do we continue to await Hannah's books? What is their hold on a culture that is, for the most part, daft for plot and character? Words. Words and sentences. Piles and piles of glorious words and sentences that no one else who is writing in English could possibly think up.

Barry Hannah is a lineal decendant of all those Southern storytellers for whom the telling was always more important than the tale. Whether it is in his deft short stories, several of which he has later reworked into longer fictions (*Geronimo* came out of an early story published in *Intro* and *The Tennis Handsome* comes out of two stories in *Airships*) or in his novels, Hannah is in love with raucous, wild, full-blooded language for its own sake. What interests him is the individual sentence, and the individual sentence is closer to the line in poetry than it is to the paragraph in the short story or the chapter in the novel. Hannah is a poet stuck in an age when poets either write song lyrics or advertising copy or support their habit by teaching somewhere. Fortunately for us, Hannah has chosen to write his poems as great chunks of fiction. These great chunks of fiction, as one of his post-adolescent masculine heroes might say, are built like brick shithouses, and every brick is marvelous. Comparing Hannah to his idol Jimi Hendrix, Will Blythe, in a 1993 *Esquire* review of *Bats Out of Hell*, wrote: "What Hendrix did with the guitar, Hannah does with prose: invent a whole new American music, viciously electric, of squawks and cries, of soul rhythms and extraterrestrial riffs. When Hannah plays his typewriter up against the speakers, as it were, the result is strangely angelic feedback about the national psyche, about how tumultuous inner lives finally spill out onto the pavement in gaudy pools of blood" (55).

[James A. Perkins]

Anne Tyler

Wrestling with the "lowlier angel"

JAMES GROVE

> Place is one of the lesser angels that watch over the racing hand of
> fiction, perhaps the one that gazes benignly enough from off to one
> side, while others, like character, plot, symbolic meaning, and so on,
> are doing a good deal of wing-beating about her chair, and feeling,
> who in my eyes carries the crown, soars highest of them all and rightly
> relegates place into the shade. Nevertheless, it is this lowlier angel that
> concerns us here.
>
> —Eudora Welty, "Place in Fiction"

Place is one of the lesser angels watching over the racing hand of Anne Tyler's
fiction. Like Welty, whom she admires, Tyler believes that character is the
highest angel of literature because of its great capacity to embody human feeling. At the same time, Tyler also supports Welty's contention that a sense of
place is essential for fiction since it helps make character sing by confining
and defining it—by creating a believable outer surface that holds and objecti-
fies what the writer strains to express (Welty, "Place in Fiction," 120, 122).
Thus, Tyler praises Welty because "in telling a story, she concerns herself less
with what happens than with whom it happens *to*, and where" ("Fine, Full
World" D1). This sense of "where it happens" makes Welty distinctly South-

ern for Tyler, who casts an eye toward her own art in this homage to her distinguished predecessor.

Tyler, like Welty, connects place to many of the recurrent concerns within her fiction: the potential for familial relations to nurture and stunt; the pressure that *time* puts on human beings; the problems and satisfactions of marriage; the mixed blessings of America's pastoralism; the precarious nature of everyday life; the difficulty of creating a coherent identity in modern America; and the deep split in the American psyche between staying put or moving on. Furthermore, for Tyler, as with Welty, place is the repository of the characters' "visible past" while being the stage for the ephemeral present (Welty, "Place in Fiction," 128-29). Since Tyler's art has a similar emphasis, it is not surprising that she has been praised for her sense of place—and sometimes defined by it. For example, Sandra Gilbert identifies one of the major attributes of Tyler's Southernness as her heavy reliance upon the same setting in novel after novel. And John Updike has written that "she is at peace in the semi-countrified, semi-plasticized, Northern-Southern America where she and her characters live. Out of this peace flow her unmistakable strengths" ("Loosened Roots" 88).

While Tyler's use of place gives her fiction a solid base of reference and a Southern flavor, it also has a persistent tenuousness which counterpoints, or at least qualifies, the "peace" Updike projects upon her. Undoubtedly, this uncertainty is rooted in Tyler's own life. Born in Minneapolis in 1941, she lived in the Midwest until she was six years old. Then her Quaker family moved to a quite insulated religious community in western North Carolina. In 1952, Tyler's family resettled in Raleigh, where she spent her teenage years as "a Northerner growing up in the South, longingly gazing over the fence at the rich, tangled lives of the Southern neighbors" ("Fine, Full World" D1). She felt both inside and outside the South—a duality reinforced and enriched in her adulthood.

In 1967, Tyler's sense of place acquired another significant dimension when she and her husband decided to settle in Baltimore, where they still live. Since *The Clock Winder* (1972), Tyler has repeatedly and extensively used this city in her fiction, for she likes its urban complexity with its "many different things to poke around in. And whatever it is that remains Southern in me has made it easy for me to switch to Baltimore" (quoted in Cook, "New Faces," 40-41). With its many pressures and opportunities, Tyler has found Baltimore to have "a lot of gritty character . . . that's good for a novel to have" (quoted in Willrich, "Watching through Windows," 506). Moreover, its identity, just like hers, straddles the North and the South—something she stresses in *Dinner at the Homesick Restaurant* (1982) when Pearl and Cody Tull, whose shared placelessness mightily contributes to their mutual enmity, cannot agree if Baltimore is a Northern or Southern city.

Tyler's identification with the South and its rich literary tradition, along with her feelings of being outside this region, have resulted in place becoming a complex and protean catalyst for her art. It is a restless presence: expanding and contracting, yearned for and rejected. It shapes her characters while being physically and symbolically shaped by them. And nowhere is her quicksilver treatment of Welty's "lowlier angel" more apparent or interesting than in the enigmatic, critically controversial, and too often neglected *Morgan's Passing* (1980), an ambitious novel about the problem haunting most place-absorbed literature: how do human beings endure and understand a world so unsatisfying in so many ways?

The first paragraph of *Morgan's Passing*, a reminiscence about an annual Easter Fair in Baltimore, idyllically revolves around images of childhood happiness, wonder, and security. Tents and rides sit on a "long, gentle hill" (3). The air smells of buttered popcorn, a kind "rabbit" hands out jelly beans, and there is an egg hunt. In *The Accidental Tourist* (1985), Charles Leary sarcastically says that Baltimore's weather is always "either too hot or too cold" (249); and it is certainly too chilly for the miserable, huddled adults in *Morgan's Passing*, who watch their egg-hunting children and who "seemed to have strayed in from the wrong season. It would have been a better fair with no human beings at all" (4). Here, the city's extreme, unpredictable climate is not only the cause but also a reflection of the grown-ups' feelings of exposure, distance, and disillusion. In the third paragraph, there initially appears a fusion of these disparate worlds as the shivering children and adults watch a puppet show where a displaced Cinderella praises the prince's palace. The audience knows her placelessness will soon end, knows that the prince is about to give Cinderella his love and protection. They count on this happy ending. But then this artificial, fairy-tale world unexpectedly breaks down—its illusion overwhelmed by the reality of displacement again—as Cinderella's voice suddenly disintegrates. The voice now "belongs" to a frightened woman about to give birth, who does not know what to do or where to go.

A six-foot rabbit. Some very uncomfortable adults. An uncompleted performance of Cinderella. A frightened young woman. With its startling juxtapositions, with its questioning what is a safe place, with its ambivalent portrait of the Baltimore landscape, and with its emphasis upon the act of pretending, this skewed opening is a brilliant preparation for Tyler's handling of her dislocated protagonist, Morgan Gower—one of the most place-confused characters in modern American literature.[1]

For some critics, however, Morgan is the most irritating and baffling protagonist in Tyler's canon. They see his characterization as a jumble of interesting, far-fetched, or ridiculous pieces. For instance, Eva Hoffman writes that

"Morgan's peculiarity seems without purpose, it drives the reader to ask the most naive questions: What's wrong with him? What does he want? Why doesn't he do something? . . . the novel remains suspended in a chilly, murky, ozone-thin limbo" (97). Others agree. They argue that Tyler fails to give Morgan's personality credibility or ironic depth. For A.G. Mojtabai, much of the complexity of Morgan's situation is lost because there is no "external vantage point from which the reader [can] reflect upon it" (99). In short, these critics see *Morgan's Passing* as one of Tyler's less successful works.[2]

This judgment is a mistake. For one thing, *Morgan's Passing* does hold answers to Hoffman's "simple" questions—albeit, very tentative ones consistent with Tyler's belief that human nature is enigmatic and that any search for truth must embrace the grayness of life. Second, this novel is not as random as it sometimes feels; it is not like Pearl Tull's diaries, where events "[flit] past with no apparent direction" (*Homesick Restaurant* 274). Of course, the practices of everyday life swirl around Morgan without any apparent cohesion or overriding meaning, and a recurrent feeling of absurdity is one cause for his placelessness. Yet Tyler also gradually gives narrative shape to this confusion, revealing it in slowly evolving patterns of behavior whose contradictions she does not try to explain away. Finally, Tyler's development of Emily Meredith— short-shrifted in most criticism—serves as a persistent "vantage point," from which the reader achieves the distance, through ironic comparison and evaluation, to appreciate Morgan's ambivalent responses to place.[3]

The causes of Morgan's placelessness form a network of identifiable internal and external forces, which have helped make his everyday environment time-worn, unconnected, and oppressive. As Edward Relph writes in *Place and Placelessness*: "Placelessness describes both an environment without significant places and the underlying attitude which does not acknowledge significance in places. . . . At its most profound it consists of a pervasive and perhaps irreversible alienation from places as the homes of men" (143). Morgan feels so much tension because he cannot reject the significance of place or accept that his alienation may be permanent. At the same time, he cannot, or will not, find an environment that will soothe his angst.

Morgan is deeply ambivalent about his "Fool house! Something had gone wrong with it, somehow." Too large and demanding, too crowded with people and possessions, too layered with memories, too much like the fragile crayoned houses his children once drew, it is a reminder that his life has not become what he wanted. If a person's home is, as place critics often stress, "a representative profile of one's very essence" (Salter and Lloyd 22), the Gowers's house with its marks of transience and imperfection speaks to Morgan's strong sense of middle-age inadequacy and unwillingness to accept the inevitable limits upon his identity.[4] The house's physical cobwebs press upon his sense of mortality. Its symbolic threads of familial responsibility entangle his confused desires for independence, space, attention, and love. His bedroom is an image of emotional and marital burnout: "The sheets were a shattered, craggy landscape; the upper reaches of the room were lit by a grayish haze, like the smoke that rises from bombed buildings" (27). Morgan's unease is further heightened because he envies and distrusts his wife's comfortable sense of place as she accepts the sloppy clutter of their domesticity. Finally, there are Morgan's children, whom he nostalgically remembers as once being less complicated and less critical of him. Now they have become another reminder of the meaninglessness of his home life, which he defines as "the particles of related people's unrelated worlds" (24).

Something has certainly gone wrong with Morgan, a fact that Tyler reinforces by highlighting his uncertain relationship with Baltimore. Although Morgan frequently appears quite at home on the city streets, he still associates Baltimore's deterioration with his abiding sense of being "unassembled." Like Willie Loman, he looks outside his house and wonders how his surroundings could have become so crowded, so noisy, so "deep in the city." Morgan believes that he cannot turn his back on this antagonistic environment; it is always chipping away at his security. To make matters more disconcerting, his place of work, a hardware store, is so far within the inner city that his family never goes there because it is not safely located. While lamenting this separation, Morgan also understands his family's apprehension. He admits always fearing for his children's safety in the city and feels something like their uneasiness when passing the neighborhood of his childhood, now lost to urban blight.

Morgan's placelessness would be less severe if he were not also carrying his father's death with him. Morgan's emptiness after his father's death fits into a major pattern within Tyler's fiction, one which connects family, place, and time to a persistent concern about human responsibility and worth. Because Morgan has never resolved the suicide, he has trouble moving past the stunted sense of place it bequeathed him—symbolized by his father's filebox filled with obsessively alphabetized instruction sheets for various household tasks. Like Pearl Tull, who only feels comfortable and strong when she fights time by fixing things, Morgan has the compulsion to order everything, an urge causing frustration and despair since he sees time's disorder everywhere. Like the space travelers in the science fiction he writes, Morgan is a caged bird of passage facing the prospect of a burned-out world: "They weren't just buzzing earth for the hell of it; they were ascertaining what equipment would be needed to transfer us all to another planet in a stabler, far more orderly solar system" (24). Thus, when feeling "ill-contained," Morgan follows his father's example and writes detailed instructions to save his loved ones from the chaos creeping up on them.

The abiding question, then, is whether Morgan, like his father, will be destroyed by this rage for order. And how will he attempt to satisfy his yearnings for a fixed, safe, and pure refuge? Will he move toward sealed-in places like Pearl Tull's insulated yet always fragile house or like Jeremy Pauling's upstairs art studio in *Celestial Navigation* (1974), a controlled world antithetical to the messy and unpredictable family life downstairs at the boarding house? Will Morgan, like Charlotte Emory in *Earthly Possessions* (1977), finally attempt to escape the whole demanding notion of place through movement for its own sake, through willingly becoming a "foreigner"? Or will he eventually acquire the stamina that Daniel Peck values in *Searching for Caleb* (1975)? The old man, who never loses his North Baltimore identity no matter where he travels, criticizes his wandering grandson for not having staying power: "He couldn't endure, he wouldn't stay around to fight it out or live it down or sit it through, whatever was required. He hadn't the patience. He wanted something new, something different, he couldn't quite name it. He thought things would be better somewhere else" (*Searching for Caleb* 8). But what will happen to Morgan if he discovers this stamina? Will it demand a soul-crunching compromise? Or will it result in a healthy reconciliation where Morgan finds that place can be physically and spiritually nourishing, even with all its imperfections?

Understanding Morgan's eccentric search for a "true country" is more difficult than identifying the causes behind his displacement. But patterns exist within his behavior. The romantic Morgan is an improviser who privately and publicly assumes one identity after another, while attempting to recreate many of the places where he *must* exist. Finding his dreams frequently stunted by everyday pressures, Morgan remains psychologically vulnerable until, like the space travelers in his unfinished novel, he ascertains how to "transfer" to a less oppressive place or role.

For example, while waiting for a bus Morgan wistfully imagines that it is "an entire civilization . . . cruising through space," much like the redemptive machines in his science fiction dreams. But when he gets on, the vehicle's violent lurching, as well as the intimidating isolation of the other passengers, destroys his daydream by scraping at his "unsupported," weak self-concept. A similar deflation occurs when his daughter gets married. Morgan tenderly contemplates living with the young couple as a "bereft old man" who would gain their love by putting their apartment in order. However, this daydream quickly dissipates when he remembers that his children would not want him around, for they know his weaknesses too well. There is also the episode in the hardware store when Morgan pretends that he and a female clerk are married and owners of a Ma-and-Pa store, that they have an idyllic relationship within their sturdy, homey business establishment. This dream—so different from the fragmentation of Morgan's actual family life—ends when he loses track of himself, calls the clerk "Ma," and scares her away. And then there is his pastoral dream, in which he and his wife escape their Baltimore clutter and "get a house in the country, maybe, live off the land."[5] However, the pragmatic Bonny Gower immediately punctures this idea by reminding Morgan that he would soon become bored away from the city. Finally, there is his imaginative reconstruction of the Merediths' domestic world. Projecting his longings for a simplicity upon them, Morgan pictures this family living a pure, uncluttered life of honorable poverty, just surviving, always just ahead of some disaster. Needing this vision of them, Morgan tries to block Emily's recurrent and resentful reminders that they live an ordinary life filled with the normal problems and pleasures, that he has misjudged them.

Yet Morgan's pretending must go on and on. He must resist the truth about the Merediths because it would take him back to mundane domesticity, and he lacks the stamina and desire for such a return. Yet in his confusion, Morgan also contradictorily maintains the illusion that he can somehow combine the idyllic Meredith household with his own, that he can somehow *escape* his home without having to leave it permanently.[6] He must continue pretending because fantasy is his primary stay against exposure and because it maintains his hope for a clean, well-lighted place where he can safely experiment with life. At the same time, the possibility always exists that Morgan's imagination will run out of alternative plots for his life—just as he has come to a standstill in his space novel, where he cannot find a way to start chapter two. This anxiety, which fuels Morgan's restlessness, is why he needs to live and work in Baltimore. While the city sometimes frightens and depresses him, its variety of stimuli, its anonymity, its constant change also give his imagination the "scope" it demands. As Frank Shelton notes, Morgan needs "a large city where the contact between individuals tends to be fleeting and a role can be sustained for the short period of time necessary" ("Houses" 856). Unlike Jeremy Pauling, who hides from the city as he creates a "pretend" world through his art, Morgan plunges into Baltimore's heart so that he can keep recreating himself within a perpetual present. Still, in the end, Morgan's and Jeremy's actions are done for basically the same reason. Both want to escape—to negate—their inability to accept how time inevitably unfixes place.

Morgan thus wanders around Baltimore, imagining permanent havens, passing through various communities, creating ephemeral identities and relationships, while paradoxically shying away from any extended attachment to a fully lived-in environment. He is most at home eating at the No Jive Cafe, soaking up the atmosphere while comfortably separated from its black customers; making his rounds as "the street priest of Baltimore"; playing upon people's sympathy as a lonely immigrant; or dancing down a strange city street, singing like Fats Domino, and bowing melodramatically—to people he really does not want to know for very long.

On the one hand, such behavior attracts Emily to Morgan, for he conveys a romantic readiness that makes the ordinary seem more spacious and interesting. It gives him the appearance of unfocused vitality. On the other hand, it is also disturbing because his behavior often seems so self-involved, so parasitic, so careless, and so temporary. Unlike Macon Leary, who increasingly connects with Muriel Pritchett's neighborhood in *The Accidental Tourist* and thus sheds his insularity, Morgan remains quite apart—comfortable only when he can feed off his surroundings without really entering them. Riding on the bus, "he sank into the lives of the scattered people sitting on their stoops. . . . A soothing kind of emptiness began to spread through him. He felt stripped and free, like the vacant windows" (39).

Morgan seems so unconventional. Yet he depends upon his routines to provide him with enough activity so that he does not have to slow down and think. Therefore, like many of Tyler's characters, he travels "the same streets for years without seeing them," his eccentric routines blinding him "to the significance of life or to the sense of self" (Gilbert 273). To temper this drifting and to gain some self-awareness, he would have to break through his frenetic role-playing and become more like Elizabeth Abbott in *The Clock Winder*, Mary Pauling in *Celestial Navigation*, Muriel Pritchett in *The Accidental Tourist*, Maggie Moran in *Breathing Lessons*, and Ian Bedloe in *Saint Maybe*. These characters do not float above the troubling yet rich surface of everyday life. Instead they courageously, foolishly, unsuccessfully, reluctantly, and humorously wade into the sometimes fast-flowing, sometimes stagnant, and always restrictive waters of place. They face its daily commitments and responsibilities. At first glance, they seem much more mundane than the mercurial Morgan. But a longer look reveals a stamina that saves themselves and others. Thus Morgan needs to quit running from himself long enough to think about his placelessness and fear of life. Only then can he achieve the balance—the hard-wrought peace—that Justine Peck and Macon Leary tentatively achieve in *Searching for Caleb* and *The Accidental Tourist*.

Tyler has been criticized for giving Morgan very little self-knowledge. As Updike remarks, "Though we are admitted to Morgan's head now and then, we never hear him talking to himself in the level, calculating voice that would make his 'act' plausible, as the strategy of a sane masculine person" ("Imagining" 100). Usually very perceptive about Tyler, Updike does not appreciate the main point behind her treatment of this character. Indeed Morgan *is* a disordered person who refuses to calculate his actions as a "sane masculine person" (whatever that means). Her characterization of him rests on the possibility that he will never come to any self-knowledge and never accept the mixed blessings of place. In fact, Tyler structures *Morgan's Passing* around the sporadic revolutions of Morgan's alienation while not allowing the novel's formal demands to undercut the complexity and persistence of his confusion. In addition, when we are admitted into Morgan's consciousness (which is more frequently than Updike indicates), Tyler reveals the pain and uncertainty behind his comic facade, behind his childlike infatuation with Emily.

Tyler's most revealing window into Morgan's mind occurs during the Gowers's vacation at Bethany Beach, Delaware, a brilliant episode which occurs halfway through the novel. It suggests the depth of Morgan's place-tension since nothing is easy for him during this vacation. Tyler does not make it easy for her audience, either, since so many contradictions flow from Morgan's dissociation.

In his role-playing, eccentricity, unpredictability, and longing for something *new*, Morgan seems set on stretching and celebrating the human search for possibility. Yet at the beach, he is disturbed by "the sound of the ocean [which] reminded him of possibilities unfolding: everything new and untried yet, just around the corner. He opened his eyes and heard the ocean . . . the very same ocean he'd lain beside with Laura Lee, but he himself was middle-aged and irritable and so was Laura Lee, he supposed" (150). One might expect, with his fears of being closed in, that Morgan would be like Jenny Tull, who would never live too far from the ocean because she "liked knowing that she could get out anytime. Wouldn't midwesterners feel claustrophobic?" (*Homesick Restaurant* 83). Just as Jenny is oppressed by the dark, cramped, and grimly spartan atmosphere of her mother's house, Morgan is depressed by the pervasive mutability and incongruent clutter of the beach cottage. But Morgan's response to the water indicates that he is even more placeless than the lonely, timid Jenny. After being traumatized by her family, after some very bad relations with men, after suffering a severe nervous breakdown, Jenny in middle-age finally finds refuge and meaning through the chaotic domesticity of her third marriage. In contrast, the middle-aged Morgan cannot relax because he is much more like Pearl and Cody Tull, who want to escape "the hazy and swarming landscape" (*Homesick Restaurant* 27) of daily life for an endlessly perfect day at the beach, for a perfectly ordered house, for the perfect life of a country gentleman — in short, for a perfect life "on such a beautiful green little planet" (*Homesick Restaurant* 284).

To Jenny Tull, then, the ocean speaks of the future, of the potential for escape and fulfillment. To Morgan, it speaks of the past: all the mistakes, the restrictive "walls," the vanished possibilities, and the lost relationships. It is a danger. And he does not like swimming in it either, for the water's relentless power demands concentration and staying power, thus throwing him back upon himself. Ironically, he wants to escape the water for the same reasons he wants to escape his run-down cottage and the over-stuffed house in Baltimore. He restlessly wants to free-float in the present, remaining placeless, consuming time without having to think about time.

However, almost everything about the vacation conspires against Morgan's desire not to think, not to remember, not to swim in time. Thus he complains, "We're city people. We have our city patterns, things to keep us busy. . . . It's dangerous, lolling around like this" (154). Forced inward, Morgan admits that he must do something with his life; admits that he's "traveling blind" (154); wonders if he is self-destructive like his father; blames his familial breakups for causing him to feel like a "foreigner" everywhere; senses that fear has undermined his attempts to start a viable "new life" (158); understands that his manic letter writing is a symptom of this fear; and even recognizes, fleetingly, that he needs to be alone to "finally have the chance to sort himself out" (173). Finally, when his brother-in-law, Robert, attempts suicide in the ocean, Morgan's anger stems from his repressed identification with this placeless man who cannot accept time. Moreover, Morgan believes that this messy act—as part of this messy vacation—reflects the persistent messiness of his family.

This vacation, which ends with Morgan's flight back to "less dangerous" Baltimore, helps readers evaluate his actions for the rest of the novel. We now have a better sense of how conscious he is and know that he is very conflicted about radically changing his life. Like Ian Bedloe, he fantasizes about doing something "violent and decisive, like leaping into space" (*Saint Maybe* 129). On the other hand, we also understand why floating remains attractive to him. Like Jeremy Pauling, he is afraid of making a sudden leap into uncertainty, of being marooned. Part of him wants to remain a "foreigner" in a circumscribed, fairy-tale world with a net allowing him to remain uninvolved, protected, and various in his identities. Yet, as Muriel Pritchett says, people "can take protection too far"; so she invites Macon to leap with her "on thin air" (*Accidental Tourist* 97, 165). Morgan would understand her advice, take her hand, and then suddenly and temporarily become "someone else" who does not want to leap. He is trapped within himself, and the novel's drama revolves around whether he will be able to resolve this potentially paralyzing inner tension.

As Morgan's infatuation for Emily Meredith becomes deeper and more loving, she increasingly serves as a touchstone for holding on to his development, because her responses to him and to her own placelessness help us clarify and remain more objective about Morgan's choices. As a teenager, Emily flees college and the South by eloping with Leon. She is afraid of drying up, like her female relatives, in the "heavily draped parlors" of her hometown, Taney,

Virginia. Like Pearl Tull, who marries Beck to escape a spinster's life in North Carolina, Emily depends upon finding refuge in a husband. This belief that marriage can automatically stabilize one's sense of place commonly occurs in Tyler's fiction; and often it leads to disillusionment because the "saving" lovers are flawed human beings, not fairy-tale princes or princesses. Either these "saviors" run away from their legitimate responsibilities or they rebel against their spouse's excessive demands. Either way, the.dependent persons discover that any answers to the problem of place fundamentally rest within themselves and not within others.

Emily's placelessness is pervasive. Orphaned at a young age, she is haunted by absence—by the smells of people long after they have left rooms or by the desolation of her suddenly quiet apartment after her child goes to sleep. Occasionally, she places the puppet, Rip Van Winkle, into strange roles where he doesn't belong, projecting her loneliness through the private "edge" this displacement gives the performance. Not a swimmer or a wader of life at the beginning of the novel, she is frightened by the "liquid darkness" of Baltimore's alleyways. She is also alienated from the iciness filling the home of Leon's parents.

Furthermore, there are her long walks and runs—ambivalent activities much like Morgan's travels through the city—which waver between confronting place and escaping it. Sometimes, Emily seems in motion just for the sake of movement—a temporary annihilation of her marital and place problems. She paradoxically can escape her everyday placelessness by becoming lost within the temporary abstraction of a run where she skims by one neighborhood after another. Tyler's vague, generic description of her movement mirrors how Emily's self-absorption often strips the surroundings of immediate meaning for her. Yet she seems to be training "for some emergency—a forced flight, a national disaster" so that she can find a more emotionally satisfying environment. Also at night, when she closes her eyes in bed, Emily specifically remembers the places she passed so absently earlier in the day, slowly, painstakingly, and vicariously connecting with them as if she *belonged*. Emily, then, is partially drawn to Morgan because they are surprisingly similar in some ways. Both are escaping hemmed-in places while searching for lost security, are ignoring everyday reality while losing themselves in the present, and are hoping for new possibilities while fearing that any change will break their present routines.

But as *Morgan's Passing* progresses, differences increasingly emerge in how Emily and Morgan react toward place, for she, despite her fears, wants to connect. This desire is even more apparent when she arrives at Bethany Beach since Emily intimately and appreciatively explores the small town and its beaches. For a change, she feels comfortable, and her happiness unsettles

Morgan, who expected her not to wade into this setting which he detests. He has wanted her to remain his "fairy dancer," true to the needs of his imagination. Later, when Morgan sees Emily's photos of the vacation, he grimaces. They hold a suspended, unreal, golden world far different from his bad vacation, where the patched road, the smelly fish, the flat sunset threatened him.[7] Yet these photos do catch the tone of Emily's "wonderful time," and this fact is also threatening because her vacation might foreshadow other dips into the waters of everyday life.

Through this vacation, Tyler suggests that it might be very dangerous for Emily to fulfill Morgan's image because she would have to remain essentially placeless. Emily has to relax in time and reflect on her past so that she can understand why she feels so "foreign." She begins to do this at the beach, and her inner journey intensifies when she travels back to her childhood home in Virginia. There Emily confronts who she once was, what she might have been, and who she has become.

At first, on the drive to Taney, it seems as if she might again be skimming away from her problems on "thinner and lighter" air, moving for moving's sake. But Tyler soon indicates that Emily is not only escaping from the city, but also noticing everything around her—in contrast to the blur of her drive to the beach with Leon: "She smiled at every driver she passed. She was fascinated by the private, cluttered worlds she glimpsed." Although still insulated in the car, Emily specifically notices the towns and farmland as she glides past them; and this landscape, familiar yet foreign, causes her to remember the world of her childhood. She doesn't feel trapped.

Caught between Taney and Baltimore, between the past and the present, between her loyalty and resentment toward Leon, Emily reaches the small Southern town and finds everything (her aged aunts, the old trees, the crowded old houses, the quiet of the Friends' meeting house) telling her something: that she made the right move fleeing this stunted place and not becoming like her aunts; that the cost of abandoning her roots was too high since it has led to a life of transience and loss; that she would always hold this world in her memory, whether she wanted to or not; that she had always wanted to join the "big group" and this has led her to "the great rush" of the anonymous, noisy, crowded city. Tyler ends this episode with Emily, overwhelmed by the closeness of this stuffy world, fleeing back to Baltimore, which she had fled a few days earlier because it was so constrictive. At this point, Emily has reached a point similar to the one Morgan reaches at the beach. She has looked inside herself, faced some things, and recoiled from what the experience might say about her present and future life.

Eventually, Morgan and Emily "leap" into marriage—a decision that ironically promises newness within the same settings that have worn them both out in the past. Will place overwhelm them again or will their relationship recreate place so that it isn't stunting and dangerous? The answer is much clearer with Emily. She thrives. Living with this eccentric man, Emily is always surprised by new stimuli. So many people and things from his former household move in with her. Her apartment's once spare rooms now overflow. She has the new baby. Everything stimulates the part of her that liked running because movement freed her from being tied to one place and gave her the sense of visiting foreign places. Now she does not have to leave her house: "You could draw vitality from mere objects. . . . They were too foreign to be hers. Foreign: that was the word. All she touched, dusted, and edged around was part of a foreign country, mysterious and exotic" (270). Such a reconciliation of the foreign and domestic is the goal behind the journeying of so many Tyler characters. The tight apartment and, later, the more crowded trailer, satisfy her in the same way that Ezra Tull's eccentric restaurant meets his emotional needs.

For Morgan, the consequences of leaping are more mixed and fluid. Bonny Gower's perceptive, albeit bitter, insights about her former husband point to why he remains so conflicted. He still has a fragmented self-concept: "All alone in the bathroom, he's no one. That's why his family doesn't count. They tend not to see him; you know how families are. So he has to go out and find himself in someone else's line of vision" (269). He also still carries the inclination to be "*every*thing." And because of these traits, he still "likes to think he's going through life as a stranger." Although he wants to find a place to rest, Morgan must struggle for, and against, the reconciliation that Emily achieves, primarily because place-tension has become so crucial to his tenuous identity.

Morgan in many ways is a loose composite of Jeremy Pauling and Duncan Peck, whose common attributes are their willful foreignness, eccentric creativity, distrust of the mundane, and connection to daily life through their wives. Being so insecure, Morgan must, like Jeremy and Duncan, tie love and place together by feeding off a woman's confirmation of his worth, by seeing her as the antidote to his placelessness, by projecting his erratic ideals of place upon her, and by worrying that the relationship he so deeply needs will inevitably imprison him again. This is a volatile combination. No wonder Bonny is disgusted with him; no wonder Emily must find various stays against his chaotic needs; no wonder we have difficulty managing his character.

After the breakup with Bonny, Tyler stresses Morgan's dependence: "He pictured having to sleep on the couch in his office forever—a man unkempt, uncared-for. Like someone who had fallen between two stepping stones in a river, he'd let Bonny go without yet being certain of Emily. He could not imagine life as a bachelor" (248). Always afraid of swimming, especially alone, this self-pitying placelessness is in tension with the expansiveness that catches Emily. It also makes us pay attention to Bonny's criticism of him and become more wary of his sustained efforts to idealize Emily as a kind of place-goddess. Soon after their affair begins, Emily visits his house, which is stifling Morgan. It is a murky "sea of bodies," with too many adults talking about too many topics, with too many fussing children, with too many Jiffy bags scattered over the floor (222-23). Emily, however, is the house's "single point of stillness." She is the "most proper person he had ever met," with her Southern small-town orderliness (224-28). Later, when he watches her run, Emily is outside of time and place for him. She has an "eternal" quality which Morgan appreciates and appropriates. He "felt himself grown weightless with happiness, and he expanded in the sunlight and beamed at everything with equal love" (230-31). Again, as he has done on the bus, Morgan empties himself and escapes his placelessness, not by accepting his environment, but by momentarily abstracting and transcending it.

Tyler's warnings about Morgan's tendency to idealize Emily raise some questions about the future of their relationship. As their marriage becomes more familiar and crowded with responsibility, will Morgan have "to go out" again, thus leaving Emily behind? How will he eventually handle not being Emily's romantic stranger? What in this marriage with a woman who increasingly loves the clutter of life will continue to satisfy his spirit?

Tyler does not conclusively resolve these issues. As a result, there have been very different readings of Morgan's final state. Shelton and Alice Hall Petry see him as achieving a "necessary balance" (Shelton, "Distance and Sympathy" 180); he is "finally a happy man, responsible to his loved ones while honoring his true self" (Petry, *Understanding*, 166). Hoffman and Mojtabai, in contrast, never see Morgan's fog of disconnection as lifting; he is in "an unfamiliar state of continual crisis, a condition for which there exists no charts or manuals ready at hand" (Mojtabai, "Continual Crisis," 100). He is permanently lost. And Gordon Taylor sees Morgan and Emily remaining "constant in their continual redelineation" of "their separate and mutual fates, free and unfree of themselves as of the world." While keeping their spirits alive, these dynamic redefinitions of self will also do "real damage" to those left behind (70).

Taylor's more provisional interpretation of the ending most effectively captures the complexity of Tyler's intentions, especially in regard to Morgan. Despite the transience of living in a trailer and being a puppeteer, Emily appears happy and settled. Morgan, however, is as restless and contradictory as ever, although there is no question that he loves Emily and their child. He wants to treat them properly, wants to be powerful for them: "Maybe he would never have any more purpose than this: to accept the assignment gracefully, lovingly, and do the best he could with it" (247). Maybe. But there are signs that this may be a very difficult task for Morgan in the long run. While climbing the steep stairs of responsibility to Emily's apartment, he is fearful that her rooms are becoming over-stuffed. While entering the "sea of hats and clothes" through his leap with Emily, he worries that he has steered off course and that he should run away with "no luggage, no fixed destination" (256). While trying to be strong for his family, he complains that he needs some place bigger—perhaps a large, bare farmhouse in the country. He cannot breathe in their crowded apartment. While trying to accept the more constricted space of their next home (the packed trailer which unsuccessfully tries to look rooted), he has a dream which suggests that "he'd been traveling so long, such a distance, that a sudden stop was impossible" (300).

Morgan is still deeply divided. He cannot stop moving or imagining different lives for himself. His makeshift solution is to journey not into the unknown, but back to the home he abandoned in Baltimore. This choice of destination is telling. He is a foreigner who deeply needs security and order; who craves adventures within circumscribed, familiar settings; who wants to be loved, but is unreliable in giving and receiving love. Making this unexpected, clandestine visit to Bonny's house thus fulfills his contradictory needs and enables Tyler to end her story on a profound note of uncertainty. On this trip, Morgan clearly indicates that life with Emily has not changed him much. He is still bothered by time and cannot make his past cohere with the present. He both laments and enjoys being an outsider to his old family. He gets a thrill by sneaking around as a "burglar" unearthing the secrets of this house. He obsessively worries about the bats in this home where he no longer belongs. And he empties himself into a "suspended state of mind," while searching for his old places within the city, while dreaming about finding Emily and Leon "still leading their pure, vagabond lives, like two children in a fairy tale" (308-9).

Because Tyler has paralleled Emily and Morgan so effectively in the latter half of the novel, she has given us the vantage point to evaluate his trip "home." It is an escape back to where he escaped from. It is yet another attempt to find himself by escaping from his present self. And, in contrast to Emily's balance, it seems rather desperate, even pathetic. He must keep redefining himself, must keep reevaluating his sense of place. So Morgan remains an enigma to the end: writing instruction lists for Bonny, pretending he is a postman, holding back other people's letters so he can discover some of their secrets, and finally feeling great joy when he sees his wife and son. "He started walking faster. He started smiling. By the time he reached Emily, he was humming. Everything he looked at seemed luminous and beautiful, and rich with possibilities" (311). Because of the many twists Tyler gives to Morgan's characterization, it is very difficult to read this very romantic ending straight, to read it without any resistance, without any apprehension for Morgan and

Emily's future together. The passage's possibilities are laced with irony, and its irony is laced with Morgan's great imaginative energy.

Morgan Gower is Anne Tyler's means for meditating on the modern predicament that Leonard Lutwack describes in *The Role of Place in Literature*:

> the despair of deracination is countered with hope of restoring attachments to remnant places, expatriation alternates with return to the impaired homeland, disaffection is answered with accommodation to the new places of our time. Writers for whom neither alienation nor recommitment is acceptable turn to other choices: escape into nostalgia, distortions of place through fantasy and hallucination, and the rejection of place altogether in favor of other dimensions of existence such as time and motion. [184]

What makes Morgan so bewildering and fascinating is that he intensively exists in this limbo between place and placelessness; and in attempting to escape it, he turns—sometimes in quick succession—to all the alternatives Lutwack identifies. As a result, the romantic, spacious, and unpredictable side of Morgan's personality continues to rub against his many fears, his passivity, and his conservative desire to find the ideal refuge. As these characteristics play off one another as the novel winds down, Morgan remains persistently elusive. This is Tyler's intent. She is asking that we not rush toward interpreting his "strange malady," but that we remain tentative, flexible, and non-reductive. She wants us to struggle with Morgan and thus struggle with the lowly angel of place. As a result, *Morgan's Passing* is yet another potent example of Alfred Kazin's thesis that the "greatest single fact about our American writing . . . [is] our writers' absorption in every last detail of this American world, together with their deep and subtle alienation from it" (*Native Grounds* ix).

Notes

1. Hoffman has noted that this opening seems "out of kilter" (95), and Spoiler says this is "a book in which things tend not to be quite what they seem. . . . The puppet world of the novel is an unpredictable place" (1221).

2. Also see Grier and Updike ("Imagining") for reserved and negative responses to the novel.

3. Gordon Taylor helpfully suggests that "an attempt to encompass *Morgan's Passing* should begin and end . . . with a sense of the narrative as surging out from, and subsiding back into, Morgan's relentless reactivity to the world" (66).

4. Many analyses of Tyler's work talk about the importance of houses in her fiction, with Shelton's "Houses" being the most focused treatment of this subject.

5. In discussing *Searching for Caleb*, Gilbert writes: "Here and always [Tyler] paints folkways with more affection. . . . This country domesticity may have added to Tyler's appeal for some readers in the last two decades, with their flourishing fads of healthful,

simple countryness" (262). Tyler's ironic treatment of Morgan's dreamy pastoralism indicates that Gilbert's statement needs to be tempered and qualified, especially since there are other instances of this irony (for example, the issue of Cody Tull's country home in *Dinner at the Homesick Restaurant*).

6. See Gullette for an excellent discussion on how this contradictory attitude toward place is pervasive within Tyler.

7. Tyler sometimes uses flatness literally and metaphorically as a negative image of place. For another example, there is Pearl Tull's suffocated response to the hot flatness of Illinois when she visits Cody there. Lutwack gives a valuable overview of how flat landscapes have been used in literature (39-40).

Bobbie Ann Mason

GUY MENDES

Searching for Home

ALBERT E. WILHELM

In the Bobbie Ann Mason story "Lying Doggo," a young woman proclaims, "One day I was listening to Hank Williams and shelling corn for the chickens and the next day I was expected to know what wines went with what" (*Shiloh* 207). In "Graveyard Day," a divorced mother observes that families "shift membership, like clubs" (167), and "a stepfather is like a substitute host on a talk show" (173). In a third story, entitled "A New-Wave Format," the developmentally disabled characters "can't keep up with today's fast pace" and "need a world that is slowed down" (217).

Such fragmentary passages, lifted almost at random from Mason's fiction, reflect her persistent concern with rapid social change and its dramatic effect on ordinary people. In the course of some fifty years, Mason has herself experienced dramatic changes in environment and lifestyle. She grew up on a small dairy farm in rural Kentucky, but immediately after college she migrated to New York City, where she wrote features for *Movie Life* magazine on teen stars such as Fabian, Annette Funicello, and Ann-Margret. As a child she sat under the apple tree reading Nancy Drew and other girl detective stories, but as a young woman she earned a Ph.D. in literature and published a scholarly study of Nabokov's *Ada*. In the early 1970s, Mason taught at a small college in Pennsylvania; now her own stories appear prominently in anthologies used by thousands of college students.

In several interviews, Mason has commented on her own sense of cultural dislocation and its importance as a theme in her fiction. In 1985 she said to Lila Havens: "I'm constantly preoccupied with . . . exploring various kinds of culture shock—people moving from one class to another . . . people being threatened by other people's ways and values" (Mason, "Residents and Transients," 95). In another interview, this one with Yu Yuh-chao, Mason contrasted her fiction with that of earlier Southern writers. "In the older generation," she said, "there was a much stronger sense of the place of the South, sense of the family, and sense of the land. I guess the newer writers are writing about how that sense has been breaking down." She then went on to emphasize the difficulty of "retaining identity and integrity in the face of [such] change" (quoted in Wilhelm, "Private Rituals," 272).

Observations similar to these are now prominent in much of the critical commentary on Mason's fiction. Darlene Reimers Hill says that "Mason's characters live in a protean world of rapid, dizzying change. Faced with finding their identities . . . in the midst of constant flux, they seek to discover something to hold on to in this modern emotional environment where one must deal with new rituals and new family patterns" (83). In a similar vein, Maureen Ryan observes that Mason's characters are "overwhelmed by rapid and frightening changes" and "must confront contradictory impulses, the temptation to withdraw into the security of home and the past, and the alternative prospect of taking to the road in search of something better" (294).

Although Mason is an acknowledged master at documenting the fluidity of contemporary culture, she has also been criticized for a degree of sameness in her stories. One reviewer of *Shiloh and Other Stories* balked at the frequent reappearance in different stories of young women who had recently been divorced or abandoned by their husbands (Johnson 197). Reviews of *Love Life* were typically quite positive but commented in passing that "characters often seem too much alike" (Freeman 1) or that "Mason dips her pen in the same ink, over and over" (Moore 7).

Insofar as these criticisms are valid, they may contain the seeds of their own refutations. In Mason's repetition we sense a sure knowledge of the characters and situations that she portrays. From apparent sameness we can derive depth and profundity of insight. Furthermore, amid those multiple accounts (almost always skillfully wrought) of separation, divorce, and adult children moving back home with their parents, Mason does offer other, strikingly different, tales of social dislocation.

In two of her best pieces of fiction, the short story entitled "Big Bertha Stories" and the novel *In Country*, Mason examines one of the most intense cultural shocks of the twentieth century—the broad effect of American involvement in the Vietnam War.[1] In focusing on the domestic consequences of this cataclysmic event, Mason portrays not just culture shock but the seismic upheaval of an entire culture. She depicts threats to individual identity and, by implication, to the larger national identity. None of Mason's stories are trivial, but these particular tales of soldiers' attempts to return home expand the theme of social dislocation to mythic proportions. In searching for the way back home, Mason's Vietnam veterans pursue an odyssey that is less extensive but even more daunting than that of Ulysses.

In "Big Bertha Stories," Mason's main character is himself a storyteller, but his narratives have many loose ends. The metafictional frame story focuses on the alienation of a Vietnam veteran named Donald. As a prominent display of this condition, the stories he tells within the frame are disturbingly disjointed. Donald actually came home from the war several years earlier and promptly acquired a good job in a lumber yard as well as a wife and a son. During the past two years, however, the war has returned to him with a vengeance, and horrible memories of destruction disrupt his family and his work. After deliberately letting a stack of lumber fall, Donald abandons his job and reverts to a symbolic war zone. In his new work, far from home in the strip mines of Muhlenburg County, we see a striking parallel between the destruction of Vietnam and his company's despoliation of the land. Mason never actually shows Donald at work, but she does portray his increasingly turbulent returns home. Since Donald never made it all the way home from Vietnam, he is caught in a relentless cycle of unsatisfactory returns from his distant job operating a giant earth-moving machine.

Donald comes home sporadically, like "an absentee landlord" (*Love Life* 116) who doesn't really belong. His sudden reappearances invariably inspire terror in his young son, Rodney, and send him off to hide in the closet. In misguided attempts to coax Rodney out of hiding, Donald loudly narrates stories about a little boy who used to live there but who has since fallen into a septic tank or been stolen by gypsies. Donald repeatedly inflicts his own pain on his family, and in these simple tales of tragic loss he is projecting his own sense of loss of identity after having been immersed in the quagmire of Vietnam. Like the fictional boy, Donald "used to live there" but can no longer find his true home.

During one of his visits, Donald shops with his family at the mall and calmly plays video games with his son. Just when his wife, Jeannette, thinks they are about to become "a normal family" (117), they encounter a reptile show in the mall parking lot. This sudden appearance of a snake in the galleria immediately produces dissension and tears. On a small scale, this episode reenacts the same mythic pattern Donald experienced in Vietnam. He remembers Vietnam as "the most beautiful place in the world"—so lush "you'd have thought you were in paradise." With his childlike Vietnamese girlfriend, Donald found a temporary Eden until the war "blew it sky-high" (130). He mentions the Bell Huey Cobra as one very efficient instrument in the destruction of paradise, and by evoking this specific reptilian name he echoes again the story of Eden's fall.

On every trip home, Donald is plagued with strange dreams that seem trivial but probably convey coded messages that he can never articulate. His dream of "hijacking a plane to Cuba" suggests extreme alienation from his homeland. Another dream about "stringing up barbed wire around the house" reflects his paranoid feelings of vulnerability. The lost doll of still another dream may symbolize the innocence of his youth lost in the jungles of Vietnam. When, after many such dreams, he rams his car "into a Civil War statue in front of the courthouse," he may be expressing his contempt for earlier war memorials because the veterans of his own war have been so nearly forgotten.

If Donald's dreams are the haunting narratives created by his active subconscious, the bizarre Big Bertha stories he tells his son are even more disturbing. Big Bertha is Donald's name for a "huge strip-mining machine in Muhlenburg County" (117), but her symbolic significance in Donald's tortured fictions is even more immense than her physical size. In various manifestations she becomes "a big fat woman who can sing the blues" (120), a trainer of racing snakes, and "a female version of Paul Bunyan" (117). Like the hero of a frontier tall tale, she creates a tornado when she belches. Like a modern superhero, she is the size of a tall building and big enough to "straddle a four-lane highway" (120). The unfathomable complexity of this fictional character is an index of her creator's inner confusion and tenuous hold on reality. The continuing inflation of her powers is a measure of his desperation.

In the most elaborate of Donald's stories, "Big Bertha and the Neutron Bomb," Big Bertha travels to California to go surfing. At first this trip seems idyllic: "On the beach, corn dogs and snow cones are free and the surfboards turn into dolphins." The story takes an ominous turn, however, when "the neutron bomb comes" and everyone except Big Bertha "keels over dead" (119). Donald claims that Big Bertha is "immune to the neutron bomb" (120), but his narrative simply stops without developing this assertion. In a later story about Big Bertha and a rock-and-roll band, the band "gives a concert in a place that turns out to be a toxic-waste dump and the contamination is spread all over the country." This story is long but confusing, and "Big Bertha's solution to the problem is not at all clear" (126).

These parables of Donald's experience in Vietnam begin with playful innocence but are soon seared with horrors. Donald desperately tries to depict Big Bertha as a potential savior, a *deus ex machina* from the coal fields, but she repeatedly fails him. As his stories become more fragmentary and disjointed, she becomes decidedly less benevolent and more menacing. In fact, as Rodney hears more of these stories, he begins to have dreams about Big Bertha that echo Donald's memories of the war.

Donald's imaginative creations merge the idyllic with the horrible because his experiences in Vietnam did the same. There he saw the hellish infuse and overwhelm the Edenic. Now his narratives sputter and falter because he has difficulty extricating any good from the apparently pervasive evil.

Lost in his obsession with Big Bertha's huge breasts and thighs, Donald is unable to accept the very real nurturing care of the woman to whom he is married. (In fact, Jeannette accuses him of being "in love with Big Bertha.") Just as a woman's breasts suggest sustenance and maternal care, Jeannette throughout the story is closely connected with food and food giving. She first met Donald while she was working at her parents' pit-barbecue restaurant, and on his visits home she conscientiously prepares pancakes and tries "to think of something original to do with instant potatoes." In this home, however, any sacramental healing value of food has been sadly lost. When they sit at the kitchen table, Donald talks about C-5As and uses a food processor blade to illustrate the destructive power of a helicopter rotor. Feeling helpless and rejected at home, Jeannette takes a job as a waitress at a steak house. Even here her accomplishments are limited because the restaurant burns down one night after a grease fire breaks out in the kitchen.

When Donald finally decides to enter a veterans' hospital, he goes "with the resignation of an old man being taken to a rest home" (130). Robbed of his youth in Vietnam and subsequently unable to assume the expected adult roles of husband and father, he becomes prematurely old. As he rides calmly to the hospital, he offers one last Big Bertha story, but now her stature is much diminished. He instructs Jeannette to tell Rodney that Big Bertha is taking him "on a sea cruise, to the South Seas" (130). In evoking a vision of a Gauguin-like paradise, Donald may still be immersed in his fictions, but they have become decidedly less flamboyant. In demanding much less of Big Bertha, he is perhaps ready to recount more healing narratives as all the veterans in his therapy group "trade memories" (131).

Left alone with Rodney, Jeannette once again becomes a professional food provider. This time "she waits on families" at Fred's Family Restaurant. In doing so, however, her performance is perfunctory, and she is just waiting "for Donald to come home so they can come here and eat together like a family" (131).

Just as the war made it impossible for Donald to be a husband and father, Jeannette's vicarious experience with Vietnam has diminished her role as wife and mother. Repulsed as a provider of comfort and sustenance, she assimilates some of Donald's debilitating obsessions. She seeks psychological counseling, but lurking within the innocuous word "therapist"—presumably an agent of comfort and health—she perceives the ominous phrase "the rapist." With Donald gone, the only man in Jeannette's life is "Mr. Bouncer," a miniature trampoline she purchases for Rodney. When she takes a turn jumping on it, she briefly experiences an exhilarating sensation of flight. But just as the war in Vietnam has robbed her of spontaneous joy, a neighbor brings her harshly back to earth by warning, "You'll tear your insides loose" (132). This dire prediction ends her play, and the same night she has a nightmare in which bouncing on a trampoline becomes "jumping on soft moss" and finally jumping on "a springy pile of dead bodies" (132).

Even if Donald never made it all the way home from Vietnam, he got close enough to spread the contagion. His nightmares have infected his son and eventually afflict his wife. The war swept away his youthful innocence and is dangerously eroding that of Rodney and Jeannette.

In "Big Bertha Stories," Mason focuses on the uncompleted odyssey of a single Vietnam veteran, but her novel *In Country* examines several returning soldiers. Throughout Donald's story the journey home is painfully repetitive and never progressive. In contrast to his aimless cyclical travel, the pilgrimage in *In Country* is linear and boldly purposeful. In traveling to the Vietnam Memorial in Washington, one veteran symbolically completes his journey home. Since all of the novel's action takes place in the United States but the phrase "in country" actually refers to the war zones of Vietnam, Mason's title is ironic. The battlefields of another country did follow Donald and many other Vietnam veterans back to America and made them displaced persons in their own neighborhoods. Even back inside their own country and presumably far from combat, they found themselves still "in country."[2] Unlike Donald, though, the protagonist of Mason's novel ultimately rediscovers and reclaims his homeland by traveling to the center of the nation's capital.

The two main characters in the novel *In Country* are Sam Hughes, a seventeen-year-old girl hovering on the brink of maturity, and her uncle, Emmett Smith, a confused veteran of the Vietnam War. Sam's father, Dwayne, was killed in Vietnam before she was born, and Emmett has never completely recovered from the psychic wounds he suffered there. Linked by blood and by some common problems, Sam and Emmett form a strange family unit.

Much of the commentary on this novel has focused on Sam and her coming of age. Joel Conarroe, for example, has called the book "a timely variation" of "the traditionally male-centered *Bildungsroman*" that "delineates Sam's quest for a father" (7). Concentrating also on Sam, Barbara Ryan's poststructuralist reading of the novel describes this search for a father as "a symbolic representation of modern man's desire for the Logos—origin of meaning and authoritative discourse" (199). While Conarroe's and Ryan's emphasis on Sam is understandable, the character of Emmett is equally important. By portraying the intertwined lives of these two characters, Mason skillfully combines the themes of the returning soldier's alienation and the young woman's initiation. Both characters display much confusion about what is worth doing in life, but both eventually gain insight. As the abandoned and mistrusted war veteran, Emmett begins the novel as an outcast—the primary embodiment of the alienation theme. In the tangled course of events during the summer of 1984, he emerges as a guide who can lead Sam and others toward maturity and wholeness. Thus, he plays a key role in the initiation theme by bringing this rite of passage to a fitting conclusion.[3]

Mason introduces the alienation theme by quoting lines from Bruce Springsteen's popular song "Born in the U.S.A" as the epigraph for her book. In an interview Mason commented that she incorporated this and many other references to Springsteen into her novel because his lyrics "reflected the themes of the book," almost "like a soundtrack" (Wilhelm, "Interview," 32). To be sure, Emmett's circumstances are not as dire as those of the speaker in Springsteen's song, but the residents of Hopewell, Kentucky, do sometimes stereotype him and other Vietnam veterans as "psychos and killers" (*In Country* 113)—"volatile specters emitting bands of alienation and derangement" (Myers 412). Hopewell is a typical small Southern town, and its name is probably an allegorical reference to the prevailing mood of shallow optimism. Like many other Americans, most of the residents of Hopewell would prefer to ignore the veterans and thus avoid the painful heritage of the Vietnam War.

When Emmett first returned to Hopewell after his tour in Vietnam, he was indeed a pariah. He and his hippie friends once tried to fly the Vietcong flag from the courthouse tower, and they were later suspected of burglarizing a local business. There are still rumors that Emmett is a dope dealer, that he sleeps with his niece, that he "killed babies in Vietnam," but gradually he has come to be regarded more as an eccentric misfit than a criminal. Although many people in Hopewell find Emmett an interesting topic for idle gossip, they remain oblivious to his suffering. We see the real Emmett in an emotional scene at Cawood's Pond when he confesses to Sam: "I'm damaged. It's like something in the center of my heart is gone and I can't get it back. . . . I work on staying together, one day at a time. There's no room for anything else. It takes all my energy" (225).

While Emmett is the primary example of the Vietnam veteran as outcast, the book contains several more veterans who display other facets of the Vietnam legacy. According to Matthew Stewart, Emmett and his friends constitute "a microcosm of veterans' problems and troubled behaviors" (176). For Tom Hudson, the primary symptom of war trauma is impotence, and his job serves as a bitterly ironic commentary on his condition. He considers himself a wreck of a man, and he works in a run-down garage—a "yawning cave-like hole"—trying to restore wrecked automobiles (76). In one car a frozen transmission defies his efforts to repair it, and this mechanical problem parallels his psychological problems of isolation and sexual dysfunction. For Buddy Mangrum, the war has left serious physical illness as well as emotional trauma.

Apparently a victim of Agent Orange, Buddy "has every symptom in the book, and the V.A. just laughs in his face" (111). Furthermore, Buddy's problems have been passed on to his daughter. Defective at birth, her tangled intestines suggest the tangled consequences of American involvement in Vietnam. The knots inside her impede the flow of life-giving nutrients just as the problems of the war have debilitated many veterans.

Pete Simms is another veteran who lives in Hopewell, but in a real sense he has never returned from the war. While in Vietnam, he had tattooed on his chest a map of the Jackson Purchase area of Western Kentucky. The map was so detailed that it indicated his street in Hopewell and even contained a tiny red dot to mark the spot where his Corvette was parked. Even though Pete has this indelible map with him always, it provides no real guidance. From the time it was created in the confusion of Vietnam, he has had to "look at it upside down," or when he tries to read it "in the mirror it's backwards." What was to be a reminder of home for a homesick soldier has become instead a tragicomic symbol of the veteran's lost condition.[4]

To make us feel the pain of these outcast veterans, Mason includes in her book several other young men who serve as foils. One notable example is Sam's stepfather, Larry Joiner. Unlike her real father, who suffered the agonies of battle, Joiner holds a cushy job at IBM and seems oblivious even to the possibility of battle trauma. His last name suggests that he is the generic organization man who fits easily into the fabric of society. Sam refers to him contemptuously as Lorenzo Jones because he is, to her, as remote and unreal as this character on an old radio soap opera. Similarly, Sam's boyfriend, Lonnie Malone, is a mindless adolescent whose greatest achievement in life was "sinking ten out of twelve jump shots" in a high school basketball game (33). Unable to get an athletic scholarship to attend college, he does little more than cruise Hopewell in his van and drink beer. Gilman describes him as "totally a creature of the present" who sets his sights "on the exigencies of the moment" (53). Like so many in Hopewell and throughout the country, he is unwilling to face the history of the Vietnam era and unable to understand how this painful past may limit the future.

If Larry and Lonnie are the local exemplars of health and normalcy, perhaps the suffering of the Vietnam veterans should be seen in a new light. Mason shows that the pain that made Emmett an outcast can also provide insight and enable him to guide others back to health. Although Emmett has no regular job, his work throughout the book displays important symbolic values. He will not sell microwaves or run a video game arcade and tells Sam that he can find no "job worth doing" in the community around him, but he does earn small amounts of money by repairing toasters and hair dryers, and he senses that, in the aftermath of war, the country as a whole stands in need of some major repairs.

Emmett's work on his own ramshackle house is emblematic of this larger task. Fearing that his house suffers from a hidden structural problem, he spends his days digging deep trenches to expose the foundations and reveal possible cracks. When his neighbor sees him at this task, she asks facetiously, "Are you digging to China?" This offhand remark suggests an ironic truth. If Emmett only could dig through to the other side of the earth, he might uncover in the swamps of Indochina the foundation of his own problems and the ominous structural flaws that threaten the larger society. Even if he can never accomplish this, his work remains therapeutic. He is engaged in what anthropologist Arnold van Gennep has termed the rituals of sympathetic magic—ceremonies "based on belief in the reciprocal action of like on like," of "the container" on "the contained," of image on "real object or real being" (4). Like Nick Adams in Hemingway's "Big Two-Hearted River," the fictional veteran of an earlier war, Emmett performs simple tasks with painstaking deliberation in an effort to set both his house and his psyche back in order.

Emmett's role as guide becomes more pronounced when he initiates the trip to the Vietnam Memorial for Sam and Dwayne's mother, Mamaw Hughes. To understand the full significance of what Emmett has accomplished by bringing Sam and Mamaw to Washington, we must examine in some detail what happens to them at the wall. For Sam, of course, this completed pilgrimage marks the conclusion of her rite of passage into adulthood. As she travels toward Washington, she notes that she has entered a "different time zone" (11). She is progressing not just from Central to Eastern Standard Time but also from adolescence to maturity. Along the road Sam listens to the radio, but the station that plays the "oldies" begins to fade away. As she puts childish things behind her, Sam can no longer hear the songs of performers with juvenile names—"Junior Walker . . . and somebody else named Junior whose name Sam doesn't catch" (8).

The dominant motif in Sam's initiation is her quest for the father she never knew. She tries to forge some link with him by reading books about Vietnam, searching for old letters, dating a Vietnam veteran much older than she is, and pretending that she is a soldier walking point at Cawood's Pond. Early in the book, she scrutinizes the only picture she has of her father and then the image of her own face in a mirror. At this point, she fails to "see any resemblance" and can therefore gain no real sense of her own identity. When Sam finally discovers her father's name inscribed on the Vietnam Memorial, she understands more profoundly who he was and what he did. Since the stone wall of the memorial is so highly polished, it becomes not merely a tablet listing names but also a mirror reflecting the images of those who stand before it. In a symbolic sense, then, at the moment Sam finds her father, she also finds herself. Later, when Sam flips through the printed directory to locate her father's name in the alphabetical listings, she literally discovers her own name there, too. Coincidentally, a young army private named Sam Hughes from Houston, Texas, was one of the casualties of the war. When Sam locates and "touches her own name" on the wall, her quest is complete.[5]

For Sam, Emmett is the guide in a ceremony of initiation, and he leads her to the conclusion of this rite of passage at the memorial. In addition, Emmett helps Mamaw Hughes to complete another important ritualistic pattern. Dwayne's funeral, the ritual of letting a dead son go, was for Mrs. Hughes tragically incomplete, and her grief has been repressed and suspended for more than seventeen years. When Dwayne was killed, the family had to wait for days to receive his body, and even then they were not permitted to open the coffin and see it. Mrs. Hughes's memory of those painful circumstances is still vivid, and she says to Sam: "It was so hard without the body. . . . When somebody dies, you're supposed to prepare the body and watch over it. It's something that brings you all together, but he wasn't here. . . . We just run around like a chicken with its head cut off" (197). With her tortured grammar and simple rural imagery, Mrs. Hughes conveys a poignant picture of the pain and confusion created by this incomplete funeral.

Although the funeral itself provided Mrs. Hughes with no tangible proof of her son's death, that ritualistic need is satisfied by her actions at the Vietnam Memorial. From deep down in this dark pit, she slowly ascends the steps of a ladder so she can place her hands on the letters of her son's name engraved in the wall. In this indirect way, she is able to feel his mortal wounds and her own emotional wounds can begin to heal. In describing the symbolic values of the Vietnam Memorial, its designer, Maya Lin, has commented that the chronological listing of the war dead should "read like an epic . . . poem. . . . Locating specific names with the aid of a directory would be like finding bodies on a battlefield" (quoted in Scruggs and Swerdlow 78). Lin says that her design was influenced by the memorial to World War I soldiers at Thiepval, France. She describes this earlier monument as a "journey from violence to serenity" (quoted in Scruggs and Swerdlow 77) and says that her own design attempts "to bring out in people the realization of loss and a cathartic healing process" (quoted in Scruggs 147). For Mrs. Hughes, such a purpose is surely accomplished, and Emmett's guiding role in the healing ritual is crucial. He not only steadies the ladder while Mrs. Hughes climbs; he is also the one who sensed her need and persuaded her to go to the Vietnam Memorial in the first place. Emmett's family relationship to Mrs. Hughes is that of a very remote in-law. He is, in fact, the brother of her former daughter-in-law. Nevertheless, this outcast from society becomes, for Mrs. Hughes, an agent of renewal and wholeness.

The scene at the Vietnam Memorial contains much imagery of wounds and healing, of death and rebirth, and this imagery relates to all who are there. As Sam and the others approach the memorial, she thinks of the V-shaped monument as "a black boomerang, whizzing toward her head" (239). For Sam and countless war veterans, the memory of Vietnam has been for many years just that—the embodiment of a destructive force that returns unerringly to attack no matter how far away they fling it. Later the memorial is described as "a black gash" in the hillside, a "giant grave" with "fifty-eight thousand bodies rotting . . . behind those names" (239). These dark images of injury and death are soon translated into images of health and rebirth. Mircea Eliade has observed that many important ceremonies of transformation "clearly imply a ritual death followed by a resurrection or a new birth" (xii-xiii). In this case, Sam and her companions must touch the open wound, must go down into the dark grave, before they can begin the renewal process. As Sam stands "deep in the pit," she feels an intense surge of energy inside her. It is so "massive and over-powering" that it "feels like giving birth" (240). Like Mamaw Hughes, Sam also ascends from the grave by climbing the steps of the borrowed ladder to touch her father's name. On the final page of the novel, Mrs. Hughes provides a simple but moving description of what she and the others have experienced: "Coming up on this wall of a sudden and seeing how black it was, it was so awful, but then I came down in it and saw that white carnation blooming out of that crack and it gave me hope" (245).

The last sentence of *In Country* describes Emmett "sitting . . . cross-legged in front of the wall" with the calmness and serenity of a Buddha. In this peaceful posture, "his face bursts into a smile like flames." If Emmett's dreams have been plagued by memories of fire fights in Vietnam, he is now the embodiment of a cleansing fire that can burn away the pain and horror of war. At this point of stasis, Emmett has progressed far beyond Donald in "Big Bertha Stories" or Springsteen's anonymous veteran in the novel's epigraph. Unlike these truncated stories, *In Country* has become a "fully realized returned veteran parable" that offers "specific narrative healing rites" (Myers 422).

At the memorial, Emmett finally completes the heroic journey described by Joseph Campbell and others. In his journey "the mythic circle includes a voyage home, the bringing of the great boon to his society, the communal dispensation of hard-earned power and knowledge" (Myers 416). By characterizing Emmett as a wounded outcast who ultimately becomes a guide for others, Mason produces a fitting transformation of a specific classical myth. In the accounts of the Trojan War, Philoctetes was a Greek warrior whose wound would not heal. Since this wound was so foul-smelling, his companions abandoned him on the island of Lemnos. After many years, however, the Greeks realized that Philoctetes was the only person who could lead them to victory over the Trojans, and they welcomed him again into their ranks.

By emerging from his alienation and becoming a guide for Sam and Mrs. Hughes, Emmett acts out a similar pattern. Emmett does not lead military forces to victory on the battlefield, but he does guide survivors to peace. As David Booth observes, it is "precisely from among the victims of war" that "healing is to be sought" (109). Furthermore, Mason suggests that what happens to Sam and Mrs. Hughes at the Vietnam Memorial can happen also to the larger community. Emmett looks forward to the time when all his friends in Hopewell can share this experience at the memorial. Near the end of the book he says with confidence, "They're all coming one of these days" (241).

NOTES

1. Mason apparently worked on these pieces concurrently. Although "Big Bertha Stories" was not published in book form until 1989, when it was collected in *Love Life,* it first appeared in *Mother Jones* in April 1985 (the same year *In Country* was published).

2. In Mason's choice of title, Owen Gilman Jr. sees "a provocative twist to the combat soldiers' terminology for actually arriving in Vietnam, turning the situation around completely" and "bringing the Vietnam aftermath fully into the open in America" (51). To emphasize the ambiguity of Mason's title, Gilman uses "In Which Country?" as the title for his own commentary on the novel. Although Mason borrowed her title from military slang of the Vietnam era, it echoes the title of another well-known war story—Hemingway's "In Another Country." There, too, the focus is on soldiers whose wounds make it difficult for them to return to the ordinary world.

3. In an essay emphasizing Mason's realism, Matthew Stewart acknowledges that "Emmett's story becomes inseparable from Sam's and is coequal in importance" (167). Stewart praises Mason's accuracy in portraying the psychological and sociological problems of Vietnam veterans, but he criticizes the novel's conclusion as a "facile, Pollyanna ending characteristic of television" (179). In labeling the final section of the novel "Fantasyland" (177), he obviously disavows Emmett's importance as a guide.

4. In David Booth's reading of *In Country,* the actual geographic setting in rural Kentucky is incidental. He contends that "the action really occurs in a universal American geography of fast-foods, malls, television serials, HBO, MTV, and pop music radio" and in the even more inclusive setting "of a 'waste land,' together with the symbols, motifs, and narrative structures of the grail legend that communicate that geography" (99). Obviously, Pete's simplistic map will be of little use because it hardly begins to chart these complex domains.

5. Mason, whose own first name could apply to either gender, had a similar experience at the wall that influenced her writing of *In Country.* In describing a visit to the

memorial in 1983, she says: "Quite by accident, my eyes fell upon my own name on the wall, a version of my name—Bobby G. Mason. I found out later that Bobby G. Mason was from Florida. I learned also that there were four guys named Robert Mason whose names were on the wall. . . . I knew then that Vietnam was my story too, and it was every American's story. Finally, I felt I had a right to tell a small part of that story" (quoted in Brussat and Brussat 2).

© MARION ETTLINGER

Cormac McCarthy

Restless Seekers

JOHN G. CAWELTI

Southerners have a favorite set of self-images involving associations with stability, tradition, and dedication to local communities, all the symbology of "down-home." But in fact the South was founded by a horde of restless seekers who left their home places behind them in pursuit of a plethora of dreams: wealth and grandeur, religious salvation, dreams of utopia, or all three in various combinations. Faulkner understood this well, and two of his most significant characters, Thomas Sutpen and Flem Snopes, represent different generations of poor whites seeking to rise in the world. Even Faulkner's great aristocratic families, the Sartorises, the Compsons, and the McCaslins, were founded by such pilgrims.

These men and women were driven by a restlessness and desperation of spirit that urged them on to glorious accomplishment or catastrophic destruction. Such extremities have also been a fundamental part of Southern culture and history. From the beginning, a key dynamic of Southern evangelical Protestantism featured saintly figures like Billy Graham vying for control of the Southern conscience with men athirst for wealth, lust, and power like Jim Bakker, Jimmy Swaggart, and Pat Robertson. The drive toward extremes may also account for the way in which Southern literature has been pervaded by a fascination with the gothic and the grotesque, plumbing the lower depths of society as well as fantasizing about chivalry and nobility. Flannery O'Connor, generally recognized as the most important Southern writer of the generation between the age of Faulkner and the present, was deeply imbued with this fascination as her parables of redemption and damnation in a modernizing South reveal. The most important contemporary inheritor of this stream of Southern literature and culture is a man many consider the most important living Southern writer, Cormac McCarthy.

McCarthy has developed in a very complex fashion, embarking in the last two decades on an almost completely new set of literary ventures, marked by his own restless quest from Knoxville, Tennessee, to El Paso, Texas, from the heart of the South to the edges of the West. In this way, McCarthy not only exemplifies some important aspects of the Southern identity as it is reshaping itself in the era of the Sunbelt, but in a deeper sense he can be seen as a postmodern avatar of that restless drive toward the West that has been a key motive in Southern culture since the first long hunters crossed the Appalachians in search of more game and the plantations began their long push from the Tidewater through the deep South to the plains of Texas.

McCarthy's literary journey embodies this great migration in mythical terms. In his first three novels, *The Orchard Keeper* (1965), *Outer Dark* (1968), and *Child of God* (1973), the protagonists are mountaineers driven or drawn out of their isolated home places into the modern world. *Suttree*, published in 1979, was McCarthy's most ambitious novel up to that time and it was also, as it turned out, his valediction to the middle South; for with his next novel, *Blood Meridian, or The Evening Redness in the West* (1985), McCarthy set forth on the fictional western quest that would soon lead to the first two novels of his announced "Border Trilogy," *All the Pretty Horses* (1992) and *The Crossing* (1994). The last two novels not only rise out of the Southern tradition, but are major reinventions of the Western, reminding us how the great tradition of the modern Western began when a Baltimorean went to Wyoming to recover his health and came back with a novel called *The Virginian* (1902), an epic account of a former Southerner's heroic encounter with badmen (and a New England schoolmarm) in the Wild West.

As McCarthy develops his mythos of the pilgrimage through the fictional world of his imagination, we realize that such quests are never simple. It is often difficult to tell whether McCarthy's seekers are mainly driven by something they flee or drawn by something they seek. Is their quest best defined in terms of a journey through space or into the soul? Is this journey best understood as moving into the future or into the past? Is it toward salvation or damnation? Are these mysterious quests ultimately as incomprehensible as life itself, or is there, in the end, some point to it all? One of the fascinating things about McCarthy is that the quest continues but each new book slightly shifts the grounds traversed by its predecessors. He too still seems to be engaged by the very quest he writes about with such mystery and passion.

Suttree is McCarthy's longest and most ambitious novel to date. It is also, along with *Blood Meridian*, a major work of culmination and transition in his career. It is in this novel that McCarthy says his symbolic farewell to the South and begins his move from gothic world of the Southern literary tradition to the leaner, more action-filled style of the Western. As a novel, *Suttree* is a culmination and transformation of literary modernism as well as of important aspects of its Southern inheritance. The McCarthy Home Page on the World Wide Web likens *Suttree* to Joyce's *Ulysses*—"the novel's evocation of Joyce's masterpiece, *Ulysses*, is often palpable"—with Suttree "like some latterday Bloom" and Knoxville as a Southern version of "dear, dirty Dublin." There's certainly some truth in this assertion,[1] but McCarthy's most direct predecessors are much closer. McCarthy himself offers homage to the greatest Southern modernist by making Suttree's very name allude to one of Faulkner's most important restless seekers, Thomas Sutpen. But Suttree is in some ways more like Henry than Thomas Sutpen, a latter-day revenant to the family home and the scene of the crime, though it's not at all clear what the crime is. However, the most direct prototype of *Suttree* is Flannery O'Connor's *Wise Blood*. Like an inverted Hazel Motes, Suttree is unwillingly driven toward a goal he does not want to seek. In addition, he is plagued by a sort of disciple whose penchant for the subhuman world takes Enoch Emery's gorilla suit several steps further and includes sexual intercourse with watermelons, a bizarre pursuit of pigs, and an explosion in the Knoxville sewers. Suttree even has relationships with women that are eerily reminiscent of Hazel's involvements with Leora Watts and Sabbath Lily Hawks. *Suttree*'s Knoxville is as much a variation of O'Connor's Taulkinham as it is of Joyce's Dublin.

Like O'Connor's major characters, Suttree is trapped in a world that has lost the sense of the presence of God. However, O'Connor's devout if offbeat Catholicism leads her to frame her stories of modern alienation by constantly hinting that, if we can look beyond the deceptive lights of the modern city, we can always see that "the black sky was underpinned with long silverstreaks that looked like scaffolding and depth on depth behind it were thousands and thousands of stars that all seemed to be moving very slowly as if they were about some vast construction work that involved the whole order of the universe and would take all time to complete" (*Wise Blood* 24).

In O'Connor's world it is always possible for the seeker to encounter transcendence. Sometimes even a person who is not actually seeking, like Ruby Turpin in the story "Revelation," is gifted with a moment of grace. McCarthy was raised a Catholic, but in his cosmos the audience sits in an empty and decaying theater and the minstrel show is long over. There's nothing left but death and silence. Whatever ultimate meaning there may or may not be can be summed up only in such enigmatic axioms as "ruder forms survive."

> The rest indeed is silence. It has begun to rain. . . . Faint summer lightning far downriver. A curtain is rising on the western world. A fine rain of soot, dead beetles, anonymous small bones. The audience sits webbed in dust. Within the gutted sockets of the interlocutor's skull a spider sleeps and the jointed ruins of the hanged fool dangle from the flies, bone pendulum in motley. Fourfooted shapes go to and fro over the boards. Ruder forms survive. [*Suttree* 5]

Suttree takes place in Knoxville in the early 1950s, a city on the verge of dramatic changes.[2] The novel ends in 1955 with the tearing down of the old slums in McAnally Flats in order to construct a new expressway, symbolizing Knoxville's hopeful participation in the Sunbelt South with its increasing commercial and industrial linkages to the rest of the country. However, the novel is not primarily concerned with the impinging of modernization on a traditional culture as it might have been had it been written by Bobbie Ann Mason, Lee Smith, Wendell Berry, or any number of other contemporary Southern writers. McCarthy chooses instead to deal with a protagonist and a group of characters whose impoverished marginality makes the new developments wholly irrelevant to them until they are suddenly dispossessed of the decaying area of the city where they live. The inhabitants of McAnally Flats form a grotesque community of exiles and escapees from the modern social order. Suttree is temporarily at home with the anarchic drunkards and grotesque thieves and madmen who live on the flats and on the waste lands along the floodplain of the Tennessee River. Deeply wounded in spirit and a restless seeker himself, Suttree is a kind of fisher king of this community of waste land outcasts. Though scion of a respectable old family, he has left the upper-middle-class world behind and become a derelict fisherman, selling carp and catfish he takes from the river to local butchers.

Yet Suttree is only hanging on in Knoxville, living marginally on its decaying fringes, held by a few residual family ties and by his loyalty to the fellow outcasts and rebels he has met along the river. Everything seems to conspire against his establishing any lasting relationships: his friends are killed by the police, hauled off to prison, or become victims of exposure and alcoholism; a perversely idyllic love affair with a beautiful girl he meets while catching mussels upriver ends tragically when his lover is killed in a rockslide; he almost settles down with a prostitute from Chicago, but just as things are going very well for them she goes violently insane and Suttree has to run for his life; finally, Suttree himself contracts typhoid fever and nearly dies. When he recovers, it is as if he has been inversely born again and everything in his former life has become dead for him. As the novel ends, Suttree passes the site of his former riverside shanty, now the construction site of a new expressway; a car stops for him, though he has not lifted a hand to signal it, and he is gone.

Whether Suttree's incessant seeking is primarily a quest for something beyond or a flight from the demons that haunt him is never fully clear. In fact, at the level of McCarthy's narrative quest and flight, seeking and running away seem to be interchangeable aspects of the same desperation of spirit. The source of this despair is McCarthy's overpowering sense of the brevity, fragility, and impermanence of human order in face of the vast but profoundly beautiful abyss of the cosmos. Above all, McCarthy's narrative gives us a sense of the macroscopic and microscopic, of the reality beyond human culture, the truth of "things known raw, unshaped by the construction of a mind obsessed with form" (427). In sudden flashes his characters reveal a primordial savagery that lurks beneath the surface of civilized society, as if "they could have been some band of stone age folk washed up out of an atavistic dream" (358). Suttree, more than most of the other characters, seems possessed with this sense of ultimate insecurity that pierces him at any moment when he lets his guard down: "he lay on his back in the gravel, the earth's core sucking his bones, a moment's giddy vertigo with this illusion of falling outward through blue and windy space, over the offside of the planet, hurtling through the high thin cirrus" (286).

Through McCarthy's vision we see that it is not the thriving New South city but the outcasts' "encampment of the damned" that is closer to reality, because it reveals the truth of man's folly and mortality: "this city constructed on no known paradigm, a mongrel architecture reading back through the works of man in a brief delineation of the aberrant disordered and mad" (3). In this world the most permanent and lyrical thing is decay, and any belief in permanence is delusion and madness. McCarthy is a veritable Tolstoy of Trash, and his pervasive and redolent poetry of rubble, garbage, and detritus are an ode to the haunting but futile beauty of the brevity and emptiness of human accomplishment against the vast geological panorama of rocks and stars.

However much he may reflect certain aspects of the Eliotic wasteland version of the grail legend, Cormac McCarthy's Suttree is no longer a Christian, nor is the possibility of Christian revelation held out to him, as is the case with Flannery O'Connor's characters. In one especially poignant scene, Suttree wanders into the unused Catholic school where he once studied, and there at this "derelict school for lechers" he finds his old desk and sits at it for a while before he notices a pathetic figure standing in the door of "this old bedroom in this old house where he'd been taught a sort of christian witchcraft." The figure is an old priest who still apparently lives in the deserted school. But there is no contact and no word. "When he came past the stairway the priest was mounted on the first landing like a piece of statuary. A catatonic shaman who spoke no word at all. Suttree went out the way that he'd come in, crossing the grass toward the lights of the street. When he looked back he could see the shape of the priest in the baywindow watching like a paper priest in a pulpit or a prophet sealed in glass" (304-5).

In *Suttree*, McCarthy's world is that of a scientific rather than a religious millenialist, though the biblical overtones of his novel are at times almost overwhelming. McCarthy views human life from the perspective of eternity, yet his version of eternity is the cosmic, geological, and biological immensity that derives from a purely naturalistic vision of the universe. In a way his characters, like O'Connor's, are "god-haunted," and his novels are secular allegories of driven souls fleeing the devil and seeking salvation in a realm across the borders of human good and evil where it is increasingly difficult to distinguish between the holy and the diabolical. This apocalyptic sense, with its implications of violence and destruction, is one aspect of the tradition of extreme individualism in religion and personal violence which John Shelton Reed identifies as a central component of the "enduring South," and which, he suggests, may be becoming an even more important characteristic of Southern culture in the postmodern era.[3]

Though he is haunted by the absence of God from the moment he first appears as a fisherman on the horribly polluted Tennessee River until he shakes the dust of Knoxville from his feet, Suttree has one significant moment of revelation during a trek up into the mountains in his second year on the river. This restless trip becomes a vision quest as Suttree gets increasingly lost and fatigue and hunger undercut his sense not only of where he is but of how long he has been there. Finally a storm that seems to have been following him for days breaks over him, and as he "crouched like an ape in the dark under the eaves of a slate bluff and watched the lightning" he has a vision of the world as a bizarre witches' sabbath with all the eras of evolutionary history mixed together:

> The storm moved off to the north. Suttree heard laughter and sounds of carnival. He saw with a madman's clarity the perishability of his flesh. Illbedowered harlots were calling from small porches in the night, in their gaudy rags like dolls panoplied out of a dirty stream. And along the little ways in the rain and lightning came a troupe of squalid merrymakers bearing a caged wivern on shoulderpoles and other alchemical game, chimeras and cacodemons skewered up on boarspears and a pharmacopeia of hellish condiments adorning a trestle and toted by trolls with an eldern gnome for guidon who shouted foul oaths from his mouthhole and a piper who piped a pipe of ploverbone and wore on his hip a glass flasket of some smoking fuel that yawed within viscid as quicksilver. A mesosaur followed above on a string like a fourlegged garfish helium filled.

A tattered gonfalon embroidered with stars now extinct. Nemoral halfworld inhabitants, figures in buffoon's motley, a gross and blueback foetus clopping along in brogues and toga. Attendants attend. Suttree watched these puckish revelers pass with a half grin of wry doubt. Dark closed about him. [287-88]

After such knowledge, what forgiveness? This vision might serve as a symbolic prophecy of the things experienced by the protagonists of McCarthy's next three novels. For Suttree, his final year on the river brings "a season of death and epidemic violence" (416). Increasingly he feels the coming of the hunter who in some mysterious way has been dogging his steps from the beginning. Finally the destruction of McAnally Flats, the one place in Knoxville he has been able to live in, drives him off the river and onto the road, where "out across the land the lightwires and road rails were going and the telephone lines with voices shuttling on like souls" (471).

Like his own protagonist, Cormac McCarthy pulled up stakes in Knoxville, leaving there in 1976, around the same time he was completing *Suttree,* and made a major geographical and creative move to the Southwest, settling in El Paso, Texas, which stands on the border between America and Mexico. This symbolic geographical location was the point of departure for McCarthy's next three novels. The book in which McCarthy began his own literary pilgrimage from Tennessee to West Texas is the extraordinary *Blood Meridian,* which combines a nightmarish series of events redolent of Southern Gothic with an anti-heroic quest set in Mexico and the future American Southwest. In some ways a strange sequel to *Huckleberry Finn* and in others, if one can imagine such a contradiction, a pre-Western post-Western, *Blood Meridian* unites the nineteenth-century tradition of western historical fiction springing from Cooper with a postmodernist vision of madness and chaos.[4] It is about the quest-initiation of a young man from Tennessee, known only as "the kid" or "he," who runs away from home in 1841 and eventually wanders westward. He becomes a member of a gang of outlaws and thieves who work the Texas-Mexico borderlands killing Indians and anyone else they think they can plunder.

The world this unnamed young man enters is a chaotic borderland, in both geographical and historical senses. It is the literal border between the United States and Mexico just after the Mexican War, when the definition of national frontiers remained in chaos and much of the land was still occupied by Native Americans hostile to both governments. Historically, the novel covers the period when the modern world first impinged upon the vast spaces of the great Southwest. The story of *Blood Meridian* is not, however, that of the traditional Western, in which heroic pioneers bring civilization to a savage wilderness. On the contrary, what the marauding Glanton gang brings to the borderlands is, if anything, more brutal and savage than the ethos of the violent peoples it encounters and seeks to exterminate.[5] The novel is as much about the twilight of civilization as its dawning.

Like many restless and alienated young men, the kid embarks on his quest looking for adventure and fortune. What he finds everywhere is horror and violence. His wanderings might serve as a nineteenth-century paradigm for the young men whose desperate quests across the border in the aftermath of World War II were the subject of McCarthy's next two "Western" novels.

McCarthy's "Western" fiction, like the transitional *Blood Meridian*, tells a story characteristic of much contemporary Western fiction: a young man's initiation into manhood. The Western version of this archetypal theme is very often connected, as were many novels of the Southern Renascence and McCarthy's own "Southern" fiction, with a deep sense of belatedness and loss, as if the world no longer offers young men the possibilities and the satisfactions of earlier times. Larry McMurtry created an important contemporary version of this story in his two early novels of Thalia, Texas, *Horseman, Pass By* (1961) and *The Last Picture Show* (1966). In *Horseman, Pass By*, the young narrator feels a deep sense of loss: "Things used to be better around here. . . . I feel like I want something back" (123). And loss does come to characterize young Lonnie's world when his beloved grandfather's diseased cattle must be destroyed and the grandfather himself is shot after being terribly hurt in an accident. *The Last Picture Show* ends with the closing of Thalia's one movie theater and with it the mythic dream of the Old West, which inspired so many of the pictures shown there. Peter Bogdanovich effectively ended his film of the novel with the great scene from Howard Hawks's Western *Red River* (1947), in which John Wayne sets off on the first great cattle drive from Texas. In contrast to this heroic moment, the young people of Thalia are lost in the vacuous emptiness of a depressed oil boomtown.

This sense of the end of the heroic West haunts such major works of the new Western fiction as Norman Maclean's *A River Runs Through It* (1976), in which an old man, haunted by memories of his long-dead father and brother and of the fishing they shared, still broods about his inability to save his brother from the violence that destroyed him. In other stories, Maclean evokes a lost world of skill with tools and heroic physical labor and shows how powerful an experience it was to be initiated into such a world. Like the mythical Western, these works celebrate a West that is largely gone, but unlike the traditional tales of wild cow-towns and cattle drives, outlaws and marshals, gunfighters and schoolmarms that populated the nation's imagined West, these stories celebrate the heroism not of gunfighters but of loggers, miners, forest service crews, and firefighters, those ordinary people who built the West and then saw it transformed into something else.

McCarthy has rapidly made himself a central figure in this literary tradition. The two novels of his Border Trilogy are among the richest and most
complex treatments of the Western themes of initiation, belatedness, and fron
tiers. They transmute the mythical fantasy world of wild Western gunfighters,
outlaws, and savage Indians into the last remnant of an age-old world of traditional work in which men are part of the unity of life and find great fulfillment
in their actions because these actions are integral with horses and the rest of
nature. Horses, which have been man's primary instrument in the use of nature and the creation of culture for centuries, are, as the novel's title would
suggest, the symbol of a traditional unity between man and the world that is
being increasingly destroyed by modern technology and industrialism. As
McCarthy portrays it, West Texas, once one of the last bastions of traditional
pastoralism in America, has become a wasteland of oil derricks.

Like McMurtry's earlier work, McCarthy's 1992 National Book Award
winner *All the Pretty Horses* begins in a depressed West Texas in the immediate aftermath of World War II. Its protagonist, John Grady Cole, is sixteen
years old and very much alone in the world. His father is separated from his
mother and is slowly dying from a condition incurred in a prison camp during
the war. Cole's grandfather is a rancher and Cole himself, loving horses and
ranching, would like nothing better than to continue the ranch, but the old
man dies and Cole's mother plans to sell the family ranch and leave the area.
To continue the work he loves, Cole crosses the border into Mexico with a
young friend, and the two find work on a large hacienda where the traditional
work with horses and cattle is still carried on.

This momentary recovery of paradise is disrupted, however, when Cole
falls desperately in love with the daughter of the great hacienda's proprietor.
When she returns his love and the two embark on a passionate affair, her powerful family has Cole wrongfully arrested. After being nearly killed in a Mexican prison, Cole is freed when his lover promises never to see him again. The
last section of the novel deals with Cole's revenge on the corrupt Mexican
policeman who has betrayed him and stolen his horses. Finally, hardened and
matured by his ordeal and deeply saddened by the loss of his love and his
encounters with death, Cole returns to Texas.

The Texas he finds is on the verge of the postwar oil boom that will utterly
destroy the traditional cattle culture, the same process further portrayed by
McMurtry in his series of Thalia novels and the background for television's
popular Western soap opera *Dallas*. While the traditional culture still exists in
the late 1940s on the great haciendas of Mexico, it too is on borrowed time. It
is significant that the wealthy *hacendado* of McCarthy's novel keeps his ranch
more as a hobby than a way of life and uses an airplane to fly back and forth
between the hacienda and his other life in Mexico City.

John Grady Cole is not only a master of horses but something of a vision-ary as well and the story is punctuated by his dreams of an eternal paradise where there are always wild horses holding out hope for man's redemption. "That night as he lay in his cot he could hear music from the house and as he was drifting to sleep his thoughts were of horses and of the open country and of horses. Horses still wild on the mesa who'd never seen a man afoot and who knew nothing of him or his life yet in whose souls he would come to reside forever" (117-18).

One of the most striking moments in the novel comes in a conversation between Cole, his young friend Rawlins, and an old man who symbolizes the traditional wisdom of the world of natural work. It is this old man who ex-presses most clearly the full spiritual significance of horses in this traditional vision of the world:

> Finally he said that among men there was no such communion as among horses and the notion that man can be understood at all was probably an illusion. Rawlins asked him in his bad spanish if there was a heaven for horses but he shook his head and said that a horse had no need of heaven. Finally John Grady asked him if it were not true that should all horses vanish from the face of the earth the soul of the horse would not also perish for there would be nothing out of which to replenish it but the old man only said that it was pointless to speak of there being no horses in the world for God would not permit such a thing. [111]

The most important thing John Grady Cole must learn in the process of his initiation into mature life is the hardest for him to accept: that such a world no longer exists for him. The Mexican hacienda is for him a Paradise Lost. Even in Mexico, the modern world of politics and revolution, technology and cities is eroding and destroying the traditions of the countryside, while in the Texas to which he must return, the only vestiges of the traditional world of man and nature are in the few remaining Indian encampments in the midst of the oil fields:

> In four days' riding he crossed the Pecos at Iraan Texas and rode up out of the river breaks where the pumpjacks in the Yates Field ranged against the skyline rose and dipped like mechanical birds. Like great primitive birds welded up out of iron by hearsay in a land perhaps where such birds once had been. At that time there were still indians camped on the western plains and late in the day he passed in his riding a scattered group of their wickiups propped upon that scoured and trembling waste. They were perhaps a quarter mile to the north, just huts made from poles and brush with a few goathides draped across them. The indians stood watching him. He could see that none of them spoke among

themselves or commented on his riding there nor did they raise a hand in greeting or call out to him. They had no curiosity about him at all. As if they knew all that they needed to know. They stood and watched him pass and watched him vanish upon that landscape solely because he was passing. Solely because he could vanish. [301]

In this profoundly elegiac conclusion McCarthy evokes that mythical Western scene of the hero riding off into the sunset, but for John Grady Cole there is no more mythical world to cross over into, there is only "the darkening land, the world to come" (302).

The Crossing, second volume of the Border Trilogy, tells a story that has many similarities to *All the Pretty Horses*. It too involves the heroic quest of a young man who seeks something he never fully understands and, in the end, discovers truths that he might prefer not to know. In fact, the hero of *The Crossing* makes three crossings into the mysterious world of Mexico, each of successively greater difficulty and risk. What he finally discovers is that life is always full of grief and evil and that perhaps the most one can hope for is to survive the night in order to struggle once again and unsuccessfully to seize the day. McCarthy's West is the world, and the true secret of the world is that it does not get any better. McCarthy's vision is as apocalyptic in its way as that of such Native American writers as Leslie Silko, though McCarthy sees only a darkening wasteland, where Silko imagines the ultimate restoration of the land through an ecological catastrophe of modern technological civilization and a return of tribal cultures.

Since the Border Trilogy is not yet complete, it is hazardous to guess where it will all come out.[6] However, there is a deep consistency throughout McCarthy's work, in spite of the dazzling changes between his "Southern" and his "Western" fiction. What haunts McCarthy as a storyteller is the way in which modern man is thrust into the world without much that he can depend on and is driven by a deep sense of frustration at being born too late for the past to be any kind of guide to action, security, and fulfillment. His desperate quest for truth and understanding is inevitably frustrated, and all the wisdom he learns cannot guarantee him anything beyond the moment in which he is alive. His heroes learn that all quests are futile, but that they have no choice but to continue their search through a world that is becoming progressively more complicated, more cruel, and more chaotic.

Cormac McCarthy links the new Western literature with that of the South through his increasing sense of the failure of white American civilization and its inescapable burden of guilt. The guilt comes from its destruction of nature and its tragic heritage of human waste represented by the extermination of great traditional cultures and by the pervasive racism of modern America. Other contemporary literary explorations of the history and culture of the South and the West, regions which were once so important as sources of romantic myths of otherness in American culture, have also produced compelling reevaluations of the basic myths of American exceptionalism and superiority and powerful critiques of the multiple failures of the American dream. It is striking, though perhaps not surprising, that these deeply critical literary movements have emerged almost simultaneously with a new surge of political conservatism and fundamentalism in America, also centered in the South and the West and seeking to manipulate the same symbolic and ideological traditions for their own very different purposes. As many commentators have noted, Ronald Reagan tried to reenact the Western myth of the shootout between the heroic marshall and the outlaw on the national and international scenes. The new breed of Southern Republicans who have recently become so important in American politics has found that a traditional Southern rhetoric of states rights, less government, family values, localism, and even a coded white supremacy skillfully disguised as opposition to affirmative action has proved highly effective on the national scene. These reactions are almost antithetical to those of serious contemporary Southern and Western writers, but they are probably different responses to the same uncertainties that have beset America in the last quarter of the twentieth century: a profound loss of confidence in America's uniqueness, moral superiority, and global omnipotence. In the context of this ongoing spiritual crisis, the South and the West, which once helped define America mythically and symbolically through their otherness, are now being pursued by both intellectual critics and conservative fundamentalists as symbols of the real truth of America.

NOTES

1. Passages like the following clearly reflect the influence of Joyce's method of amassing incredibly detailed catalogues of the people and things that haunt the Dublin streets:

Every other face goitered, twisted, tubered with some excresence. Teeth black with rot, eyes rheumed and vacuous. Dour and diminutive people framed by paper cones of blossoms, hawkers of esoteric wares, curious electuaries ordered up in jars and elixirs decocted in the moon's dark. He went by stacks of crated pullets, plump hares with ruby eyes. Butter tubbed in ice and brown or alabaster eggs in ordered rows. Along by the meatcounters shuffling up flies out of the bloodstained sawdust. Where a calf's head rested pink and scalded on a tray and butchers honed their knives. [*Suttree* 67]

In spite of the Joycean model, McCarthy imparts his own distinctive aura to the scene.

2. Perhaps there's some hint of James Agee's nostalgically beautiful "Knoxville: Summer, 1915," that haunting evocation of a bygone way of life from *A Death in the Family*, in McCarthy's Knoxville of the 1950s.

3. Cf. John Shelton Reed, *The Enduring South: Subcultural Persistence in Mass Society* (Lexington, Mass.: Lexington Books, 1972). Also Clyde N. Wilson, ed., *Why the South Will Survive by Fifteen Southerners* (Athens: U of Georgia P, 1981).

4. The protagonist of *Blood Meridian* leaves Tennessee at the age of fourteen, about the same age Huck was when he decided to go down the river and then to run off to the "territory." The Southwest where the kid goes might well be an extension of the "territory" and the historical period is the same, the 1840s. The kid is a Huck-like innocent who encounters a world of terrible violence and corruption and grotesque characters Twain would surely have appreciated. But this is the West as well, and the theme identified by Michael Herr as "regeneration through violence" is precisely the mythos that Richard Slotkin characterizes as the dominant theme of the myth of the frontier. I'm not sure, however, that there's much regeneration in *Blood Meridian*. Rather, the book lives up to its subtitle, *The Evening Redness in the West*. (Michael Herr's comment is quoted on the cover of the paperback edition of *Blood Meridian*. Slotkin's important three-volume analysis of the myth of the frontier began with *Regeneration through Violence* [Middletown, Conn.: Wesleyan UP, 1973].)

5. It's pretty clear that *Blood Meridian* is also, like such sunnier post-Westerns as Thomas Berger's *Little Big Man*, a tacit commentary on the American invasion of Vietnam.

6. Rumor has it that the third volume tentatively titled *Cities of the Plain* will appear in the near future.

Alice Walker

The Color Purple as Allegory

WINIFRED MORGAN

Since the 1982 publication of *The Color Purple*, Alice Walker has continued to publish essays, poetry, and fiction. She has also maintained a high profile in news media for her role in spearheading a campaign against the primarily African practice of female genital mutilation, clitorectomy. Regardless of these accomplishments, Walker remains best known for *The Color Purple*. Since its publication, buoyed up by the enthusiastic support of feminists and black studies departments, the novel has enjoyed considerable success. This was true both before and after Stephen Spielberg's cinematic revisioning of the novel.[1] Walker's novel certainly has appealing qualities which generally sell—strongly drawn characters, a sense that these characters embody the experience of many people, memorable contrasts between the oppressors and oppressed, a downtrodden central character who overcomes both horrendous abuse and deprivation to bloom into a strong person, and, above all, an optimistic, some say a fairy-tale, ending.

Whether they praise or condemn the novel, few readers react with less than passion to Alice Walker's *The Color Purple*. The considerable critical disagreement which has developed about the novel reflects these emotional responses. Beginning with the novel's publication and continuing through the 1985 premiere of the film version, one group of reviewers and critics has lavished praise even as others have questioned both the novel's and the film's artistic validity, particularly their verisimilitude, and their depiction of black men.[2]

From the first reviews to the most current criticism, writers have analyzed, adulated, and excoriated the novel's structure. A number of scholars, with a glance toward Terry Eagleton's comments on the epistolary novel in *The Rape of Clarissa*, have concentrated on Walker's use of letters. Most (for example, Gates) find the choice fortuitous, allowing Walker to move beyond the limitations of first-person narration while still encouraging readers to identify with the central character. Most critics also find Nettie's letters the least satisfying part of the novel.[3] A few critics (for example, Katz and Heraldson, in Bloom) enjoy the use Walker makes of this inherently didactic form usually associated with eighteenth-century tomes. They believe that Walker uses this traditional, even old-fashioned form, to overturn expectations of traditional social structures.

Still other writers have placed the novel in the existential tradition (Christophe) and that of the parable (Scholl). Yet the most obvious tradition that the novel belongs to beyond that of the epistolary novel is that of the slave narrative. The common narrative pattern encountered in slave narratives—an innately good, morally superior person is unjustly confined and maltreated by a corrupt individual; through heroic efforts, the victim escapes and lives to tell the tale and to work against the evil institution—continues to influence African-American literature almost a century and a half after the legal abolition of chattel slavery in the United States.[4] In fact, Walker's echoing of that form[5] accounts for a good deal of the angry reaction to the novel since black men, accustomed to seeing themselves vindicated in African-American literature, encounter little vindication in this novel.

Although critics have made much of the tie between *The Color Purple* and the slave-narrative tradition, concentrating on the similarities between the form of this novel and that of slave narratives may distract critics from the novel's allegorical possibilities, what Hernton refers to an "ironic analogy" between racism and sexism. A traditional definition reminds students that allegory is

> a form of extended METAPHOR in which objects, persons and actions in a NARRATIVE are equated with meanings that lie outside the NARRATIVE itself. . . . *Allegory* attempts to evoke a dual interest, one in the events, characters, and settings presented, and the other in the ideas they are intended to convey or the significance they bear. The characters, events, and settings may be historical, fictitious,

or fabulous; *the test is that these materials be so employed that they represent meanings independent of the action described in the surface story.* [Harmon and Holman 12; my italics in the last clause]

With this novel, Alice Walker joins other late-twentieth-century feminists in building up, and on, an allegorical construct which personifies the traditional gender roles of woman as constituting slavery.[6] In fact, Kathleen Barry even equates domestic abuse and incest with slavery: *"Female sexual slavery is present in ALL situations where women or girls cannot change the immediate conditions of their existence; where regardless of how they got into those conditions they cannot get out; and where they are subject to sexual violence and exploitation"* (40; Barry's italics and caps).

Not only does the novel play upon the form of traditional slave narratives, as an allegory *The Color Purple* provides a devastating critique not only of racism but also of the sexism that has doubled the burden of those women whom Zora Neale Hurston has one of her characters call the "mules of men."[7] Furthermore, the novel speaks against all forms of oppression. Readers do not have to be poor, black, ugly, unable to cook, or female to feel its central character's plight.

A striking allegorical representation of a kind of continuing slavery occurs in *The Color Purple*. Unnerving similarities exist between Celie's twentieth-century existence in the early part of the novel and that of her slave ancestors and other black women's lives under slavery. Before the novel opens, Celie's birthright has been stolen as her stepfather, Alphonso, has usurped her inheritance. If, as a sage in one of the medieval Spanish *ejemplos* argues, stealing is "the greatest villainy," then that is what has been practiced against Celie. Not only has her stepfather taken over her inheritance, his physical and sexual abuse have almost obliterated her sense of self. Hence, when fourteen-year-old Celie attempts to write her first "letter to God," her second sentence begins with a false start as she crosses out "I am." The adolescent Celie's rape by the man she believes is her father parallels the rape of slave women whom plantation theory considered "children" of the patriarchal owner. In common with generations of slave women, Celie then has her infant daughter and son taken from her. Her stepfather tells her that they are dead when, in fact, he has given — perhaps sold — them to a childless couple.

Five or six years later, when he hopes to unleash his sexual abuse on her younger sister, Nettie, Alfonso connives to get rid of Celie by having a neighbor, Mr. _____, a widower with four children, marry her. During their negotiations, Alfonso's description, "she ain't fresh," identifies Celie with milk-producing animals, and the way he makes her turn around for Mr. _____ to examine her body recalls the way slave women were bought and sold. Like them, Celie is handed on to Mr. _____ for reasons slave women were bought—their ability to endure hard physical labor and their potential as sexual objects.

In common with her ancestors, Celie is lied to and lied about. In fact, her stepfather tells Mr. _____ that "She tell lies" (10). Until Celie finally breaks loose from Mr. _____—whom she refuses to, perhaps dare not, call by his first name, Albert—she is almost constantly abused and intimidated by him. Celie spends her first day of married life fleeing Mr. _____'s twelve-year-old son, who nonetheless manages to wound her in her head with the rock he throws at her. She then cooks dinner under primitive conditions and untangles the long-neglected hair of Mr. _____'s little daughters. When night comes, she spends her time thinking about her sister, Nettie, and Shug Avery while Mr. _____ is "on top" (13) of her. Mr. _____, it quickly turns out, is a brute who alternates between beating her and beating his children (22). Living with Mr. _____'s brutality, Celie inures herself to maltreatment and tells herself she is a "tree" (22). "I don't say nothing. . . . What good it do? I don't fight, I stay where I'm told. But I'm alive" (21). Celie lacks power and skill. All she can do is survive and persevere. All she retains of ego is her "voice," and in the presence of her masters, that she keeps silent.

The stories of the other black women in the novel provide variations on Celie's story. They also serve as catalysts. As a matter of fact, from the first mention of Sophie twenty pages into the novel, Celie's existence *starts* to improve—if only because she has someone to talk to. The intersection of the other women's lives with that of Celie allows her for the first time to envision other possibilities. First Sophie, then Shug, but even Mary Agnes (Squeak) and Nettie move from being dominated to liberated. Each of them starts out "freer" than Celie, but none travels quite as far as she. As Shug comments to Mr. _____'s brother, Tobias, "All women's not alike" (52).

The Color Purple looks at what the dynamics of power between men and women, and particularly between some black men and women, currently achieve. The novel finds them so appalling that they evoke the image of conditions under slavery. No other image has quite the same potential for inciting horror, repulsion, and anger among African-Americans. Having raised this dreadful specter and dramatized the similarities between slavery and patriarchy, the novel, in effect, asks, "Can men and women find 'another way' of dealing with one another? What might this new dynamic look like? How might it come about?" The novel then pictures a world in which such new relationships might unfold. The novel's allegory implies that if such changes and new relationships could occur in the life of the downtrodden, humanly almost obliterated Celie, surely a new life with different alternatives could be possible for anyone.

In a sense each person's life, even that of a single cell, recapitulates that of the entire race. Yet Celie's experience in the first two-thirds of Alice Walker's *The Color Purple*—until she leaves Mr._____ and moves to Memphis with Shug and Grady—has such specific parallels with the experiences of slave women that the novel emerges as an allegory of the black woman's experience of slavery in America. Calvin Hernton labels the novel "an emulation of the slave narrative" (3). But as an allegory, and not merely a novel utilizing "a classical (primal) literary genre" (Hernton 3), the novel becomes an even stronger statement of the parallels between the domestic slavery found in some homes and marriages and the situation of black women under the system of chattel slavery existing in the United States before the Civil War. Although he never actually uses the word *allegory,* Hernton does interpret the novel as an allegory of patriarchy (13-14). Celie's declaration of independence from Mr._____ contrasts with her earlier comment that "I don't fight. . . . But I'm alive" and echoes what is probably the best known epiphany found in the slave narrative genre, Douglass's insight into Covey's tyrannous reign (Douglass 81).[8] When Celie turns on Mr. _____ and challenges him with the warning that "Anything you do to me, already done to you. . . . I'm pore, I'm black, I may be ugly and can't cook. . . . But I'm here" (176), she changes her life dramatically. "What women want" is respect. But then that is what all human beings want and need. The ending of the novel projects "what might be" if men and women respected one another.

One wonders whether the novel's allegorical message helps to explain its popularity, which took even Walker by surprise. Readers respond to this novel at an emotional level, suggesting that something is influencing them at a subliminal as well as a conscious level. One explanation might be that in *The Color Purple,* Walker has written an apparently realistic novel that also functions as an allegory of the slave woman's experience. But since the story does not, after all, take place during slavery times, readers are left with the impression that for some black women, at least, their condition after slavery hardly changed. Orlando Patterson's definition of slavery resonates with a chilling familiarity when one thinks about Celie's situation at the opening of the novel. As Patterson explains, "on the level of personal relations . . . *slavery is the permanent, violent domination of natally alienated and generally dishonored persons*" (13).[9] Although not born a slave, as the novel opens, for all practical intents and purposes, Celie is a slave.

One has to ask "Why has the condition of women like Celie changed so little?" Many people respond that racism alone does not explain this fact. Both the excitement and the outrage that the novel has generated are understandable, even to be expected, when one realizes that inadvertently or not, the novel lends itself to an allegorical interpretation explicating the lives of many poor black women both during and after slave times. The fragmented, epistolary, almost inchoate early part of the novel also deflects readers from suspecting that Walker might be using a seemingly outdated technique like allegory. By setting the novel in the not-too-distant past, Walker makes clear that slavery did not end with the Emancipation Proclamation nor even with the end of the American Civil War. Nor—despite the novel's apparently happy ending—does slavery end until people grow into an appreciation of themselves within a human community. Celie's story starts in slavery but goes on to suggest not so much how slave women of the antebellum period could choose to be free (they could not) as how those who continue to suffer a kind of slavery might participate in their own emancipation.

The central narrative in *The Color Purple* certainly works as an allegory, and the allegorical nature of the novel may help to explain why critics delight in finding multiple interpretations. It mimics aspects of the slave-narrative pattern because it harks back to a defining experience in African-American culture: the unavoidable historical fact of chattel slavery. But Walker seems to use that experience as a foil or mirror, forcing her readers to acknowledge the equally formative experience of sexism under patriarchy.[10]

Unlike the "temptation" which C.S. Lewis warns readers to avoid lest they attend to an allegory's larger meaning to the detriment of its poetry, to find allegory in *The Color Purple* in no way encourages readers to attend to an intellectual abstraction or any other kind of construct in preference to the novel's verisimilitude. On the contrary, most readers are far more likely to get so caught up in the fiction's highly charged details that they ignore any larger significance. Yet, in fiction as in poetry, "the more concrete and vital the [work] is, the more hopelessly complicated it will become in analysis: but the imagination receives it as a simple—in both senses of the word" (Lewis 345).

Yet the critical reaction to *The Color Purple* illustrates that, however easy it is to summarize its plot, the novel is not simple. That Walker should have produced a work with allegorical overtones flows organically from her rural Southern upbringing in which the tradition of African-American religious music has always spoken symbolically. Allegory works through symbols, and as Don Cameron Allen reminds readers, symbols allow communication that is larger than simple reality. "It is also the nature of the symbol to communicate to others those intuitions which seize us" (Swann and Krupat 566). The emotional reaction to the novel seems to suggest that many readers have felt that it speaks to their intuitions. Allegory, according to Angus Fletcher, has been "omnipresent in Western literature" as long as there has been such an entity, and often the surface of an allegorical tale works perfectly well by itself but achieves greater depth with interpretation. In any case, allegory serves to get past defenses, to speak to those intuitions of which Allen speaks, intuitions that might otherwise be repressed.

By its nature allegory is open to interpretation. Since readers respond to a piece of literature and interpret it according to individual experiences, not surprisingly, contemporary readers do indeed find *The Color Purple* a "moral tale" as Walker originally subtitled the novel. While, *of course,* the novel reflects the experience of only a portion of black women, enough of them relate to the central character's vicissitudes that, for example, during the movie's showing in some theaters, black women's voices sang out their encouragement of Celie. On the one hand, many African-American women could reasonably interpret *The Color Purple* as an allegory of both the racial and sexual oppression that black women have endured during and since slavery. Many white women, on the other hand, respond to the novel as a "womanist" (with its emphasis on choosing a course of action rather than accepting one's fate as biologically predetermined) allegory. Anyone can read the novel as an allegory of every human being's need for respect.

The novel's most adamant critics have objected to its supposed lack of realism and what they insist are vicious stereotypes of black men. But if *The Color Purple* is allegorical, the criticism of the novel as a fairy tale or unrealistic or improbable loses some of its validity. *The Color Purple* is about reclaiming one's history, gifts, inheritance, language, skills, song, and voice—and thereby throwing off the yoke of slavery. Though the action in the early part of the novel closely parallels that of black women under slavery, the novel's conclusion has moved far beyond that. Questions both about whether it is unfair that some black men are depicted as violent and whether the story achieves adequate historical accuracy are beside the point. As an allegory, the novel does not have these as primary concerns. In any case, why cannot the story of a poor black woman's liberation also help to set free others of both sexes, all classes, and all races?

NOTES

1. The movie subtly alters and even subverts some of the novel's feminism, but that's another essay. As Jacqueline Bobo reminds readers, "the film is a commercial venture produced in Hollywood by a white male according to all of the tenets and conventions of commercial cultural production in the United States" ("Cultural Readers" 93).

2. See, for example, Bartelme, Baumgaertner, Bovoso, Graham, Heyward, Hiers, Kelley, Pinckney, Prescott, Dinita Smith, Tickle, Towers, and Watkins.

3. See, for example, Barbara Christian's comments in an early essay on Walker (in Evans 470).

4. During the early 1990s, William L. Andrews led NEH Summer Seminars at

the University of Kansas exploring how this tradition functions in African-American literature. I was fortunate to be part of the 1991 seminar.

5. The assumption that *The Color Purple* echoes the slave narrative is so common as to be almost a truism. See, for example, Awkward and Hernton.

6. This is, of course, hardly a new connection, since radical eighteenth-century feminists insisted on the same similarities. More recently, Kari Winter's *Subjects of Slavery, Agents of Change* delineates some of the parallel strategies utilized by women slave narrators and women writers of gothic fiction. Winter's book also carefully delineates the limits of the rhetoric linking women under slavery and other, for the most part, less harsh patriarchal forms of domination.

7. In *Their Eyes Were Watching God*, Janie's grandmother gives this warning to the still youthful, romantic central character.

8. This is, of course, the section of Douglass's autobiography where he determines to fight back. In an extended brawl he beats the bully Covey; and years later, recalling his insight from that experience, Douglass muses that "I now resolved that, however long I might remain a slave in form, the day had passed forever when I could be a slave in fact. I did not hesitate to let it be known of me, that the white man who expected to succeed in whipping, must also succeed in killing me" (81).

9. In David Brion Davis's explanation, "the slave has three defining characteristics: his [sic] person is the property of another man, his will is subject to his owner's authority, and his labor or services are obtained through coercion." Without irony, Davis goes on to note that "various writers have added that slavery must be 'beyond the limits of the family relations'"(31).

10. Michael Awkward explores what he believes is Walker's conscious construction in *The Color Purple* of a tale about black women's creativity in order to counter false images developed over the years in the fiction of black men. Her portrayal, even if a "dream" or "utopian," nonetheless offers a picture of what a black community that had advanced beyond patriarchy might look like (163-64).

Fred
Chappell

Midquestions

Randolph Paul Runyon

Born in western North Carolina, in 1936, Fred Chappell has drawn increasingly on his Appalachian heritage in recent years. His best works—the epic poem *Midquest* (1981) and the novel *I Am One of You Forever* (1985)—are rooted in a quasi-autobiographical network of recurring hill-country characters, including his parents and grandparents, various eccentric uncles, and general-store proprietor Virgil Campbell, whose prankish independence harks back to Sut Lovingood but whose first name has a deserved Old World resonance.

This is particularly true in *Midquest*, which takes place in the Dantean middle of the protagonist's life, his thirty-fifth birthday (as well as Fred Chappell's), and where Virgil is, if not guide, at least a constant presence. The poem is actually four books of eleven poems each in which "the first poem is mirrored by the last," according to Chappell in the Preface, "the second by the next to last, and so on inward. But the sixth poem in each volume is companionless in that volume, and concerned with a garrulous old gentleman named Virgil Campbell, who is supposed to give to the whole its specifically regional, its Appalachian, context" (ix-x). As David Paul Ragan has pointed out, however, this is somewhat "misleading" in its implication "that the regional context is conveyed primarily through [the Campbell poems] alone"

185

(22). For plenty of the other poems in *Midquest* provide that regional context, too.

More troubling is Chappell's misleading the reader in the matter of the placement of the Virgil poems. Of the four volumes in the poem—*River, Bloodfire, Wind Mountain,* and *Earthsleep*—of only the first and last is it true that "the sixth poem is . . . concerned with . . . Virgil Campbell." The Virgil poem in *Bloodfire,* "Firewater," is the seventh poem; in *Wind Mountain* it is the eighth, "Three Sheets in the Wind"—a circumstance that is not immediately apparent in the table of contents, which does not display subtitles. If it had, such a misstatement could hardly have escaped notice, for the poem's full title is "Three Sheets in the Wind: Virgil Campbell Confesses."[1] If the Preface is wrong in this particular, can we believe what else it says?

It is unusual for a poet to go to such trouble to detail the hidden architecture of his text. In the case of Fred Chappell it may even be a little suspicious. For in an essay first published in 1989, eight years after *Midquest,* he wrote in not entirely approving tones of the "modern epic poet" who "shall tell us" that his poem "'has a secret structure that is hidden by its bewildering surface.' Then he proceeds to point out to us"—as did Chappell himself—

> arcane principles of structure, unnoticed axioms of organization, subterranean networks of relationships, correspondences, and associations. And so it turns out that this object which has appeared to be so haphazard and patchwork can actually be clarified with a diagram. Aren't we all now reassured of the poet's sanity?
>
> Perhaps we are. Perhaps not. For it is a wild connect-the-dots scheme, this construction of the contemporary epic. [*Plow Naked* 89]

What kind of modern epic poem is he talking about? He goes on to allude to Pound's *Cantos,* Williams's *Paterson,* Olson's *Maximus Poems,* Zukovsky's *A,* and Crane's *The Bridge.* But is he also talking about *Midquest*? Perhaps not. Instead of "patchwork," the model his Preface claims is the "sampler," a display of fancy stitches: terza rima, tetrameter, rhymed couplets, chant royal, among others. Yet that refers not to the possible symmetrical relation of the poems to each other on the grounds of theme and language but to their various forms.

A more fitting description may be the "crazy-quilt" of the flesh of Dr. Frankenstein's creation in *Bloodfire*'s ninth poem, "Burning the Frankenstein Monster" (85). Particularly because this "innocent wistful crazy-quilt of dead flesh" in the Frankenstein poem seems to participate in the "balancing act" Chappell claims is going on in *Midquest,* an element in the mirroring that poem does of its symmetrical companion, "My Father Allergic to Fire," the third poem in *Bloodfire.* The Frankenstein monster was unnaturally afraid of fire: "Why must poor Karloff . . . die, fire-fearing, / In the fire?" (85). Fred's father, despite the title, is allergic to only "One kind of fire." The Klan's burn-ing crosses make him vomit. When he was nine, he spied on a Klan meeting, was caught, and forced to join. They took matches and heated a pocket knife to burn a cross onto his shoulder. In recounting this episode, he "Peeled back" his clothes to show the cross to his son, who found he couldn't see it. "I stared into my father's skin. / A little pimple in a square of gray-pink flesh. / . . . no cross at all. / 'Can't you see it?' He pleaded like a child. // My father's innocent shoulder I almost kissed" (64). Fred subsequently yields to his father's desire and lies, saying that he can see the cross, though it's "awfully small." His father is relieved, for it loomed so large in his memory that it had to be there. If the reader of *Midquest*, mindful of the Preface's promise, stares at these two po-ems long enough, something will indeed appear: the father's "innocent" "flesh" will reappear, as if in a mirror, in the "innocent . . . flesh" of the "crazy-quilt" of which the monster was made.

In "Burning the Frankenstein Monster," Chappell increases the mirror-ing effect by drawing out the father-son relationship between creator and mon-ster, thus recalling the father-son situation grounding "My Father Allergic to Fire": Dr. Frankenstein "has fathered / A son" (86). Creator and created are "Father and son, with one instant of recognition between them." Fred's not being able to see the cross but saying he could might be termed a sort of false recognition. In another echo, in "My Father Allergic to Fire," the father "*Peeled back* two layers / Of undershirt" (64) to bare his shoulder, while Fred's "vividest memory" of the Frankenstein film is the scene where the monster first sees sunlight, "pouring / Through the roof *peeled back* little by little, at last" (85).

This echoing effect is self-referential, and in an unsettling way. Fred fibbed when he told his father he could see the cross. Chappell, similarly, is not quite truthful when he tells us that the sixth poem will always be about Virgil Campbell. Is he telling the truth when he speaks of the mirroring effect of the poems? They certainly mirror in this instance, but we find ourselves in the very act of looking for evidence of it curiously foreshadowed by the poet's per-sona in "My Father Allergic to Fire." Is Chappell drawing us into such a situa-tion only to then suggest that we would be as untruthful as the son if we said we could see it?

To answer that question it might help to determine if the mirror effect is at work elsewhere, even though to do that might still be to play Chappell's game, even to fall victim to what may be a "rusty" on his part. But let's see where it takes us anyway. Consider "Firewood" and "Firewater," the fifth and seventh poems in *Bloodfire*. In "Firewood," Fred is chopping at a particularly difficult piece of oak, "blow on blow not yielding at all until / 28 strokes tear a jag / of shadow-lightning across the grooved / round top." Coincidence or not, this is the sixteenth of the forty-four poems in *Midquest* (which is divided into four books of eleven poems each), which means there are as many left as the number of strokes it will take to make a tear in the log. "Numbers," Chappell writes in the Preface, "are obviously important in the poem" (ix).[2] Are they important enough for there to be an allegorical parallel between the reader's hacking at *Midquest* to open up its secret (by rereading it over and over to find the promised mirror echoes, for instance) and the poet's chopping away at the oak?

Fred wields his ax to find what secret the wood will disclose, but discovers that its secret was already laid bare. The wood "at last torn open shows that all the secret / was merely the hardness itself" (68). A log is text, or at least texture: "there is I tell you in the texture of this log that / which taunts the mind." But in the end "nothing happens except that matter retains its smirking / hardness & just sits there" (72).

This smirking and sitting is mirrored in the tale Virgil Campbell tells in "Firewater." Big Mama, a notorious but never apprehended moonshiner, is invited to parade a model still down Main Street for the Hayesville centennial. "Sitting on a rocking chair on a wagon" and "Grinning grinning grinning," she waves to the deputy sheriff. For this is no pretend still, but a real one, "smoke just boiling out / Pretty as you please" and disabling the mule in the wagon behind, who passes out dead drunk from the fumes (79). Like the log displaying its secret that is no secret at all and that "smirking . . . just sits there," Big Mama sits in her chair "Rocking and grinning and rocking." For ten years the authorities had been trying to catch her at her trade, but they had not expected that she would respond to their invitation so literally. Yet she was breaking the law. The deputy stepped forward to announce that she was under arrest. Her sons then "stood up . . . / And threw down on the deputy three shotguns" (79). "Firewood" appropriately supplies the right term for such an impasse: "Mexican stand off is the closest you'll get," matter in the form of a near-impenetrable walnut log tells Fred (72).

Verbal echoes reveal that numerous elements of one poem have their counterparts in the other. "A cat would've by God laughed" in "Firewater" to see Big Mama still in action under the deputy's nose (79). Feline reaction to the main event is foreshadowed in the first line of "Firewood," where "the cat is scared" by the fury with which Fred attacks the log (67). Near the end, Fred rests from his near-futile labor: "it could go / on like this forever since it forever has, better take / a moment's cigarette" (73). Similarly, at the end of "Firewater" Big Mama forsakes the moonshine business ("Ain't no profit in it" any more) for cigarettes: "Growing these Merry Widow cigarettes, / That's where they make their money" (80). "I will sit on this log & breathe bluegray smoke," Fred says in "Firewood," anticipating this time the mule that followed Big

Mama's wagon: "Drunk as an owl, / Just from breathing the smoke that was pouring out / From Big Mama's *model* still" (79; italics in original).

Fred muses about finding "our unguessable double" in the heart of the log, not realizing that Chappell leads his readers, along the trail running from the Preface's remarks about mirror effects to such examples of it as these, to guess that his double may be an inebriated mule.

In the mirror effect "Susan Bathing" and "My Grandfather Gets Doused" (poems V and VII in *River*, to adopt Chappell's roman numeral numbering system) enact, one finds Fred's wife's double in the water that baptized his grandfather, and the doubling effect finds another self-referential description in the form of recycled Lucretian atoms. Fred imagines Susan's body "remaining yet sailed / away on streams on streams of atoms into the winds . . . sweetening now zephyrs / by Bermuda & Mykonos" (22), while the grandfather, repenting of having undergone a Baptist immersion in the waters of West Fork Pigeon River, is consoled by the thought that "The water that saved him was some place / Else now, washing away the sins / Of trout down past McKinnon Trace. // . . . 'What damn difference / Will it make?'" (33). Like the streams of atoms that make up Susan and the stream itself, atoms from one poem are "some place / Else now" (in fact, *now* itself is just such an atom, having first appeared in "sweetening now zephyrs" but now turning up here), drawn into another poem.

Likewise "a single tear reflecting my chest & face" (21) on the bathing Susan becomes a "double tear" in his grandfather's eye that is also a sign of Fred's presence: "He frowned // When he saw me gaping. A double tear / Bloomed at the rim of his eye" (31). Animals in "Susan Bathing" "go robed churchly in / white" (24) while the baptismal candidate had likewise been "togged . . . out in white" (31). In more general (and thus perhaps less interesting) terms, Susan's immersion in her bath anticipates the grandfather's in the river.

Similarly, the well-scrubbing in "Cleaning the Well" is reflected by the milk can-cleansing in "My Grandmother Washes Her Vessels" in *River* poems IV and VIII, though it is hardly surprising that two paired poems should be about such similar subjects in an eleven-poem sequence devoted to water. More intriguing is the fact that both the well into which the boy is let down by his grandfather and the channel into which his grandmother plunges her vessels reek of mortality. The "*spring*-run" is "a concrete grave" (34), while the deep and chilly hole into which the fearful boy descends is the "well*spring* of death" (16). Coming out at last, his task completed, he feels like "Jonah, Joseph, Lazarus," risen from the dead. With a taste for symmetry, Chappell has the formerly "white sun" of noon (14) turn "Yellow" (17) when the boy emerges an hour after he went in (yellow, and "Thin," it is too cold to warm him up that December day after his brush with chilly death), while just the opposite will happen in the other poem: The "Yellow light" of the August six-o'clock sun "entering / The bone-white milkhouse recharged itself white" (34).

If we went by titles alone, we might have been tempted to say "My Grandmother Washes Her Vessels" would have made a better match with "My Grandmother Washes Her Feet," the third poem in *River*. But, going by the numbers, as Chappell implies we should, that poem is paired with the ninth, "Science Fiction Water Letter to Guy Lillian." The connection arises from what Fred's grandmother tells him about how "We sprouted from dirt" and that he should never forget it. "No Mam," he says, assuring her he won't. "Don't you say me No Mam yet. / Wait till you get your chance to deny it" (12-13). In the letter to Lillian, Fred outlines a projected science fiction novel in which "once upon this earth / Words had not the shape that now they shine in" (41). They lay upon the ground like objects; men had no ears to hear them with, no understanding of their possibility of signification. "The notion / Of *word* had not yet squiggled into being. / But there they were, twitchy to be discovered, / All words that in the world ever were or will." An extraterrestrial woman from Nirvan, "who'd been awarded / Mother of the Year" on that planet, lands on earth, and instructs the first man who comes along in the art of words (42). She takes him to a mountain, tells him this is what *"Water"* is, and the mountain, "Finally collapsing, like jello in an oven, to liquid" (43), becomes it. The man sprouts ears, and words now take on meaning at last, words like "Pomegranate. Baseball. Mouse. / Cadillac. Poem. Paradise. Cinnamon Doughnut." That first man called himself Adam, and Chappell calls his teacher "Our Lovely Mother" (43), as if, despite her origins, she were Eve, mother of us all.

This ultimate grandmother, mother of the human species, recalls Fred's grandmother in the other poem. Not just because she instructs her grandson concerning dirt, but because she does so concerning words. And in particular concerning words whose meaning and appropriate use will only become clear at some later time: she won't let him say "No Mam" to her yet. Later, she lets fall a word Fred doesn't know, and for that word too—like the words in the science fiction novel—its existence as an incomprehensible and unusable entity must long precede its use and comprehension: "'Fatback just won't change to artichokes.' // 'What's artichokes?' // 'Pray Jesus you'll never know. / For if you do it'll be a sign you've grown / Away from what you are'" (12).

The jello that the mountain turns into as it liquefies recalls the "ancestral jelly" (13) into which Fred imagined himself "forcing warm rude fingers," which then sends us back to the other poem to meditate on the role of fingers there: "S-f [science fiction] is / . . . less pleasurable to / the fingers; a deliberate squeamishness obtains" (38). Though he has respect for some practitioners of the genre, and outlines a science fiction novel himself, Fred finds it too sterile. At this point we can start to see the real connection to the other poem. Fred here and his grandmother there are saying, at bottom, the same thing. We are born from dirt and we shouldn't pretend otherwise. "It's not the skeleton" in science fiction and ghost stories "that rattles me, but the flesh— / or want of it." It has the color of blood "but not its taste." Science fiction "has no feel for pastness" (39). The grandmother does, though, and knows that "Just about the time you'll think your blood / Is clean, here will come dirt in a natural shape / You never dreamed" (12). Science fiction is guilty of the willful forgetting of the necessary connection between dirt and life the grandmother warned Fred against.

Elsewhere in *River*, the narrator's ascent to "this hill at midnight" (45) in "On Stillpoint Hill at Midnight" (X) was anticipated by the moon's "Climbing the steep hill of void" (7) "on a midnight full / of stars" (6) in "Birthday 35: Diary Entry" (II). Looking up from the riverbank to the hill the moon illumined, Fred in the latter poem "saw nothing human, / . . . No animals . . . only moon / Upon moon, sterile stone" (7), while in the other poem the opposite takes place as he considers "how stones will burgeon / into animals" (45), given enough geological time. The animals evolving from stone will eventually be "gnawing the ruled streets and lot corners / of suburbs" (45), thus demonstrating that life will emerge despite the present appearance of death, a situation in which the poet includes himself: "(I glow amidst the dead)." In "Birthday 35" gnawing is likewise the sign of life: "this gnawing worm shows that I'm not dead" (5).

Verbal echoes between the first and last (eleventh) in each book are for some reason sparser, though these poems always recount the same situation, the poet in bed with his wife at dawn (though this is less clear in "Wind Subsides on the Earth River," the last poem in *Wind Mountain*, where it is night but not necessarily the end of night). As Chappell points out in the Preface, each of the four books together cover "the same twenty-four hours of the speaker's life" (ix). Only the first and last poems tend to evoke the same hour. As Karen Cherry points out, trees figure in the opening lines of each of the four first poems (117):

Deep morning. Before the trees take silhouettes
    ["The River Awakening in the Sea" (1)]
Morning. / First light shapes the trees
    ["Fire Now Wakening on the River" (55)]
Early half-light, dawnwind driving / The trees
    ["Dawn Wind Unlocks the River Sky" (97)]
The cool deep morning / Begins to fashion the trees
    ["Earth Emergent Drifts the Fire River" (145)]

The first line of the last poem in *River*:

Again. Deep morning. ["The River Seeks Again the Sea" (50)]

recalls the first line of the first:

Deep morning. ["The River Awakening in the Sea" (1)]

And what Fred's forehead does in one his mind does in the other:

My forehead suckles your shoulder [1]
my mind suckles your shoreless lonesomeness. [50]

The first poem of *Bloodfire* continues this theme, recalling the first poem of *River*: "My forehead enters your shoulder" ("Fire Now Wakening on the River" [55]).

Bloodfire's first anticipates its last through poison and sizzle:

Boiled juices of poison oak [56]
the poison / wild cherry [93]
Torn sheet of light sizzles in the mirror [56]
sizzle on the hard / vine ribs [93]

And Orion makes an appearance in both (56, 92).

More worthy of note, or at least more easily interpretable, is the way Baudelaire and Rimbaud, featured players in "Rimbaud Fire Letter to Jim Applewhite" (II), return in "Bloodfire" (X): "Here I turned / Back to the books that nurtured me / When I met evil first, learned / An implacable philosophy" (89). It is a literal turning back that is evoked here, inviting the reader to turn back to what the Preface said would be the companion poem to "Bloodfire," "Rimbaud Fire Letter," where Fred makes it pretty clear that the books that had nurtured him were Rimbaud and Baudelaire. "That decade with Rimbaud I don't regret. / . . . Rimbaud was genius pure; / . . . Kind of a handbook on how to be weird and silly" (58). Baudelaire, in whose *Flowers of Evil* Fred apparently "met evil first," played an important role, too, in those formative years: His high school teachers "stood up for health and truth and light, / I stood up for Baudelaire and me" (59) — Baudelaire, in that formulation, representing a glorification of *le mal* that ran counter to all that health and truth and light.

"Let's don't wind up brilliant, young, and dead" (61), Fred says to Applewhite in the "Rimbaud Fire Letter." Which is exactly what happens to the young man whose fate is recounted in "Bloodfire," who immolates himself in protest against the war in Vietnam. He "never could belong / To another army" (88) than that of the war protesters, while Fred in the other poem tried to enlist in the military, in pre-Vietnam days, but "They turned me down for the army" (60).

In the remaining pair in *Bloodfire* not yet mentioned, the "sickness" and "silver fire" of "Feverscape: The Silver Planet" (IV) find echoes in the episode Fred recounts in "My Father Burns Washington" (VIII) of how his father, "sick" of having to think "of nothing but money" (82) in the depths of the Depression, took out a dollar bill and set it on fire. "Money," the father complains. "It's the death / *Of the world*" (82; emphasis added), recalling the feverish boy's statement in the other poem: "I know well what sickness comes trembling over / the edge *of the world*" (66; emphasis added). Listening at night to his parents, downstairs lamenting their penury, the boy in "My Father Burns Washington" feared that "Money would climb / The stair . . . and, growling, try / The doorknob, enter upon us furiously" (81). Likewise, in the fever of various childhood illnesses, in "Feverscape" he finds his bedroom invaded by the silver planet whose "vast leaping / coronas fingered the medicine space I suffered in" and whose "White tentacles of camphor-smelling flame . . . lashed me" (65, 66).

His father breaks into open revolt against money's oppression. Likewise, Fred in the other poem declares that "Too long we have bared our backs, we / have bent our heads beneath the cruel silver fire" (66). In the context of "Feverscape" alone, it is not clear (at least to this reader) what Fred is talking about here, for the silver planet seems now (at the conclusion of the poem) to mean something significantly broader than the fever-induced hallucination it had been in his childhood. In the context it shares with "My Father Burns Washington," however, a context Chappell's Preface makes licit, it seems that it may have something to do with money. Silver, after all, is money—though not the paper variety that lends itself so well to combustion. "It might have helped if I had known some French," as Fred says in "Rimbaud Fire Letter" (58), a language that makes that equation self-evident.

In elegant self-referential symmetry, a mirror that becomes a window ("The mirror like a burning window" [97]) in the first poem of *Wind Mountain* ("Dawn Wind Unlocks the River Sky") finds its mirror reflection in windows that become mirrors ("reflections of Buicks in supermarket windows" [141]) in the last ("Wind Subsides on the Earth River"). In the next pair, "The weepy *eaves* peep down into the *rooms*" as "Wind and water drive against the windows" (emphasis added) in "The Highest Wind That Ever Blew: Homage to Louis" (II), while the wind and rain in "Hallowind" (X) "tear the ragged *eaves* as if / The world outside weren't *room* enough" (135; emphasis added). In "Second Wind" (III), Fred's grandmother is renewed by a welcome "cooling wind" after the death of her husband, though before it showed itself the day was so "hot and still" that there had been "Not the least little *breath* of air" (103; emphasis added), while in "Remembering Wind Mountain at Sunset" (IX), there is no wind but an ill one, whether it be the one that blows down from Freeze Land in winter or the coal stove wind of summer that hasn't "a *breath* of soothe in it" (132; emphasis added). The wind in "Second Wind" "was the breath of life to me," exclaimed the grandmother (106), while in "Remembering Wind Mountain at Sunset" we find "the wind robbing / them [the poor] of breath" (129). The opposition between the life-restoring wind in one poem and the death-dealing one in the other is internalized in "Remembering Wind Mountain at Sunset" by the realization that "the funny part is, come summer / same wind out of the same place" has the opposite effect from what it had in winter. Then, it went "over you / ice water," but now it "feels like it's pouring out of a coalstove" (131, 132). It is, in other words, another moment of self-reference, the same-yet-opposite quality of the wind in poem IX duplicating, and thus alluding to, the opposite-yet-same quality of the wind that blows through both poems.

Why then should Chappell declare in the Preface that *Wind Mountain* does *not* include such mirror effects as these: "each of the volumes (except *Wind Mountain*) is organized as a balancing act"? "In order to suggest the fluid and disordered nature of air," he says later in the same paragraph, "*Wind Mountain* was exempt from some of these requirements," the requirements just then mentioned being (1) that the poems be symmetrically paired, (2) that the sixth poem be "companionless" and devoted to Virgil Campbell, (3) that the fifth be "given to stream of consciousness," and (4) that each volume be "dominated by a different element of the family" — *River* by the grandparents, *Bloodfire* by the father, and *Earthsleep*, "the part most shadowed by death," constituting a "family reunion." It is just after this sentence that he grants the third volume its exemption "from some of these requirements." But from which ones exactly? From the second to be sure, for Virgil appears there in the eighth poem, not the sixth. But this prompts the question why his is the *seventh* poem in *Bloodfire*, when no such exemption was granted that volume. *Wind Mountain* fulfills the third requirement, its fifth poem, "The Autumn Blast of the Weathervane Trombone," being as much in the stream-of-consciousness genre as "Susan's Morning Dream of Her Garden," the fifth in *Earthsleep*,[3] though not perhaps as Joycean as "Susan Bathing" (in *River*) and "Firewood" (in *Bloodfire*). Evidently he was thinking of the fourth requirement (the one he had most recently mentioned) in alluding to the freedom granted his third volume, for grandparents, mother and father appear with about equal frequency there.

But this does not exempt Chappell from the contradiction between the Preface's description and the reality of his poem with regard to the "balancing

act." The Preface's account of the poem gives rise to more questions than answers, for *Wind Mountain* is in no way exempt from that requirement, as the
two remaining pairs (and the three preceding) show. It obliges the reader who
follows Chappell's implied advice to seek out the mirror echoes to risk discovering that Chappell not only fibbed about what would be found in the middle
of each volume (not more than half the time is it Virgil Campbell) but did so
as well about the structure of *Wind Mountain*.[4]

"My Mother Shoots the Breeze," the fourth poem in that volume, finds
some remarkable reflections in the eighth, "Three Sheets in the Wind: Virgil
Campbell Confesses." Fred's mother tells her son how she first met his father,
who taught science in the high school where she taught languages. He asked
for the loan of her slip so that he could make a kite to demonstrate Ben
Franklin's lightning experiment. For her it was sexually arousing: "my slip, /
Scented the way that I alone could know, / Flying past the windows made me
warm" (108). J.T. went too far, however, flying the kite every day for two weeks.
"It's time to show that man that I mean business." So she borrowed her father's
shotgun and "blew the fool out of it, both barrels. / It floated up and down in a
silk snow / Till there was nothing left. I can still remember / Your Pa's mouth
open." They were married within a month. Sexuality is rampant, too, in "Three
Sheets in the Wind," in which Virgil Campbell confesses how his youthful
indiscretions came to an end when his wife caught him in bed with another
woman. "I leapt out / The window . . . praying that the shooting wouldn't hit
me." But "The wind lifted a sheet" on the backyard clothesline and Virgil fell,
knocked out cold with the sheet wound about him (126). When he came to,
all he could see was whiteness. "It came to me that I was dead—/ She'd shot
my vitals out—and here's the shroud / They buried me in." He tried to claw
his way out, but she had sewn him in and was flailing away with a curtain rod.
"*pow*! Pow pow pow." He thought it was the beginning of the tortures of hell,
prelude to burning oil and pitchforks. The parallels between these poems are
as striking as any in *Midquest*: the slip and the sheet, both lifted up by the
wind; the windows; the shooting; the sexual, and conjugal, context.

In the remaining pair, "The Autumn Bleat of the Weathervane Trombone"
(V) anticipates the Dantean vision of "In Parte Ove Non E Che Luca" (VII),
which begins as a translation of *Inferno*'s fifth canto, by imagining the afterlife
of poets. The "fancy" that comes to Fred as he plays his trombone is that "poets after the loud labor of their lives / Are gathered to the sun," where they
"speak in flame" and "lie a lot" (112). George Garrett will be there, and
Applewhite and Tate and at least eight others. Fred, too, though the thought
gives him pause. "Trapped in a burning eternity with a herd / Of poets, what
kind of fate is that for a handsome / Lad" like him? There are poets too—
Byron and James Dickey—in the "inferno" (121) the other poem describes.

While the solar afterlife in "The Autumn Bleat" is a kind of heaven and this one hell, the poet's paradise is nevertheless "a burning eternity." In the mirror reversal these poems enact, what's positive in one is negative in the other. Fred's trombone-induced fancy leads him to see himself in a falling leaf of tulip poplar as a poet "cast from heaven," the heaven of all those poets in the sun. "It's too much *love of earth* that draws him thither, / . . . *The flesh* the earth it suits me fine" (113; emphasis added). This is precisely reversed (as in a mirror) in the other poem when "Into this pain the *lovers of flesh* are thrust" (122; emphasis added), lovers like Casanova, Byron, and Dickey. The parallel—and the reversal—could hardly be more clearly drawn.

A brief look at the final volume will round out this tour of *Midquest*'s mirrors. While *Earthsleep*'s first and last poems, like those in the preceding three volumes, appear less tightly linked than other pairs in the same volume, a "Tree of Fire" appears in each (150, 186). Both "My Mother's Hard Row to Hoe" (II) and "Stillpoint Hill That Other Shore" (X) speak of fatigue. When the mother was a child her day was filled with such unending farm chores that "It was a numbing torture to carry on." She always obeyed her mother's commands, "no never-mind how tired / I was" (151). In the tenth poem, "our limbs quiver, / exhaustion of stale guilt" (184), and the narrator "is avid for . . . sleep" (185).

In "My Father Washes His Hands" (III), Fred's father would like to wash his hands of farming and of the guilt of having had to break the dead mule's legs to get her to fit in the grave that blue clay made undiggable. "Two feet down we hit pipe clay as blue / And sticky as Buick paint." Nothing but "Blue glue" (153). Blueness becomes an echo internal to the poem when, sad at having broken Honey's legs as her dead eyes stared up at him, "The harder down I dug the bluer I got" (154). In "My Grandfather Dishes the Dirt" (IX), another grave poem, the grandfather speaks from his tomb and gives blueness a connotation the precise opposite of what it had in the other poem when the father got bluer the deeper he dug: "blue May days / Leap out in my grave sleep / Like sun-drunk butterflies" (181). Both Honey's grave and the grandfather's are full of blueness.

The ninth poem's title is somewhat misleading, as the grandfather has no dirt to dish, nothing much to say, except that he's content to remain ("I *like* it here" [italics in original]), awaiting Judgment Day. "Death disinherits / Us of wanting," though it is "kind of lonely" (181, 182) down there. "The dead I'm here to say have nothing to say. / . . . Let's let each other alone, for Jesus' sake" (182). The father in the other poem would have welcomed that sentiment, for, to his dismay, the dead mule has plenty to say and will not leave him alone. "Honey's not gone, / She's in my head for good and all and ever" (155). In her sleep he can "see her pawing up on her broken legs / Out of the blue mud . . .

in her eyes the picture / Of me coming toward her with my mattock; / And talking in a woman's pitiful voice: / *Don't do it, J.T., you're breaking promises*" (italics in original).

The talking mule in "My Father Washes His Hands" is succeeded in the following poem, "The Peaceable Kingdom of Emerald Windows" (IV), by talking horses. "Bay Maude says to Jackson: 'Don't let's stop / At windrow-end, good fellow, I feel the edge / Of the world just barely beyond my hooftip'" (161). Indeed, *Midquest* is probably as rich in sequential echoes as it is in symmetrical ones. Donald Secreast points out, for example, that "Cleaning the Well" is preceded by Bubba Martin managing to fall into the well after shooting himself in "My Grandmother Washes Her Feet," and that "the reflection of the lightbulb on the grandmother's glasses mirrors the two suns which the boy sees as he enters the well" (41).

The horses' conversation is part of a symmetrical echo as well, however, for in "My Grandmother's Dream of Plowing" (VIII) we again encounter "Jackson and Maude whose heads went up and down / Like they agreed on what they were talking over" (178). In the grandmother's dream the horses' plow uncovers what appears to be "a big and shining lump of gold." They'd never have to worry about money again. Then she hears her husband's voice behind her: "*Is that your baby that was never mine?*" (italics in original). She looks again and it *is* a baby, "And this gold child was / Speaking to me. . . . / Except I couldn't hear" (179). And then it turns into a goblin. She found herself wishing it would die, and it does. It "sighed a sigh, and lay in my arms stone dead. / / . . . It turned into a stone, / And it was all my fault, wishing that way" (180). She wept. "And then you woke up," her grandson tells her. "'And now I know,' she said, 'I never woke.'" It's quite a nightmare, suggesting a whole other side to Fred's grandmother. As Dabney Stuart writes, "the revelation of this buried secret from her past casts a sharp light on her preoccupation in the previous poems about her with the 'Shadow Cousins'"—in "My Grandmother Washes Her Feet" (12)—"the profound hesitation she experienced before committing herself to marrying Frank, and our seeing her in two situations where she is washing something (her feet, her milk cans)" (214). And as Chappell says in the Preface, *Midquest* is "something like a verse novel" (ix).

Midquest should be read as a novel, and in connection with *I Am One of You Forever* and *Brighten the Corner Where You Are*, novels in which these characters recur, but it should also be read within the context it creates for itself, and in that respect it is intriguing that "The Peaceable Kingdom of Emerald Windows" should begin with talk of dreams and hidden babies: "Tree-dream, weed-dream, the man within the tree, / woman within the weed, babies inhabit / Tea roses" (156). This is a stream-of-consciousness poem, more so really than "Susan's Morning Dream of Her Garden," which, as the fifth poem in *Earthsleep*, should, according to the Preface, have been the volume's example of that genre—yet another of the Preface's strange misstatements. In its stream may be found the essential elements of the grandmother's dream: babies to be found, as noted already; but also a "dream of stone" (156) to match the grandmother's dream of a stone dead baby turned to stone; hidden there too (like the babies in tea roses) may be found "the grandmother's tear of parting" (157), anticipating the grandmother's bitter tears at the baby's demise ("I . . . cried so hard I felt my eyes dissolve" [180]). Even the sex behind the grandmother's guilt is present here, with an echo involving sacks: the baby when it was just a lump of gold was "About as big as a twenty-five-pound sack / Of flour" (178), while in "The Peaceable Kingdom" "we can get it on / On the sacks of cottonseed meal . . . / No one not even the rain has such big tits, / Lend me your lip a minute, willya, lovechile?" (157). Not to mention the "Rains of semen."[5]

Finally, the last remaining pair: "Susan's Morning Dream of Her Garden" (V) and "How to Build the Earthly Paradise: Letter to George Garrett" (VII). Susan dreams of a garden where "the sweet rose invites her oriental suitors all // iridescent in green and *oil*" (164; emphasis added), while Fred dreams up an earthly paradise where with "Green / plants for / the heart's delectation, the rough-red / singing vine glows with fire-*oils*" (175; emphasis added). In her garden "into ground lean the lonely / and elaborate dead . . . / burbling one to another always"; in his, "the dead / are troublous in their cool sleep, they stir / and grumble." She reflects on "the way my hand goes into the dirt"; he imagines "a dirt so rich our warm rude fingers / tingle inside it." But their dreams diverge as well: Susan would improve upon the garden the natural world provides, importing elements from another world and time: "I am not replete or reconciled. // Garden, garden, will you not grow for me / a salon full of billets-doux and turtledoves? / . . . I long to belong to / the chipper elegance, those centuries where / the hand of man has never said an ugly word" (165). Fred, on the other hand, is happy with the way things are: "That's / how I'd / build it, the Earthly Paradise: no / different, how could it be?, from what / it was ever dreamed. . . . Is / it true / already, what if it's true already? and / we have but to touch out to see it" (176-77).

Thus it is that Susan wishes to retreat from the real world into her garden, and does not want to wake: "I'd be a fool, a woman's a fool, to be drawn back / into the waking world. . . . I'm snugging / deeper in the larder of dream" (165-66); while Fred "never no more will turn my back / upon" (177) the real world which is "no / different . . . from what . . . was ever dreamed." Fred wakes willingly from his dream, emerging from the door of his lair: "I'm coming belchlike out of / the cave, make way my friends make way, / here gleaming with unspotted dream"; Susan, however, has found another door, not the way out but a way deeper inside: "I'm diving to a door I sense below, / . . . that opens truly into the garden //. . . and can draw / my waking body in and there no one / can draw me out again."

And thus *Midquest* ends—that is, its trail of mirrors ends—the same way *I Am One of You Forever* concludes, with the uncanny phenomenon of shared dreams. In the last chapter of the novel, Jess discovers that Johnson Gibbs, Uncle Luden, and his father all appear to be dreaming the same dream, each saying the name "Helen" in their sleep. Then the three sleepers sit bolt upright in their beds and stare at the same vision, which the boy thinks he can maybe see, too, but he's not sure: "If something had actually appeared . . . if I had seen something . . ." (182). Fred is less uncertain concerning what his father thinks he should be able to see, the cross on his shoulder in "My Father Allergic to Fire." Yet these are surely parallel moments in Chappell, the moment of instant recognition ("Father and son, with one instant of recognition between them" ["Burning the Frankenstein Monster" (87)], "all in a single instant—I saw something. I thought that I saw" [*I Am One of You Forever* (182)]) in which one seems to catch a glimpse of something one has seen before: "the features blurred . . . and yet familiar. . . . I was disturbed most of all by the unplaceable familiarity of the vision" (182-83). The poems in pairs, not just the last pair but all of them, seem to dream the same dream. The reader, given the conundrums the Preface poses, may never be quite sure that what he or she sees is what the poet sees. But Chappell seems to have written that quandary into his text.

NOTES

1. It did not escape the notice of Henry Taylor, though he denies it any significance. "It turns out that in *Bloodfire.* . . Virgil Campbell holds forth in the seventh poem. . . . In the more loosely arranged *Wind Mountain*, he gets the eighth poem, as it happens; he does not settle back to the middle of a part until *Earthsleep*. My point is not to show that there is a mistake in the order of the poems, or even in Chappell's description of it; it is rather to notice that it is just as effective to give Virgil poems VI, VII, VIII, and VI, as it is to give him VI every time. It is only the prefatory remark that brings attention to this matter" (75). The Preface, in Taylor's view, doesn't count as part of the text.

2. Four, he goes on to say, "is the Pythagorean number representing World, and $4 \times 11 = 44$, the world twice, interior and exterior. Etc., etc." (ix).

3. Though, as I will later suggest, "Susan's Morning Dream of Her Garden" is not in fact *Earthsleep*'s stream-of-consciousness poem. That honor belongs to the fourth poem, "The Peaceable Kingdom of Emerald Windows."

4. David Paul Ragan, who pointed out that the declaration about Virgil Campbell giving *Midquest* its Appalachian context is a gross oversimplification, suggests what I

have made explicit here, that the Preface is full of other misstatements as well: "like many of the statements in that Preface," the one about Virgil "is perhaps misleading" (22).

5. Or these lines: "We'll look up the dresses of tan-legged women oh boy / See the mouth in the moss. See Spot run. / World-wound, come and get me, I'm dying for blood" (158).

Josephine Humphreys

"Hope's last stand"

ELIZABETH A. FORD

Few bodies of literature more seductively invite historically informed criticism than Southern fiction. From Faulkner to Warren, from Welty to Mason, great Southern writers have reveled in conflicted time and troubled place, and their combined pages yield up an embarrassment of cultural riches. Yet, the application of history to literature is itself a conflicted endeavor, as a current *PMLA* forum on interdisciplinarity demonstrates.[1] Although many bemoan the methodological and theoretical difficulties that plague the intersection of literary and historical analysis, we keep producing such studies because, as Clarisse Zimra states, "we cannot resist boldly going where no one has gone before" ("Forum" 292). Yet, if the object of such quests is a perfect synthesis of historical and literary analysis, Carolyn Porter says scholars have not yet succeeded: "No, we are not being historical yet. But that is not for lack of trying" (781).[2]

Perhaps we are trying too hard, double-focusing so resolutely on the interdisciplinary challenge that we ignore what the works we examine might reveal about method. Southern fiction may invite historically based criticism, but it also provides abundant models of writers "being historical" successfully. Josephine Humphreys belongs to that tradition, and her preoccupation with the constructed past links her to current debates about the nature of history. Humphreys understands "the advantages of indirection—of choosing to ex-

201

ploit flawed evidence, whose greatest value may reside in its irreducible imperfection" (Wilkinson 81).[3] I examine Humphreys's use of history in her first
novel, *Dreams of Sleep* (1984), as a way of answering the criticism that her
work is "important, if imperfect,"[4] an epithet I would rephrase as *important
because imperfect.*

Although she has set three of her novels in her history-laden hometown of
Charleston, Humphreys is a reluctant Charlestonian, ambivalent about its history: "I didn't want to go back there to live, but I did." "Holding on to the past,"
she claims, is "the danger" of living in a city where "the past is everywhere,
and you can't get away from it" (Humphreys, "Continuity and Separation,"
792). Nevertheless, she imbeds her city's history in her fictions, if not with the
pedagogic zeal revealed in Walter J. Fraser's introduction to his history of
Charleston: "The academic historian has an obligation to synthesize history
for the inquisitive lay person; otherwise who will keep the educated public
aware of the paradoxes and complexities in history and its significance to their
daily lives?" (xi). Although less burdened by the "obligation" Fraser rashly promises to fulfill, Humphreys does ask readers to recognize the complexity of the
dialogue between the past and present, a theme she has continued to examine
since she wrote *Dreams of Sleep.*

Humphreys revised her recent novel *The Fireman's Fair* (1991) to incorporate Hurricane Hugo's devastation of Charleston, an event that occurred
while she wrote ("Continuity" 793). This response—to make her creation reflect reality—implies she values the mimetic relationship between fiction and
history. While Humphreys changed her text to trap "reality," she drew attention instead to the analogy between external and internal processes, comment-
ing in the same interview that *The Fireman's Fair* was "already filled with images
of ruin and disaster" (793), and that Hugo simply added a "reason." Hugo's
devastation and the community's response mirror the disintegration and re-
building of the protagonist's life.

History functions as analogy in Humphreys's second novel, *Rich in Love*
(1987), narrated by seventeen-year-old Lucille Odom, who says she does not
understand "how events are linked in the world." Lucille relates linked events
nevertheless as she tells of a troubled transitional period in the Odom family
history. During that six months, Lucille comes to terms with her own sexuality
and with the disintegration and reassembly of her family. Lucille, who learns
that "everything is history," often uses the past to footnote the present, as she
does when she compares the "progress" that has paved the space between
Charleston and Mount Pleasant to the lava flow that covered Herculaneum
(11).

Often in *Rich in Love*, history foreshadows action. The ugly trouble brewing beneath the surface in the Odom family escalates after an African-American family friend glosses a "guided" tour of historic Charleston. Rhody points out that slaves and pirates were hanged on Charleston's showplace, the Battery, events not usually included in the guide's narrative. Lucille Odom and Rob Wyatt grew out of Humphreys's fascination with similar characters—Iris Moon and Will Reese, whom she created in *Dreams of Sleep,* her richest work, and the novel most concerned with history; her "imperfect" mimetic and analogic representations of the past begin here.

A third-person narrative, *Dreams of Sleep* chronicles Alice Reese's response to the revelation that her husband, Will, is sleeping with his receptionist; Will's mother tells Alice about the affair. Stunned by Marcella's "news," Alice begins to contemplate her past, trying to discover some basis for action. Will, too, replays his childhood and his life with Alice, certain that he wants to continue the marriage, but just as certain that he loves Claire.

Trying to be helpful, Marcella encourages Alice to hire a baby-sitter for her daughters, Marcy and Beth. Queen, Marcella's African-American cook, suggests seventeen-year-old Iris Moon, her son Emory's best friend.[5] The product of a wildly dysfunctional family, Iris, fresh from a nervous breakdown, seems an unlikely catalyst for family healing, but her strength helps Alice decide to stay in the marriage. Alice repays Iris by beginning to think of her as family.

Humphreys's central characters, Alice, Will, and Iris, have engrossing, detailed individual histories that no plot summary could capture; Humphreys's skilled character development has attracted critical attention. I will focus, not on those personal histories, but on the constructed past that deepens and widens *Dreams of Sleep.* Humphreys relies upon historical evidence to explicate her narrator's claim: "Growing up in an old city, you learn history's one true lesson: that history fades. Nothing sticks together for very long without immense effort" (*Dreams* 112). *Dreams of Sleep* could be deconstructed on the pivot of that assertion, but only if you read "fades" as "disappears." To illustrate the ways in which history fades, Humphreys assembles disparate pieces that have not disappeared: an historic site, a myth, and a piece of material culture.

Fort Sumter recalls Charleston's catalytic role in the Civil War. From their perch on the Battery Wall, Marcy and Beth Reese could see this important historical site, if they wanted to: "The summer heat made Fort Sumter a dancing dot in the blue-gray harbor, air and water shimmering together so that the line of separation between them swam. Only a few gulls broke the flat, ribbony gray. The children seemed to sit at the edge of the world; everything was precarious" (6). Here, "on April 12, as Lincoln's relief expedition neared Charleston, Beauregard's batteries began shelling Fort Sumter, and the Civil War began" (Nash, Jeffrey, et al., *American People,* 503). The diary of Miss Emma

Holmes offers a firsthand account of the shelling: "at half past four [in the] morning the heavy booming of the cannons woke the city from its slumbers" (25). The Battery was "soon thronged with anxious hearts," and "through a telescope," Holmes watched "the shots as they struck the fort."[6] The collage of history in this short paragraph briefly illustrates the variety of available historical views of the Fort. The first excerpt, from an American history book, focuses on those in power, Lincoln and Beauregard, and the action they precipitated, while Emma Holmes interprets the response of onlookers to the momentous event going on before their eyes.

Humphreys paints a diffused view of the site, a fort distorted by heat, distance, and time into a pointillist's dot, part of a kinetic seascape. The only threat in this vignette comes from the position of the children sitting "at the edge of the world." Humphreys abstracts history into an allusion that functions as good allusions do. During this scene, Marcella detonates the action of the plot and starts a small, parallel civil war, as catalytic to Alice as falling off the edge of the world. Alice's union is threatened, so she reconnoiters; she goes to Will's office to stare at her rival. Alice secedes; she withdraws into herself to think over her dreamlike past. Marcella orders action, but Alice's action is to retreat and run South, taking her children with her. Still, her action brings the battle to a head, resulting in a reconnected, if fragile, union. Humphreys places her present action against the background—the start of the Civil War— provided by her allusion to Sumter. She foregrounds the same site to illustrate history's morph into product.

Marcy and Beth sit across from Sumter in front of Grandma Marcella Reese's ostentatious house "with columns," on the Battery, the historic waterfront promenade and park that now form Charleston's prime real-estate property. Here history wears a For Sale sign. Marcella's second husband, Ohioan Duncan Nesmith, loves his "fake plantation house," just as he adores the old, false South: "Ohioans love what they think is the South. Boiled shrimp, debutantes, the Civil War—they're gaga over every bit of it, fueling the tourist industry in Charleston and Savannah and New Orleans and every town that has a plaque or a monument" (*Dreams* 46).

In a memoir of her childhood, Humphreys describes Charleston as "the odd city where Christmas is warm and a black man drives buggyloads of Northerners around" ("My Real Invisible Self" 9). In *Dreams of Sleep*, she explains what those "Northerners" are seeking: an idealized Southern past. They are willing to reconstruct it by buying or building properties that fit their vision. Will Reese's label, "Ohioans," stands for all outsiders, and Duncan Nesmith's description of potential investors shows from how far "outsiders" can come— "there's a bunch of Kuwaitis," he brags, "making me offers already." Duncan's Middle Eastern investors recall an actual transaction; Fraser mentions the

Kuwaiti sheikdom that bought Kiawah Island off the coast of Charleston (*Charleston!* 426).

Although Will doesn't like to hear it, Duncan makes him understand that not only outsiders participate in the marketing of Charleston; complicit insiders use "Ohioans" as a front (*Dreams* 181). If the historic site once belonged to Charlestonians, it now belongs to whoever can afford it. Whether a century-old home or a new home with a view of Sumter, Battery houses become objects of desire labeled with a powerful designer logo: history.

Here, Humphreys avoids judgment. Her characters cannot be stamped "good" or "bad" on the basis of their attitudes towards the commodification of history. Will Reese doggedly seeks out unspoiled places and rails that "no Charleston man" would be faithless to its history; he derides his mother for marrying Duncan and for helping to sell Charleston. But Will, a weak-willed dissembler, proves faithless to his wife, while Marcella, real-estate agent supreme, is loving and strong.

Well-heeled outsiders are not the only customers for Charleston's classy past. Iris Moon, whose family screams "poor white trash" to Southern fiction junkies, should resent the wealth ranged before her. She gazes, instead, at the Fort and the Battery and dreams of ownership. The narrator describes Iris's reasoning, a process that might reduce a good Marxist to tears: "if all the world is rich enough to allow such houses as these, maybe somewhere in it is a small one for her. The world's wealth gives her a hope, even if now she has nothing of it, not a scrap, not an invisible crumb" (218). Iris, generally neither a fool nor an idealist, cannot resist the dazzle. Infused with a subtle politic and hardly isolated in a regional bubble, *Dreams of Sleep*, published at the end of Ronald Reagan's first term, resonates to external as well as internal history.

The selling of Charleston's most historic site reflects the '80s feeding-frenzy of international buyers questing for high-profile U.S. real estate; this wave peaked in 1989 when Sony bought Columbia Pictures and the Mori Development Group bought Rockefeller Center (Greenwald 83). And surely Iris, almost tasting her morsel of the big pie, is hoping for trickle-down Reaganomics to work.

Humphreys's evocation of this historical site could be called "imperfect." After all, the history embedded in her story consists of an allusion to past action, some conversation, a factual detail, a reflection of the current national context. But the American history text that conflates site and action is, at least, incomplete, as is Miss Emma Holmes's view of the crowd watching the event. Humphreys's fragmented presentation of the Fort and Battery through literary device, through time, through filter of character, resembles current historians' refusal to fix a historic site into a single view. Although he is discussing memory as reflection of history, James Wilkinson's comment about the transitory nature of the thing remembered fits well here: "while the site (defined in the broadest sense) remains constant, memory does not. Interpretation and use change continually in response to a variety of events" (86).

Epiphanic moments disclose history's slipperiness to Humphreys's characters. Alice Reese, newly aware of hew husband's faithlessness, realizes that everything fades; she cannot halt the flow of time carrying her beyond her moment of enlightenment. But the Fort and the Battery, in a state of permanent impermanence, wait for present meaning.

What happens when present interpretations of the past depend upon myth? Duncan Nesmith thinks of Disneyesque pirates when he dreams of his not very original theme park on the Battery, and his tackiest plan for "improving" Charleston introduces them into the narrative: "We'll have . . . pirate ships that actually go out . . . to Drum Island, where we'll give [tourists] maps to dig for buried treasure. Everything will have the pirate theme. . . . It's a natural because there really were pirates here. One of them was hanged on the Battery. We plan to reenact it" (178). The pirates who plagued Charleston more than a century before the shelling of Sumter certainly have not been mythologized into regional heroes comparable to Jefferson Davis, but they *have* been transformed into eternal parrot-toting goodfellows, providers of Halloween costumes and jolly pirate speak: "Avast, Yo Ho Ho, You landlubber." Well, you get it. To validate his sleazy plan, Duncan emphasizes the provable presence of the pirates who plagued South Carolina's coast, like Blackbeard and Stede Bonnet, who "really were" there.

Mrs. St. Julien Ravenal mentions Blackbeard and Bonnet in her popular history of Charleston in a chapter called "The Conquest of the Pirates" (1929). She does not, however, detail their raids on the shipping trade between Charleston and England. Instead, she relates humanizing anecdotes. Blackbeard, she explains, only kidnapped Charlestonian "Samuel Wragg and his little son" so that he could trade them for drugs to treat his sick crew (*Charleston: The Place and the People* 71). Clever Stede Bonnet, "a gentleman by birth and education" (73)—class distinction operates even with regard to pirates—captured the sympathy of the public at his trial, but was hanged in 1718 and buried on White Point Shoal, which "has been filled up and is now the Battery Garden" (78). Mrs. Ravenal's portrayal of Charleston's famous pirates recalls Robert Louis Stevenson's creation of Long John Silver, the pirate captain in *Treasure Island* (1881), whose good impulses and cleverness leaven his wickedness.

At least partially through the influence of Stevenson's classic text, pirates have become the province of childhood, as children have inherited myth, folk, and fairy tale. Their piratical inheritance, however, is a motley thing. Mrs. Ravenal emphasizes behavior that mediates the archetypal "shadow" status of both pirates; they are villains who may have souls. The current "information" books for children I examined dispense anecdotal capsules of lore, but rely primarily on the appearance and accessories of pirates. Young readers will undoubtedly enjoy knowing that Blackbeard liked to increase his perceived ferociousness by braiding "lit hemp fuses into his hair and beard" (Wright, *Pirates!* 6). Fortunately this is not one of the many suggested projects, although kids are encouraged to craft pirate flags like Blackbeard's, which featured a skeleton and a bleeding heart. In these pirates-for-kids texts, synecdoche triumphs. The trappings of piracy—flags, eye-patches, and rumpled treasure maps—become the whole, and a very '90s whole at that. These heavy-metal, MTV pirates are freaky in a familiar way.

Humphreys never calls Owen Moon a modern pirate, but an early image—a part that stands for the whole—seems to connect him to that legacy. Marcy and Beth Reese find "buried jewels" in their driveway, but Alice makes them throw away the "emeralds" that really are "pieces of broken Coke bottle. Trash" with "sharp edges" (10). Owen wears "blue jeans, a dark green T-shirt" and footgear reminiscent of those dangerous emeralds: "boots of worn black leather studded with bits of green and silver in star designs" (20).

Owen's persona and equipage pale in comparison to those of past pirates. He lacks the pyrotechnics of Blackbeard, the polish of Bonnet, and instead of a ship, he drives a "purple Dodge" on his frequent coastal raids between Florida and Charleston. In an era of terrorism and corporate crime, Owen defines petty piracy. A bigamist with a second wife in Florida, and not even a "professional" pirate's code of conduct, he preys on his own, abusing his family with ease, charming while he repels.

Apparently he will settle for cheap booty, driving from Florida to lift "Fay's stereo . . . steak knives . . . and a driftwood table lamp" (20). But he once came back to seduce, beat, and abandon her, and he has "kidnapped" his troublesome teenage son. If he would stay in Florida, Owen could become the myth his wife has tried to tell, a combination of "false hopes and artificial memories" (226). Fay elevates Owen and the history of their marriage into the stuff of romance: "we were the finest things ever seen in town, and neither one of us ever needed money to be happy, we just spent ourselves" (19). But Iris quickly reduces Owen to his parts, noticing that her father is "not dressed in adult's clothes," and understanding the "cold, mean tint" in his green-blue eyes (20). Humphreys does not create a detailed history for Owen. Instead she presents the myth in the making, Owen himself, and Iris as revisionist historian.

This triple perspective gives Owen just enough dimension to keep him from becoming a stereotype. Humphreys hints that he may be a villain with a soul, but his character cannot be deduced satisfactorily from the available snippets of evidence. Although class usually determined punishment for crimes of piracy in the past: "poor pirates" were hanged in Charleston, while "rich ones appeared publicly and were not molested in the least" (Fraser 12); this is not the case in *Dreams of Sleep*. Owen is not the only outlaw in the text.

Humphreys connects the lower-class Moon and middle-class Reese families, beginning with the image of the false emeralds. As well-to-do and well-educated as Stede Bonnet, Will also hurts and deceives, and Alice Reese, not Owen, performs the most conclusive act of piracy. Driven to despair by Will's behavior, Alice kidnaps Marcy, Beth, and Iris and runs South, "down the angled coast of the state" (205). The water-riven moonlit landscape that once hid Bonnet and Blackbeard gives Alice and Iris the space to transcend barriers of age and class, and Iris teaches Alice a lesson she needs. Debunking the myth of family perfection, Iris assures Alice that in every family "the setup is always flimsy" and that "you live with the possibilities" (201). Alice commits an act of piracy, and her temporary outlaw status frees her. Owen, a habitual outlaw, only knows how to escape. Trapped into traversing the same no-man's-land, he scuttles from point to point. As a modern incarnation of a dark archetype, Owen suffers a postmodern fate. While Fay constructs his myth, Iris simultaneously deconstructs it, leaving his identity suspended in limbo.

In Owen's case, and perhaps for the pirates before him, myth as historical evidence is certainly imperfect. Whether memory or observation build the story, the object is subject to the whim of the teller. About the teller, however, myth discloses at least some "irreducible truth." Duncan wants an execution he can market; Mrs. Ravenal needs pirate personalities to warm up her history; and Rachel Wright, the author of *Pirates!* thinks graphic villainy will interest kids in the past. Fay Moon must shore up the myth she has made of her marriage, while Iris must tear it down to find a starting place for her own reconstruction. Only when Iris can look into a sliver of mirror and see her lovely face does she begin to see her father as a person.

Humphreys intertwines strands of analogy and mimesis: present-day lives mirror history's patterns, while "reality" alters the patterns, even as they are being embraced. However, neither mimesis nor analogy describes Humphreys's method of constructing the past via a material object—an antique bed made by "Queen's great-grandfather, the freed slave, Dave-Nero Jones."

Appropriately, many pivotal scenes in *Dreams of Sleep* take place in bed. Few are as tranquil as the novel's cinematic opening, in which early morning sunlight streams in to wake a reluctant Alice (1). In fact, Humphreys presents a history of disturbingly bad-bed images. The narrator reveals that Alice Reese's bed—the center of that tranquil opening—actually makes her "short of breath" (61), and that one of her worst experiences, a miscarriage, took place while she was "half-sitting, half-lying against the headboard" of a bed in her student apartment (43). Fay Moon soils her own bed, catatonic over Owen's desertion (86), and Iris responds by making herself a little bed of "warm laundry" at the laundromat, an act that precipitates her nervous breakdown (88). Will Reese's pained moment of enlightenment comes as he stands over his mistress' bed, watching her sleep with his best friend (191).

Good-bed scenes are less common. Alice and Will do finally sleep comfortably together, "gambling" on making their marriage work (231), and Iris's rented room contains a positive emblem of her new, direct approach to life — a clean, spare bed: "a mattress and a metal frame with wheels" (61). The most comfortable and comforting bed by far belongs to Queen. Iris knows "it is easy to sleep in [this] bed" (24). Here, when she visits Emory and Queen, she can forget Fay's filthy apartment and her brother's smelly mattress.

Iris likes Dave-Nero's signature "carved on the back of the headboard" because it reminds her that when he was "nineteen and living a life not his own, he was sure enough of his worth to put his name on his work and let it stand for him" (24). A freed slave who "got rich from feed stores and insurance," Dave-Nero has made it into "the South Carolina history textbook" (24).

Although this sounds inspiring, an artifact that can stand nobly for its creator, Queen wonders about the impact of "a stick of furniture" when "all of us is still maids," and she orders Iris to "get up out of that bed now, girl" (24). Humphreys's thumbnail history of Dave-Nero is sketchy. It reads like one of those "enrichment" sections thrown into current history books to "recover the past" through primary evidence — patriotic paintings, magazines, political campaign artifacts — instead of a historian's narrative. Dave-Nero's mini-biography, however, conceals more than it enlightens. What gave him self-confidence? How did he begin a feed store? What kind of insurance did he sell, and to whom? Did he stay in Charleston? Did he like the "fancy English furniture" he bought as well as the bed he built? Was he happy after he carved his affecting signature?

"Like any piece of historical evidence," one American history text counsels, a piece of material culture "must be approached critically and carefully" (Nash, Jeffrey, et al., *American People*, 366). I would be glad to analyze the bed carefully, if that were possible. But the bed, like Dave-Nero's history, offers little concrete evidence. It is "old," and it hides its creator's signature "in the dark cobwebbed shadow against the wall" (24); except for those details, the deed is a blank.

Joseph Millichap sees imperfection in Humphreys's creation of "the black characters" in *Dreams of Sleep*. He complains that they "seem obscure figures, shadowy reflections of the whites" (249). I agree that Queen and Emory are not fully developed characters. Like Dave-Nero Jones and his bed, they tease out questions. But in such imperfections dwell larger, historic issues of silence and recovery.

Humphreys identifies "imagining the experience of others" as part of a writer's job ("Continuity" 798). She does not, however, imagine complete interior lives or past histories for African-American characters. One could argue that the "shadowy" nature of these characters only demonstrates their peripheral status, yet their presence in the text matters. Queen brings Iris and Alice together; Iris's only previous support comes from Queen and Emory; and Dave-Nero's bed can hardly be considered a peripheral image in a text that repeatedly presents images of uncomfortable beds and unquiet sleep.

A deconstructive critic would analyze the gaps, and Alice and Iris offer a way into such a reading. Both women hold similar world views which acknowledge "holes" that "open up in solid ground," making "previous rules into nonsense" (*Dreams* 79). A deconstructive reading, however, would fill the holes, and present a negative unification of the text. I believe that the "holes" in *Dreams of Sleep* refuse even that kind of unity. Instead they offer a parallel to the world of historians and literary critics who see holes and "wish to hear the voices and feel the passions of a cast of hitherto silent actors," yearning which "has created a powerful tension between the desire to know and the availability of materials from which to derive that knowledge" (Wilkinson 82).

Dave-Nero's bed, which is not described and cannot be read, suggests a shaping step beyond mimesis or analogy. Alice Reese finally acknowledges her passivity, her tendency to watch and wait, because it promises "regeneration," the promise of possibility, "the purest shape that hope can take. Hope's last stand" (230). Perhaps hesitation to fill the gaps, to assume knowledge, to own history, is the "purest shape that hope can take," for fiction writers and interdisciplinary literary critics.[7] Carolyn Porter imagines a criticism "free from static 'world pictures' and 'world views,' and faced with the opportunity to approach literary texts as agents as well as effects of cultural change, as participating in a cultural conversation" (782). Josephine Humphreys models such an approach in *Dreams of Sleep*.

NOTES

1. See "Forum: Forty-one Letters on Interdisciplinarity in Literary Studies," *PMLA* (1996). Most forum participants agreed on the difficult necessity of understanding and incorporating current discussion in non-major disciplines. Although critics may understand current debate in their own areas, it is convenient to assume a static state in "other" disciplines.

2. Porter argues that not all new historicists can or should be grouped under a Marxist blanket, but that all new-historicist critics do need to acknowledge political agendas in their work.

3. James Wilkinson argues that the range of evidence now accepted as suitable for study is at once a strength and a weakness.

4. Millichap characterizes Humphreys as "traditional," applauding her skill at plot-

ting, creating setting, and developing character. Yet he claims that Humphreys's "strength" at creating character is also her "weakness" because she fails "to focus on any single character" (249).

5. Emory later finds out that Queen is not his mother, a revelation that shocks Iris, but frees Emory (152).

6. My use of Holmes's diary does not indicate that I accept her single view as fact instead of interpretation. I readily admit choosing this piece of evidence because it fit my task.

7. Edward Said identifies knowledge that leads to ownership as a kind of colonization in *Orientalism*.

Richard Ford

Postmodern Cowboys

JEFFREY J. FOLKS

Richard Ford approaches the mythology and literary conventions of Western fiction from the perspective of a native Southerner who has spent most of his life in the South and the East, and, following the publication of *Rock Springs* and *Wildlife*, he has not returned to the Western subject. As Russell Martin puts it, in explaining Ford's absence from his 1992 anthology of contemporary Western writing, Ford is among those "writers with strong connections to this Western country whose lives and work are now focused elsewhere" (xxii). But why should Ford have decided to write about the West at all? Why, one must ask, should a native Southerner, educated in the Midwest and resident more recently at Chicago and Princeton, elect to devote a substantial portion of his creative life to an alien and marginal culture?

As a writer from outside who briefly entered the literary culture of the West, Richard Ford is hardly an anomaly. The audience for cowboy myth in its classic form—in dime novels, popular fiction, film, or television—was created for consumption by a national and, in practical terms, largely an Eastern audience.[1] The classic Western story, which gradually came to center on male initiation experiences,[2] was adapted for each subsequent generation of readers. In the 1930s and 1940s, the "singing cowboy" (in the person of Gene Autry,

Roy Rogers, and Tex Ritter) sentimentalized and softened the cowboy's rugged image. A third generation of Westerns, identifying the cowboy with the gunfighter, appealed to audiences in the 1950s and 1960s concerned with defending American democracy against Cold War enemies. A fourth-generation cowboy myth, popularized in film and country music during the 1970s, introduced the cowboy "drifter" and "outlaw," as defined in songs like Waylan Jennings's "My Heroes Have Always Been Cowboys" (1976). In his outlaw persona, the cowboy projected "a peculiar blend of nostalgia and pessimism" (Savage 90). In the decade after 1975, the outlaw figure was featured in a succession of popular songs, collected on such albums as Willie Nelson's *Red-Headed Stranger* (1975) and *Wanted: The Outlaws* (1976), which repeated "the isolation, violence, and inconsolable sorrow habitually associated with the genre" (Dunne 227). As Michael Dunne notes, one important feature of outlaw mentality is the awareness of a life of lost opportunities. As Waylan Jennings suggests in "My Heroes Have Always Been Cowboys," the cowboy is a kind of poet *manqué* who has wasted his life (230).

In its more extreme variants, as Malone writes, the outlaw figure verges on dangerous forms of survivalist figuration. Hank Williams Jr.'s song "A Country Boy Can Survive," for example, "was virtually a survivalist hymn with its emphasis on rural independence and its underlying hint of violence" (Malone 393). Richard Ford's more radical examples of Western "independence" similarly echo, in a prescient manner, the militant antigovernment sentiments that reportedly led to the actions of those responsible for the Oklahoma City bombing in 1995. For the most part, however, his protagonists are too demoralized even for resistance. What they do share with the militant extremists is an embittered loss of faith in American society, particularly as it relates to the traditional roles of young white males, who feel increasingly marginalized and have reacted either by dropping out, in acts of passive resistance (as Ford's protagonists do), or by striking back, either in literal or fantasized gestures.

Like the popular media, Ford draws on the figures of the drifter and outlaw—those romantic losers forever unsettled in love and in trouble with the law. At the same time, the social realism of Ford's writing continually undercuts the element of fantasy in Western myth and implicitly interrogates the often commercialized and colonizing usages of regional myth. Indeed, by exploring radically different geographical locales for his writing, Ford asserts a powerful artistic independence which frees his work of parochial attachments to particular "subjects" as such. The more profound aspects of social limitation, forms of human oppression which are not localized or culturally specific, are the focus of his art. At the heart of this form of social oppression is the control of consciousness through the processing of cultural images and linguistic authority.

In Ford's postmodern Western, the social and economic dilemmas of America as a whole are not escaped but only magnified by the desolate, ecologically damaged New West which, as Craig Lesley has written, "contains working people living a hardscrabble existence and trying to stay ahead of the bills and banks" (2). Ford's protagonists live just such lives "on the edge" where economic survival is unsure and social relationships are unstable. As Martin perceptively writes, the American West, more so than other regions of America (but no more so than Ford's native South), is the product of colonialism, as Eastern and European financial interests have historically "developed" its resources: "The entire region, perhaps inevitably, became a kind of colony, a place whose wealth was channeled elsewhere and that suffered, therefore, a colony's classic sense of inferiority as well as its gnawing, troubled urge to assert its independence" (xviii). In this colonial scheme, human beings are subjected to the same shortsighted economic forces as the environment: both are stripped of value until they are exhausted and then abandoned. Like Earl Middleton in the title story of *Rock Springs*, they are colonials whose injured mental life "leaves something out" (9). Within this society, Ford's postmodern cowboys are utterly out of place; they stumble through life, hoping at best to avoid being hurt or causing harm to others and aspiring only to understand and communicate their anxiety.

In the story "Rock Springs," Ford presents three characters who are immediately recognizable as victims of a restrictive social environment: a father fleeing imprisonment on a "bad check" charge, his young daughter, and his current girlfriend. En route to Florida in their stolen Mercedes, this hapless family cannot help but suggest and parody the typical western "family vacation," as the three characters comment on the scenery and search for a motel where they may spend the night. Along the way, Ford's protagonist, Earl Middleton, stumbles upon the fabled "gold mine," the object of all generational escatologies, but finds that its wealth is controlled by corporate owners and that its workers subsist in a grimy boomtown of trailers that only resemble "homes." A potentially more valuable discovery is Earl's chance meeting with an elderly black woman and her grandson. Within her cramped trailer home, the woman seems to have created "something good and sweet, instead of just temporary" (14). Unlike Earl himself, who has refined lying to an art, the black woman appears to speak sincerely of love and family, and in questioning Earl about himself, she "seemed to want truth" (15). Together with her exemplary husband, off working hard in the mine, she has uncomplainingly taken responsibility for a brain-damaged grandchild, apparently abandoned by the child's parents. In this chance encounter, as presumably in all such encounters, Earl is easily seduced by his own conventional paradigm of family happiness, and it is clear that he seizes on this idealized family as a nostalgic reminder of the kind of homey goodness and responsible stability that he associates with "real" families. Yet his idealization of "family" is a gauge of the disruption of his own social existence; it seems a misguided and desperate effort to secure meaning. It is precisely the instability and rootlessness of his life, and his inability to escape his limitations, that make Earl a figure of particular narrative interest. His "leaving something out," a feature that his girlfriend, Edna, identifies as his chief character trait, admits an absence denied by others; his disorganized flight from authority suggests the limited opportunities of his environment.

Like several stories in *Rock Springs* ("Going to the Dogs" and "Fireworks," for instance), the title of the story "Great Falls" refers allegorically to social breakdown as well as to the literal meaning—in this case, the setting of Great Falls, Montana. The story traces a series of "great falls"—adultery, maternal desertion, premature death of the father, and a son's loneliness—that come to seem inevitable to the Westerners who stoically accept and even take pride in their barren lives. When Jackie's father, Jack Russell, retires from his job at an air base in Great Falls, he elects not to return to his "home" in Tacoma, Washington, and one imagines that it is the "placelessness" and dissociation of Great Falls that he finds attractive. Russell's transgressing of the legal system, as he supplements his income by selling illegally procured fish and game to local caterers, resembles the widespread resistance to federal governance of western lands, a part of a regional culture in which federal "law" is connected with a long history of colonial intrusion. It is not surprising, in a way, that when Russell confronts his wife's lover he asks first about Woody's home and if his parents are living, as if to position the younger man in relation to communal boundaries which he himself lacks. Russell's rootlessness and indifference to the law are liberating but also place him and his family at risk, as his son, Jackie, comes to understand after his parents' breakup when he says, "We were all of us on our own in this" (48).

Ford connects Jack Russell's rootlessness with the kind of work he performs: first at the air base in Montana and later following the oil boom in Ely, Nevada, where he is killed in an accident, his labor is temporary and dissociated from society. Military bases are established or closed according to national priorities (or politics) and mining and drilling operations are even more transient. As Martin notes, "at the close of the twentieth century, the West's frontier legacy of boom and bust still hasn't abated. Immigrants continue to barrel into the region, certain that it harbors those things that their lives have always lacked, and they continue, most of them, to end up disappointed" (xviii).

Jackie's mother is also uncomfortable in the confinement of settled relationships—so much so that when she abandons Jackie, she explains tersely, "'I'd like a less domestic life, is all'" (47). At the end, Jackie can only say of his mother that he has seen her "from time to time—in one place or another, with one man or another—and I can say, at least, that we know each other" (49). The verb "know" in this sentence suggests mere acquaintanceship rather than friendship or intimacy, and when Jackie and his mother do meet by accident in a grocery after many years of separation, they have only a few words to say to each other. As Gilles Deleuze and Felix Guattari have written in theorizing "minor literature," an author from a marginal culture must find a point of "underdevelopment" and must develop a *patois* to express forms of deterritorialization. Paradoxically, a regional writer such as Richard Ford, whose work is embedded in a sense of place (albeit a *shifting* sense of place) may be best situated to utilize the "impossibilities" of marginal culture (by writing outside the dominant language and national culture). His writing does not attempt to reterritorialize its subject by reauthorizing traditional referents of place (in the sense that Gabriel García Márquez may attempt through the amassing of local myths, legends, and particulars of place); rather it embraces its deterritorialized condition by exploring the gaps and incongruities of language. In the story "Sweethearts," for example, Ford employs the nuances of provincial speech. On the morning he is to enter prison for a year, Bobby is still anguished by love for his ex-wife, Arlene, who is now married to Russell. Bobby's admission that he had considered murdering Arlene and perhaps killing himself or Russell terrifies his ex-wife, as one might expect, but it is also a kind of archaic assertion of romantic love that seems out of place in his oppressed situation. How can Bobby assert faithful love for Arlene in a society where he cannot even be assured of employment, to say nothing of physical freedom. When Arlene and Russell toss Bobby's pistol into the river after driving him to prison, it is as much a purification—against the displaced conventionality of Bobby's awkward fidelity—as an expression of their fear.

As Deleuze and Guattari have suggested, within marginal literature, all personal relationships are "shadowed" by political facts. "Children" is a story set in the Hi-line section of northern Montana, near the Canadian border, "an empty, lonely place if you are not a wheat farmer." Like the Four Corners region of the Southwest, which Martin describes as "not the absolute end of the earth back then [in the early 1950s], but . . . close enough to make you sort of skittish" (xiii), the Hi-line's very emptiness constrains the lives of its inhabitants. Driven by anger, escapism, or sheer boredom, its young people seem to respond destructively to the mere vacancy of the land. The association of the narrator George and his "friend," Claude Phillips, is as arid as the mechanized farming culture of the Hi-line. George comments that he didn't really know Claude nor anyone else very well, and he implies a connection between his separateness and the environment: "You did not learn much of other people in that locality" (70). In the culture that the "children" of the story are enter-

ing, maturity involves learning to live "on your own" in a frighteningly complete sense. George understands that the young runaway Lucy, separated from
her family across the Canadian border and temporarily paired with Claude's
father and later with Claude, "was already somebody who could be by herself
in the world" (94)—a fact that seems disturbing because it is so much an accepted part of George's experience. Perhaps because he is trying to come to
terms with his own mother's desertion—he notes that her leaving "that part of
Montana" was "not unusual" (82)—George finds nothing remarkable in Lucy's
promiscuous independence: she seems to him pretty much a "normal girl."
The fact that she is "running away" is not unusual and doesn't seem "a bad
thing" to George.

It is clear that the conditions of George's childhood, in its dissociation of
feelings and experience, have resulted in the creation of a new idiom. When
Lucy says that she "loves" George and Claude and claims that she would rather
spend the night with them than with Claude's father, George understands it
as "just talk": "I knew that wasn't what she meant. It was just a thing to say, and
nothing was wrong with it at all" (90). Nor do Claude's actions—his disrespect
and hatred for his father and his casual affair with Lucy, whom his father puts
under his "protection"—trouble George, who sees that "nothing you did when
you were young matters at all" (98). In fact, little that one does *as an adult*
matters to the larger world, "a place that seemed not even to exist, an empty
place you could stay in for a long time and never find a thing you admired or
loved or hoped to keep" (98).

The quest that all of Richard Ford's adult protagonists undertake has everything to do with this definition of experience as "an empty place." While
they seem cowboys—transient laborers with few loyalties or social ties—it is
evident that Ford's protagonists are at least shadowed by the absent virtues that
George lists: a full place where you *can* find attachment, things you *can* admire and love and hope to keep. In their failure to obtain such a place or to
find something to admire or love, Ford's characters construct a unique *patois*
based on absence and failure rather than success. In *Rock Springs*, narrators
such as Les Snow in "Winterkill" and "Communist" or Frank Brinson in "Optimists" carve their own right way to act and speak, appropriate to their own
experience.

In representing the impossibility of these lives, Ford draws on the nuances
of regional working-class speech as it creates unexpected meanings from familiar words. Expressions such as "you could trust me to . . .," "that's a sure
fact," or "I had known him to . . ." cite but simultaneously undermine conventional meanings of "trust," "fact," and "know." Presumably the difference between a simple "fact" and a "sure fact" is a context in which a "fact" is not
"sure," a linguistic distinction which nicely captures the uncertainty of regional

culture. It is urgent for Ford's characters to express their tentativeness of experience in carefully drafted speech, but what they invariably discover is that the stories of their lives are inconclusive or even inconsequential. It means a great deal, however, to arrive at the conviction that nothing matters.

In "The Language of African Literature" (the first chapter of *Decolonising the Mind*), Ngugi wa Thiong'o writes of the centrality of language to cultural identity: "The choice of language and the use to which language is put is central to a people's definition of themselves in relation to their natural and social environment, indeed in relation to the entire universe" (4). The imperialist domination of African languages and cultures resulted in a colonial alienation of African identify, for the repression of language closes off communication between self and others, between self and nature, and indeed "between me and my own self" (15). Particularly ironic is the fact that so many African writers, under the mental control of imperialist cultures, participated in the devaluation of their own local cultures and the exaltation of European languages and cultural models. One of the worst effects of this process was the exclusion "of the participation of the peasantry and the working class" from the cultural debate (26).

It is not coincidental that Richard Ford, like so many regional writers before him, should focus on a region's particular oral language. Like Faulkner, O'Connor, Wright, Welty, and Morrison, Ford understands that the writer's work is one of recovering or at least utilizing repressed speech, particularly the orality of marginalized social groups. Like his predecessors, Ford creates art out of excluded forms of orality. Indeed, Ford himself, as a writer whose works have achieved critical approval, appears to stoically accept the possibility that his work might at any time fall out of favor, or that he might not continue writing at all. As he told Kay Bonetti, "if next year I decided I didn't want to write another book, or if I couldn't write another book, it wouldn't be the worst thing in the world to happen to the world or to literature or to me; it would just be something else that happened" (84). In this, Ford admits that his literary reputation, and experience in general, is largely beyond his control. The outside world is filled with potential harm, largely as a result of the fact that art is so little understood and "employed," so that Ford's narrative focuses on language as a way to admit and confront the emptiness of experience. While Ford's comments on his role as an artist are characteristically "cool" and indifferent, he is deeply engaged in opposing internal colonialism and reversing its effects. His meticulous uses of regional and working-class orality are inseparable from a political consciousness of the repression of local cultures within an assimilationist model of American democracy (a model meticulously analyzed in Sacvan Bercovitch's recent book, *The Rites of Assent* [1993]). Ford's comments on the precision with which he renders regional and class speech betray a serious artist compelled by both technical and ethical concerns.

Richard Ford has admitted that, as an individual, he found the "voice" of *Rock Springs* similar to his own ("Interview" 95). In the expression of a provincial working-class culture, Ford brings to postmodern writing the voice of the aggrieved, excluded provincial, forever denied significance within the national culture. Ford's own self-conception as a writer involves a belief that language affords "consolation" against the kind of anxiety produced in an unreflexive, colonized use of language. In the interview with Kay Bonetti, Ford stated that Faulkner "treated me with and to language which was about things that made the world more orderly to me." On the next page, Ford explained that literature "*can* be consoling. It *can* say the thing not before said. . . . We think we know what love is; we think we know what passion is; we think we know what hatred is. We know, in fact, a lot about those things. And literature's opportunity is to say about those concepts what hasn't been said yet, so that we know more about them, so that we'll find a way to take some solace in them" (80). For this writer from a fractured and excluded culture, immediate experience is always inarticulate and inherently painful, but presumably, experience *does* become more "orderly" as the myths we live within are better understood.

In any provincial culture, the cultural mythologies have been created or at least largely shaped from the outside by hegemonic cultures. In his Western fiction, the mythology of individual opportunity which the national culture has for long associated with the Western frontier occupies Ford in several stories. "Empire," for example, another important story in *Rock Springs*, is a fable of the duplicity of personal freedom. Riding the Great Northern line between Spokane, Washington, and Minot, North Dakota, Victor Sims enjoys the pleasant illusion of detachment that he associates with train travel: observing others from his compartment without being observed, crossing a near-wild landscape without personal risk. Sims believes that he need exercise no control over events in his life, but that, paradoxically, his life is continually getting better: "Things you do pass away and are gone, and you need only to outlive them for your own life to be better, steadily better" (136). Several ominous events in the story suggest that this philosophy is not reliable: Sims's seduction of Cleo, a neighbor's sister, leads to a phone call from Cleo's biker friend, Loser, who threatens Sims's wife. Like some repressed voice of conscience, Loser charges that Sims has been an "asshole" who has betrayed his wife and "doesn't deserve her." A similar suggestion of consequences is implied by the wildfire that threatens the lives of all the train passengers.

It is in the context of what Ngugi calls cultural alienation that Sims's benign fatalism "makes sense." When a culture has been denied the opportunity for coherent significance, all expression must be accidental and purposeless.

For example, Sims's brief tryst with Doris Benton is only one episode in a life-time of disengagement, suggested at the beginning of the story by his answers to his wife's personality quiz (for every question, he answers "None of the above"). Even his marriage to Marge is largely accidental, for he had been almost equally attracted to Marge's sister, Pauline. Indeed, when he first met Marge, he at first thought she *was* Pauline, whom he had once dated. Both Marge and Pauline presumably attracted Sims because of their "imagination for wildness" (116), a quality which involves all of them in accidental and bizarre relationships—such as the pairing of the neurotic and superstitious Sims with the unsentimental, mechanical Sergeant Benton. Like George in "Children," Sims does not feel that "things you do" have any lasting impact; his actions matter so little that he invents stories about his past, including the falsehood that he had served in Vietnam during the war. If Sergeant Benton catches him in this lie, which he regrets only because he is caught, she is equally unconcerned. For her part, Marge shares Victor's attraction to a de-ceptive freedom. Even as she watches farmers in the distance battling the flames, their farms destroyed by the wildfire, she remarks: "'The world's on fire. . . . But it doesn't hurt anything'" (147). With her sense of "how happy I am" and his feeling of being "alone in a wide empire, removed and afloat, calmed, as if life was far away now" (148), Marge and Victor travel within a discourse of illusory freedom, chance events, and inconsequential preoccupation.

In one of the finest stories in *Rock Springs*, "Winterkill," the adult Les Snow describes his and Troy Burnham's meeting with Nola Foster. All three characters are victims of a harsh, unforgiving economic system, and their con-dition is intimately connected with internal colonialism and with their status at the bottom of that system. At the beginning of the story, Les is represented as an individual alienated from all society—"alone, where I didn't mind being at all" (168). Les's conception of "trust" is oddly mechanical, based on "pre-dictability" rather than social obligation. If one could *predict* that Les will act in a certain manner, one could "trust" him to act that way. By his own code, Les is faithful toward his friend, Troy, whose paralysis below the waist leaves him physically impotent, but, as we learn at the end of the story, Les is simul-taneously attractive to Nola (herself a wanderer who spends her days in bar-rooms in the company of various men). For his part, Les finds it difficult to enter a long-term relationship since he is frequently out of work and waiting for better times, which may require geographic removal. Yet, the economic system is only part of a quiescent culture in which Les's posture is that of "wait-ing." Ford peoples his fiction with characters who are, in more than a literal sense, "out of work" and "waiting" for their luck to change. The question of their survival is posed well by Frank Bascombe near the conclusion of *The Sportswriter*: "Where do sportswriters go when the day is, in every way, done, and the possibilities so limited that neither good nor bad seems a threat?" (339).

Understandably, the best Les Snow can imagine is a life in which harm "stays away" and in which he hurts no one, rather than a system in which he "acts." When the freezing river yields a dead fawn, one of the unprotected creatures that die in the course of the winter, Les takes the "winterkill" as further evidence of the world's ubiquitous danger. For Les at the end of the story, Troy and Nola, whom he leaves together undisturbed, appear as two further examples of winterkill—damaged individuals who can only find momentary comfort in one another, but who are unable to change their condition.

Frank Brinson is another character in *Rock Springs* who finds that the cultural myths of individualism and economic opportunity associated with the West are particularly unreliable. In the story "Optimists," Frank's father, a switch-engine fireman on the Great Northern Railway, believes that his union has created a "workingman's paradise" until he finds his job threatened by layoffs. By late 1959, the railroads have begun to cut workers: "everyone knew, including my father, that they would—all of them—eventually lose their jobs, though no one knew exactly when, or who would go first, or, clearly, what the future would be" (172-73). Under this pressure, at the end of a horrifying night when he sees a hobo cut to pieces by a train and bleed to death on the tracks, Roy Brinson snaps. After he is insulted by Boyd Mitchell in his own home, Roy lands a single punch which kills his abusive neighbor. He spends five months in prison for manslaughter, but his entire life unravels afterward.

From this episode, Roy's son, Frank, concludes that, as he says, "situations have possibilities in them, and we have only to be present to be involved" (181)—a strikingly agentless analysis of social repression. As Frank comments: "The most important things of your life can change so suddenly, so unrecoverably, that you can forget even the most important of them and their connections, you are so taken up by the chanciness of all that's happened and by all that could and will happen next" (187). Frank's reaction to the catastrophe is impassive, just as, in cowboy music, there is a conventional lack of protest to the "loneliness, social alienation, poverty and the strain of arduous physical labor" (Dunne 227). Yet protest of a sort is implied—at least from the perspective of the narrative if not from that of Frank—in the very act of recording the cowboy's voice.

If Ford's text registers the distress of the working-class culture he narrates, it is practically impossible for Ford's Western characters to articulate their own resentment. As Ngugi puts it, "it is the final triumph of a system of domination when the dominated start singing its virtues" (20). Just how out of place cultural criticism is in the American West is illustrated by the story "Communist" in *Rock Springs,* in which Glen Baxter fantasizes a network of communists in Montana and suggests an impending social revolution. Ford, however, undermines Baxter's rhetoric by showing that his personal crises have driven him outside society and that his political radicalism is a measure of his control by others rather than his independence. Baxter, currently unemployed and living with Les Snow's mother, competes with her for Les's approval. If Aileen hopes for a middle-class future for her son, Baxter attempts to inculcate his radical ideals and, at a deeper level, to pass on his heritage of futility and stoic acceptance to the boy. While Glen Baxter seems to have been only a minor influence on Les, he, in fact, turns out to be an important substitute for Les's father. The entire point of Les's retelling Baxter's story twenty-five years later is that Les hopes to better understand his own situation by rehearsing that of his exemplar. Despite his mother's opposition, Baxter's influence has been lasting.

By contrast, Aileen's authority has been slight. Les feels that he doesn't know his mother very well and in fact feels more comfortable when she is absent. At the time he tells the story, Les is forty-one and admits that his last real communication with his mother occurred when he was sixteen. In the last paragraph, in what is also the last line of the collection *Rock Springs*, Les speaks of the separation from his mother with sad resignation, suggesting that he has accepted the loneliness and fragmentation of his social environment: "I am forty-one years old now, and I think about that time without regret, though my mother and I never talked in that way again, and I have not heard her voice now in a long, long time" (235).

Stories such as "Communist" explore the role of the male code of stoic acceptance within a colonized Western culture. Paternal and maternal ideals compete for Les's approval, since Baxter's passion for hunting reiterates the boxing lessons that Les received from his father before his death. His father had trained him to "stay on" his opponent "until he falls"—an implicit irony since Les's father soon "falls" himself and his place in his wife's bed is taken by the younger, fitter man, Glen Baxter. Baxter, in his turn, imparts a similarly fatalistic male code to Les. When, for example, Baxter returns from months of drifting following his sister's funeral in Florida, his "story" seems to Aileen Snow unreliable, and Les, who better comprehends his incoherent desperation, comments that "A light can go out in the heart." Baxter has crossed the line beyond which it no longer matters whether his life can be imagined coherently: he can poach while claiming he is not poaching, he can live with one companion or another, he has lost whatever protection language affords. In an episode in which Baxter and Aileen argue over leaving a wounded goose to die on the freezing lake, he attempts to pass on a stoic masculine code that accepts the harshness of the outside world and that insists on the limits of pity. Aileen understands perfectly well what Baxter is attempting to teach, and her fury over his leaving a suffering bird on the lake is more deep-seated: although her vision of life is never developed in the story, it is clear that she is uncomfortable in the "half-wild" country in which she lives and that she opposes the male code of killing and fighting. She even has hopes of Les's attending college—the ultimate apostasy, apparently, for the cowboy hero!

While the West, with its store of cowboy myth and frontier ideology, is especially well suited to Ford's purposes, a similar absence of social discourse is apparent in all of the author's works, including those set in suburban New Jersey (*The Sportswriter* and *Independence Day*), the American South (*A Piece of My Heart*), and expatriate American society (*The Ultimate Good Luck*). The American West offers a convenient symbolic landscape for expressing the rootlessness of an increasing number of Americans, for in the West, pursuing quintessential myths of freedom and opportunity, Americans have typically preferred to "pick up stakes" and "move on" rather than confront communal problems. Yet the cowboy and frontier myths encode cultural values and mask social problems shared by the nation as a whole.

Like Ford's protagonists in *Rock Springs* and *Wildlife*, Harry Quinn and Rae in *The Ultimate Good Luck* lead transient and rootless lives, and they are essentially early sketches for the outlaws who appear later in his fiction. Rae, who appears at the beginning of the novel traveling in the company of a bronco rider and car thief named Frank Oliver, "figured out that what she was doing was simply craziness and nobody in his right mind would be doing it, but it was all she could bear to think about longer than a minute" (41). Against the backdrop of the seventies drug culture in the expatriate American community in Oaxaca, Mexico, Quinn is also something of a colonial amnesiac, a figure who attempts to follow a merely personal code (which includes loyalty to "buddies") which leaves out any collective vision, as for example in his respect for the use of weapons without regard for their social damage. When Quinn's attorney, Bernhardt, toward whom he feels some sense of attachment, is shot to pieces by a campesino, and the entire magazine is unloaded into his body (stopping only "when there wasn't enough left to shoot at"), Quinn remarks laconically: "It was skilled work, something Bernhardt wouldn't have expected"(155).

Like Ford's Western characters, Quinn learns from experience to suspect all settled relationships or institutions, and his rule is to avoid human connection altogether. At one point Quinn recalls a childhood experiment of placing a frog in a pan of water over a gas flame. As he gradually increases the heat, the frog sits calmly in the water until it realizes the danger, but it is now helpless to move, staring "out past the time when it could move even if it needed to." The lesson for Quinn is that human beings are in the same position: the frog is "an illustration of how people let certain things they're used to go on so long that they don't know that the things they're used to are killing them" (152). His solution is to remain mobile and in apparent control of his life.

The Sportswriter and its sequel, *Independence Day*, focus on the character of Frank Bascombe, a divorced suburbanite who resembles Ford's Western protagonists in his reflections on the illusory myths of individualist society. At the beginning of *The Sportswriter*, Frank compares his own experience with the myth of the American Dream as he reflects on "the good life" he had expected with his wife and three children: "Just exactly what that good life was—the one I expected—I cannot tell you now exactly, though I wouldn't say it has not come to pass, only that much has come in between" (3). In contrast with Ford's Western characters, to some degree Frank's social isolation is masked by a more benevolent suburban environment (he after all continues in a lucrative job, lives in the same community, and retains some of the same acquaintances), but Ford's artistic purposes in the New Jersey novels are not essentially different from those in his Western fiction. The middle-class enclaves of central New Jersey are represented as equally desolate and shallow, equally lacking in communal attachments. In his unique *patois* of sports-talk, the suburban male expresses an absence similar to that of Ford's Western figures. It may be, however, that the Western material allows a more blatant representation of alienation. Like the physical environment of the West, which must weather greater extremes of climate and geography, its social environment subjects human beings to unusual stresses of isolation and trauma.

Perhaps because of the severity of their conditions, many of Richard Ford's Western characters are shown to vividly imagine their now lost families and childhood communities. As he records an ambiguous definition of "family" and the tentativeness of all social relationships, Ford's language employs the colonial tropes of emptiness and impossibility: the ways in which parents fail their children, the loneliness of adults "out in the world" without families, the "chanciness" of all social ties.

Like Earl Middleton moving furtively in the parking lot of a Ramada Inn in Rock Springs, Wyoming, Ford's protagonists often experience a sense of *déjà vu* as they observe the apparently purposeful lives and ordered communities of others. Like Earl, peering into the windows of "a Pontiac with Ohio tags"—an imperial sort of family car loaded for a Western vacation—they undergo the colonial's startled admission into the presence of the colonizer. As Earl puts it: "It all looked familiar to me, the very same things I would have in my car if I had a car. Nothing looked surprising, nothing different. Though I had a funny sensation at that moment" (26). Earl's "funny sensation" is associated with the unfamiliar and uncomfortable knowledge that he is being observed; however much he tries to escape notice of the controlling legal and social systems, he is always within the jurisdiction of cultural hegemony.

Like all of Richard Ford's postmodern cowboys, Earl Middleton wants mostly to be left alone, to find "solace" from the pain of his alienation, "to put things like this out of your mind and not be bothered by them." As Earl reflects at the end of "Rock Springs," what he wants out of life is not more freedom and opportunity but less adversity and grief, not more of the American Dream but less: "Fewer troubles, fewer memories of trouble"(26).

NOTES

1. "Western" art was indeed often the creation of Eastern writers who had little actual contact with the West—as in the case of Clarence E. Mulford, inventor of the Hopalong Cassidy figure, who never visited the West until seventeen years after his first published Western story (Savage 143-44).

2. The trail ride, from the Southern Plains to markets in the North, may have actually served the purpose of initiation, if we are to judge from memoirs and historical accounts. The long trail ride provided the first extended period away from home for many young men from small towns and rural backgrounds, and it offered a memorable, and in many cases one-time, adventure for youths destined to return to their isolated communities (Savage 14 ff).

Andre
Dubus

"Never Truly Members"

LUCY FERRISS

> "They were never truly members of that faith, and so could not have
> left it." —Dubus, "Rose"

With Andre Dubus's writing life still in its summertime, we, his readers, seem
already to have planted him in the patch of ground we most wanted to fill —
that fertile place, looking out on the human condition, that was being shunned
by the metafictionists and minimalists of the seventies and the eighties. Critics
have praised Dubus's keen realism, his craftsmanship, the care he takes to remove the scaffolding that obscures our suspension of disbelief. According to
the one book-length study of his work, by Thomas Kennedy, Dubus's fiction is
"consistently concerned with an existential Christian vision of a real world in
which real human beings must live" (ix). Connected to this realist label is
another that has always been attached to Dubus: that he is a writer's writer.
Had he not existed, we might venture, the literary community would have
invented him.

    Without denying the evident truth of some characteristic observations of
Dubus—his classic opening lines, his attention to tangible physical detail—I
would like to focus on his concerns with Roman Catholic sexual politics, as
well as his connection to the literary tradition of his native South. Read in

these ways, Dubus's fiction may seem less a corrective to the experiments of writers like William Gass, John Barth, and Donald Barthelme and may afford his work both a more distinctive and more problematic status.

Dubus himself regards his separation from the South as "complete": "For years," he stated in an interview with Jon Holmes, "I worked on Southern stories and a novel that was filled with miscegenation and lynching and the like. Then . . . I discovered . . . I was writing about Faulkner's South, not my own life" (8). Yet Dubus has listed his favorite writers as Katherine Anne Porter, James Dickey, Robert Penn Warren, and William Faulkner. Despite Dubus's adamant insistence on Haverhill, Massachusetts, as the setting for most of his mature fiction, he carries with him the legacy of his birth and upbringing among New Orleans Catholics and the heritage of a central emphasis on storytelling in his craft. Comparison of opening lines from Dubus's classic "A Father's Story" with those by his mentors yields a remarkable resonance of concern with voice, place, and time:

> My name is Luke Ripley, and here is what I call my life: I own a stable of thirty horses, and I have young people who teach riding, and we board some horses too. This is in eastern Massachusetts. [Dubus, "A Father's Story"]

> At that time I was too young for some of the troubles I was having, and I had not yet learned what to do with them. [Porter, "Holiday"]

> It unrolled slowly, forced to show its colors, curling and snapping back whenever one of us turned loose. The whole land was very tense until we put our four steins on its corners and laid the river out to run for us through the mountains a hundred and fifty miles north. [Dickey, *Deliverance*]

> Mason City. To get there you follow Highway 58, going northeast out of the city, and it is a good highway and new. Or was new, that day we went up it. [Warren, *All the King's Men*]

> Once (it was in Mississippi, in May, in the flood year 1927) there were two convicts. [Faulkner, "Old Man"]

Without forcing a definition of Southern writing into which Dubus or anyone else might fit, these selections resemble one another most in what Eudora Welty called shape, "the contours of some continuous relationship between what can be told and what cannot be told" ("Words into Fiction" 143). It is within that shape that the writer renders "justice to reality," a reality itself imbued with the myth-making impulse.

In Dubus's case, that mythic reality is grounded in the sacramental life as defined by the Catholic Church and in sexual relations between men and women. "I see the whole world as a Catholic," Dubus has said, "so I can't help but see my characters through the eyes of a Catholic. . . . I think it pervades my writing" (Kennedy xx). That his religious viewpoint penetrates the bedroom implies not prudishness or censorship but a heightening of the power of sexual love: "To love one must almost live like a saint. . . . Love doesn't fail us. We fail it. We are defeated by our pain" (Kennedy xx).

Thus, love of God and love of another human being are continually equated in Dubus's fiction, but he cannot avoid at least one significant difference: in the human realm, the beloved is an erotic being and the definition of human love contains an erotic element. Moreover, just as Catholicism and sexual love are the abiding concerns of the texts, each has its dark, destructive side. According to Dubus, the Catholic Church, in its rigid, moralizing manifestation ("If They Knew Yvonne"), represses and warps the human psyche, just as shallow, egoistic sex ("Voices from the Moon") destroys the very love it purports to express. But Dubus's careful, conscious balancing of sacramental and erotic realms contains an important flaw. In the relationship of lover to beloved represented in the Catholic Church, the lover is God, denoted as "He" and embodied in a male Son; the beloved is God's Church, denoted as "she" and figured by the virgin mother. What happens to the interweaving of erotic and sacramental love when the lover in the human realm is female?

Luke Ripley is revealing a deeply Dubussian and deeply Catholic sentiment when he observes in "A Father's Story," "it was womanhood they were entering, the deep forest of it, and no matter how many women and men too are saying these days that there is little difference between us, the truth is that men find their way into that forest only on clearly marked trails, while women move about in it like birds" (462). Initially, the forest figures womanhood. But as such, it soon devolves to metaphoric nonsense, since women would naturally be more comfortable in womanhood (as men in manhood), and its forest would not be one a man would find his way into except as a voyeur—hardly a blow struck for an advocate of *la différence*. Rather, the forest quickly broadens to figure sexually aware adult life. Following Dubus's metaphor in this sense, we find that women do not encounter that life but are part of it, just as they enjoy freedom of movement but no control over their destiny, whereas the men marking trails appear to envy those who "move about in it like birds," without expressing any desire to trade places with them. Here is food for thought, and a striking articulation of Luke's—and Dubus's—"truth."

Recent Catholic apologists create similar figurations. According to Catholic doctrine, woman "is created as the perfecting element . . . the 'being-in-relation'" (Tavard 8). Pius XI's 1930 encyclical offers a scripturally based hierarchical structure for marriage: "For if the man is the head, the woman is the heart, and as he occupies the chief place in ruling, so she may and ought to claim for herself the chief place in love" (15). The investigations of Catholic psychologist F.J.J. Buytendijk have produced theories of male and female movement that read like echoes of Luke Ripley. Finding that men emphasize the concluding phase of each step while walking whereas women's steps are less accentuated, he writes that "the movements of males consist of countless *endings*; the movements of females are *endlessly continuous*" (quoted in Hauke 89).

Closely entwined with such gender-based imagery is a pattern in Dubus's writing which is at first startling but in the end consistent with Church doctrine: no woman in the stories ever attempts to construct a dialogue with the divine or to carry on a spiritual life outside the symbolic dimensions of sexual or maternal love. For men, Dubus has pointed out the need to transcend the sexual relation; the idea of a woman satisfying "all [a man's] spiritual yearning . . . is, I think, damned near impossible" (Kennedy 99). Thus the male characters who embody promise in the stories either appear to reject false religion for true or are able, as in "Voices from the Moon" and "A Father's Story," to cut straight to the notion of communion with God. Conversely, religion (meaning Catholicism) exists for female characters *only* as the superficial, outworn strictures—as when the tragic Rose's "Catholic beliefs" cause her to "practice rhythm" or when Polly in "The Pretty Girl" thinks of Mass mostly as a masquerade where "she did not pray with concentration, but she did not think either, and her mind wandered from the Mass to the faces of people around her" (88).

In the patristic tradition, of course, virgins and female religious figures have privileged access to God. Great female mystics like the medieval Margery Kempe, who bore fourteen children before turning to a life of pilgrimage, took vows of chastity in order to carry forward a dialogue with Jesus. None of Dubus's women, however, is inclined toward abstinence, and so it is the Church's figuration of non-celibate women we need to examine. And that traditional figuration has "tended to separate . . . the liturgical service of the Lord from contact with women" (Tavard 119).

Dubus has been lauded for his deeply felt characterizations of women and his ability to tell stories from a female point of view. "Thus, in Dubus's fiction about women," writes Kennedy, "we find central questions of identity and intimate human communication" (22). My focusing attention on the absence of female dialogue with God may seem either an attempt to qualify that praise or a new and cynical questioning of the inherent value of religious transcendence in Dubus's work, but I intend it as neither. The recent debate over the ordination of women in the Catholic Church has raised issues of gender difference and valuation in doctrinal terms; what Dubus accomplishes is a remarkable presentation of those issues, and of his Catholic stance on them, in fictional terms. The following discussion of the two stories Dubus himself has named as his strongest, "Adultery" and "Molly," will explore that stance further.

Although their physical forms vary, Dubus's fictional women generally conform to the image of Christian womanliness as conceptualized by contemporary Catholic theologians like Manfred Hauke.[1] Edith, of the long short story "Adultery," who is "conscious of her size . . . small and slender," is no exception. She is having an affair with an ex-priest, Joe Ritchie, a figure who embodies Dubus's idea of the sacrament of human love. As Dubus said in an interview:

> I guess Joe Ritchie and I are set in that line—the lover must look outward toward the beloved. . . . To love, one must almost live like a saint, as one must live like a saint to perform really well in everything else; by that I mean the focus, the commitment, the control of self that a saint must have. . . . What Joe Ritchie wants and does get is the spiritual love merged with physical. He wants the love which is in harmony with his love for God, for the deity, in harmony with his spiritual love, not a substitute for it, but a movement *toward* it; a commitment as total as his commitment to Christ. [Kennedy 99]

The spirituality of Joe's secular love is inconceivable without his religious devotion, which is both freely and deeply felt, unbound by institutional caveats. Of course, Joe's brand of Catholicism is no longer threatened by birth control or the stigma of masturbation. Further, the story of his priesthood and his decision to leave it, which follows and parallels Edith's story of her marriage to Hank and its corruption, contains within it the story of the women confessors who provide the window through which he can envision his future life. These women sin (as Edith will sin, with him), but their sins are "instinctual," having "nothing to do with God"; they are also exclusively sexual, as opposed to the "calculated" and multivalent sins of men. Women thereby become "their own temples," their confessions "a distant and dutiful salute to the rules and patterns of men" (443); in effect, they are either sinful *by nature* or free of the sort of sin a priest might absolve. It is this inward-dwelling nature of women that provides Joe the "female reception he had to have" (442). And it is this same analysis of female nature that leads Hauke to write, "The fact that women are guided more strongly by intuition and feeling also means that they are more open to concrete experience, whereas men always behave more critically" (93); this unreservedness leads in turn to "a greater readiness for devotedness," which in turn both places higher stakes on a woman's capacity for sin and denies women the more "decisive" action of turning toward God "even if doing so clashes with some current mood or feeling" (94). Hauke is preparing an argument for a male priesthood; Dubus is laying the ground for Edith's literal and figurative epiphany with the dying Joe.

Edith is not unaware of sin and redemption. When she has her first extra-marital affair, before Joe, she immediately categorizes it as a sin, one to which she has "committed herself" and in which she takes a certain pride. ("She was able to sin and love at the same time" [429].) By considering her pride, not in its late twentieth-century translation as self-esteem, but with its original connotation of sin, we can understand the self-deception of Edith's pose. Heady with her own triumph, she considers words like "sin" and "cleansing" without acknowledging their moral thrust; her psychological gesture is "a distant and dutiful salute to the rules and patterns of men." Although she *is* sinning, she does not yet understand in what way. The difference between Edith and Joe at this early stage finds its correlative in the ways they each frame fear. Edith's fear, akin to that of the lonely farm-woman whose story she hears, is every-where and nowhere, "the house enclosing and caressing her with some fear she could not name" (437). Joe's fear is specific and exhilarating; it lies in his repeated thought, "I must have a woman" and engenders not loneliness but kinship "with all those alive and dead who . . . suddenly made the statement whose result they had both feared and hoped for" (441).

Joe, a Catholic man, surmounts his fear through transcendence, through a "leap of the heart of man toward the heart of God" (444)—a movement echoed in the Catholic notion, described by Hauke, of a "thrust outward" from the "center of the subject . . . the essence of the masculine qualities" (142). Moreover, he equates his connection to God with his sexual connection to Edith:

> He believed that faith had no more to do with intellect than love did; that touching her he knew he loved her and loving her he touched her; and that his flesh knew God through touch as it had to [in] a leap caused by the awareness of death. Like us, he had said. . . . When we make love, he said. We do it in the face of death. . . . Our bodies aren't just meat then; they become statement too; they become spirit. [444]

Remarkably, Joe speaks to Edith of this sacramental union, pushing the parallel of Eucharist and lovemaking to the point where it seems to demand an equivalent notion of transcendence from her. To a reader whose frame of reference lies outside Catholic constructions of gender, her lack of response is disappointing. When Joe asks, "If we can do that with each other then why can't we do it with God, and he with us?" she replies, "I don't know . . . I've never thought about it." But *Joe* is not disappointed: "Don't," he tells her, "it's too simple" (444). And when he later pushes the question further he makes clear what form her transcendence can take, how she can escape being "just meat": "He maintained and was committed to the belief that making love could parallel and even merge with the impetus and completion of the Eucharist.

Else why make love at all, he said. . . . But if she were free to love him, each act between them would become a sacrament, each act a sign of their growing union in the face of God and death" (445). In other words, it is not necessary to have Edith commune with *God* in order for the act of lovemaking to do so; she only needs to commune with *Joe*—lovingly and freely, free of Hank. Hank becomes, as it were, her false Church, Joe her true, so that at the end "she is telling Hank good-bye, feeling that good-bye in her womb and heart" (453)—her movement from false to true occasioned, like Joe's, by a sudden recognition of death.

Edith's ability to locate transcendence in a love for Joe accords with the doctrinal view of women's immanence, whereby "women are more strongly embedded in the near world," their "dynamics . . . less expansive than that of men" (Hauke 141). This same doctrine houses "the central idea that woman-hood is essentially receptive" (Tavard 132). At one time, Dubus writes, Edith "wanted to fall in love with God" (428); now, having been through the fire of adultery and love for the dying Joe, it is Joe she encounters instead. Making love, her pleasure comes when Joe "kisses her and enters with a thrust she receives . . . [and] she knows she holds his entire history in her body" (413). As Joe himself receives the Eucharist in last rites, she parallels that sacrament's desire for union with the holy as she "has the urge to fleshless insert her ribs within his, mesh them" (453). If Joe must feel an "earth-rooted love for God in order to live with certainty as a man" (444), Edith must feel an earth-rooted love for a man in order to live as a woman. In Joe, and not beyond, lies her salvation.

"Adultery" might be held realistic in the movement of its narrative—the characters' small, clumsy gestures and half-finished sentences represent life as most of us know it—though its concern with thematic parallels and with words like "receive," "know," "touch," and "body" lifts the story to a symbolic level. But in the story "Molly," Dubus's most profound experiment in female perspective, he abandons the assumption of realism altogether. When Molly is nine, Dubus writes, her divorced mother, Claire, talks to her during their "cocktail hour." And not only talks but discourses in long monologues about things like sex and the Vietnam War:

> And there I was with my little life. Working with real-estate agents, and lawyers, and banks—Jesus: *banks*—and architects and building contractors. And I think everything would have been blurred. For me, anyway, if it weren't for the war. I think I would have figured this is the way the world is. And maybe that's how these people got that way when they were young. Maybe they just figured this was it: lying and fucking over people. . . . I was pregnant with you. And I sat

there and knew we did not live alone anymore, me and you inside of me. I was part of the war. [121]

Claire has been drinking; but these are not meant as alcoholic monologues, the sort of gibberish that sends the listening child a single message: your parent is out of control. Instead, "By the time Molly was nine she was a sensitive and eager listener who understood everything, it seemed, that Claire told her. . . . Molly was able to connect her own moral landscape with Claire's" (122). Dubus has stepped out of the "real" world of mother-daughter relations—possibly because he does not understand those relations, but more likely in order to create a gendered point of view based not on a particular female character but on the ways that women use language to construct action. Likewise, "Molly" does not refer explicitly to religious faith but uses the narration of Claire's moral universe and Molly's rite of passage to realize the hollowness of life without transcendence, which is also the life these women lead.

In place of the references to sexual union as *sacrament* or *touch* in "Adultery," Dubus in "Molly" plays variants on the theme of carnal *knowing*. Claire has learned "that the desire to know another, and to be known by him, was futile" (122); but to Molly she can still describe the illusion of love as one of feeling "known." The failure of Dubus's male characters to achieve intimacy reflects the unspoken Catholic grounding of his fiction. Turning again to contemporary Catholic theology, we find the idea that "women are more capable than men of paying attention to another person" (*Mulieris*, par. 18), whereas men "tend more to see the world in terms of obstacles and means" (Hauke, 92). Raymond, Claire's ex-husband, is in these terms a monster of manhood, focused entirely on "obstacles and means" and relating more closely to potsherds than to his wife. But the project of knowledge fails with all men, Claire claims; and following the dichotomy above, she, in her turn, can be judged unwilling to understand the other—abandoning her own inherent "sensitivity to values" and construing knowledge as a tit-for-tat exchange rather than the fruit of union.

The question in "Molly" is whether Claire has passed her failure on to her daughter. Dubus dangles answers before us: after having oral sex with her best friend's brother, Bruce, Molly tells her mother she wants to go out with him "to know things," and later Molly and Bruce talk:

> "I don't even know you."
> "Only for eight years."
> "Belinda's big brother. You don't know me."
> "I know you're a fox."
> "For eight years?"

"Three."
"So what are we doing?"
"I don't know." [168]

The focus on knowing in this exchange, and its denial, implies that Molly and
Bruce are treading the same ground that Claire has worn bare. The actual
lovemaking between the young people is as painful in its superrealism as Claire's
monologues are in their surrealism. As if to prove not only the authenticity of
Molly's point of view but the raw factuality of the event, Dubus records everything from the car's gear shift in Molly's back to the blood on her pants.

More important than the act itself, however, are two motifs preceding it
that work to frame Molly's loss of virginity in terms of both the story itself and
of Dubus's Catholicism. The first is Molly's repeated intention not to make
love with Bruce that night, to wait. Bruce has condoms but "won't need them,"
she tells her mother; and to Bruce she announces, "I didn't come out here to
make love" (169). Yet she does, and the change seems to come from the same
awareness that prompts Edith's decision to divorce Hank: the imminence of
death.

> It frightened her, that large black space that was not sea and sky at all, yet
> she stared at it, as though looking at the night of her death. . . . All she saw was
> Molly Cousteau, not scattered ashes now, nor ashes drawn back and contained
> again by flesh and voice, and eyes with vision; but Molly as one tiny ash on the
> surface of the earth, looking into the depth of the universe, at the face of eter-
> nity. [170-71]

Concurrent with Molly's gradually fading denial is her growing feeling
concerning Bruce, that "she was his girl" (170). The naming of her status creates a new identity for Molly, much as Edith's early desire "to be a nice girl
someone would want to marry" (413) creates her identity in her courtship and
early marriage with Hank. In an earlier Dubus story, "Miranda Over the Valley," Miranda states the desire baldly: "I want to be owned" (6).

Love for these women involves the dissolution of the autonomous self, a
dissolution that feels much the same whether it stems from a sudden awareness of the enormity of death or from what Dubus has called the saintliness of
the beloved, a figure he takes from Catholic theologian Henri Nouwen: "Becoming the Beloved means letting the truth of our Belovedness become
enfleshed in everything we think, say, or do. . . . To become the Beloved we,
first of all, have to claim that we are taken" (39, 43).

To surrender one's original self in love, to find freedom in submission, is a
Christian directive for all people, but especially for women, whose guiding
force, Jesus' mother, Mary, represents "the cosmos' power of surrender in the

form of bridal woman" (Hauke 306). Paul VI's address to the Second Vatican Council envisioned woman not just as man's companion, but as the embodiment of self-gift, "le don supreme de l'amour . . . l'heroisme habituel de sacrifice" (Col. 1923). The trouble, for Molly and Edith and other Dubus women, starts either when no one appears strong enough to take possession (as in "Miranda"), or when the intersection of love and death is a falsely imagined one, like Molly's concatenation of herself and Bruce with Hemingway's nova-like lovers in *For Whom the Bell Tolls*: "[Later] she could not give words to what she had felt holding Bruce under the trees. She only knew she would never feel it again. Long after she had wept for Maria and Robert, reading in bed on a summer night, she could only think: *There is no Madrid*, but she could not say that to Belinda, or even to Bruce as they lay on her bed after school" (175).

Contrary to James Yaffe's assertion that "'Molly' opens up the possibility for motherhood and family happiness in a young girl" (150), the story seems one of closure. The callow, forgivable mistaking of a fleeting notion of death for true awareness of death, and of dating status ("his girl") for true possession by a lover, together close off the possibility of sacramental love and replace it with a series of love-encounters ("the others waiting, in high school and college and afterward" [176]), bringing Molly back in line with her mother, Claire, who believes "there was nothing harmful in living a lie if you knew you were. . . . How else could you live, except to will yourself into an alteration of the truth you were dealt at birth?" (123).

And yet Molly's gesture toward Bruce, the gesture she will strive to hold onto in memory—"she stepped forward and tightly held him, her heart weeping but not with sorrow, her body quivering but without passion or fear" (175)—is actually more maternal than sexual. The nonprocreative nature of sex with Bruce (like sex for Edith with Joe) denies Molly the divine role accorded women by Augustine, who could not envision "in what sense the woman was made as a helper for the man if not for the sake of bearing children" (75). But the intensity of Molly's postcoital gesture invokes the other side of the doctrinal coin: Bishop Fulton Sheen's injunction to women to "realize" some "form of motherhood," whether physical or symbolic (Yzermans 202). It is Molly's "self-gift" to Bruce, not to receive his seed, but to make him feel that what he has done is all right, for "he stood at the edge of remorse, and if she did not hold him, she would lightly push him over" (175). It is through her nurturing attention to Bruce's adolescent need, rather than through her deflowering, that Molly achieves womanhood.

Far from being a realistic coming-of-age story, "Molly" is an *exemplum*, its moral so closely woven into the fabric of its narrative as to be invisible without an accompanying sermon. To ask how Molly will fare, for instance, in the "real" future awaiting her is to ask the wrong question. More to the point is the vision of womanliness and love presented, first by Claire and later by Molly. Does the vision accord with the reader's ideals? No, despite that pure gesture toward Bruce. Where then, Dubus begs, have Claire and Molly gone wrong?

Dubus's answer to this sort of question, like his answer to the question Joe Ritchie implicitly poses for Edith ("Else why make love at all?" [445]) poses a challenge to late twentieth-century feminism. Women who are "their own temples," women who move about like birds in the forest, quickly become women whose participation in the temple or forest of the larger world is iconographic and impressionistic: their interest lies in the ways that the world inscribes itself in them. Thus in Dubus they consistently receive, as Edith Milton puts it, "a sexual answer for a spiritual need" (137). Claire, and to a lesser extent Molly, fail to recognize the power of self-gift. As Molly drifts toward a future where she cannot envision "something new waiting for her, something she had not done," she tries to recall the sanctified moment: "[But] she still could not see them holding each other, with the rubber and her bloody pants near their feet, her body quivering with his. Bruce's voice gave her another image: a boy she did not even know . . . and she shivered and opened her eyes to the snow and the dark sky" (176).

Insofar as the power of Dubus's writing lies in his Christian, Catholic view, his women—the most essential aspect of that writing—need to be understood within that Christian, Catholic framework. Ironically, it is because of that framework itself—that is, because of doctrines differentiating male from female in both quotidian and spiritual life[2]—that the Catholicism in Dubus's view of women is less apparent than in his view of men. The faith of men like Joe Ritchie, Luke Ripley, and Richie Stowe is expressed not only in the ways they live their lives, but explicitly, in their religious creeds and doubts. When they equate love of God and love of another human being, they do so consciously and by comparison.

For Dubus's women, viewed as they are through the lens of his faith, sacramental love is achieved not along with, but through, secular love. Expression of love toward another human being, whether erotic or maternal, is itself a kind of prayer or communion with the holy. According to Thomistic thought, woman "sanctifies herself by making herself available to those in need"—often to a man "who associates with a woman and in love enters a realm which is far deeper and wider than the two persons concerned" (Tavard 132, 141). Dubus figures this ethic in his view of Edith, cleaning the house to which her lover Joe will never return:

> She looks out at the bright snow and the woods beyond: the spread and
> reaching branches of elms and birches and maples and tamaracks are bare; there

are pines and hemlocks green in the sun. She almost stops working. Her impulse is to throw herself against the window, cover it with her body, and scream in the impotent rage of grief. But she does not break the rhythm of her work: she continues to push the vacuum cleaner over the carpet, while behind her [Joe] watches the push and pull of her arms, the bending of her body, the movement of her legs. [449-50]

Theologian George Tavard has written, in a spirit of conciliation, that "it is in her relationship to man that woman discovers herself as woman; and she does not exist as woman except in that relationship" (228). The difficulty for a deeply Catholic writer like Andre Dubus may be that it is also in her relationship to the godhead that woman discovers herself as woman. That divine relationship accomplished (as it was, say, in mystics like Margery Kempe), she is no longer available for definition through human heterosexuality. Conversely, the sexual relationships in which Dubus's women find themselves come to comprise the woman-definition, in a way that they do not for men, whose relationship to a patriarchal God is not symbolically heterosexual.

With his religious viewpoint in mind, we can return to the issue of Dubus's Southernness. Flannery O'Connor's statement that the Southern writer does "justice to reality by telling a story" bears a close relation to Dubus's fiction, which probes the truth of human spiritual experience by an attentive telling of stories. That O'Connor's fiction is peopled less by realistic characters than by grotesques does not undermine her thesis, for she is speaking not of *representation of* but of *justice to* reality. It is very much justice that Dubus is after, a rebalancing of our morally skewed world by virtue of stories whose actions and consequences depend as much on moments of epiphany and conversion as they do on the choices of realistically modeled characters.

NOTES

1. "Because of the nature of the female reproductive organs, women are, to a greater extent than men, 'sexual beings.' . . . The body's bone structure tends . . . to be weaker in women than in men. . . . A woman's skin is softer. . . . The female figure appears to converge more toward the center of the trunk. . . . The male, accordingly, is more strongly directed toward the 'outside,' and the female, toward the 'inside'" (Hauke 87-88).

2. Jean Vanier, a close colleague of Dubus's spiritual mentor, Henri Nouwen, has written that "the difference between man and woman is a radical and fundamental one which permeates the depths of our consciousness and affects *all human behavior*" (49; emphasis mine).

Clyde Edgerton

Death and Dying

James A. Grimshaw Jr.

> "It's just one big happy family that cooks,
> and talks about dead people . . ."
> —Edgerton, *The Floatplane Notebooks*

"Dying is a part of living," Pearl tells her sister, Mattie Rigsbee, matter-of-factly in Clyde Edgerton's second published novel, *Walking across Egypt* (1987). And she believes it too. Pearl's words may serve as an overall thematic statement for Edgerton's fiction from 1985 to 1995 because when readers enter Edgerton's fictive world, they enter a mind-set focused on death and dying. Rhonda's observation in the epigraph captures that thematic essence pointedly. In his six published novels—the other five are *Raney* (1985), *The Floatplane Notebooks* (1988), *Killer Diller* (1991), *In Memory of Junior* (1992), and *Redeye: A Western* (1995)—the major themes, which R. Sterling Hennis Jr. identifies in his bio-bibliographical essay on Edgerton in *Contemporary Fiction Writers of the South*, are inextricably tied to death and dying. Those themes deal with love, familial relationships, the clash between past and present values, the extended family, and the struggle to live the good life, that is, a Christian life; they constitute the other parts of living and are connected by the underlying theme of death and dying.

Place transcends the geographical location in which Edgerton sets the action of his novels. Thomas Hardy has his Wessex, William Faulkner has his Yoknapatawpha County, and Clyde Edgerton has his Hansen County, North Carolina. They represent not just a mere postage stamp of earth but more significantly the history, the people, the families that have existed there for generations. The shift in emphasis, as C. Hugh Holman has noted in *The Immoderate Past: The Southern Writer and History*, replaces the standard view of the present and space with the Southern concept of the past and time. Or, as Jack Burden observes in Robert Penn Warren's *All the King's Men* (1946), we must accept our past in order to live the present and hope for the future (461). The Southern writers' absorption with, and in, history and the burden their history has placed on them are well documented and illustrated. Edgerton's communities are small towns — Listre, Bethel, Summerlin, and White Level — made up of Faulknerian families: Bales, Bell, Copeland, McCord, Purvis, and Rigsbee. Outsiders also bring new ideas and different values to Hansen County: Wesley Benfield, the orphan; Ted Sears from a military background; the Shepherds from Atlanta, Georgia; and the Trents from Michigan.

More than three hundred characters populate the pages of these five novels; approximately 10 percent of them are dead. Their deaths and their dying, however, carry the weight of these families' relationships. We should not be surprised, for example, when, in *In Memory of Junior*, Tate Bales's love of flying is traced historically from Uncle Grove McCord back to Albert Copeland, the keeper of the floatplane notebooks and a cousin of Uncle Grove.

Edgerton links *The Floatplane Notebooks* and *In Memory of Junior* stylistically as well as through location and characters. The form offers various points of view, and each section bears the name of the narrator, similar to Faulkner's *As I Lay Dying*. *The Floatplane Notebooks* carries six narrators, one of which is the wisteria vine started by Caroline Copeland at the back of the Copeland graveyard; *In Memory of Junior* has twenty-one narrators and the action is advanced by the variety of voices.

Both novels center on a graveyard. In *The Floatplane Notebooks*, the Copeland family's ritual is to gather the first Saturday each May for a gravecleaning. The occasion serves as a family picnic, and all available members are expected to attend. Stories of deceased family members are retold; and young and new members of the clan, such as Bliss Copeland, Thatcher's eighteen-year-old wife, are initiated into family history and lore. The ghosts that sit and talk in the moonlit graveyard share details of the family history that corroborate or contradict the legends that are passed on among the living. (Incidentally, Edgerton uses italics for those dialogues, a variation on a Faulknerian technique of typography.)

In *In Memory of Junior*, Uncle Grove, who has fallen from family grace because of his lesbian sister, Evelyn, and because of his wild shenanigans as a young man, lives in Cutler, Arkansas. Notwithstanding his alienation from family members, he decides he will be buried with his family in Listre, North Carolina. In a series of farcical episodes that begin when he ships his tombstone to his nephews, Faison and Tate Bales, he concocts a plan to have his own grave dug, to have a specially designed coffin built with an inside latch delivered to the grave site, to lie down inside his coffin and commit suicide, and, as prearranged, to have the hired gravediggers bury him. The entire scheme is as bizarre as Addie Bundren's burial. One mistake leads to another, but two incidents ultimately stave off the gruesome end for Uncle Grove.

Morgan, Uncle Grove's grandnephew, is a typical sixteen-year-old who copes with his emotionally wrought existence as he is shuffled between divorced parents by escaping into the world of computers. Morgan's long hair, earring, and slovenly dress indicate to Uncle Grove an individual attempting to escape his situation. In some ways, Morgan represents a young, modernized Uncle Grove. Uncle Grove wins over Morgan through his own free, maverick spirit; and for $100 he persuades Morgan to drive him to the graveyard and to ensure that his plan is fulfilled.

The second event involves Tate Bales, Uncle Grove's nephew and Morgan's father. Tate has purchased a used '46 Super Cruiser airplane like the one Uncle Grove flew "off a pole." Tate's purpose is to interest Morgan in flying maybe and in life definitely. Tate is educated, teaches at Ballard University, and is a local hero because of the Silver Star he earned in Vietnam as a Navy fighter pilot. When Uncle Grove appears unannounced in Summerlin, Tate accepts him, unlike the other relatives, who resent him. He takes Uncle Grove flying; later, and without Tate's knowledge, Uncle Grove "borrows" Tate's plane by himself and buzzes the graveyard where he was to have been buried. Both Tate's and Morgan's acceptance of Uncle Grove seem to have altered his view of dying in spite of his prostate cancer, and Uncle Grove gains the emotional support he needs to go on living.

Although Edgerton's six novels interconnect through members of these local communities, two other novels also pair up more directly. *Walking across Egypt* and *Killer Diller* follow the change in Wesley Benfield, change wrought through the love and care provided by Mattie Rigsbee. *Walking across Egypt* is Mattie's story. She is a seventy-eight-year-old widow whose grown children, Robert and Elaine, have not married and have gone their own ways, in spite of Mattie's attempts to influence their lives. When Wesley Benfield, a sixteen-year-old juvenile delinquent, escapes from the Young Men's Rehabilitation

Center (YMRC), he finds his way to Mattie's house. In keeping with Mattie's Christian beliefs, her loneliness, and her amazing innocence and boundless forgiveness, she adopts Wesley as her grandson. In *Killer Diller*, eight years later, Wesley resides in the Back on Track Again (BOTA) House and still visits Mattie Rigsbee and calls her his grandma. He takes care of her and frees her from the entrapment of the nursing home before he flees BOTA House and exploitation by an overzealous university president, Ted Sears. In his escape, Wesley "adopts" a sixteen-year-old retarded youth, Jules Vernon Jackson, a "killer diller." Wesley orchestrates the BOTA House Noble Defenders of the Word Band's departure and takes with him his first genuine love, Phoebe Trent.

Mattie Rigsbee reminds us of the grandmother in Flannery O'Connor's short story, "A Good Man Is Hard to Find." Like O'Connor's grandmother, who wants the family to travel in clean underwear in case they have a wreck, Mattie thinks she would just die if someone came into her house and found a sink full of dirty dishes. Although Edgerton's characters are clearly his own and not clones from other authors, other traces of O'Connor's characters emerge briefly: Wesley, an older version of O'Connor's John Wesley in "A Good Man Is Hard to Find," and Robert and Elaine, older versions of John Wesley and June Star in the same story. Robert and Elaine also combine some characteristics of Wesley and Scofield, Mrs. May's children in "Greenleaf," and Hulga in "Good Country People." However, later in *Killer Diller*, Wesley's religious conversion has parallels with Hazel Mote's initial conversion in *Wise Blood*. Not unlike O'Connor's primary female characters, Mattie, her sister Pearl, and other female characters in Hansen County are widows. They are left alone in a rapidly changing world to cope the best way they can.

On one occasion in *Walking across Egypt*, Mattie and Pearl go to the funeral home to select their coffins and to make arrangements for their funerals. Dying is truly a part of living to them, and neither seems to fear death. Their visit with Mr. Crosley is satirically humorous and is reminiscent of Charles's general criticism of funeral homes in *Raney*. Charles is addressing the Funeral Home director:

> "Mr. Simmons, do you realize that some families can't afford a two thousand dollar funeral? Do you realize that by displaying those expensive caskets the way you do, you make people feel guilty if they don't get one? Do you realize that?"
>
> Mr. Simmons stayed composed. "We—"
>
> "Why don't you display the cheaper caskets for people to decide on—especially poor folks?"
>
> "We believe that—"
>
> "I know what you believe. I've read about what you believe. You believe you can squeeze two thousand dollars from some grieving widow who can't think

straight—rather than explain to her that a funeral does not *have* to be so damned expensive. Your 'profession' has carried this whole business to the extreme. And I can't believe you people stand up there in your casket display room and talk about how one vault is guaranteed not to leak within fifty years and another within one hundred years and that kind of garbage." [135]

In a more Horatian mode in *Walking across Egypt*, Edgerton again targets the exploitation of the dying, especially the elderly. In *Killer Diller* the satire shifts from morticians to university administrators who also know how to get along with widows in hopes of generous bequests to their school; those administrators spend their energies raising funds at the expense of the health and life of their university. In his continued examination of death and dying, Edgerton shifts the emphasis from dying with dignity to exploitation of the dying.

Edgerton's first novel, *Raney*, was not the first novel he had planned to write. *The Floatplane Notebooks*, which includes the first story Edgerton wrote, might have been the first; but he felt it was not right and turned to *Raney*. *Walking across Egypt* evolved from an actual incident in which his mother sat in a rocking chair without a bottom in it and got stuck. In an unpublished interview conducted by Jean Marie Elliott on December 1, 1987, Edgerton explains that he wrote a short story about that incident, and that story grew into a novel.

Those insights into the development of his first three novels provide additional support and understanding of the linkage throughout his work. *Raney* deals primarily with the trials and tribulations of a young couple, Raney Bell and Charles C. Shepherd, in the first two years, two months, and two days of their marriage. They have very little in common other than their love for one another: Raney is Baptist, Charles is Episcopalian; Raney's family members are small-town, working-class people who share a tight familial bond; Charles's family is urban, educated, and rather aloof—"God's frozen chosen." Family values and questions dominate the surface of the novel, and the thematic emphasis on death and dying appears only subtly. Nevertheless, nine deaths furnish sufficient reason for characters, especially Raney, who narrates the story, to reflect on the end of life. Matter-of-factly, Raney mentions Uncle Nate's former wife, Joanne, who is dead. Also gone but not forgotten are Uncle Frank and Uncle Forrest, and Uncle Newton's and Uncle Nate's passing touch Raney and raise questions in Charles's mind about the relationship of the survivors and the deceased. To Charles, taking food to the grieving family, visiting the funeral home, and viewing the body seem primitive acts. But, then, Raney cannot be too surprised because Charles "never had the heart to" hunt, another death-related activity that he found to be unnecessary and primitive. The fact that such "primitive" acts might have deep, psychological meaning to the participants eludes Charles.

Having noted briefly the general predominance of death and dying as a thematic focus in Edgerton's six novels, we may still question the extent of its effect on the characters, their language, and their values. Clyde Edgerton has created an imaginary rural Southern community of characters who have individual hardships, who have maintained hope in spite of obstacles, and who have emerged with a deeper love for one another. Yet, Edgerton has achieved this creation with humor, a keen ear for dialect, and astute psychological insight.

Edgerton's main characters are individuals in some ways and choruses of voices in others. Raney, Mattie Rigsbee, Wesley Benfield, Uncle Grove, and Bliss Copeland perhaps to a lesser extent, are figures for which individual voices can be heard. In *In Memory of Junior*, the twenty-one narrators compose a choirlike sound, a community of voices. Gloria Palmer, a slightly more aggressive Dilsey, speaks from the perspective of domestic help; Faison and Tate Bales, as heirs apparent, provide a center for the other voices' focus. Uncle Grove clearly sings solo. These characters are the survivors, the members of their communities who learn, or are learning, their lessons from others. They affirm what Shannon Ravenel, fiction editor for Algonquin Books, told R. Sterling Hennis Jr.: Edgerton explores "the message of hope and revival of life that is to be found in the mysteries of love" (120). That love comes from hope; and in consonance with Dr. Sherwin B. Nuland's theory in his provocative book, *How We Die: Reflections on Life's Final Chapter*, the hope that brings peace is found in the memory the survivors can create and in the meaning the deceased person's life would have for those after his death.

Notwithstanding their different backgrounds, Raney's love for Charles grows, in part at least, through their discussions about values, their compromises about familial obligations, and their shared losses. Their biggest argument, which almost ended their marriage, was over Uncle Nate Purvis's death and his sister Doris's guilt. Uncle Nate suffered a disabling wound in World War II and returned home to be cared for by his family. Charles's accusation hurts Raney: "It was a whole family's refusal to look for alternatives to a . . . a way of life. To read—to become educated about a problem staring you in the face. Given the self-righteousness of . . . fundamental Christianity in this family, your Uncle Nate didn't have a chance" (153).

Raney defends her family's caring and responsibility for family members, and she and Charles agree to go to a counselor, Dr. Mary Bridges, who facilitates their reconciliation. Raney comes to realize that it is difficult for her "to think about marriages when all the men" in her family have died. Raney's revelation reminds us of Robert Frost's "Mending Wall" when she observes: "Rules get set by somebody hundreds of years ago and they are hard to break, like rules about what you can and can't talk about" (174). In *The Floatplane*

Notebooks, Bliss Copeland, the outsider who marries into the family, faces similar frustrations, though Bliss is not as outspoken as Raney.

Similarly, in *Walking across Egypt* most of the women are widows. Mattie Rigsbee's husband, Paul, died of a heart attack when she was seventy-three years old; her father had died when she was eight years old. She takes on Wesley Benfield, to whom she refers as "the least of these my brethren," as a project. Edgerton told Elliott in her telephone interview that "the least are usually very unattractive" and, therefore by implication, are not the ones most sought after by those proffering help. Mattie prevails against the protests of her grown children, both of whom are single, and becomes Wesley's legal guardian. After her telephone conversation with her daughter Elaine, who fears Mattie has lost her senses, Mattie thinks: "*Somebody* needed to get married." Mattie recognizes love as a stabilizing force.

In *Killer Diller* Wesley seems to have assimilated Mattie's convictions about love. As the BOTA House Band members run away in a bus repaired by Jules Vernon Jackson's father, Holister, the owner of Sunrise Auto Repair Shop, Wesley dreams. His dream contains memories of his past with Mattie Rigsbee and a religious conversion with visions of his future as an accepted member of society with Phoebe and Vernon by his side.

The deaths from which Wesley learns about life are metaphorical deaths of society's biases against difference. In *In Memory of Junior*, the characters learn from real deaths, particularly the death of Junior. Their lesson learned is reminiscent of the lesson in Robert Penn Warren's poem, "Grackles, Goodbye," in which the persona concludes: "only, / In the name of Death do we learn the true name of Love" (117). Faison develops a better understanding of June Lee's feelings, and Tate grows closer to Morgan. Uncle Grove, who had considered suicide, reveals the reason Evelyn, Faison and Tate's mama, had deserted her family: Evelyn fell in love with another woman, Honour Walters. Tate is stoic about the truth; Faison has a more difficult time reconciling that truth. He decides finally "why the hell should I worry about something happened over forty years ago. It's all history. I can't do a thing about it" (200).

Toward the end of the novel, the references to death come from the two sons, Morgan and Junior. After his near-death experience of the airplane crash and the rattlesnakes, Morgan has his "first story" to tell; and he tells it to his girlfriend, Teresa. Morgan has almost joined the human race. Although Junior is dead, his fifth-grade journal records his thoughts about family, pets, flying, war, and marriage—values he had already begun to learn from his family and from Uncle Tate. His journal is his voice from the grave.

The language Edgerton chooses is subtle and perhaps achieves the understated humor in conversation and in the dialect that he admires so much in the writings of Mark Twain, especially in *Adventures of Huckleberry Finn*.

Because death and dying seem to be applicable to most considerations in Edgerton's novels, they become focal points in the language, action, history, and myth in Hansen County. For example, in addition to direct references to literal death, the characters use idiomatic expressions that incorporate images of death: at one point, Charles looks "bored to death"; "I'm going to kill you when we get home," the man in the Hansen County Mental Health Clinic tells Oscar, who reminds us of Mary Grace in Flannery O'Connor's short story, "Revelation"; Charles's parents view the language of Raney's family as dying: Raney says, "It embarrassed me to death," she is "nervous to death," and she is "surprised to death"; Sneed gives down-home philosophy with, "You only live once"; "Pearl would die laughing," thinks Mattie Rigsbee; later Mattie feels as if she is "slowing down," a euphemism for dying; and she thinks of dying close to morning at the "still moment"; Mattie's metaphor for Wesley is "a dry, dying plant"; when Alora fantasizes about Wesley raping her, she blurts out that "she would just die"—with a possible bawdy pun on Edgerton's part on the word *die*; "what Papa would die if he knew about," muses Noralee; Rhonda loves "that song to death"; Meredith, who can groan like he is dying, almost frightens Noralee to death; thunder dies away to rain as Wesley exits the BOTA House via his third-floor window; Ben, who refers to the difficulty of obtaining a pass to enter Eastern LinkComm, says, "We're gon' dry up and die"; Gloria proclaims that her "granddaddy would die" if he knew; Ansie tells Morgan that the Baleses "would have fought to the death to keep from taking something given to" them; Glenn Bales's room has the smell of death; Faye tells Faison, "Over my dead body there will be an autopsy of my mother"; and of more than 156 total references to death, one more—Jimmy Knight reports that he read in the newspaper about Duke University's "dead white males," a curriculum controversy he fails to comprehend.

These expressions crop up in moments of tension or in extreme reactions to a crisis; perhaps they suggest a readily accepted response to death itself, that is, a tenseness girded in fear or apprehension. Many of them are clearly hyperbolic, not reflecting seriously contemplated action. And in that framework, they create part of the subtle humor that helps prevent an otherwise morbid subject from being morbid.

Folk expressions, however, are perpetuated because they contain a grain of truth that allows insight into a society's values. Edgerton's sustained use of that language points to a strong awareness of the relationship of death and dying to the surface of life. Yet, even facing its presence in their everyday speech and actions, the characters take a realistic view of death. They do so in contrast to what the French social historian Philippe Ariès calls a modern phenomenon, the "Invisible Death." Nuland offers the following explanation of the term: because dying is viewed as ugly and dirty, death is therefore to be relegated to hospitals where today 80 percent of American deaths occur. "Medicine's humility," Nuland maintains, "in the face of nature's power has been lost, and with it has gone some of the moral authority of times past" (259).

In Edgerton's Hansen County, the characters are caught between the moral authority of the past and the modernization of the present as change encroaches on their community. They begin a descent into a familiarity with death, the center of which seems to be the Copeland graveyard and the ghosts the Vine sees. This underworld, this underlying theme, seems further tied to a journey, sometimes literal and sometimes symbolic. Several examples are the annual summer trip of Raney's family to the beach; Mattie Rigsbee's falling through her rocking chair and getting stuck, beginning her journey into an awareness of her mortality; the Copeland's annual grave-cleaning and their trip to Silver Springs, Florida, to hunt and fish; Wesley and the BOTA House Band's journey in search of a new life; and Uncle Grove's trip from Cutler, Arkansas, to Summerlin, North Carolina, his fishing trip to McGarren Island, and his airplane trip with Tate.

These journeys are not without difficulties, catastrophes, and potential death. The annual trips are ritualistic, almost a rite of initiation for the young and new members of the families. On these trips, values are discussed, debated, and shared. Verbal battles are waged over such issues as hypocrisy in religion, suggesting the death of faith; about misfits in society, suggesting the death of tolerance and Christian love; and about the rivalries and fragmentation in families, suggesting a death of family values. Charles's theory about Uncle Nate's depression and attempted suicide targets a family who protect and love someone to death, who smother someone with love. Other values are equally threatened. Ballard University's overzealous, egotistical administrators threaten the death of educational standards. The consumption of alcohol, hunting, war (especially Vietnam), divorce, homosexuality, crime among the young, society's treatment of "the least of these my brethren," and the care of the elderly—all of these issues touch on values in peril in the modern world.

The remedy in Edgerton's fictive world might be summarized in the word "love." Love is manifested in various ways, not the least of which is the acceptance of death as a necessary process of nature that permits us to continue through our own children and the children of others, as Nuland so succinctly phrases it. Suffering, endurance, hope, and love are the best conception of life's sequence. The past helps us understand and accept our present. The future holds at the end but one conclusion, death. The dignity of the inevitable event then rests with the life that precedes death. Based on love, our memory continues and helps future generations. As Uncle Grove so candidly observes, "[We] are history longer than [we] are fact" (47).

JOHN ROSENTHAL

Lee Smith

Ivy Rowe as Woman and Artist

ELIZABETH PELL BROADWELL

Although her short fiction about life in the suburbs appears regularly in anthologies of contemporary Southern literature and has won several prizes, Lee Smith is best known for her novels set in the mountains of Appalachia. Having grown up in the southwestern corner of Virginia, where the hills and hollows have been scarred by the coal mining and logging industries, she creates characters who are alienated from their modern environment and who have been fragmented by a past that, in some cases, lacks the vitality to sustain them.

In six novels set in the Appalachian region, Smith's protagonists often struggle to achieve wholeness in a culture that circumscribes rather than nurtures them. *Black Mountain Breakdown* (1980) portrays a young woman's unsuccessful attempt to achieve selfhood in a contemporary mountain culture that has been stripped of its vitality and its natural resources. *Oral History* (1983), Smith's first experiment with an intergenerational novel, spans a hundred-year period with thirteen different points of view; in each generation these mountain people long for something their environment does not provide or will not tolerate. In *Family Linen* (1985), which also uses multiple points of view, family members gain access to their own unexplored consciousnesses when they gather to attend to their mother, whose sudden illness and death uncover family secrets long buried. *Fair and Tender Ladies* (1988) presents a sustained and powerful female voice that tells of a life of hardships from young age until death. In two recent novels, *The Devil's Dream* (1992) and *Saving Grace* (1995), Smith portrays the Southern subcultures of country music artists and religious snake handlers, respectively: *The Devil's Dream*, which traces the history of a country music family from the 1930s in the Virginia mountains to modern-day Nashville, ends with a contemporary singer's efforts to reclaim the gospel and folk music of her childhood. *Saving Grace* portrays a woman who struggles to find her own identity as she grows up in a snake-handling family and later marries a minister. In these highly praised novels set in the mountains of Appalachia, Smith evokes an unmistakable sense of place, captures the voices of the past, uses language richly expressive of its mountain heritage, often experiments with narrative point of view, and weaves together family and cultural history in novels that span generations. She explores themes of memory, the presence of the past, and an individual's search for identity and wholeness in a culture that is often fragmented.

Of all of her novels, *Fair and Tender Ladies* is perhaps her most critically acclaimed and certainly her best loved. In 1989, following the novel's publication the previous year, Lee Smith received the Appalachian Writers Award and the W.D. Weatherford Award for Appalachian Literature. Identified in early reviews as the author's best book to date, the novel has been critically assessed, in general, as evidence of Smith's integrated world view. Although his remarks are largely based on *Oral History*, Fred Hobson has shown how Smith, like other contemporary Southern writers, accepts her world rather than feels the postmodernist need to invent it. Lucinda MacKethan has compared *Fair and Tender Ladies* to Alice Walker's *The Color Purple*, showing how both epistolary novels present a woman's alienation from and search for self, her discovery of sisterhood, her reunion through language with her lost self, and her restoration to wholeness. Dorothy Hill, who offers a feminist reading based on mythology, argues that in Ivy Rowe, who is a synthesis of Aphrodite and Demeter, Smith reconciles the conflicts which have fragmented her earlier protagonists. For Katherine Kearns, who believes that Ivy confronts but does not solve the conflict of her two roles as mother and artist, the novel is evidence of Lee Smith's own growing acceptance of her identity as an artist.

While critics have offered various assessments of the book, Lee Smith's many readers have responded to the book's appealing protagonist. Women particularly have found the indomitable Ivy Rowe to be personally inspiring, so much so in fact that, according to the author, at least four babies have been named for her heroine (Guralnick 27). Indeed, Lee Smith has acknowledged that the book was very "strength-giving" for herself as well. Her mother was dying and other family members were in the hospital while she was writing the book; Ivy Rowe, she says, was a role model she created for herself during this difficult period of her life (Virginia Smith, "On Regionalism," 785).

Lee Smith's *Fair and Tender Ladies* is an epistolary novel about a woman born at the turn of the century in the mountains of Virginia. In letters written to friends and relatives from the time she is twelve until the end of her life in her seventies, Ivy Rowe tells her own story—a story of passion and sacrifice. As a young girl, she wants to become a writer who writes about love, but she becomes instead a mother and a wife. In acknowledging Ivy's personal development, critics who have written about the novel generally have neglected the origin and scope of Ivy's conflict and its persuasiveness even in the language of the book. Indeed, Ivy's failure to integrate her creative and sexual passion is inherent in the value system of the coal-mining community itself. In its separation of subjective and objective reality, the community fragments modern consciousness, creating a dualism between self and society, between self and other, and, finally, between woman and artist that is mirrored in language itself. Smith uses images of baby/child, clothes, water, fire, and height to reinforce her central themes of fragmentation, identity, and self-discovery.

Smith's protagonists are often limited by having parents who embody different spheres of reality. In *Black Mountain Breakdown*, Crystal Spangler's parents seem to represent the fragmentation of the private and the social spheres—her father is associated with imagination and artistic expression and her mother with business acumen and practicality. In *Fair and Tender Ladies*, Ivy Rowe's parents, Maude and John Arthur, are complementary, extreme examples of the severing of the sexual and the creative spheres. Smith's use of fire and water imagery in two related incidents emphasizes Maude's incomplete sense of identity. When she was only fifteen, Maude ran away from a possessive, wealthy father in Rich Valley (who wanted her to learn "how to act like a lady") to elope with John, a man considerably older than she. Having ridden up the mountain toward her new home with John, double astride on his horse Lightning, Maude blindly followed her own passionate nature and gave in to her own impulses. When they stopped at the creek, Ivy remembers that her mother said her face was "burning hot as fire" and when she looked at her reflection in the pool of the creek, she "looked so wild, she culd not of said who she was, she culd not of called her own name" (12). Literally having seen nothing but John riding in front of her on the horse, she loses her sense of identity. Ironically, Ivy prefers this story of her mother's passionate youth and romance to the present reality of the effects of time and age on her, all worn out with eight children, her beauty vanished. The Maude that Ivy knows still has a passionate nature but is constrained by circumstances—by years of hard times and caring for children. Although her eyes still burn inside her head, she goes to Pilgrim Knob, stands unprotected in the wind, and "sits out in the snow and cries," saying "she's a fool for love" (24). Whereas the image cluster of fire and water in the initial journey emphasizes Maude's passion ("Lightning," "burning hot as fire") and foreshadows Maude's loss of identity as she peers into the water, the cluster of fire and *snow* in her later walk emphasizes her fragmentation and isolation.

If Ivy Rowe's mother's intensity drives her into the cold (isolation and suicidal thoughts) rather than toward the heat, her father can never get warm enough. A heart condition inherited from his father causes him to grow weaker and weaker until he spends his last years, always cold, curled on a pallet in front of the hot fire. Just as his horse Lightning (as his name implies) was used up fast in his service to their union, the creativity and vitality John embodies are weakened figuratively in domesticity and in union. In contrast to her mother, who discourages Ivy from reading too much because it will just fill her head "with notions," her father John is associated with artistic expression. He loves to tell old mountain stories rich in folklore and to play the guitar and sing. He is allied with that which is sensuous, natural, and vital. He used to take Ivy and her brothers and sisters berry-picking in the mountains and swimming in the Levisa River. Ivy remembers how he took them up on the mountain in the early spring to tap a birch and get the sap. Once when he gave her a piece of bark to lick the inside, he said "slow down, slow down now, Ivy. This is the taste of Spring." By urging her to live in the present moment, he is suggesting that she live in a time-bound world that follows desire and creative response.

The dualism embodied by her parents' union is further emphasized in the presence of their twins, which, Ivy notes, runs in the family. Indeed, of her parents' eight children, half are twins; Ivy herself later has one set of her own. The older twins—her brother and sister, Babe and Silvaney—embody two different spheres of reality—the earthly and the ethereal. Babe, who was born healthy, has many plans and schemes but they are largely channeled into violent, destructive activities. Silvaney, on the other hand, was tiny and blue and barely breathing at birth, and, at the age of five, had a high fever for a week that damaged part of her brain. The precariousness of Silvaney's physical condition at birth and her sickness as a child suggest the frailty of imagination and creativity in the domestic environment in which she lives. Silvaney makes no plans; she is just a spirit that, as her name suggests, enjoys the woods where she often wanders. Silvaney, who is Ivy's favorite sibling, has "slept in the same bed [with her] all their lives" and they "have done everything as one," their identification suggesting Ivy's alignment with the world of the imagination as well as her own fragmentation.

Because they each embody a fragmented condition, both twins are associated with childhood. Silvaney, who is the possessor of the family's only doll-baby, is characterized as being very childlike, choosing to communicate almost entirely with body language and primitive sounds. Babe's own nickname reinforces the effect of the fragmentation on him—without imagination, he lacks maturity and exists in a crudely physical sphere. Moreover, his (implied) incestuous behavior toward Silvaney and Ivy further underscores the difficulty of establishing a healthy dynamic when the physical and spiritual worlds are divided. Smith often creates siblings who represent different realms of reality, and she makes one of them impaired, or even retarded, thereby symbolically suggesting the limitation of such a partial world view; in some novels, incestuous activity further illustrates the dangers of such dualism.

In *Fair and Tender Ladies*, the contrast in Babe and Silvaney's approach to sexuality, which is reinforced by phallic imagery, highlights their differences. Babe, who is described as mean as a snake, kills a snake that had posed a threat to Ethel before Ivy snatched her younger sister to safety. Silvaney, on the other hand, is scared of snakes. Once when she and Ivy went with the Conaway boys and Oakley and Ray Fox up the mountain to pick berries, she ran away when they encountered a snake. It is significant that it was during Silvaney's absence that Ivy experienced her first kiss. Similarly, when Silvaney is institutionalized and sent away after Babe's death, Ivy (who, according to her mother, was the only one who could do anything with Silvaney) has sexual intercourse for the first time and becomes pregnant. Just as Ivy, at twelve, had intuitively recognized the conflict for women between, on the one hand, being a writer and being in love, and, on the other, having babies, she seems to become incomplete when Silvaney is absent—her passion becomes specifically sexualized and she loses a sense of autonomy. The rest of the novel—most of which is comprised of letters to Silvaney—is both her compensation for being a mother and wife instead of a writer and her achievement for her endurance, her capacity to be nurturing, and her hard-won self-discovery. Indeed, Lee Smith has said that in *Fair and Tender Ladies* she was writing about the importance of women's heroism and of women's creativity, which is often different from, and takes different forms than, men's (Virginia Smith, "On Regionalism," 787).

Ivy's conflict between her desire to love and be loved and her desire to be creative and artistic is manifested early in the novel in her response to her boyfriend, Lonnie, whom she meets in the boardinghouse in Majestic where she and her mother move. Her decision to let Lonnie sleep with her results directly from her confusion as well as her teacher's confusion of sexual and creative passion. When Ivy, who is inspired by her drawing lesson, suddenly realizes her teacher is making sexual advances, in an excited state she flees back to her own room where she finds Lonnie waiting. After she and Lonnie make love in her room, she looks out her window from which she can see the entire town—a vantage point she normally enjoys. Suddenly, she feels as if she has "lost it"—the town and the room—because of Lonnie's presence there. In her use of a double entendre she expresses a sense of loss for these places, which are metaphors for the self. Her association of sexuality and loss of self foreshadows the pregnancy, which results from their union and does, indeed, conflict with her aspirations to be a writer.

Before she realizes she is pregnant, as she says good-bye to Lonnie, who is going off to war, she still thinks she can choose to accept her teacher's offer to live with her and go to school in Boston if she wants to and, if she does not like it there, even choose to return home. In the letter she writes Silvaney recounting the good-bye scene, she describes herself almost as if she were a fictional character she can control who is "free to come and go" as she pleases. Even the language that she uses suggests the stasis of being caught in time: "So picture me Silvaney," she says (120). Ironically, as she describes the scene, she and Lonnie are standing on the bridge with the river flowing beneath them. Like the water below, time is rushing on, making it impossible to have future choices not determined by those made in the past.

Following Lonnie's departure, Ivy initially feels as if her "whole self came rushing back" again and all the poems she ever knew came "rushing and tumbling" into her head (119); however, the return of her creative passion is short-lived when she realizes she is pregnant. Ivy's fears of losing her identity are projected in images of the baby and submersion. When she learns her condition, she feels "I *was* that little baby caught inside of my own self and dying to escape. But I could not. I could never ever get out, I was caught for ever and ever inside myself" (122). In a dream Ivy sees herself riding on a raft down the river with Silvaney; Granny Rowe, the community's midwife and herbalist, holds out a hand but is too far away to help. Both Silvaney and Ivy fall into the dark water. Although she provides no help, Granny Rowe's appearance here in Ivy's dream and later at significant moments in her life is life-sustaining. An independent woman who has great intuitive knowledge and is attuned to nature, Granny Rowe foreshadows what Ivy will become at the end of her life.

Ivy's identification with the trapped baby and with a Silvaney who is lost reinforces the fear that her imaginative, creative self will be trapped or lost permanently to her. In fact, she does nurture that part of the self for years afterwards but in a different form. The daughter she bears, Joli, who grows up to be a successful writer, becomes that self she wanted to cultivate. In contrast to her earlier awareness of the absence of poetry when she was with Lonnie, when Ivy gives birth to Joli she says that "all the poems I ever knew raced through my head" (148). The birth itself, attended, significantly, by Granny Rowe, seems to symbolize the unleashing of the creative imagination, represented by the child, Joli. The child is, however, still a child, who mirrors her mother's own creativity in an arrested stage. Indeed, Ivy's language even underscores her own regression: she says that in Joli she has "a doll-baby all my own" now (144).

Ivy's move to her sister Beulah's house on Diamond Mountain marks the first stage in her alienation from her past and her childhood identity. Unlike Silvaney, Beulah is the sister whose dreams and aspirations are solely material-istic. Specifically, they are tied to seeing that her husband advance in the coal company, which means for each earned advancement, being able to live liter-ally higher and higher on the mountain, where row upon row of houses are ringed in socially stratified tiers. There is a parallel between Diamond Moun-tain, which contains valuable resources of coal, and Ivy's body growing big with the pregnancy; moreover, the exploitation by the coal company of Dia-mond Mountain, where so many people live "it's like bees in a honeycomb" (137), foreshadows what will happen to Ivy, who later marries a miner and has so many children that her own sense of her self is almost lost.

Ivy's affair with Franklin Ransom, the son of the mine superintendent, reflects her vulnerability to the forces of materialism and signifies her loss of identity. Wearing a dress borrowed from Beulah, Ivy is sitting on a rock black-ened by coal dust with her hands and feet submerged in the creek when Franklin startles her out of a half-sleeping, dreaming state. Smith uses water, which traditionally represents life, sexuality, and imagination, to emphasize Ivy's own dreaminess and her openness to sexuality. However, just as Ivy's bor-rowed dress suggests her assumed identity, the rock blackened by coal dust ironically suggests that what is stable on Diamond Mountain is also exploit-ative. Indeed, as his name suggests, Franklin Ransom embodies the material-istic and dehumanizing aspects of the coal company to which his family is aligned. Ironically, when he meets Ivy he tells her that he likes his horses and his girls "to have some spirit" (154).

It is significant that, although she is dressed in Beulah's clothes during her first meeting with Franklin, she later affirms her own identity and, finally, asserts her unwillingness to have unequal status in their relationship. Just as the sun prevented Ivy from seeing Franklin very well when he startled her out of her dreamy state by the creek, Franklin's sense of entitlement and his irre-sponsibility prevent her from ever being able to "see his outline" clearly or to know who he is (164). However, their lovemaking causes her to be more acutely aware of her body, and as a result of their relationship she becomes more self-directed. The night that she and Franklin make love at his parents' house on the top of the mountain, Ivy looks in a full-length mirror and, for the first time, sees her whole self naked. Realizing that she is truly beautiful, she is symbolically approving of her own identity. Later, she refuses Franklin when he tries to get her to wear one of his mother's dresses to a roadhouse. If Ivy refuses to play the mother to Franklin, who has skin "like a baby's" (165), she also refuses to assume a childlike identity in their relationship. When he calls her "baby" and wants to keep driving farther than they have gone before, despite her own longing to go with him, she says "I am not your baby. . . . I have got a baby of my own" (169). By insisting that he turn back, she starts to take responsibility for her daughter, Joli, and for nurturing her own independent self.

In deciding to marry Oakley Fox, the first man who kissed her years before when she had wandered into a cave picking blackberries, Ivy both chooses to live in the present and, simultaneously, longs to retreat to the past. When there is a big explosion at the mine and hundreds of workers are feared dead or disabled, Ivy joins a big crowd walking down Diamond Mountain, where she lives with her sister's family, and is carried along to the scene of the disaster as if she were "riding a raft downriver" (174). As she watches the black, smoking bodies being hauled out of the gaping hole, she thinks of how fast time has gone by since Joli's birth—"eight years which had rushed pell mell, like high water under the bridge at Majestic" (175). Then, when she sees Oakley Fox walking out of "the mouth of the mine . . . like he had been spared, or like he had just been born" (176), she knows that he is the reason she rushed down the mountain to wait at the mine.

Ivy's sudden realization of death and the passing of time, which is reinforced by water imagery, makes her choose to live more fully in the present and to marry Oakley, whose presence suggests stability and order and who reminds her of her childhood. While she had believed eight years earlier that she could choose another direction as she had stood still on the bridge above the swirling river, now she moves as with a current. The mine, which recalls the cave in which Ivy was kissed when she went berry-picking, is associated with sex and death. Years earlier, in the cave where Oakley kissed her, Ivy unknowingly crushed the berries in her hands and stained her dress with berry juice, an image suggesting her own sexual awakening and foreshadowing her union with Oakley. Later, as Ivy waits to see if his corpse will be brought out of the mine, Oakley emerges as if newly born. As she summarizes in a letter to Silvaney, "The mine fell in, and I got married" (164), not only reinforcing the association of death and sexuality but also, ironically, suggesting by the unusual parallelism that both actions—the mine's collapse and her marriage—are death to the spirit. Indeed, as he emerges from the mine when he hears her voice, Oakley calls "Baby, baby, it's you" (177).

The fragmentation of the different aspects of herself that the marriage forces on her is suggested by her association with the baby image and is foreshadowed in an earlier scene when Ivy's identity is associated with her mother's. When she is bent over the kitchen sink washing her hair, Oakley suddenly appears, pulls her up by the hair, kisses her, and tells her she is his girl. At the

time, Ivy is dressed in "some old wrapper" of her mother's, the clothing symbolizing the identity Oakley embraces and foreshadowing the one she will be
forced to assume in their union. Indeed, the separation of the child/mother
selves is the result of being consumed in the role of parent to a growing number of children while the imaginative, creative self is repressed and remains
only in an infantile stage. It is significant that when Ivy marries and returns to
Sugar Creek, her childhood home, she plans to take Silvaney with her; however, instead of Silvaney, who, she learns, had died in the institution ten years
earlier, she takes Martha, a young girl from Diamond Mountain whose mental capacities are limited but who knows how to keep house. The substitution
of Martha for her beloved sister symbolically suggests that in her marriage she
replaces her imaginative, creative self with a "retarded" self who knows how to
cook and clean but is unaware of time passing.

Indeed, even the structure of the house Ivy and Oakley inhabit at Sugar
Creek symbolizes the fragmentation embodied in Ivy and exacerbated by the
marriage. By returning to live in Ivy's parents' old house, they symbolically
return to the past and choose a marriage much like the one her parents had.
When they find the breezeway between the double cabin broken apart and
overgrown with ivy, Oakley "shore[s] it up" and makes the cabin again inhabit-
able. The doubleness of the cabin as well as the ivy that clings to both halves
foreshadows Ivy's own fractured state in the marriage. Just as Oakley repairs
the breezeway, which would have involved tearing down the ivy, he inadvertently strips the woman Ivy in order to shore up the social structure of the marriage, which is dualistic in its division of labor and in its fragmentation of
dimensions of personal fulfillment. Ivy says the breezeway is a good place to
do "piecework," but her mother found little time for such activities. Just as her
father used to sit out there and "play a tune," Oakley sits on the breezeway and
whittles, which, Ivy says, "he is really good at," while she shells beans or sews
some (183). When the women do have time for artistic pursuits, they do "piecework," the name reflective of the design as well as the fragments of time they
have to devote to such artwork.

When Ivy uses a beautiful crazy quilt on her marriage bed that her mother
had intended as a burying quilt, the act underscores her choice to live in the
present but also, ironically, foreshadows her own burial in her marriage. Oppressed by child care, hard work, and the alienation of her imaginative, creative self, Ivy writes only perfunctory, abbreviated letters during the first ten
years of her marriage. As the years go by, she realizes that she has been "caught
up" in a "blackness so deep and so soft" that you could "fall in there and get
comfortable and never know you are falling at all" and that she has been "frozen, locked in time." In fact, it is after she sends Joli away to school that she
begins to be conscious of her depression and of the distance that has grown up

between Oakley and her and is able to write about these changes. In a letter to Silvaney, whom she had not written in ten years, she describes how she took Joli up the mountain and told her some of the mountain tales remembered from her own childhood. By recollecting the stories high up on the mountain and then releasing Joli into the world, Ivy symbolically unleashes her own newly emerging imaginative self and, consequently, realizes her own dissatisfaction.

Ivy's trip up the mountain with Joli, with whom she passes on stories remembered from the Cline sisters, both foreshadows her later trip with Honey Breeding and is prefigured by her earlier trip up the mountain with Granny Rowe, who instructs her on how to gather life-sustaining food at a time when she is depressed and in need of physical and spiritual nurturance. When Ivy meets Honey Breeding, the community bee man, she knows an intense longing within herself has gone unfulfilled. Just as significant encounters with Lonnie and Franklin are associated with water, with her daughter LuIda in tow she first meets Honey at the family springhouse, symbolically the source of life and literally the place Ivy associates with letting her imagination wander. When Ivy leaves her family for five weeks and climbs with Honey past the treeline up to the top of Blue Star Mountain where she can see for miles and miles, she leaves the familiar world which sustains life as she knows it and journeys toward self-discovery. In contrast to being with Franklin naked in the dark on the top of Diamond Mountain, Ivy lies naked with Honey in the sunshine on top of the highest mountain she has ever climbed. Height here is associated with personal fulfillment and artistic vision rather than with social status and materialism. By telling stories that recall her father's storytelling and making love to her in ways she never dreamed possible, Honey enables her to reclaim her artistic self and reintegrate her body and her mind. Moreover, just as her room at the boardinghouse, which was as high as the church steeple, has religious associations, Honey himself generates a sense of spirituality within Ivy. When she is on the top of Blue Star Mountain, she feels as if he has given her back her "very soul" (232). Later, after she returns to her family, as the sunlight floods the kitchen and she eats a biscuit covered with honey, she "*felt* like church" as she watched the ordinary events of the day unfold with her family surrounding her (248).

While it is appropriate (since Smith's world is a dualistic one) that Ivy's self-discovery occur in relation to another human being, Honey does function primarily as a symbol of Ivy's own passionate, imaginative nature. Indeed, with his godlike appearance and his role as rumored father of many of the community's children, Honey, like Eudora Welty's King MacLain, exists primarily on a mythic rather than a literal level. Moreover, just as Ivy cannot see Lonnie's face when he is standing on the bridge and can never see Franklin's outline, she has difficulty seeing Honey when she first encounters him on the steps of the springhouse outlined against the sun. He seems like a man she "had made up in the cool dark springhouse, like a man [she] had imagined until he came true" (214). Indeed, Ivy herself later wonders if she made Honey up because she needed him so much. When she is with Honey on top of Blue Star Mountain, all the poems that she ever knew come rushing back over her body and she feels as if she had gotten a part of herself back that she had lost "without even knowing it was gone" (232). Honey's association with Silvaney, which is suggested by Ivy's referring to each as her "soul," is emphasized by Ivy's parallel discovery of her voice in writing her most intimate thoughts to Silvaney, and her later recovery of her voice with Honey as she relates all the stories that she thought she had forgotten. Indeed, Honey himself reminds her of a poem. Just as she had once imagined the Brontës' Rochester and Heathcliff to be ideal love interests, she says of Honey, "he *is* me and I am him," echoing Catherine's words about Heathcliff and, simultaneously, foreshadowing, in the allusiveness, the difficulty of sustaining this union (230). As Ivy reintegrates her passionate, imaginative self with the rest of her being, she suddenly realizes her autonomy: "*I could of climbed up here by myself, anytime,*" she says (233).

When Ivy returns from her trip up the mountain with Honey, she learns that a snake was found in the house and had been killed and discovers that LuIda has died in her absence. Just as LuIda represents Ivy's child-self, her death, as well as the associated appearance and death of the snake, which recalls Silvaney's aversion to snakes, suggests the death of innocence and the beginning of Ivy's real independence and maturation. It is significant that LuIda, who is with Ivy when she first meets Honey at the springhouse, reacts by crying and clinging to her mother's legs. Earlier still, after the birth of LuIda's younger sister, Ivy remarks that LuIda has "her [doll-] baby and I've got mine," the parallelism drawing an identification between the child and herself. Moreover, the appearance of the snake and LuIda's subsequent death, suggesting the symbolic interrelatedness of sex and death, parallel Ivy's own attraction to and union with Honey. Like her mother blindly following her husband up the mountain, Ivy follows Honey to the top of Blue Star Mountain where they live in a cave for five weeks, nourished by stories more than by berries and nuts. Just as the image cluster of fire and water associated with Maude suggests both passion and loss of identity, the image cluster appears, too, in Smith's portrayal of Honey, whom Ivy meets at the springhouse, and Ivy, who feels "on fire." Indeed, Ivy finally becomes so mesmerized by Honey's presence there that she can "see nothing but him"—not "the valley below, nor any part of the world." While her withdrawal from the world and her union with Honey initially afford her an expansive view, Ivy's continued isolation and consequent self-focus in a womblike cave, where she nearly starves, suggest the seductiveness as well as the dangers of the artistic vision that is removed from the world.

In the years following her trip up the mountain with Honey, where she turns inward and becomes aware of her own self, Ivy's continued development is marked by the marriages of Martha and Joli, her "retarded" caretaker self, and the developing aspect of her imaginative, creative self. Since the time Ivy had gone away with Honey, Martha had become much more independent and accomplished. As she is preparing for Martha's wedding, Ivy wonders, "if you *treat* somebody as simple, does it *make* them simple," the question recognizing her own responsibility in retarding Martha's development. During Martha's wedding ceremony, which symbolically suggests the maturation of Ivy's mother self and its reintegration with other aspects of herself, Ivy recognizes the Shakespearean sonnet that is read—"Let us not to the marriage of true minds admit impediment"—a poem that significantly speaks of bridging a dualism. Later, when she ponders Joli's upcoming wedding, which she is unable to attend because of Oakley's illness, she holds a jar of lightning bugs, watching the lights blink and change in her hands, and the lightning bug lantern reminds her of Joli—glowing and always changing. When Ivy unscrews the lid of the jar and dumps the bugs out, she symbolically releases both the child Joli from her care and her imaginative self from its childlike state.

Ironically, it is only after Oakley dies that Ivy's letters emphasize his artwork and present him as an artist. Ivy's experience of him was as a man dedicated to his work, his religion, and his community. She saw him as a statue bent over, engaged in work. Just as Oakley used to sit in the breezeway whittling while Ivy worked, it was easier for him to be an artist than for Ivy, whose time and energy were consumed in childcare and cooking. In her older age, however, and with Oakley gone, she surrounds herself with Oakley's carved animal statues, which function as reminders of the artist who carved them and of her own imaginative interests. The aging Ivy makes a list of positive self-assertions of what she can do, including "I can make up my own life now whichever way I want to, it is like I am a girl again, for I am not beholden to a soul," and "I can act like a crazy old woman if I want to which I do" (277).

In the opening letter of *Fair and Tender Ladies*, the twelve-year-old Ivy writes to Hanneke, a little Dutch girl she hopes will be her pen pal: "I take a interest in Love because I want to be in Love one day and write poems about it. . . . But I do not want to have a lot of babys though. . . . So it is hard to think what to do" (15). Although her qualifying statement recognizes the conflict for women between enjoying the roles of wife and mother on the one hand, and artist on the other, her mountain culture fragments these spheres of reality, retarding the development of the imagination and, consequently, constraining, if not silencing, the female voice. In a letter she writes to her dead father,

Ivy asks him about the childhood sickness that resulted in Silvaney's brain damage: "Oh Daddy were you ther when Silvaney took so sick, did you watch by her side? . . . Were you ther when she walked in the fire?" (66). Echoing the spiritual "Were you there when they crucified my Lord?" Ivy questions him, admonishing him for what appears to be his neglect. In writing to her dead father about Babe's activities and Silvaney's present mental state, she wants the past to integrate the two spheres of reality that the twins represent—the physical, earthly sphere and the imaginative, ethereal sphere. Smith seems to suggest that patriarchal society or the fathers of the past are responsible for the failure to integrate the imaginative, ethereal world that Silvaney represents with the real world. The penetrating questions Ivy asks her father reflect the crux of the conflict that she identifies in her first letter and that she herself comes to embody.

In a description from that first letter, the gender divisiveness of the culture and its language is reflected in the contrast between the men who talk and enjoy community and the women who singularly go about their business in silence. At Stoney Branham's store, all the men gather around a woodstove waiting for Bill Waldrop, the mail carrier, and "talk and talk about who has seed a bear or who is laying up in the bed sick or who has been bit by a snake or where lightning has struck last, or they will tell a tale, and the womenfolks that is in ther will be lookin at thread or may be some flowered piecey-goods" (16).

Just as the men here are the ones associated with the community's tales as well as with written and oral communication, Ivy's father is the one who relates most of the tales his daughter hears. It is because of his passion for stories that Ivy knows the community's women artists, who are sister storytellers who pass a story back and forth between them until it is completed and who always visited Ivy's father when he was young on Old Christmas to tell their stories. It is significant that the sister storytellers, like Ivy and Silvaney, appear as a pair, suggesting the strength that is drawn through female bonds. However, while the Cline sisters are virtually sustained by stories, they live significantly in isolation and without husbands or children, thereby further emphasizing the isolation of the female artist. Moreover, although many of their tales are about transformation and human relationships, including the story told especially for Ivy—"Whitebear Whittington"—that story in particular has a subtext which depicts not only the father's and the husband's control over the woman's destiny but also the husband's silencing of his wife.

While this story is about transformation, its subtext both recalls Ivy's recognition of the dilemma of the woman artist and parallels conflicts in her own life. In its portrayal of a husband who warns a wife against speaking and who punishes her by withdrawing his love, "Whitebear Whittington" recalls the dilemma between loving and writing, which is a way of speaking or having a voice. Although they enjoy a very fulfilling love relationship, Ivy, in effect, is *silenced* in her marriage to Oakley. Her only writing is contained in letters. Following her marriage to Oakley and her discovery that Silvaney has been dead for a number of years, it is ten years before Ivy writes again to her dead sister to describe a "darkness" she has fallen into. While Ivy is the one who wants to be an artist, it is, ironically, Oakley who becomes one. Moreover, through his artistry—his carving of wooden bears—Oakley is identified with Whitebear, the silencer in the tale.

Fair and Tender Ladies both tells the story of Ivy's growing discovery of the power of language and demonstrates the limitations of language. As the story shifts from letters to Hanneke, the Dutch girl she hopes will be her pen pal, to Molly, who truly becomes her friend, to Silvaney, the sister who is her soul mate, Ivy moves closer and closer to the self, locating meaning less in Other than in Self. Recognizing the primacy of the kind of intuitive knowledge her sister represents, Ivy believes that Silvaney "knows a lot more than you think" (17). It is Silvaney's institutionalization following her breakdown that creates the occasion for Ivy's letters, which reveal her deepest thoughts. The institutionalization itself is suggestive of society's suppression of the imaginative reality Silvaney represents. In a letter to her teacher, who apparently instigated her sister's institutionalization, Ivy disparages not only Mrs. Brown but the doctor who signed the warrant against Silvaney and the officer who served it, thereby admonishing all of society's institutions—academic, medical, and legal—which conspired against her sister.

Given Silvaney's own association with semiotic discourse, Ivy's letters to her are both an expression and a validation of interiority that does not seem to exist elsewhere in the world of the novel. They attempt to reconcile the language of the body with the language of the mind. Ironically, these letters chart Ivy's own developing awareness of the limitations of language and of her *need* to write as a way of interpreting and understanding her own experience. Her earliest letters show that the twelve-year-old Ivy learns that the written word is judged and that it is powerless to evoke the response that the writer intends. Although Ivy had not known that her teacher would read her letter to Hanneke, Mrs. Brown reads it, judges it "not appropriate," and makes suggestions about the subjects Ivy should include in the revised letter. Moreover, neither Hanneke nor Mr. Castle, Ivy's grandfather, to whom she writes a request for money, responds in any way to her letters.

In her letters to Silvaney, Ivy validates the process of writing itself. When she acknowledges her need to tell Silvaney things that she wouldn't tell anyone else, she admits that language is a human construct that cannot adequately express internal reality: "I feel that things are happening two times allways, there is the thing that is happening, which you can say, and see, and there is another thing happening too inside it, and this is the most important thing but its so hard to say" (102). In the course of writing, Ivy begins to realize that knowledge itself is dependent on her use of language: "Sometimes I despair of ever understanding anything right when it happens to me," Ivy says. "It seems like I have to tell it in a letter to see what it was, even though I was right there all along" (183). Following the long period after she marries Oakley and learns of Silvaney's death, when she writes almost no letters, Ivy affirms her belief in writing as a process of self-discovery. It is during the course of writing her first letter to the deceased Silvaney that Ivy *realizes* her emptiness. Later, when she writes about her affair with Honey, when all the poems that she ever knew come rushing back, she is validating writing as a way of creating herself. In reclaiming her artistic self, she recovers her early desire to integrate mind and body and gains a sense of artistic vision and personal fulfillment.

At the end of her life, when the letters to her dead sister are discovered, in a final act of self-discovery Ivy burns all the letters she had written Silvaney over the years, her soul feeling lighter and lighter with each letter burned. Realizing that "it was the *writing* of them, that signified" (313), Ivy comes to understand that living passionately in the present is what matters, affirming the notion that in writing she creates herself and the view of writing as process. Ironically, however, as readers we still hold Ivy's letters, the ones she burned, in our hands. Moreover, Ivy's statement, which *seems* to comment on life as well as art, *can* be read as not holding any *meaning* at all. Indeed, on one level, Ivy seems to be saying that it was the *act* of writing that signified or was important. On another level, however, the statement is about language. It is the writing that signifies or uses signs. Read this way, Ivy's statement, which seems to describe the *mechanical* nature of symbolic discourse, indirectly affirms the semiotic language of pure experience.

After the letters to Silvaney are burned and Ivy herself is weak and near death, there is a final letter to Silvaney, which appears to be the stream-of-consciousness of Ivy's last moments. This final letter is a prose poem which recalls the freshness of the young Ivy not burdened by hard work and childcare. In its collage of important images from her life, lines from favorite poems remembered from youth, and phrases from the "To every thing there is a season" passage from Ecclesiastes (3:1), it serves as a powerful testimony to the world that Ivy encompassed, the love that she felt, and the personal fulfillment that was her final accomplishment.

Works Cited

Allen, Don Cameron. *Mysteriously Meant: The Rediscovery of Pagan Symbolism and Allegorical Interpretation in the Renaissance.* Baltimore: Johns Hopkins UP, 1970.

Augustine, Saint, Bishop of Hippo. *The Literal Meaning of Genesis.* Vol. II, bk. 9. Ramsey, N.J.: Paulist, 1982.

Awkward, Michael. *Inspiriting Influences: Tradition, Revision, and Afro-American Women's Novels.* New York: Columbia UP, 1989.

Barry, Kathleen. *Female Sexual Slavery.* New York: New York UP, 1984.

Bartelme, Elizabeth. "Victory over Bitterness." Rev. of *The Color Purple,* by Alice Walker. *Commonweal* (11 Feb. 1983): 93-94.

Baumgaertner, Jill. Rev. of *The Color Purple,* by Alice Walker. *The Cresset* 46 (May 1983): 28-30.

Bloom, Harold, ed. *Alice Walker.* New York: Chelsea, 1989.

Blythe, Will. "Hannah and His Sentences." *Esquire* (March 1993): 55.

Bobo, Jacqueline. *"The Color Purple:* Black Women as Cultural Readers." *Female Spectators: Looking at Film and Television.* Ed. E. Deidre Pribam. London: Verso, 1988. 90-109.

Booth, David. "Sam's Quest, Emmett's Wound: Grail Motifs in Bobbie Ann Mason's Portrait of America after Vietnam." *Southern Literary Journal* 23.2 (1991): 98-109.

Bovoso, Carole. "Main Events: Books." Rev. of *The Color Purple,* by Alice Walker. *Essence* (Oct. 1982): 20.

Brussat, Frederic, and Mary Ann Brussat, eds. "A Film Guide to *In Country.*" New York: CIStems, 1989.

Burke, James Lee. *The Convict* (stories). Baton Rouge: Louisiana State UP, 1985.

———. *Heaven's Prisoners.* New York: Pocket Books, 1989.

———. *The Neon Rain.* New York: Pocket Books, 1987.

Chappell, Fred. *I Am One of You Forever.* Baton Rouge: Louisiana State UP, 1985.

———. *Midquest: A Poem.* Baton Rouge: Louisiana State UP, 1981.

———. *Plow Naked: Selected Writings on Poetry.* Ann Arbor: U of Michigan P, 1993.

Cherry, Kelly. "A Writer's Harmonious World." *Parnassus: Poetry in Review* 9.2 (fall-winter 1981): 115-29.

Christophe, Marc-A. *"The Color Purple:* An Existential Novel." *CLA Journal* 36 (1993): 28-90.

Conarroe, Joel. "Winning Her Father's War." *New York Times Book Review* (15 Sept. 1985): 7.

Cook, Bruce. "New Faces in Faulkner Country." *Saturday Review* (4 Sept. 1976): 39-41.

Croft, Robert W. *Anne Tyler: A Bio-Bibliography.* Westport, Conn.: Greenwood P, 1995.

Davis, David Brion. *The Problem of Slavery in Western Culture.* Ithaca: Cornell UP, 1966.

Deleuze, Gilles, and Felix Guattari. *Kafka: Toward a Minor Literature*. Minneapolis: U of Minnesota P, 1986.

Derrida, Jacques. *Dissemination*. Trans. Barbara Johnson. Chicago: U of Chicago P, 1981.

Dickey, James. *Deliverance*. Boston: Houghton Mifflin, 1970.

Douglass, Frederick. *The Narrative and Selected Writings*. Ed. Michael Meyer. New York: Modern Library, 1984.

Drake, Robert. *Amazing Grace*. Philadelphia: Chilton, 1965.

———. *Amazing Grace: Twenty-fifth Anniversary Edition*. Macon: Mercer UP, 1990.

———. "Appendix." *My Sweetheart's House: Memories, Fictions*. Macon: Mercer UP, 1993. 183-84.

———. "The Fifth Wheel." *The Single Heart*. Nashville: Aurora, 1971. 120-25.

———. *The Home Place: A Memory and a Celebration*. Memphis: Memphis State UP, 1980.

———. *My Sweetheart's House: Memories, Fictions*. Macon: Mercer UP, 1993.

———. "The New Bridge: *Cui Bono?*" *University of Tennessee Daily Beacon* (14 Jan. 1977): 2.

———. "An Interview with Robert Drake." By Jeffrey Folks. *Mississippi Quarterly* 43 (spring 1990): 226.

———. "On the Side Porch." *Survivors and Others*. Macon: Mercer UP, 1987. 96-103.

———. "Robert Drake." Interview by Ashby Bland Crowder. *Writing in the Southern Tradition: Interviews with Five Contemporary Authors*. Ed. Ashby Bland Crowder. Amsterdam: Rodopi, 1990. 119-51.

———. *The Single Heart*. Nashville: Aurora, 1971.

———. *Survivors and Others*. Macon: Mercer UP, 1987.

———. Telephone interview with James A. Perkins. 18 Feb. 1991. Unpublished.

———. "The Three States of Tennessee." *Tennessee: A Photographic Celebration*. Helena, Mont.: American Geographic Publishing, 1990.

———. "The Trains in My Life." *Phoenix* (fall 1973): 23.

———. "Under the Bluff." *The Burning Bush*. Nashville: Aurora, 1975. 33-40.

Dubus, Andre. "Adultery." *Selected Stories of Andre Dubus*. 406-54.

———. "A Father's Story." *Selected Stories of Andre Dubus*. 455-76.

———. "If They knew Yvonne." *Selected Stories of Andre Dubus*. 174-97.

———. "Miranda Over the Valley." *Selected Stories of Andre Dubus*. 1-19.

———. "Molly." *The Last Worthless Evening*. Boston: Godine, 1986. 117-35.

———. "The Pretty Girl." *Selected Stories of Andre Dubus*. 65-120.

———. "Rose." *Selected Stories of Andre Dubus*. 198-232.

———. *Selected Stories of Andre Dubus*. Boston: Godine, 1988.

———. "Voices from the Moon." *Selected Stories of Andre Dubus*. 288-358.

———. "With Andre Dubus." Interview by Jon Holmes. *Boston Review* 9.4 (July 1984): 7-8.

Dunne, Michael. "Romantic Narcissism in 'Outlaw' Cowboy Music." *All That Glitters: Country Music in America*. Ed. George H. Lewis. Bowling Green, Oh.: Bowling Green State University Popular Press, 1993. 226-38.

Edgerton, Clyde. *The Floatplane Notebooks*. Chapel Hill, N.C.: Algonquin Books, 1988.

———. *In Memory of Junior*. Chapel Hill: Algonquin Books, 1992.

————. *Killer Diller*. Chapel Hill: Algonquin Books, 1991.

————. *Raney*. Chapel Hill: Algonquin Books, 1985.

————. Telephone interview with Jean Marie Elliott. 1 Dec. 1987.

————. *Walking across Egypt*. Chapel Hill: Algonquin Books, 1987.

Eliade, Mircea. *Birth and Rebirth*. New York: Harper, 1958.

Evans, Mari, ed. *Black Women Writers, 1950-1980: A Critical Evaluation*. Garden City, N.Y.: Anchor/Doubleday, 1984.

Faulkner, William. "Old Man." *Three Famous Short Novels*. New York: Vintage, 1961. 77-184.

Fletcher, Angus. *Allegory: The Theory of a Symbolic Mode*. Ithaca: Cornell UP, 1964.

Flora, Joseph M., and Robert Bain, eds. *Contemporary Fiction Writers of the South: A Bio-Bibliographical Sourcebook*. Westport, Conn.: Greenwood P, 1993.

Ford, Richard. "An Interview with Richard Ford." By Kay Bonetti. *Missouri Review* 10.2 (1987): 71-96.

————. *Rock Springs*. New York: Vintage, 1987.

————. *The Sportswriter*. New York: Vintage, 1986.

————. *The Ultimate Good Luck*. New York: Houghton Mifflin, 1981.

————. *Wildlife*. New York: Vintage, 1989.

"Forum: Forty-one Letters on Interdisciplinarity in Literary Studies." *PMLA* 111 (1996): 271-311.

Fraser, Walter J. *Charleston! Charleston!: The History of a Southern City*. Columbia: U of South Carolina P, 1989.

Freeman, Judith. "Country Parables." *Los Angeles Times Book Review* (19 Mar. 1989): 1+.

Freud, Sigmund. "Medusa's Head." *Sexuality and the Psychology of Love*. Ed. Philip Rieff. New York: Collier Books, 1963. 212-13.

————. "Some Reflections on Schoolboy Psychology." 1914. *The Standard Edition of the Complete Psychological Works of Sigmund Freud*. Ed. and trans. James Strachey. 24 vols. London: Hogarth, 1953-74. Vol. 13, 241-44.

Frost, Robert. *Complete Poems of Robert Frost*. New York: Holt, Rinehart and Winston, 1964.

Garrett, George. Rev. of *A Visitation of Spirits*, by Randall Kenan. *Chicago Tribune Book Reviews* (Aug. 13, 1989): 6.

Gates, Henry Louis, Jr. *The Signifying Monkey: A Theory of African-American Literary Criticism*. New York: Oxford UP, 1988.

Gates, Henry Louis, Jr., and K.A. Appiah, eds. *Alice Walker: Critical Perspectives Past and Present*. New York: Amistad, 1993.

Gennep, Arnold van. *The Rites of Passage*. Trans. Monika B. Vizedom and Gabrielle L. Caffee. Chicago: U of Chicago P, 1960.

Gibbons, Kaye. *Charms for the Easy Life*. New York: G.P. Putnam's Sons, 1993.

————. *A Cure for Dreams*. Chapel Hill: Algonquin Books, 1991.

————. *Ellen Foster*. New York: Vintage Contemporaries, 1987.

————. *Sights Unseen*. New York: Putnam's, 1995.

————. *A Virtuous Woman*. New York: Vintage Contemporaries, 1989.

Gilbert, Sandra. "Anne Tyler." *Southern Women Writers: The New Generation*. Ed. Tonette Bond Inge. Tuscaloosa: U of Alabama P, 1990. 251-78.

Gilman, Owen W., Jr. *Vietnam and the Southern Imagination.* Jackson: UP of Mississippi, 1992.

Gordon, Jaimy. "The Lazarus of Appalachia." Rev. of *Gospel Hour,* by T.R. Pearson. *Book World* (10 Mar. 1991): 6.

Graham, Maryemma. "Skillful but Disturbing Novel." Rev. of *The Color Purple,* by Alice Walker. *Freedomways* 23 (1983): 278-80.

Gray, Paul. "Digressions." *Time* (14 July 1986): 64.

Greenwald, John. "Sure, We'll Take Manhattan." *Time* (13 Nov. 1989): 7.

Grier, Peter. "Bright Novel That Overstretches Credibility." Rev. of *Morgan's Passing,* by Anne Tyler. *Christian Science Monitor* (14 Apr. 1980): B9. Rpt. in Alice Hall Petry, ed., *Critical Essays on Anne Tyler,* 101-2.

Grisham, John. "Book 'Em." Interview by Tom Mathews. *Newsweek* (15 Mar. 1993): 78-81.

———. *The Client.* New York: Doubleday, 1993.

———. *The Firm.* New York: Dell, 1992.

———. "The Grisham Brief." Interview by Robin Street. *Writer's Digest* 73 (July 1993): 32-34.

———. *The Pelican Brief.* New York: Dell, 1993.

———. "The Rise of the Legal Thriller: Why Lawyers Are Throwing the Books at Us." *New York Times Sunday Book Review* (18 Oct. 1992): 33.

———. *The Runaway Jury.* New York: Doubleday, 1996.

———. "Tales Out of Court." Interview by Kim Hubbard. *People Weekly* (16 Mar. 1992): 43-44.

———. *A Time to Kill. 1989.* New York: Dell, 1992.

Gullette, Margaret Morganroth. "Anne Tyler: The Tears (and Joys) Are in the Things." *The Fiction of Anne Tyler,* ed. C. Ralph Stephens. Jackson: UP of Mississippi, 1990. 97-109.

Gunn, John C. *Domestic Medicine, or Poor Man's Friend.* Knoxville, Tenn., 1830.

Guralnick, Peter. "The Storyteller's Tale." *Los Angeles Times Magazine* (21 May 1995): 15-17, 27-28.

Hammontree, Patsy G. "Comic Monologue: Robert Drake's Community of Voices." *Kennesaw Review* 1 (spring 1988): 67-68.

Hannah, Barry. *Airships.* New York: Knopf, 1978.

———. "The Crowd Punk Season Drew." *Intro #1.* Ed. R.V. Cassill. New York: Bantam Books, 1968. 3-19.

———. *Geronimo Rex.* New York: Avon, 1973.

———. *Ray.* New York: Knopf, 1980.

Harmon, William, and C. Hugh Holman. *A Handbook to Literature,* 7th ed. Upper Saddle River, N.J.: Prentice, 1996.

Hauke, Manfred. *Women in the Priesthood? A Systematic Analysis in the Light of the Order of Creation and Redemption.* San Francisco: Ignatius, 1988.

Henley, Ann. "Space for Herself: Nadine Gordimer's *A Sport of Nature* and Josephine Humphreys' *Rich in Love.*" *Frontiers* 13 (1992): 81-89.

Hennis, R. Sterling, Jr. "Clyde Edgerton." *Contemporary Fiction Writers of the South: A Bio-Bibliographical Sourcebook.* Ed. Joseph M. Flora and Robert Bain. Westport, Conn.: Greenwood, 1993. 112-22.

Hernton, Calvin C. *The Sexual Mountain and Black Women Writers: Adventures in Sex, Literature, and Real Life.* New York: Anchor/Doubleday, 1987.

Heyward, Carter. "An Unfinished Symphony of Liberation: The Radicalization of Christian Feminism among White U.S. Women: A Review Essay." *Journal of Feminist Studies in Religion* 1 (1985): 98-118.

Hiers, John T. "Creation Theology in Alice Walker's *The Color Purple.*" *Notes on Contemporary Literature* 14.4 (1984): 2-3.

Hill, Darlene Reimers. "Use to the Menfolks Would Eat First: Food and Food Rituals in the Fiction of Bobbie Ann Mason." *Southern Quarterly* 30.2-3 (1992): 81-89.

Hill, Dorothy Combs. *Lee Smith.* New York: Twayne, 1992.

Hobson, Fred. *The Southern Writer in the Postmodern World.* Athens: U of Georgia P, 1991.

Hoffman, Eva. "When the Fog Never Lifts." Rev. of *Morgan's Passing,* by Anne Tyler. *Saturday Review* (15 Mar. 1980): 38-39. Rpt. in Alice Hall Petry, ed., *Critical Essays on Anne Tyler,* 95-97.

Holman, C. Hugh. *The Immoderate Past: The Southern Writer and History.* Athens: U of Georgia P, 1977.

———. "No More Monoliths, Please: Continuities in the Multi-Souths." *Southern Literature in Transition.* Ed. Philip Catille and William Osborne. Memphis: Memphis State UP, 1983. xiii-xxiv.

Holmes, Emma. *The Diary of Miss Emma Holmes, 1861-1866.* Ed. John F. Marszalen. Baton Rouge: Louisiana State UP, 1979.

Hood, Mary. "After Moore." *And Venus Is Blue.*

———. *And Venus Is Blue.* New York: Ticknor & Fields, 1986.

———. *Familar Heat.* New York: Knopf, 1995.

———. *How Far She Went.* Athens: U of Georgia P, 1984.

———. Letter to David Aiken and Della Jean Aiken. 14 Oct. 1993.

———. "The Real Life of Mary Hood." Interview by Don O'Briant. *Atlanta Weekly* (25 Jan. 1987): 6, 8.

———. "A Stubborn Sense of Place." *Harper's Magazine* (Aug. 1986): 36.

Humphreys, Josephine. "Continuity and Separation: An Interview with Josephine Humphreys." By Rosemary M. Magee. *Southern Review* 27 (1991): 792-802.

———. *Dreams of Sleep.* New York: Viking, 1984.

———. "The Epistle of Paul to Titus." *Incarnation: Contemporary Writers on the New Testament.* Ed. Alfred Corn. New York: Viking, 1990. 247-56.

———. *The Fireman's Fair.* New York: Viking, 1991.

———. "My Real Invisible Self." *A World Unsuspected: Portraits of Southern Childhood.* Chapel Hill: U of North Carolina P, 1987. 1-13.

———. *Rich in Love.* New York: Viking, 1987.

Hurston, Zora Neale. *Their Eyes Were Watching God.* 1937. Urbana: U of Illinois P, 1978.

John Paul II. "*Mulieris Dignitatem,* Apostolic Letter of the Supreme Pontiff John Paul II on the Dignity and Vocation of Women on the Occasion of the Marian Year." *Catholic Resource Network,* Aug. 15, 1988.

Johnson, Greg. "Stories of the New South." *Southwest Review* 68.2 (1983): 196-97.

Joyce, Alice. "Tough, Gentle Tim McLaurin, '85." *Carolina Alumni Review* (Winter 1989/90): 44-53.

Kazin, Alfred. *On Native Grounds*. New York: Harcourt Brace, 1942.

Kearns, Katherine. "From Shadow to Substance: The Empowerment of the Artist Figure in Lee Smith's Fiction." In *Writing the Woman Artist: Essays on Poetics, Politics, and Portraiture*. Ed. Suzanne W. Jones. Philadelphia: U of Pennsylvania P, 1991.

Kelley, Ernece. Rev. of *The Color Purple*, by Alice Walker. *CLA Journal* 27 (1983): 91-96.

Kenan, Randall. "Conversation with Randall Kenan." Interview by Dorothy Allison. *Village Voice Literary Supplement* 188 (Sept. 1993): 26.

———. *James Baldwin*. New York: Chelsea House, 1994.

———. *Let the Dead Bury Their Dead*. New York: Harcourt Brace, 1992.

———. "The Strange and Tragic Ballad of Mabel Pearsall." *The Christ-Haunted Landscape*. Ed. Susan Ketchin. UP of Mississippi, 1994. 261-77.

———. "The Virtue Called Vanity." *The Rough Road Home*. Ed. Robert Gingher. Chapel Hill: U of North Carolina P, 1992. 131-50.

———. *A Visitation of Spirits*. New York: Doubleday, 1989.

Kennedy, Thomas. *Andre Dubus*. Boston: Twayne, 1988.

Lane, Anthony. "Against the Law." Rev. of the film *The Pelican Brief*. *New Yorker* (27 Dec. 1993–3 Jan. 1994): 148-52.

Langbaum, Robert. *The Word from Below: Essays on Modern Literature and Culture*. Madison: U of Wisconsin P, 1987.

Lawrence, D.H. *Studies in Classic American Literature*. 1923. Rpt. New York: Penguin, 1977.

Lecture notes by David Aiken. University of Georgia. Athens, Ga., 1 June 1993.

Lesley, Craig. "Introduction." *Dreamers and Desperadoes: Contemporary Short Fiction of the American West*. Ed. Craig Lesley and Katheryn Stavrakis. New York: Laurel, 1993.

Lewis, C.S. *The Allegory of Love: A Study in Medieval Tradition*. New York: Oxford UP, 1958.

Lutwack, Leonard. *The Role of Place in Literature*. Syracuse: Syracuse UP, 1984.

Machann, Clinton, and William Bedford Clark, eds. *Katherine Anne Porter and Texas: An Uneasy Relationship*. College Station: Texas A&M UP, 1990.

MacKethan, Lucinda H. "Postscript: Writing Letters Home." In *Daughters of Time: Creating Woman's Voice in Southern Story*. Athens: U of Georgia P, 1990.

Madden, David. "Barry Hannah's *Geronimo Rex* in Retrospect." Rev. of *Geronimo Rex*. *Southern Review* 19.2 (Apr. 1983): 309-16.

Malone, Bill C. *Country Music, U.S.A.* Rev. ed. Austin: U of Texas P, 1985.

Marius, Richard. *After the War*. New York: Knopf, 1992.

———. *Bound for the Promised Land*. New York: Knopf, 1976.

———. *The Coming of Rain*. New York: Knopf, 1969.

———. "The Home That Lies Always in Memory." *Touchstone* (spring 1986): 5-9.

———. "How I Write." *Writers on Writing*. 2 vols. Ed. Tom Waldrep. New York: Random House, 1985-88. 2: 101-18.

———. Interview by Missy Daniel. *Publishers Weekly* (25 May 1992): 34-35.

———. Interview by Randy Brison. Atlanta, Georgia. 5 Nov. 1993. Unpublished.

———. "Interview with Richard Marius." By Carroll Viera. *Southern Quarterly* 33 (fall 1994): 113-25.

———. "On Laughing All the Way to the Gallows." *Soundings* 75 (1992): 229-42.

———. "The Middle of the Journey." *Sewanee Review* 85 (1977): 460-67.

———. "Musings on the Mysteries of the American South." *Daedalus* 113.3 (1984): 143-76.

———. "Reflections on Writing the Biography of a Saint." *The Portrayal of Life Stages in English Literature, 1500-1800: Infancy, Youth, Marriage, Aging, Death, Martyrdom.* Ed. Jeanie Watson and Philip Pittman. Lewiston: Mellen, 1989. 175-202.

———. "Ruleville: Reminiscence, Reflection." *Christian Century* (23 Sept. 1964): 1169-71.

———. *A Short Guide to Writing about History.* 2nd ed. New York: Harper Collins, 1994.

———. "The War between the Baptists." *Esquire* (Dec. 1981): 46-55.

Martin, Russell. "Introduction." *New Writers of the Purple Sage: An Anthology of Contemporary Western Writers.* New York: Penguin, 1992.

Mason, Bobbie Ann. *In Country.* New York: Harper, 1985.

———. "An Interview with Bobbie Ann Mason." By Albert E. Wilhelm. *Southern Quarterly* 26.2 (1988): 27-38.

———. *Love Life.* New York: Harper, 1989.

———. "Residents and Transients: An Interview with Bobbie Ann Mason." By Lila Havens. *Crazyhorse* 29 (1985): 87-104.

———. *Shiloh and Other Stories.* New York: Harper, 1982.

McCarthy, Cormac. *All the Pretty Horses.* New York: Knopf, 1992.

———. *Suttree.* 1979. New York: Random House, 1992.

McLaurin, Tim. *The Acorn Plan: A Novel.* New York: W.W. Norton, 1988.

———. *Cured by Fire.* New York: Putnam, 1994.

———. "Dreamers and True Grit: Booking Passage." *News & Observer* [Raleigh] (11 Apr. 1993): 5G.

———. "Fighting Back: A Writer Confronts Cancer." *Spectator Magazine* 12.21 (12-18 Apr. 1990): 3+.

———. Interview by Sue Laslie Kimball. Chapel Hill, N.C., Aug. 1994. Unpublished.

———. *Keeper of the Moon: A Southern Boyhood.* New York: Doubleday, 1991.

———. "What I Learned from Doris Betts." *The "Home Truths" of Doris Betts: With a Bibliography.* Ed. Sue Laslie Kimball and Lynn Veach Sadler. Fayetteville, N.C.: Methodist College P, 1992.

———. *Woodrow's Trumpet: A Novel.* New York: W.W. Norton, 1989.

McMurtry, Larry. *Horseman, Pass By.* College Station: Texas A&M UP, 1985.

Miller, Mary E. "An Adventure to Live for and to Live Through." *News & Observer* [Raleigh] (4 July 1991): 1E-2E.

Millichap, Joseph. "Josephine Humphreys." *Contemporary Fiction Writers of the South: A Bio-Bibliographic Sourcebook.* Ed. Joseph M. Flora and Robert Bain. Westport, Conn.: Greenwood P, 1993. 244-54.

Milton, Edith. Rev. of *Adultery & Other Choices,* by Andre Dubus. In Kennedy, *Andre Dubus,* 134-37.

Minor, Valerie. Rev. of *Let the Dead Bury Their Dead,* by Randall Kenan. *The Nation* 255 (6 July 1992): 28+.

Mojtabai, A.G. "A State of Continual Crisis." Rev. of *Morgan's Passing,* by Anne Tyler.

New York Times Book Review (23 Mar. 1980): 14, 33. Rpt. in Alice Hall Petry, ed., *Critical Essays on Anne Tyler*, 98-100.

Moore, Lorrie. "What Li'l Abner Said." *New York Times Book Review* (12 Mar. 1989): 7+.

Morrison, Toni. *Playing in the Dark*. Cambridge, Mass.: Harvard UP, 1992.

A Moveable Feast: Profiles of Contemporary Authors: T.R. Pearson. Videotape. Our Time Arts Media. Hosted by Tom Vitale. Atlas Video, Inc., 1991.

Mullins, C. Ross. "Flannery O'Connor: An Interview." *Conversations with Flannery O'Connor*. Ed. Rosemary Magee. Jackson: UP of Mississippi, 1987. 103-7

Myers, Thomas. "Dispatches from Ghost Country: The Vietnam Veteran in Recent American Fiction." *Genre* 21.4 (1988): 409-28.

Nash, Gary B., Julie Roy Jeffrey, et al., eds. *The American People*. New York: Harper, 1990.

Ngugi wa Thiong'o. *Decolonising the Mind: The Politics of Language in African Literature*. London: J. Currey, 1986.

Nichols, Ashton. *The Poetics of Epiphany: Nineteenth-Century Origins of the Modern Literary Movement*. Tuscaloosa: U of Alabama P, 1987.

Nouwen, Henri J.M. *Life of the Beloved: Spiritual Living in a Secular World*. New York: Crossroads, 1993.

Nuland, Sherwin B., M.D. *How We Die: Reflections on Life's Final Chapter*. New York: Knopf, 1994.

O'Connor, Flannery. *Three by Flannery O'Connor*. New York: Signet, 1983.

———. *Wise Blood*. New York: Harcourt Brace, 1952.

Panofsky, Erwin. "Et in Arcadia Ego: On the Conception of Transience in Poussin and Watteau." *Philosophy and History: Essays Presented to Ernst Cassirer*. Ed. Raymond Klibansky and H.J. Paton. Oxford: Clarendon, 1936. 223-54.

Patterson, Orlando. *Slavery and Social Death: A Comparative Study*. Cambridge: Harvard UP, 1982.

Paul, Robert S. *Whatever Happened to Sherlock Holmes? Detective Fiction, Popular Theology, and Society*. Carbondale: Southern Illinois UP, 1991.

Paul VI. "Second Vatican Council." Address. *La Documentation Catholique* no. 1482, col. 1923 (1966).

Pearson, T.R. *Call and Response*. New York: Linden P, 1989.

———. *Cry Me a River*. New York: Henry Holt and Company, 1993.

———. *Gospel Hour*. New York: William Morrow and Company, 1991.

———. *Off for the Sweet Hereafter*. New York: Linden P, 1986.

———. *A Short History of a Small Place*. New York: Ballantine, 1989.

Petry, Alice Hall, ed. *Critical Essays on Anne Tyler*. New York: G.K. Hall, 1992.

———. *Understanding Anne Tyler*. Columbia: U of South Carolina P, 1990.

Pinckney, Darryl. "Black Victims, Black Villains." Rev. of *The Color Purple*, by Alice Walker; *The Color Purple*, a film by Steven Spielberg; and *Reckless Eyeballing*, by Ishmael Reed. *New York Times Book Review* (29 Jan. 1987): 17-20.

Pius XI. "Encyclical Letter of Pope Pius XI on Christian Marriage." Boston: St. Paul Editions, n.d.

Plato. *The Collected Dialogues of Plato*. Ed. Edith Hamilton and Huntington Cairns. Princeton: Princeton UP, 1961.

Porter, Carolyn. "Are We Being Historical Yet?" *South Atlantic Quarterly* 87 (1988): 743-86.

Porter, Katherine Anne. "Holiday." *The Collected Stories of Katherine Anne Porter.* New York: Harcourt Brace, 1979.

Prescott, Peter S. "A Long Road to Liberation." Rev. of *The Color Purple,* by Alice Walker. *Newsweek* (21 June 1982): 67-68.

Ragan, David Paul. "At the Grave of Sut Lovingood: Virgil Campbell in the Work of Fred Chappell." *Mississippi Quarterly* 37.1 (winter 1983-84): 21-30.

Ravenal, Mrs. St. Julien. *Charleston: The Place and the People.* New York: Macmillan, 1929.

Relph, Edward. *Place and Placelessness.* London: Pion, 1976.

Richards, Jeffrey. "Through McLaurin's Mirror, Darkly." *News & Observer* [Raleigh] (13 Aug. 1989): 4D.

Routley, Erik. *The Puritan Pleasures of the Detective Story.* London: Gollancz, 1972.

Ryan, Barbara T. "Decentered Authority in Bobbie Ann Mason's *In Country.*" *Critique* 31.3 (1990): 199-212.

Ryan, Maureen. "Stopping Places: Bobbie Ann Mason's Short Stories." *Women Writers of the Contemporary South.* Ed. Peggy Whitman Prenshaw. Jackson: UP of Mississippi, 1984. 283-94.

Said, Edward. *Orientalism.* New York: Vintage, 1978.

Salter, C.L., and W.J. Lloyd. *Landscape in Literature.* Washington, D.C.: Association of American Geographers, 1977.

Salwak, Dale, ed. *Anne Tyler as Novelist.* Iowa City: U of Iowa P, 1994.

Savage, William W., Jr. *The Cowboy Hero: His Image in American History and Culture.* Norman: U of Oklahoma P, 1979.

Schafer, William J. "Twirl and Bob and Flop and Lurch: The Novels of T.R. Pearson." *Appalachian Journal* (spring 1992): 381-25.

Schmitt, Cannon, and Donald Ulin. "Teaching the Social Text: England, 1859—Brushing History against the Grain." *Teaching Contemporary Theory to Undergraduates.* Ed. Dianne F. Sadoff and William E. Cain. New York: Modern Language Association of America, 1994. 205-17.

Scholl, Diane Grabrielson. "With Ears to Hear and Eyes to See: Alice Walker's Parable *The Color Purple.*" *Christianity and Literature* 40 (spring 1991): 255-66.

Scruggs, Jan C., and Joel L. Swerdlow. *To Heal a Nation: The Vietnam Veterans Memorial.* New York: Harper, 1985.

Secreast, Donald. "Images of Impure Water in Chappell's *River.*" *Mississippi Quarterly* 37.1 (winter 1983-84): 39-44.

Shelton, Frank W. "Anne Tyler's Houses." In C. Ralph Stephens, ed., *The Fiction of Anne Tyler.* Jackson: U of Mississippi P, 1990. 40-46.

———. "The Necessary Balance: Distance and Sympathy in the Novels of Anne Tyler." *Southern Review* 20 (1984): 851-60. Rpt. in Alice Hall Petry, ed., *Critical Essays on Anne Tyler,* 175-83.

Simpson, Lewis P. *The Fable of the Southern Writer.* Baton Rouge: Louisiana State UP, 1994.

Skube, Michael. "One Writer's Long Wait in Seattle." *News & Observer* [Raleigh] (2 Apr. 1990): 4J.

Smith, Dinita. "'Celie, You a Tree.'" Rev. of *The Color Purple*, by Alice Walker. *The Nation* (4 Sept. 1982): 181-83.

Smith, Lee. *Black Mountain Breakdown*. New York: Putnam's, 1980.

———. *The Devil's Dream*. New York: Putnam's, 1992.

———. *Fair and Tender Ladies*. New York: Putnam's, 1988.

———. *Family Linen*. New York: Putnam's, 1985.

———. "On Regionalism, Women's Writing, and Writing as a Woman: A Conversation with Lee Smith." Interview by Virginia Smith. *Southern Review* 23 (1990): 784-95.

———. *Oral History*. New York: Putnam's, 1983.

———. *Saving Grace*. New York: Putnam's, 1995.

Somerville, John N., Jr. "Thomas Reid Pearson." *Contemporary Fiction Writers of the South: A Bio-Bibliographic Sourcebook*. Ed. Joseph M. Flora and Robert Bain. Westport, Conn.: Greenwood, 1993. 343-47.

Spoiler, Nicholas. "Taking of parts." *TLS* (31 Oct. 1980): 1221.

Stace, W.T. "Man against Darkness." *Atlantic Monthly* (Sept. 1948): 53-58.

Stavrakis, Katheryn. "Introduction." *Dreamers and Desperadoes: Contemporary Short Fiction of the American West*. Ed. Craig Lesley and Katheryn Stavrakis. New York: Laurel, 1993.

Stephens, C. Ralph, ed. *The Fiction of Anne Tyler*. Jackson: UP of Mississippi, 1990.

Stewart, Matthew C. "Realism, Verisimilitude, and the Depiction of Vietnam Veterans in *In Country*." *Fourteen Landing Zones: Approaches to Vietnam War Literature*. Ed. Philip K. Jason. Iowa City: U of Iowa P, 1991. 166-79.

Street, Robin. "The Grisham Brief." *Writer's Digest* 73.7 (July 1993): 32-34.

Stuart, Dabney. "Spiritual Matter in Fred Chappell's Poetry: A Prologue." *Southern Review* 27.1 (winter 1981): 200-20.

Swann, Brian, and Arnold Krupat, eds. *Recovering the Word: Essays on Native American Literature*. Berkeley: U of California P, 1987.

Tavard, George. *Women in Christian Tradition*. Notre Dame: U of Notre Dame P, 1973.

Taylor, Gordon O. "Morgan's Passion." Stephens, *The Fiction of Anne Tyler*, 64-72.

Taylor, Henry. *Compulsory Figures: Essays on Recent American Poets*. Baton Rouge: Louisiana State UP, 1992.

Tickle, Phyllis. "Raising the Brown Curtain." *Publishers Weekly* (27 June 1986): 100.

Towers, Robert. "Good Men Are Hard to Find." Rev. of *The Terrible Twos*, by Ishmael Reed, and *The Color Purple*, by Alice Walker. *New York Review of Books* (12 Aug. 1982): 35-36.

Tyler, Anne. *The Accidental Tourist*. New York: Knopf, 1985.

———. *Breathing Lessons*. New York: Berkeley Books, 1989.

———. *Celestial Navigation*. New York: Berkeley Books, 1984.

———. *Dinner at the Homesick Restaurant*. 1982. New York: Berkeley Books, 1983.

———. "The Fine, Full World of Eudora Welty." *Washington Star* (26 Oct. 1980): D1.

———. *Ladder of Years*. New York: Knopf, 1995.

———. *Morgan's Passing*. New York: Knopf, 1980.

———. *Saint Maybe*. 1991. New York: Ballantine Books, 1992.

————. *Searching for Caleb.* 1975. New York: Berkeley Books, 1983.

Updike, John. "Imagining Things." Rev. of *Morgan's Passing,* by Anne Tyler. *New Yorker* (23 June 1980): 97-101.

————. "Loosened Roots." Rev. of *Earthly Possessions,* by Anne Tyler. *Hugging the Shore.* New York: Knopf, 1983. Rpt. in Alice Hall Petry, ed., *Critical Essays on Anne Tyler,* 88-91.

Vanier, Jean. *Man and Woman He Made Them.* Foreword by Henri J.M. Nouwen. Mahwah, N.J.: Paulist P, 1985.

Voelker, Joseph C. *Art and the Accidental Tourist in Anne Tyler.* Columbia: U of Missouri P, 1989.

Vollmann, William T. "The Search for Miss Polaroid." *New York Times Book Review* (11 Apr. 1993): 11-12.

Walker, Alice. *The Color Purple.* New York: Harcourt, 1982.

————. *In Search of Our Mothers' Gardens: Womanist Prose.* San Diego: Harcourt, 1983.

Warren, Robert Penn. *All the King's Men.* New York: Harcourt Brace, 1946.

————. *All the King's Men.* New York: Bantam, 1951.

————. "Grackles, Good-bye." *New and Selected Poems, 1923-1985.* New York: Random House, 1985.

————. *Selected Essays.* New York: Vintage, 1958.

Watkins, Mel. "Sexism, Racism and Black Women Writers." *New York Times Book Review* (15 June 1986): 1+.

————. "Some Letters to God." Rev. of *The Color Purple,* by Alice Walker. *New York Times Book Review* (25 July 1982): 7.

Welty, Eudora. *Conversations with Eudora Welty.* Ed. Peggy Whitman Prenshaw. Jackson: UP of Mississippi, 1984.

————. *One Writer's Beginnings.* Cambridge: Harvard UP, 1984.

————. "Place in Fiction." *The Eye of the Story: Selected Essays and Reviews.* New York: Random House, 1978. 116-33.

————. "Words into Fiction." *The Eye of the Story: Selected Essays and Reviews.* New York: Random House, 1978. 134-58.

Wilcox, James. *Modern Baptists.* Garden City, N.J.: Dial, 1983.

Wilhelm, Albert E. "Private Rituals: Coping with Change in the Fiction of Bobbie Ann Mason." *Midwest Quarterly* 28.2 (1987): 271-82.

Wilkinson, James. "A Choice of Fictions: Historians, Memory and Evidence." *PMLA* 111 (1996): 80-92.

Willrich, Patricia Rowe. "Watching through Windows: A Perspective on Anne Tyler." *Virginia Quarterly* 68 (1992): 497-516.

Winter, Kari J. *Subjects of Slavery, Agents of Change: Women and Power in Gothic Novels and Slave Narratives, 1790-1865.* Athens: U of Georgia P, 1992.

Wright, Rachel. *Pirates!* New York: Knopf, 1994.

Yaffe, James. Rev. of *The Last Worthless Evening: Four Novellas and Two Short Stories,* by Andre Dubus. In Kennedy, *Andre Dubus,* 147-50.

Yzermans, Vincent, ed. *American Participation in the Vatican Council.* New York: Sheed, 1967.

Contributors

David Aiken, assistant professor of English at Charleston Southern University, is the author of numerous articles on Southern literature, including essays on Samuel Henry Dickson, William Gilmore Simms, John Beauchamp Jones, John Esten Cooke, E.D.E.N. Southworth, William Faulkner, and Flannery O'Connor. In 1991-1992 he founded and directed the Southern Studies Program at the University of Georgia.

Doris Betts, Alumni Distinguished Professor of English at the University of North Carolina at Chapel Hill, is the author of many articles and stories as well as eight books of fiction, the most recent being *Souls Raised from the Dead*, published in 1994. She taught Randall Kenan when he was an undergraduate at Chapel Hill.

Elizabeth Pell Broadwell is professor of English at Christian Brothers University in Memphis, where she teaches Southern literature, contemporary literature, the modern novel, and women's literature. She has published interviews with and articles on Lee Smith, Erskine Caldwell, and Elizabeth Spencer. Currently she is working on a book on Lee Smith.

John G. Cawelti is professor of English at the University of Kentucky. Specializing in American literature and popular culture, he has published seven books, including *Adventure, Mystery and Romance* and *The Six-Gun Mystique* as well as numerous essays. His latest book is on the African-American novelist Leon Forrest. He is working on a book on changing images of the South and the West in American culture.

Charlene Kerne Clark is public relations officer for the Sterling C. Evans Library at Texas A & M University. In addition to publishing articles on Carson McCullers, she has contributed essays to books and periodicals devoted to library development issues.

William Bedford Clark is professor of English at Texas A&M University and has published widely in the field of American literature. He is the author of *The American Vision of Robert Penn Warren*.

Lucy Ferriss is assistant professor of English and creative writing at Hamilton College. Her fourth novel, *The Misconceiver*, and her critical book, *Sleeping with the Boss: Female Subjectivity and Narrative Pattern in Robert Penn Warren*, were both published in 1997. Her short fiction is widely published, and she writes frequently on issues of gender and narration in fiction.

Jeffrey J. Folks has taught at Indiana University, Tennessee Wesleyan College, and Miyazaki International College, where he is professor of literature. He twice served as senior Fulbright lecturer in Eastern Europe. His publications include *Southern Writers and the Machine: Faulkner to Percy, Remembering James Agee, Second Edition* (with

David Madden), and articles in *Southern Review, Southern Quarterly, South Atlantic Review, Studies in Short Fiction, Southern Literary Journal, Critique,* and other journals.

Elizabeth A. Ford teaches in the English Department at Westminster College in Pennsylvania. In addition to her work on Josephine Humphreys, she writes critically about children's literature as well as modern British literature. She is currently working on an essay on Christopher Hampton's film *Carrington.*

James A. Grimshaw Jr., Regents Professor at Texas A&M University at Commerce, has written and edited seven books on Robert Penn Warren, Cleanth Brooks, and Flannery O'Connor. Among his forthcoming works are *Cleanth Brooks and Robert Penn Warren: Their Literary Correspondence, "All the King's Men": Three Stage Versions* (with James A. Perkins), and *Understanding Robert Penn Warren.*

James Grove is professor of English at Mt. Mercy College in Cedar Rapids, Iowa, where he teaches a seminar on Southern fiction. From 1989 until 1990 he was a Fulbright lecturer in Czechoslovakia. He has published on American and Czech literature, including articles and interviews in the *New England Quarterly, American Literature, Critique, Prairie Schooner, Iowa Woman, The Review of Contemporary Literature,* and *The High Plains Literary Review.* Currently he is working on a study of contemporary midwestern fiction.

Mary Bozeman Hodges teaches English at Carson-Newman College. Her first novel (unpublished) is based on her experiences growing up in a mining community and is heavily influenced by the stories told to her by her father and her friends. She also has written and published a number of short stories.

James H. Justus is professor emeritus of English at Indiana University. With Donald L. Cook and Wallace E. Williams he edited *The Current Voice: Readings in Contemporary Prose.* In 1981 Justus established himself as an important contributor to modern criticism with the publication of *The Achievement of Robert Penn Warren.*

Sue Laslie Kimball, professor emerita, taught at Methodist College for seventeen years and founded the Southern Writers Symposium. She co-edited three books: *Reynolds Price: From* A Long and Happy Life *to* Good Hearts; *Paul Green's Celebration of Man;* and *The Home Truth of Doris Betts.* She has been editor of the *Robert Penn Warren Newsletter* and compiles the annotated bibliography "Who Speaks for Robert Penn Warren."

Nancy Lewis is the coeditor, with her husband, R.W.B. Lewis, of *The Letters of Edith Wharton.* She has written on Jill McCorkle and on the sixteenth-century painter Bronzino. At present she is at work with Lewis on a volume based on portraits from the National Portrait Gallery in Washington, D.C.

David Madden directs the United States Civil War Center, which grew out of his research for *Sharpshooter,* his latest novel. He has published eight novels, two books of stories, and more than thirty works of criticism on James Agee, James M. Cain, Wright Morris, Nathaniel West, and the tough guy and proletarian writers of the 1930s, among others. He co-edited, with Peggy Bach, *Classics of Civil War Fiction*.

Winifred Morgan is a professor of English at Edgewood College, Madison, Wisconsin. She is the author of *An American Icon: Brother Jonathan and American Identity* as well as essays in the *CEA Critic* and *American Studies*. In recent years she has been engaged in a longer study of tricksters in modern American literature.

James A. Perkins teaches public relations and contemporary literature at Westminster College in New Wilmington, Pennsylvania. He has published criticism, three books of poetry, and two volumes of short stories, including *Snakes, Butterbeans, and the Discovery of Electricity*. He has written articles on Lee Smith, Robert Penn Warren, and Robert Drake.

Randolph Paul Runyon is professor of French at Miami University of Ohio. He is the author of *Delia Webster and the Underground Railroad, Reading Raymond Carver, The Braided Dream: Robert Penn Warren's Late Poetry, The Taciturn Text: The Fiction of Robert Penn Warren,* and *Fowles/Irving/Barthes: Canonical Variations on an Apocryphal Theme*. He is currently working on a study of textual architectonics in Montaigne, La Fontaine, and Baudelaire.

Hugh Ruppersburg is associate dean of Arts and Sciences and a professor of English at the University of Georgia. He is the author of *Voice and Eye in Faulkner's Fiction, Robert Penn Warren and the American Imagination,* and *Reading Faulkner: Light in August*. He has also edited two collections of Georgia writing: *Georgia Voices: Fiction* and *Georgia Voices: Non Fiction*. He has published essays on Faulkner, Warren, John Irving, Jack Kerouac, John Kennedy Toole, Thomas Wolfe, and other writers, as well as on film.

Carroll Viera is a professor of English at Tennessee Technological University and a staff member of Tennessee's Governor's Academy for Teachers of Writing, a two-week summer program directed by Richard Marius. She has published an interview with Marius in the *Southern Quarterly* and articles on him in *English Journal, Tennessee Philological Bulletin,* and *Tennessee English Journal*. In addition, she has published articles on a number of nineteenth- and twentieth-century writers and on the teaching of writing.

Albert E. Wilhelm is a professor of English at Tennessee Technological University. His previous scholarship on Bobbie Ann Mason includes two essays, a published interview, and several conference papers. He has written on several other American writers, including John Updike, John Cheever, Robert Penn Warren, Thomas Wolfe, and Breece D'J Pancake.

Index